Change My Life

An Inner Transformation

Author's Note

Hello, my name is Jack and I would like to welcome you here and congratulate you on getting this book, which is your *second* action on your new journey to inner transformation, the first action being to have the thought to do something about the situation you are currently in (most people do not get this far).

If you consume this information, the way you will see life thereafter will be changed forever.

The reason *I* went on a journey of inner transformation was to change my predominant negative thoughts, my isolated views on life and my beliefs which i didn't entirely believe in. Something was missing in me that was stopping me becoming fulfilled. I had an idea of who I wanted to be and what I wanted in life but I was getting in my own way. Like a new computer with old software, the potential was there somewhere, I needed a software upgrade.

This upgrading process began 10 years ago and will no doubt continue for the rest of my life, my mind has been opened, my life is now fulfilling. Looking back over the last few years I have achieved things I could never have dreamt of before.

What I have learnt goes way beyond this book but this is where I started and where I feel you will benefit from starting too. Of all the studying of great philosophers, influential speakers, successful business people and spiritual leaders I've condensed the teachings down to a few key areas which are laid out for you in this book.

Take in the information until you understand it, it will take time for your mind to digest, that is ok, I explain why this is throughout the book.

Follow the tips and take action, keep doing this until it becomes who you are.

Remember to be successful in anything you simply have to not give up.

If you enjoyed this book I am glad, if you would be so kind as to leave a review I would be forever grateful, it is very helpful for me as an author and the future direction of my books.

If you would like a *FREE* copy of the *Life Changing Daily Reminders* Ebook please use the link below when you are next using the internet. Use the Information in the Ebook to repeat and remember the fundamental points key to changing your life.

https://jackthomasbooks.ck.page/0abef4b456

Table of Contents

Introduction 1

Chapter 1: *The Toughest Start, a Realization* 6

Chapter 2: *They Are NOT Your Beliefs* 19

Chapter 3: *Is that Really the Way It Is?* 33

Chapter 4: *This Will Stop Everything* 47

Chapter 5: *Something Powerful that We Don't Do Enough* 62

Chapter 6: *This is the Person You Should Love the Most* 75

Chapter 7: *Getting in Our Own Way* 88

Chapter 8: *The Most Important Step to Take* 101

Chapter 9: *The Goal Is to Set Goals* 118

Chapter 10: *Believe in Yourself, Believe in the Process, Have Faith* 131

Conclusion 144

References 149

Introduction

Unfortunately, life isn't perfect. We all encounter obstacles and face challenges that are out of our control. We all experience hardships we didn't deserve, encounter conflicts we didn't instigate, and see the most carefully laid plans sidelined by something unexpected. For the most part, there's not much that we can do about this — sometimes life just throws you lemons.

If you feel this way, then you've come to the right place. This book is here to tell you that you have a lot more power over your life circumstances than you've ever realized. This isn't to put blame or insinuate that you are somehow responsible for life circumstances that have left you feeling powerless or unhappy. Instead, this book is about taking back autonomy over your own joy and emotional well-being. It's true that there is much about life that we can't control, but there's a lot more of life that we can control, and it's simply about taking a step back and making adjustments to the way we think.

This book will help you take that step back. Through simple tasks and exercises for you to do at your own pace, this book will help you discover where many of your thoughts, beliefs, and values come from. Once you have a deeper understanding of how you think and what forces contributed to help make you who you are, then you can let go of patterns that are no longer serving you. As the title suggests, this book will take you deep within yourself, discovering the root of what makes you who you are so you can free yourself from... well, from yourself.

I believe that many of us are suffering from cognitive traps. We are so entangled in our own thoughts, belief systems, and value sets that we can no longer see the world as it really is. This entanglement stops us from solving problems that are solvable. It stops us from feeling happy, fulfilled, or powerful. The more we struggle to free ourselves, the more tightly restricted we are by our own thoughts.

I know this to be true because this was once my situation. I was quite frustrated as a teenager, especially in my late teens. I felt a great deal of pressure in high school to conform to certain social mandates. I would work hard to fit myself into the typical stereotypes of "cool kid," "sports guy," or "geek," worried that I wouldn't be able to make friends if I couldn't find a way to belong to a pre-set social grouping. I strove to be good in the subjects I was told were important, even if I didn't enjoy them. This thought pattern was positive — it drove me to be ambitious and take my learning seriously. However in other ways, this thought pattern was negative — I felt a great deal of pressure to be "successful" without really knowing what that word meant or how I wanted it to manifest in my own life. I believed that if I didn't excel in school, then I would struggle in life. However, I felt restricted and misled by this same belief. Because of this inner conflict, my life began to feel more and more out of control. Instead of taking charge over my own life, I felt pressured and resentful. If I got bad grades, I would blame the teacher for not helping me learn enough to pass the test. If other kids came to school wearing the newest trainers, I would blame my parents for not having the money to buy me new clothes.

These thought patterns of stress and resentment followed me on my way to university. There, however, things started to change. I was exposed to many kinds of people who came from very different backgrounds, cultures, and even countries. Eventually, a university friend recommended a book called *The Secret,* by Rhona Byrne. At first, I scoffed. This was a "self-help" book, something silly and mindless that I would never waste my time on.

This thought pattern was reinforced when I mentioned the book to my brother, who laughed and dismissed it as a book about "thinking happy thoughts." His attitude was like mine. Life just happens, and you have to brace yourself and try to make the best of it.

Finally, I overcame my negative thought pattern, and I'm happy to say that I gave *The Secret* a shot. After reading it all the way through five times, I knew that something in me changed forever. For the next 10 years, I poured through literature and books by people from a variety of different life circumstances who were all saying different versions of the same message: your mind holds the key to your own happiness.

Today, I work with people daily, helping them break free of restricting thought patterns like the ones that crippled me in high school. Over and over again, I see how understanding one's own mind can unlock doors of possibility that once seemed impossible to open. Too many people are trapped in their own thoughts, believing that there's nothing to be done about their own lives and blaming external forces for the things that cause them unhappiness (Canfield, 2015).

This book is not about "just thinking happy

thoughts,"— it's about cultivating an intimate understanding of how your mind works so you are no longer caught in its workings. Understanding how and why you think the way you do will help you recognize thought habits for what they are. Once you understand how your mind works, then you can let go of thought habits that are no longer serving you and take back control of your own happiness.

Now it's time to turn the page and begin learning how to transform your mindset into one of happiness and success. No matter where you are in your life's journey, it's never too late to improve your life and start reaping all the benefits you deserve.

Chapter 1

The Toughest Start, a Realization

In your life, the only thing that needs to change is you! Harsh words, I know. But even if your boss is awful and your hours are long, you can make a change from within. If your partner is selfish, boring, or even abusive, you can make a change from within. If your parents don't understand or support you, you can make a change from within.

This change isn't about accepting bad circumstances, and it's not about thinking it's ok for people to abuse or mistreat you. It's about standing your ground and taking responsibility for your own happiness. This is the secret in *The Secret,* the idea that you truly can have, do, or be anything that you want. Solving problems, achieving goals, and feeling fulfilled have very little to do with outside circumstances. More often than not, the person preventing you from living the life you want to live is you! Upon hearing this truth, many people's first reactions (including mine) are to become defensive.

They may say something like "I can't help it if my boss is awful!" or "It's not my fault my job has long hours. What do you want me to do?"

Insisting that you have the power to change your life isn't about placing blame or pointing fingers. It's about telling you that your life circumstances now don't have to be defined by what happened to you in the past. No matter how many bad things have happened to you, there's nothing stopping you from making a change now. If you feel unfulfilled or unsuccessful, the number one obstacle to your happiness or success is your mindset. It is not your boss or your wife, your salary, your education, or your relationship with your parents. You have power over your future, and you always will.

But what stops many of us from accessing this power is identity. We define ourselves by our previous actions, and this can stop us from growing or moving forward into the future. If we fail to stand up to our boss, we decide "I'm a coward," or "My boss is stronger than I am," and from that moment on, we define our entire lives around one negative incident.

This, however, doesn't have to be the way it is. You don't have to be beholden to your past self, nor do you have to rely on others to make you happy. You can't change your boss' behavior, but blaming your boss for making your life unhappy doesn't serve you either. No matter how hopeless the situation, there is almost always something that you can do to change it. You have more power than you know, but your own thought patterns may be holding you back.

Thoughts are some of the most intimate experiences we have as humans. No one else can read our minds, and no one around us can really understand what's going on in our heads. Our thoughts are as unique and personal as our physical brains or the DNA coding that makes up our cells. Our thoughts are who we are. They give us our identities. They form our opinions, and they help us understand our feelings, fears, desires, hopes, and dreams. However, because our thoughts are so intimate, we believe that our thoughts are completely created by us. You might say, "My thoughts are my own." No one else can put a thought into my head, just as I can't put thoughts into the heads of other people.

But this is not strictly true. Many of our thought patterns result from cultural, familial, and social teachings that are impressed upon us in childhood and beyond. To survive certain social (or even physical) situations, we adopt certain thoughts, behaviors, and beliefs that help us interact with the other people around us in a healthy and harmonious way. However, the situations that engender our thought patterns don't last forever. But long after that situation has changed or faded away, we are still thinking in the same way, applying the same worldviews, belief systems, or social norms to every situation we find ourselves in. Some thought patterns help us again and again. But some thought patterns can stunt our growth. They prevent us from seeing our situations, relationships, or even ourselves, for what they truly are, and instead cause us to become stuck in an emotional trap of our own making.

In the words of John Assaraf, your present self is a product of past thoughts. This means that who you are today results from all the many you's of the past. However, this also means that the thoughts you are having now are actively creating your future self. If you can change your present thoughts, you can change your future reality (Byrne, 2006).

This may sound silly or "new age," but our thoughts eventually turn into actions. If you are constantly thinking things like "I can't do this," or "I wish I didn't live here," or "I'll never be able to pass this test," then that's exactly what will happen. We all encounter strokes of good luck, and we all sometimes need to reach out to friends and family for emotional support. But if we are constantly undermining our success with every thought we have, then these moments of good luck will sparkle and fade, and we will remain stuck in the same negative life patterns.

Great life moments or achievements rarely happen spontaneously. The Wright Brothers didn't just happen to learn how to fly — it began with a thought, an idea or even a wish. Some people have a great deal handed to them in life, but most people who are living happily or are achieving great things are doing so because they are *thinking* in a way that facilitates success. We all have doubts, of course. But think of someone like Martin Luther King, Jr. This is someone who saw and experienced horrible social pressures, the dangers of being a black man in a racist society. He was truly in danger, and there was nothing he could do about it. How could one man change an entire society, right?

But you know that's not true. You know there was a great deal that Martin Luther King, Jr. could and did do about his situation. The world that we live in today owes a great deal to him. This doesn't mean that you have to be as influential as Martin Luther King, Jr. or the Wright Brothers to be fulfilled or successful. But none of the great people of history would have been able to do what they did without first freeing themselves from their own mindset. Imagine if Queen Elizabeth I of England had accepted the idea that women can't be powerful or effective monarchs. Imagine if Beethoven had accepted the idea that deaf people can't write or play music. Every single one of Beethoven's symphonies began with one thought — I can do this. Without that kind of mindset, he wouldn't have been able to write a single note.

Does this mean that Beethoven never doubted himself? Of course not! But even the most determined of us can fall prey to our mindset. Often, the key to success is not changing what we are thinking about, but how we are thinking about it. For example, in *The Secret,* we see an example of a thought many of us in the 21st century have thought: "I hate being in debt." While you might think this thought would inspire you to do everything you can to beat your debt, it can have the opposite effect. By thinking this, you are shifting the focus of your thoughts from you to your debt. Instead of taking responsibility for your situation, you are blaming your debt for your unhappiness, and therefore taking away your power to change your situation (Byrne, 2006).

"I want to get out of debt" is better. It doesn't lay blame or reinforce negative feelings, 153 but it still doesn't give you power over the situation. The unconscious implication behind this kind of thought is "I want to get out of debt *but I can't*." So you might think that the best kind of mindset would be to think the opposite:"I can get out of debt." This definitely puts you on the right track, but there's still one more problem.

Thinking to yourself "I can get out of debt" puts all of your focus on the debt, and none of your focus on the solutions. Even if you are working hard and making payments all the time, you will only see the debt, and you won't be able to appreciate all the progress you are making with it! And if you aren't making progress, thinking"I can get out of debt" puts you on the right track emotionally, but it doesn't do much in the way of offering you a solution. There may be a very good reason you're in debt and thinking positively by itself won't get you out of it.

To truly succeed, you have to change your focus. In keeping with the debt example, set a goal for yourself, something simple and doable. It can be as small as "I can pay my minimum on time this month" or as big as "I will put 10,000 on my loan by the end of the year." That's it! You can worry about the details of your plan later. But first, set yourself that intention. Don't focus on the entirety of your loan, or the entirety of your debt. Focus, instead, on your intention, and when the month comes and you are able to pay your minimum on time, you'll feel amazing!

Instead of focusing on what you don't have or what you can't do, set an intention and work toward something that you *can* do. Shift the focus of your inner dialogue and ask yourself positive questions, like "What can I get done today?" instead of negative questions like "What do I have to do today?" You're essentially asking yourself the same thing, but the first question sets you up to look for achievements and get excited about your accomplishments. The second question sets you up to feel overwhelmed by your To-Do List. Even if you get a lot done, your focus is on reaching the end of the list, and so you won't be able to recognize how much you've accomplished.

This kind of positive orientation doesn't apply only to goal setting. Think about the way that you talk about yourself to others. When you're catching up with an old friend, what are you more likely to share? Do you tell them about all the projects you're working on, the goals you want to achieve, and the things that you're looking forward to? Or do you tell them about all the things that are going wrong, all the ways that you are frustrated, and all the things that are bothering you? We all need to vent from time to time, but if you pay attention, you'll notice that certain people talk about positive things, while others seem to complain endlessly. Those happy people don't have perfect lives, any more than those negative people are leading tragic existences. Almost always, the difference between a happy and an unhappy person isn't life circumstances, it's their perspective on those circumstances.

This is the basic premise behind the idea commonly referred to as the "Law of Attraction." Essentially, it means that you get from life what you expect from it. If you are thinking positive thoughts, then you'll be open to the positive things around you. You'll have a mindset that enables you to see and appreciate the positive things when they appear for you. If, however, you're thinking negative thoughts, then the opposite is true. You will be closed to the positive things, and you may feel like only bad things are happening because you're missing the good things when they appear!

Whether you believe this is about sending energy out to the universe or is a form of cognitive-behavioral therapy doesn't really matter. Spiritual or psychological, there's a great deal of testimony out there to suggest that perspective really makes a difference. If you're still skeptical, here's an example. Perhaps there's a hardware store at the end of your street. You've lived on that street for almost ten years now. You drive past that store five days a week on the way to work, and then again when you come home. But you won't notice it until the day you need a fuse or a length of rope.

What happened? Did your vision magically improve on the very day that you needed something from the hardware store? Did the store magically appear to provide you with the thing you needed? Of course not! What changed was your perspective. You could only see the hardware store when you were thinking about hardware. When your thoughts were focused on buying hardware supplies, the solution to your problem appeared in front of you. It may seem like magic, but the hardware store was there the whole time.

This analogy can be applied to far more abstract concepts. This is why changing your focus is so important. If you are constantly thinking about being unemployed, then all you will see is your unemployment. If you are thinking about sending out resumes or practicing for interviews, however, then you will see more opportunities to send out your resume and start getting more interviews. Did those opportunities magically appear out of nowhere? No, they were there the whole time, but your mindset literally blinded you to them.

Those who believe in the Law of Attraction describe this phenomenon as putting the idea out into the universe, or setting an intention. More religious people will say that this is God answering your prayers. Those who are more scientifically minded believe this is purely psychological, and that your brain can only focus on so many things at once. Regardless of how you view this process, the results are the same. When you adjust your focus to the things you want or the things you have, then that is what you will see. If you are focused on the things you don't want or the things you don't have, then that is what you will see.

Using this practice of intention-setting gives the power back to you. You can't change anyone else, so you can't rely on others to make you happy. We all need friends, family, and partners for emotional support. No one can live life on their own. However, there's a big difference between leaning on someone for support and expecting them to carry you through life. You can't help if your boss is a jerk or if your parents are emotionally distant. You can't change someone's abusive behavior or horrible attitude. But you can change yourself. If you can embrace the idea that your own perspective may trap you in a bad situation, then you can embrace your own power to get yourself through anything that life throws at you. It's not just "thinking happy thoughts," it's adjusting how you view the world so that the good things are easier to see. It's changing your focus so that your opportunities are at the forefront of your vision, not your challenges. Intention setting isn't about fixing what you don't have, it's about prioritizing the things important to you.

Though this may be difficult to accept, the hard truth of inner transformation is that working on your life means working on yourself. To do this, you must resist the temptation to blame bad circumstances on others, on the world, or even on yourself. When tragedy strikes, like a car accident or even an illness, it's easy to become bitter and resentful. We may ask, "What did I do to deserve this?"

But the answer is... nothing! You are not responsible for the tragedies that happen in your life, and inner transformation is not about blaming yourself for everything that's ever gone wrong for you. Nor, however, is it about blaming other people, or blaming the universe. Ultimately, it's about not placing blame at all. Most of the time, bad things just happen. No one intended them, it's just how the cards fell. Even many fights or conflicts are the results of bad communication, with neither side intending to hurt the other. When we blame, whether that blame is directed inward or outward, we close our minds to the possibility of solution. Laying blame is a form of denial — it prevents us from fully accepting the reality of a situation. When faced with terrible circumstances, this is only natural. It's a way that our minds protect us from grim realities.

To reach true fulfillment, we must push through this defense mechanism. Though it can be comforting to place blame and deny the circumstances in front of us, denying reality doesn't make it any less real. Denial doesn't make the problem go away, and too often, it makes the problem more difficult to overcome. Taking responsibility for your happiness doesn't mean believing that you cause all of your problems. It means believing that you have complete control over how you respond to those problems. Ultimately, it's your response that makes all the difference.

Chapter 2

They Are NOT Your Beliefs

What do you believe in? God? Human rights? Freedom? Although this may be difficult to accept, none of these are your beliefs. No matter how ardently you follow them, none of the values, ideological, or spiritual beliefs that you hold originated with you. This is hard to swallow, but take a moment to think about it. When you were born, how did you know what was right or wrong, good or bad? The beliefs and values that you hold dear now had to be taught to you by your parents, grandparents, teachers, and even media like television, literature, or the internet. Almost everything we know about the world does not come from our own empirical observations of reality, but from how we are taught to think by our familial, religious, and ethnic communities. In fact, many of our beliefs are transmitted to us before we are even born!

Traditionally, we are taught to think of our development in terms of "nature" and "nurture." Much of medical study is about determining whether certain behaviors, emotions, thoughts, and even diseases are the product of "nature" or "nurture." If we follow the mentality of "nature," we believe that physical and mental illness, destructive thoughts, and antisocial behaviors or emotions are encoded into our genes. This is the mentality that often causes us to blame others for our life situations. "I can't help it," we say when we're depressed, sick, or angry, or "That's just how I'm wired." When we follow this mentality, we often try to change our lives with physical interventions. If you have trouble getting along with your co-workers, you start taking anti-anxiety or anti-psychotic medications to "fix" what you perceive to be a faulty brain. If you are prone to high blood pressure or bad digestion, you start taking medications or looking into surgical options to "fix" what you perceive to be a faulty heart or digestive tract (Lipton, 2016).

If we follow the mentality of "nurture," we believe that physical and mental illness, destructive thoughts, and antisocial behaviors or emotions are things that were taught to us as young children. If we suffer from anxiety or depression, we once again blame others. Instead of saying "That's just how I'm wired," we say "That's just how I was raised." We blame our upbringing for our problems instead of our biology, but ultimately the effect is the same. Instead of taking medications we go to therapy, but it still doesn't get us anywhere because we are waiting for the therapy to fix us, instead of using the therapy to help us fix the situation.

Dr. Bruce Lipton, however, believes that "nature" and "nurture" are really just two sides of the same biological, genetic, and psychological coin. According to his (and other cognitive) theories, humans have one brain, but two minds: the conscious and the subconscious. The conscious mind can be thought of as our "creative" mind. This mind shapes our personal identities, our spiritualities, and is the mind often being referred to when we talk about "mindset," "attitude," or "thoughts."

The subconscious mind is far more passive. Dr. Lipton describes it acting almost like a tape recording device, recording information from the environment and storing it as behaviors. Whenever similar patterns in the environment appear around us, the subconscious mind hits the "play" button to initiate those behaviors. This part of our mind is the non-thinking mind, the mind that shapes our habits, our emotions, and is most in touch with the rest of our bodies (Lipton, 2015).

Both the conscious and subconscious mind are integral to who we are and how we live, but you may be surprised to learn that 95% of your mental processes are governed by the subconscious mind, with only the remaining 5% percent coming from the conscious mind. Too much psychology, personal growth, and even spirituality teaches us that changing our mindsets is a matter of willpower, but if only 5% of our mental activity is governed by conscious thinking, then this can't be the whole story. To change your mindset, it's not enough to change the patterns in your conscious mind. You must change the patterns in your subconscious mind as well.

So where do the patterns in the subconscious mind come from? While the subconscious mind is always growing and developing throughout our lives, most of our subconscious behaviors are formed during the first six years of our lives. By age six, you already have a fully formed subconscious profile that much of your mental activity today is still based on. Before this age, we have almost no conscious mind at all. Young children operate almost entirely through the subconscious, because the subconscious brain is still forming. The brainwaves of children under the age of six primarily operate at a very low EEG level, sending waves we call "theta" waves. The theta state is a very calm, even dreamlike consciousness state. You are in a theta state when you are between sleeping and waking. The cognitive process of hypnosis puts your brain into a theta state, which is why many people have used hypnosis techniques to change their subconscious programming.

Young children live almost entirely in a hypnotic state. The first five years of our lives are spent in a trance. This is so that our brains can primarily engage with the environment through observation. As the subconscious mind forms, the brain records and stores all these observations as the foundation which the worldviews and belief systems of the conscious mind will be based upon.

Even then, however, the forming of the conscious mind doesn't come entirely from within our individual brains. The "blueprint" of the conscious mind comes primarily from observing our parents. From the moment of birth, the first thing a child's brain does is record the patterns of its parents' faces. Within just a few days, a human child can distinguish the faces of their parents from all other human faces. As the brain develops, observations of these faces becomes more sophisticated. Human children learn to recognize fear, anger, happiness, and contentment in the faces of their parents within the first few weeks of their lives. While the subconscious is being developed, we use the faces of our parents to inform how we understand the world. When a child encounters something new in the environment, they instinctively look to the faces of their parents to determine how they should react. If the child sees fear or worry in their parents' faces, then they, too, will react to that situation, person, environment, or object with fear and worry. This is to help the brain gather information on what is dangerous and what is safe. The opposite is also true — if the child sees happiness or smiles on their parents' faces, then they will also react to that situation, person, environment, or object with happiness and relaxation (Lipton, 2019).

Our basic understanding of what is safe and dangerous, good and bad, right and wrong, comes from these early formative experiences, which are primarily informed by two factors: 1) the kinds of situations, people, environments, and objects we are exposed to in our formative years, and 2) how our parents reacted emotionally to those situations. So if our parents are living in fear or concern when we are young children, then we will grow up to fear or be wary of different kinds of situations, people, environments, or even objects. Even if you know in your conscious mind that something isn't dangerous, your emotional and even behavioral patterns will continue to follow the fundamental patterns laid by the subconscious mind.

This might seem like a bizarre way for nature to program us, but it's actually efficient at keeping us alive and healthy for most of our young lives. The brain forms for optimal survival in the world we are born into, and long after our subconscious has been formed, many of those subconscious patterns continue to help us learn, grow, and thrive in that environment. If your parents are living in anxiety or concern, for example, it's probably because the world you've been born into is a dangerous world. As such, those subconscious patterns will help you recognize the dangers in that world, and subsequently help you avoid them.

The trouble comes when our environments change. For the most part, the world that we are born into tends to be the world that we live in well into our teens and twenties. But by the time we are in our thirties, forties, and fifties, much in our environments has probably changed. Things that we learned to fear as children may not be dangerous anymore. The behavioral patterns that brought us social or physical rewards as children may no longer serve us as adults. The trouble that many adults face is that they don't recognize their habits, behaviors, and even emotions as coming from the subconscious mind. Many of us believe that we can change the subconscious (95% of the mind) with the power of our conscious mind (only 5% of our brainpower). This results in many people feeling frustrated, unfulfilled, or held back in life. We think because we can't change ourselves, then the problem must be something external that we have no choice but to accept as part of our world.

But how do you change your subconscious mind? Natal and prenatal science now tells us that our personalities are probably half formed before we are even born, shaped by emotional chemicals and growth hormones that have been passed to us through the placenta. Does this mean we are the product of genetic make-up in the womb, and that we can never change the patterns of our subconscious minds? Of course not! However, thinking about it is only 5% of the battle. Many of your behavioral and emotional patterns were formed before you even had a conscious mind, so thinking your way out of limiting behaviors or emotions won't be enough to change your mindset. Instead, the way to change the subconscious is to change the environmental information upon which it bases your behaviors and emotions. Though the subconscious is fully formed by age six, it never stops observing or reacting to its environment. The world that you developed in becomes the foundation for your mindset, but it's not set in stone. Patterns that no longer work can be changed, but they must be changed through experience, not through thought (Lipton, 2012).

The good news is that you don't have to reprogram your brain completely if you want to change your mindset to improve your life. Remember that 95% of you is your subconscious mind. So take a look at your life. The things that are working for you work because of beneficial beliefs in your subconscious. That mental programming doesn't need to be changed — it's your brain doing exactly what it needs to do to keep you happy and healthy in the world you've been born into. Changing your mindset is about looking at what's not working. Obstacles, challenges, and setbacks may not necessarily be coming from the universe, or even from other people. Many times, we struggle with things because we weren't "programmed" to deal with them as children. The behaviors and emotions with which we react to certain things are there to protect us from danger, but that protection may be misplaced. As a result, your own behavioral and emotional patterns may be what's holding you back from achieving whatever it is you want to achieve, whether it's a promotion or a healthy relationship with your mother-in-law.

To overcome these limiting subconscious programs, our conscious minds can only take us so far. It's not enough to think we want to change, or even change our conscious thoughts. We have to replace the current subconscious program with a new program. The behavior or emotion that limits you can't simply be deleted; it has to be replaced with a new behavior or emotion that serves you. To help you achieve this, each of the chapters in this book will end with a few different tasks you can implement to help you "reprogram" the limiting patterns of your subconscious mind. As you undergo the process of inner transformation, be patient and forgiving with yourself. Remember that it took six years to form the subconscious patterns you currently have! You're not going to reshape your mindset overnight. Open yourself up to the journey, allow yourself to grow at your own pace, and start by observing yourself. Learn who you really are by observing your subconscious patterns and not worry so much about labelling them as "limiting" or "enhancing" your personal growth. As you become more in-tune with your own mind, you will slowly understand where your own mind is limiting you, and where it enables you to grow and thrive.

Inner Transformation Task - Observing Habits

After the age of seven, the primary way in which our brains acquire and edit subconscious programming is through repetition and habit formation. For example, perhaps you grow up with an innate fear of dogs. Now you're twenty-seven, and you've started dating a man who owns two big dogs. Your conscious mind knows that dogs aren't inherently dangerous, but your subconscious mind reacts with fear. However, if you commit to walking the dogs with your partner every week, you'll have good experiences with those dogs. The repetition of this good experience every week will slowly but surely change your emotional programming from one of fear to one of love and affection.

This is one concrete example, but repetition and habit formation works like this on a variety of different levels, and in response to a variety of different emotions and behaviors. However, you can't realistically form new habits until you understand the habits you currently have. This task is an observation and reflection task. You can choose to use the information you gain from completing this task and structure your observations however you want. This could be taking notice, keeping a journal, recording your observations artistically, or even making a spreadsheet! Just remember to record them in a way that you can return to, as you will use this information at the end of the task, and in more active tasks later in the book.

However you do it, try to notice your habits. Start at the very beginning of your day. How do you wake up? Do you have an alarm? Do you have several alarms? Is that alarm on your phone? Do you hit the snooze button or do you wake up right away? Do you feel groggy and tired when you wake up, or do you feel refreshed and energized? Do you wake up at the same time every day? Do you wake up early in the morning or late into the afternoon?

This might sound like it's overanalyzing, but it's not. Try to cultivate this kind of hyper-awareness throughout the day. You may be totally surprised by what you "see" yourself doing throughout the day. You may observe actions, thoughts, or emotions that you feel almost every day of your life, but that you've never actively taken notice of before. Observing your daily habits and routines might seem small or pointless, but they have a lot more to do with the bigger patterns in our lives than we realize. Observation of your habits doesn't just mean observing your behavior — remember to observe your emotions too. For example, if the way your office partner greets you in the morning annoys you, record this annoyance. There's no logical explanation for this kind of emotion, no concrete reason that a friendly greeting should make you grind your teeth. This annoyance is an emotional habit. It may have anything to do with your partner at all! Instead, this may be a subconscious program that's been engaged. Something about your partner's energy, body language, or tone of voice has tripped a subconscious emotional pattern deep within you that causes you to respond to their greeting, not with warmth and openness, but with anger and irritation.

After you've observed your habits for about a week, look back over your findings and find places where you felt unhappy or frustrated. For example, if you hate waking up in the morning, return to that moment and ask yourself what is making you unhappy. If you had full control over how you wake up every day, how would you do it? There may truly be factors of your situation that you can't change. But you will probably find that you have more control over your life than you've previously believed. Often, the things stopping us from living how we want are imaginary. They are emotional and behavioral patterns coming up from the subconscious. It's difficult to explain or recognize these patterns because they aren't coming from the conscious mind. It's something you literally do without thinking, and so you assume that, because you didn't consciously think about it, it must come from something external.

Chapter 3

Is that Really the Way It Is?

We think our perspective is the product of our conscious minds, and that our worldview is a logical belief system based on a lifetime of experiences that confirm how we see things. However, perspective is rarely, if ever, based on cold rationalism. Our emotions, past experiences, and internal dialogues all work together to color how we see the world. This gives us a unique view of the world, but it also means that, if we can't stop and question our perspective, we can become stuck in a perspective that doesn't have anything to do with objective reality.

Police officers, detectives, doctors, lawyers, and journalists all understand how subjective human perspective truly is, because they spend most of their lives listening to multiple people telling the same story. For example, after a car accident, police officers will take statements from as many witnesses as they possibly can. Why? Because every witness' version of the event will be slightly different. This is not because people are lying or delusional. It's just that everyone has a slightly different way of interacting with the world, and those interactions are based just as heavily on thoughts and emotions as they are on objective observations (Bozak, 2019).

The reason that 12 different people can all experience the same event and tell a different story of what happened is because "experience" is more than just observation. Scientists don't experience photosynthesis or the growth of cancer cells; they watch these events happen. Experience, however, is what happens when we give meaning to our observations. When you witness a car crash or a fistfight, you aren't coldly observing these events under a microscope. You are watching these events unfold within the context of your own life. You may identify with one person or the other in the fistfight, and so may perceive aggression on either side that the person standing next to you didn't see. You might have been daydreaming about buying a red car just like the one in the lane next to you, and that's why you saw the driver spin out, but other witnesses didn't.

We are constantly interpreting everything that happens around us through the filter of our own memories, culture, spirituality, and values. These interpretations form our beliefs about our own identities, the nature of our relationships, and our general worldviews. The meaning that we will give to future events is then interpreted against the mental backdrop of these beliefs, which will either be strengthened by how we interpret the event, or be challenged and therefore slightly altered.

We are constantly making judgments and forming opinions about events happening around us, and that's not necessarily a bad thing. These judgements and opinions are necessary for identity formation. They help us understand who we are, how we interact with the world, and how we want to interact with the world around us. Our beliefs, in short, make us who we are.

Our core belief system is divided into three parts: how we view ourselves, how we view others, and how we view the world (or the universe) at large. While some of our core belief system is influenced by our conscious minds, most of our core beliefs come from our subconscious mind. There are a number of subconscious forces that are constantly at work to influence and shape our core belief system.

The first of these forces is the influence of past experiences. The subconscious mind is constantly at work observing the environment and recording experiences as behaviors. Whenever you encounter a similar experience, your subconscious mind automatically activates the behavioral or emotional pattern that got you through the experience the last time. Experiences that leave behavioral or emotional programs in our subconscious minds are the formative years of our early childhood, cultural rituals, religious or spiritual rituals and value-based experiences (social situations in which you were explicitly praised and rewarded for being "good" or judged and punished for being "bad"). Every time we encounter an experience like this, our subconscious minds are either imprinted with a new program, or they automatically play the program that helped us through similar experiences in the past. Biological and genetic factors have a part to play in our subconscious programming as well, but these are but one of the myriad of influences that combine to form our belief systems.

For example, those who are bullied, hurt, or abused by others have a very different perspective from people who have not had those experiences. Being bullied or hurt by others, especially multiple times, changes the core belief system. You believe that the world is a dangerous place and assume that other people are antagonistic and motivated to harm you. You may develop passive behaviors, going along with what others want to avoid conflict. Many years after the experience that shaped this core belief, you may still have this passive demeanor. It got you through the dangerous times, and may even earn you a deserved reputation as being easy-going. However, this passive behavior (fueled by the core belief that others are willing to do harm) may hold you back. Perhaps you're missing opportunities at work or are overloaded with responsibilities at home. You blame others — your boss is demanding, your partner is taking advantage — and this makes perfect sense to you. After all, your core beliefs are telling you that others are actively looking to harm you.

What this perspective is hiding from you is that it may be your own passive behavior that's holding you back. The conflict-avoiding behaviors that saved you from humiliation and violence in the past are now holding you back. Is your boss demanding, or is your boss assuming that, because you never complain, that you are managing your workload just fine? Is your partner taking advantage of your good nature, or is your partner assuming that you enjoy helping out? Even situations that others might find relaxing or peaceful you might find stressful or threatening. Words, actions, and even facial expressions that may be intended to be friendly you will be constantly analyzing for danger. "Did they mean that?" you might think, or "They're only being nice because they feel bad for me." Your perspective is that the world is a dangerous place, and so you are constantly looking for danger. Like the example of the hardware store, once you look for danger, you'll see it everywhere. Even if you know in your conscious mind that you are with friends, your subconscious mind will scan parties, business meetings, and casual conversations for signs of danger, and at the slightest trigger, will activate the associated behavioral or emotional programs.

In this example situation, you are stuck in a strange perspective-feedback loop. Your experiences cause a change in your core belief system. This change causes your subconscious to program certain behaviors to help you handle the situation. These behaviors help you out of the situation which validates your core belief system. Every time you encounter a similar situation, your subconscious mind activates the behavior program. However, the behaviors that helped you survive past experiences create new dynamics that hold you back, validating the need for those behaviors in the first place, and you are stuck going in circles of frustration and unfulfillment.

This is only one example of a perspective-feedback loop. No matter what your experiences are or how your subconscious programming is trapping you, the trick is to gain perspective on your perspective. If you can shine a light on the specifics of your core beliefs and question them, you can then start to more honestly identify the subconscious behavioral or emotional programs that validate those core beliefs. This can be extraordinarily difficult to do, and no matter how much of a handle you think you have on your own mind, remember that a staggering 95% of your brain is run by these subconscious behavior programs!

This is why it can be so difficult to change or challenge your core belief systems by yourself. One of the trickiest social examples of this is racism. If you are a white person raised in a racist society, you have an awful lot of subconscious programming that validates a racist core belief system. You consciously might not be racist. You may understand on a deep level why and how racial constructs are harmful and dangerous. And yet... you do or say things that are offensive, frustrating, or outright harmful to people of color. How does this happen? Because your subconscious mental programs are nearly impossible to change on the strength of your conscious mind alone.

Our subconscious is incredibly good at reshaping new information to make it fit to your pre-existing belief system. Remember that while young children are still developing their subconscious minds, their brain waves are operating at a very low frequency. In this hypnotic state, the subconscious mind is flexible, and open to new stimuli. Once the brain functions at higher frequencies; however, the subconscious mind becomes much more difficult to change. Even new information is changed, edited, or dismissed to protect pre-existing belief systems. This is why conscious willpower alone is not enough to change your perspective, or your core belief systems. To change your core belief system and truly shift your perspective, you have to engage the subconscious mind.

So how do we do that? Though the psychological terminology is relatively new, humans have been struggling to overcome their subconscious programming as long as there have been humans. One of the most sophisticated mechanisms humans devised over the centuries for challenging our core belief systems is art. Literature, music, theater, and even visual art have the important cultural function of both cataloging and critiquing belief systems, whether those core beliefs belong to one individual or an entire society. Why is art so effective as a core belief challenger? Because it activates both the conscious and the subconscious minds at the same time. Art is an experience. Yes, you have to think about it (conscious) but you also have to feel it (subconscious). This is why a movie about the Holocaust is far more effective at challenging our subconscious beliefs about race, religion, or oppression than an essay about the Holocaust. The essay only engages the conscious mind, while the movie engages the subconscious by stirring up powerful emotions in the viewer's mind.

So believe it or not engaging with art can be an effective way to challenge your core belief systems. If you are consistently having trouble at work, for example, watch a movie, read a book, or even listen to music. Notice what comes up for you. Do certain characters annoy you? Who do you identify with? Which situations make you laugh, which frustrate you, and which characters are you rooting for? Engaging actively with art can help to give you a fresh look at your own behaviors and emotions. It can help you see your own actions through the eyes of other people, and can give you insight into how those around you may view the same situation.

For the same reason, it's also worth it to look at the art you naturally gravitate toward and what kinds of art you reject. We all have our favorites when it comes to TV shows, movies, books, and music. What kinds of art do you like? Do you have any favorite plays or musicals? Do you gravitate toward specific kinds of fashion or even interior decoration? We love the art that validates and reflects our core beliefs back at us, and oftentimes that's ok! Our core beliefs aren't always destructive - in fact, they are what has kept us alive and healthy for so long.

But if you're feeling like the world is against you and life is holding you back, it may be time for a perspective change. One of the easiest ways to do that is to engage with art that you either don't like, or know anything about. Take a chance on a new TV show or an album by a musician you've never heard of before, but this time, pay attention. Do you like it? Do you hate it? Why? Why not? Pay attention to the emotions and thoughts that come up as you listen, watch, or read. What triggered those emotions? What does this tell you about your subconscious emotional programming?

We hear the word "triggered" a lot in today's slang, but many of us don't understand where the word comes from. In psychological terms, a trigger is something that activates a defense mechanism in the mind of someone who has suffered serious physical or emotional trauma. The problem with triggers is that they aren't always predictable. For example, a military veteran may abstain from the Fourth of July celebrations, because they know that the explosive sounds of the fireworks are triggers that make them feel anxious or even activate flashbacks. However, that same veteran may find themselves extremely irritated during a business meeting or have a panic attack in the waiting room before a routine dentist appointment. These extreme emotional responses aren't the product of a faulty brain. Something about the business meeting or the dentist's waiting room engaged the veteran's subconscious programming. Since their past experiences have been so extreme, their subconscious behavior programs are probably extreme as well. But in one way or another, all of us have the same problem as the traumatized veteran. Our subconscious minds register the booming of fireworks as the explosion of bombs, and engages behavior patterns that helped us survive the war in the past, but make us seem like crazed, violent lunatics at our neighbor's cookouts in the present.

Inner Transformation Task - Helicopter View

Have you ever heard the expression "You can't see the forest through the trees?" This idiom is an ancient way of expressing the problem of perspective. If you believe other people are dangerous, you will interpret every look, action, and sentence as coded, threatening, and potentially harmful. If you believe America is the greatest nation on earth, you will register any criticism of America as unpatriotic or an international threat. If you believe your partner has your best interests at heart, then you will always find something you did "wrong" to explain away their abusive language or behavior.

The helicopter view is a way for us to gain perspective on our perspective. It helps us to take a proverbial step back from our problems and finally see the full expanse of the forest that we couldn't see on the ground among the trees. This is quite a challenging task and is one that you will have to repeat many times in order to begin engaging with your subconscious programs. However, with time and patience, this task will help to expose your own personal biases, and free you from your own mindset traps.

To gain the helicopter view, whenever you begin feeling negative feelings or thinking negative thoughts, the first step is to stop. Notice that you are feeling angry, frustrated, sad, despairing, or whatever other negative feelings come up. Remember that it's ok to be unhappy — these feelings are signals from the subconscious that we need to take action! Negative feelings are the mind's way of protecting us from danger. The true test of character is not whether or not we feel negative emotions, but how we act on them.

So you've encountered a situation that makes you react in a negative way. Take a minute to ask yourself four questions:

1) **What am I reacting to?** For example, if you hate your boss, examine your interactions. Are you angry about what they said, or how they said it, or both? Are you disappointed that they confronted you, or disappointed that they didn't? Are you frustrated that you haven't been recognized for what you did well, or are you feeling betrayed because they didn't point out this problem sooner? No matter the situation, take a moment to think about what's bothering you.

2) **What would this look like to others involved?** Imagine the same situation from the point of view of another co-worker or family member. Imagine being the boss you hate or the sibling you want to strangle. Is there anything you could do differently to diffuse the situation? Is there something you're doing or saying that another

person could misinterpret?

3) **What would this look like to someone who is not involved?** Imagine your best friend could secretly watch the conversation between you and your boss. Imagine the woman who sits next to you at work could secretly watch the fight you had with your partner. What would this stranger think? What kind of advice would they give you? Would they agree with you that the other person is the source of the problem? Why or why not?

4) **Is there anything I can do to change the outcome?** This is the most difficult part of this task, and sometimes this question needs to be asked over and over before a truly fresh perspective can be gained. Even if you're right, and your boss is a jerk or your mother-in-law is pathologically manipulative, what can you do? How can you change your behavior to change the situation? It's very rare that we face situations that are 100% out of our control. Sometimes even the slightest change in tone, gesture, or timing can make a world of difference in the way others interact with us. But small changes in behavior can sometimes require an enormous amount of mental effort.

Chapter 4

This Will Stop Everything

The most limiting perspective loop we can get ourselves into is a negative one. Negativity can be limiting when it invades our subconscious programs. It's ok to plan for disaster or prepare for the worst. But negativity is when you start expecting bad things to happen and believing that there's nothing you can do to stop or change them.

Negativity, too, can trap us in a perspective loop. The more negative you are, the worse you feel. The worse you feel, the more your negative beliefs are validated. This spiral can keep you stuck in some terrible situations, and worse, negative energy can cause others to avoid you. Negativity is contagious, and so positive people who don't want to get caught in your negative perspective loop will start to distance themselves from you. This can cause problems in your social and professional life that you may feel unable to explain or solve (which then makes your negative feelings even stronger) (Alban, 2019).

When we develop negative core belief systems, it can be difficult to change them. Our subconscious will change any information that comes to us to fit into our negative worldview. Things that are positive and good your subconscious will twist. You may feel suspicious, anxious, or uncomfortable in situations that others find relaxing and peaceful.

Almost every human has a bit of negativity built into their core belief systems. There are two physiological reasons for this. The first is that our brains are constantly on the lookout for danger to protect us from harm. When our brains sense that we are in danger, our bodies chemically switch from our normal "rest-and-digest" state into "fight-or-flight" state. This is what gives the strength, stamina, and mental clarity to run from tigers or mad-axe murderers when we need too. However, many of the dangers we humans face now are social, not physical. Spotting a bear in the woods and spotting an eviction notice in the mailbox both trigger the same fight-or-flight response. But running from the bear is a situation that is quickly resolved, and once we are out of harm's way, our bodies can return to normal. The eviction notice, on the other hand, isn't something you can run from. Nor are high workloads, steep student loan payments, or alcohol addictions. These dangers take a long time to resolve, and they often lead to more problems that also activate the fight-or-flight response.

Living under constant fear, pressure, or anxiety is called chronic stress, and unfortunately, it's something that's practically universal in contemporary society. Our lives are extraordinarily pressurized, and stress can come from almost every area of our lives. Continuously living in fight-or-flight mode can have disastrous consequences for our bodies and minds. Negative and traumatic experiences can have huge, long-lasting impacts on the subconscious mind. Chronic stress means that positive or affirming experiences can be far and few between and living this way can make it very easy to develop a negative mindset. This means that, in a high-stress world, we have to do a lot of work to combat the effects of negative experiences before they become subconscious programs and core beliefs.

The second reason is that our parents are constantly on the lookout for danger when we are young children to protect us from harm. Again, there's nothing wrong with this — it means that our parents loved and protected us! But when we are small children, our brains rely a great deal on our parents to help form our core belief systems and our foundational subconscious programming. If our parents are constantly worried or fearful for our safety, then many of our core beliefs will be built around worry and fear. No matter how well-intentioned, negativity in our formative years can turn into limiting negative mindsets and perspective loops when we are adults (Elmer, 2019).

Perspective is intimately connected to focus. Your mind sees what it's looking for. If you have a negative worldview, then you will always see the darkness in the world. Your focus will be on what is wrong or absent, and so you will miss the things that are good and present. A negative perspective tends to paint your world in grayscale, and it can become difficult to see or feel positivity, even when you are surrounded by it. It's probably not difficult to imagine why such a mindset can cause us to feel a great deal of unnecessary unhappiness.

It's also important to remember that a negative perspective is no more "realistic" than an overly optimistic one. Culturally, we view pessimism as being pragmatic and rational, while optimism is viewed as flighty, romantic, or out of touch. But a truly realistic mindset is balanced. Someone who can see life for what it is has the most realistic perspective and is the person who will be most able to make the necessary changes to live the life they want to live. If you can't see the good things around you, then you are just as blind as someone who lives in denial and refuses to admit they have problems.

Changing a negative mindset is not about living in denial or pretending that your life is perfect. Developing a positive mindset is about examining your core belief system and identifying negative behavior or emotional patterns that are stopping you from accessing the good things in life. Developing a positive mindset isn't about exchanging one bias for another; it's simply about shifting your focus and removing your blind spots, so you can see all the positive things that were previously hidden from you.

Negative core beliefs can be about any area of our life, including self-esteem, productivity, finances, relationships, career, and sexuality. Often, negative core beliefs appear in one area, but as those negative beliefs become validated by our toxic behaviors, they affect all areas of our lives. For example, if you have negative self-esteem, you probably call yourself a lot of names. You might feel lazy, useless, or unlovable. This negative self-image will affect your productivity (you don't believe you can do it, and so you don't put in all the effort you could), your finances (your low productivity stops you from getting jobs or promotions you want), your relationships (believing that you are worth less than others attracts manipulative or abusive people who take advantage of your unhappiness), your career (you settle for low-level jobs you're good at because you don't believe you have what it takes to do what you really want), and even your sexuality (believing that you are essentially ugly or unattractive stops you from properly caring for yourself, which makes you seem sickly and unattractive to others).

As you can see, a negative mindset can quickly spread, and can easily trap you in perspective loops. The worse you feel, the more your subconscious activates negative behavior patterns, and those behavior patterns contribute to negative life situations, which then validate your negative core beliefs. To break yourself out of this cycle, the first thing to do is identify your negative behavior patterns.

Remember that behaviors come up from the subconscious. You may be negative in ways or situations that you don't even realize! Identifying your negative behavior patterns will make you more aware of how and when you are negative, which will then help you identify the core beliefs that are the source of your negative behaviors. Negative behavior patterns can take on many forms, but the most common are:

- complaining,
- blaming,
- criticizing,
- being attracted to drama or gossip,
- feeling victimized or attacked,
- expecting the worst,
- depression,
- taking things personally, and
- being unable to stop thinking about bad news.

Do you do or feel any of these things? If so, you may want to pay attention to when and why these negative behaviors appear. If you complain a lot, start to notice when you complain. What triggered your complaints? Is there something you can actively do to solve the situation you're complaining about? Is there a certain person or group of people you complain to more than others? Is there a certain situation that you complain about more than others? Understanding what instigated your complaining will help you uncover your negative core beliefs. Complaining is a negative behavior pattern initiated by your subconscious. When you start paying attention, you'll probably realize that you complain a lot more than you even realized!

This constant complaining may make your situation even worse.

This entire chapter is devoted to negativity because there are so many ways that negative mindsets can limit us or stop us from achieving our full potential in life. Those who live in constant fear hold themselves back. They never take risks, and so they are unable to seize or even see opportunities when they appear. Negative mindsets can lead to a very long list of mental illnesses, including eating disorders, drug or alcohol addictions, and mood disorders like depression, anxiety, and bipolar. Battling with mental illness can make life difficult, and create serious problems in our relationships, professional lives, and even impact our physical wellness.

When you pay attention to your negative behaviors, it's also important to notice who you are with when those feelings or behaviors pop up. Negativity is infectious. Negative people bring out more negative feelings within us. Sometimes this is clear — you might already know that you feel badly around a certain family member or group of co-workers. But sometimes this isn't clear. People who we may think of as good friends or close family may be the very people validating our negative behaviors. It doesn't matter who started it; once you contribute your own negativity, then you become part of the toxic group dynamic. Negative behaviors can encourage negative mindsets in the people around you, including your friends, co-workers, and family members. Those especially vulnerable to your negative behaviors are your children, who, if continuously exposed to your negativity, can then grow up to have negative core belief systems of their own.

So how do you combat negativity and cultivate a positive mindset? Though negativity can grow deep roots, you'll be happy to find that cultivating a positive mindset isn't as difficult as it seems. All the tasks at the end of this chapter will help you change your perspective and rewrite your subconscious programming to help you bring positivity into your mindset and your life.

Inner Transformation Task 1 - Creating Distance

If you suspect that the people around you are contributing to your negative worldview, then this task is right for you.

First ask yourself the question: Who in your life is negative?

The first step toward cultivating a positive mindset is to surround yourself (as much as possible) with people who make you feel loved, safe, and capable. People who leave you feeling fearful, depressed, angry, or hateful are people that you want to create a distance between.

The second part of this task is actively working to distance yourself from negative people. It may not always be possible to cut toxic people out of your life — you can't stop seeing your boss or your mom, for example. But can reduce the amount of contact that you have with them. Make small changes to your schedule or routine that will eliminate contact with negative people. Stop making plans to see or hang out with toxic people. Most important, eliminate negative people from your social media.

Coldly cutting people out of your life isn't always the answer. If you have family members, friends, or co-workers who are toxic people, it's not always right to cease speaking to them. But reducing your contact with them gives you the opportunity to find some mental clarity. Free from their negative influence, you can decide on the next step that's best for you. Can you change the way you interact with these people to make your interactions with them more positive? Are they feeding off of your negativity just as much as you feed of theirs? Are there certain things you can overlook for the benefit of their love, friendship, or support? Or are you clinging to toxic people that really aren't contributing anything positive to your life?

Whatever you decide to do, don't feel guilty about removing negative people from your life. There's nothing wrong with choosing to spend time around people that bring you peace, joy, and happiness. No relationship is obligatory. While there are often changes we can make or conversations we can have to work through negative patterns in our close relationships, negativity is rarely a one-man show. Sometimes people close to us react with anger, hurt, or manipulation when we do things that are positive and affirming for us. No matter how much we love those people, it's sometimes necessary to let go of people who don't want us to be happy.

As you create a distance or work on setting better boundaries within your negative relationships, be mindful of conflict and drama. Guilt tripping, accusations, and picking fights are all negative behaviors, and are all behaviors that you should no longer tolerate in yourself or in others. Engaging with these behavior patterns only validates the other person's negative mindset. It teaches them that guilt and anger are things that you will respond to, and so when they want your attention in the future, they will use the same negative patterns.

But it's not enough to limit your contact with negative people. The third part of this task is to increase your contact with positive people. Make more time for people who make you feel loved, happy, and supported. If you find that you don't have a lot of positive people in your life, it's time to take your new positive mindset out into the world and try to find some. Making new friends can be scary, but if you actively engage in positive behaviors, you find that other positive people will naturally become attracted to you. Just as negativity attracts negativity, positivity attracts positivity. The more positive people are around you, the more you will emulate and internalize their positive behaviors. Believe it or not, surrounding yourself with positive people is actually the easiest way to rewrite negative subconscious programs.

If you're not sure how to find new friends or positive people, start with a hobby. Choose an interest or activity that you love. It can be anything, as long as it's something that you enjoy. From creative writing to playing tennis to working with animals, whatever your hobbies or interests are, it's almost a given that there are other people out there with similar interests. Join a club or local group. Go to events like shows, conventions, or festivals that are themed around your interests. Find blogs, forums, Facebook groups, or Reddit feeds that are themed around your hobby, so you can meet new people both online and in person.

Meeting new people in the context of a passion or hobby is actually the best way to meet positive people. Why? Because when you are engaged in something that brings you happiness, you are at your best self. No matter how negative your mindset, it's impossible to be negative while engaged in something that you love. If you meet new people through this positive experience, then you will inevitably find yourself surrounded by people who are positive and supportive.

Inner Transformation Task 2 - Working with ANTs

Thinker John Asseraf talks about ANTs, or Automatic Negative Thoughts, and how these ANTs can quickly grow from momentary thoughts to core belief systems. ANTs are a natural part of the brain's protective system. In an unknown situation, your brain will automatically scan for signs of danger, and so will bring up the negatives first to keep you safe. Asseraf's advice for dealing with new ANTs is to thank your brain for bringing you this information, acknowledge the risk, and then let the thought go. This approach can help you to filter out ANTs that are unnecessary so they don't become part of your subconscious programming.

John Asseraf's ANT task is about examining our self-talk. When you are in a new situation, do you automatically think things like "This won't happen" or "There's no way this will work" or "I can't do this?" These are all examples of ANTs that have become part of your subconscious programming, and are now a critical part of your thought process. These self-limiting thoughts will cause you to hold yourself back unconsciously from opportunities and prevent you from taking the necessary actions to achieve your goals and fulfill your needs.

To begin the ANT task, make yourself an ANT notebook. Whenever you feel frustrated, fearful, or discouraged, write down your ANTs. Then write down empowering statements called affirmations, to challenge and change them. Here is an example:

ANT: I could never do (task, action, achievement).

Affirmation: I am capable of (learning, doing, or thinking) new things.

ANT: (Task, action, solution) will never work.

Affirmation: I see learning opportunities in every situation.

Whenever you think the ANT, automatically respond with the affirmation. Slowly but surely, when you face new or challenging situations, your brain will start reaching for the affirmations instead of the ANTs, and you will find yourself with more power and motivation than you ever believed you had!

Chapter 5

Something Powerful that We Don't Do Enough

Gratitude. Giving thanks for what we have is essential to our emotional, spiritual, and even social well-being. A daily habit of gratitude is one of the best ways to break out of self-limiting core beliefs because it shifts your mental focus away from what you don't have and places it on what you do have. Instead of focusing on what you can't do, a daily gratitude practice shifts your focus onto what you have already accomplished.

Focus, as we know, makes a huge difference in mindset. Remember the example of the hardware store? You don't see it until you need to buy an extension cord. A daily gratitude habit works much in the same way. Being thankful for what you have changes your focus. Suddenly, you will see more and more things to have gratitude for. Are all these good things appearing in your life by magic? No. In fact, they were always there, you just weren't able to see them (Mager, 2014).

However, gratitude works on a much deeper level than a simple change in focus, because gratitude is more than just a thought. It's also a feeling, which means that expressing gratitude engages both your conscious and your subconscious mind at the same time. Gratitude is an extremely easy and powerful way to rewrite limiting or negative subconscious programs. We just don't do it enough, mostly because it seems way too simple a solution for big and complex life problems. What we don't realize, however, is that gratitude (often as simple as a smile and a "thanks!") is an entire mindset of its own. Gratitude is all-encompassing, affecting our thoughts, imagination, mood, and actions. This is why gratitude is so powerful. It doesn't just make you feel good; it makes you act good, think good, and imagine good things. Your entire relationship with the world can be changed by gratitude if you allow more of it into your life.

Gratitude is a mindset of love, and it puts you in tune with the loving power of the universe. When we appreciate others, we are showing them love. When we appreciate ourselves, we are showing ourselves love. When we appreciate objects or situations, we are sending love out into the universe. This appreciation for the things we love acts as a powerful attractive force, bringing more and more love into our lives.

The secret to cultivating a gratitude mindset is to make it a habit. Too many people wait until they are feeling angry, irritated, or unhappy to practice gratitude. If you're feeling angry, thinking grateful thoughts might help you in the moment, but it doesn't solve the underlying dynamics that caused you to feel anger in the first place. It's another example of trying to change subconscious programs with conscious thinking. However, if you're listening to a favorite song or out with friends, thoughts and feelings of gratitude will come up easily and naturally.

This is why many daily gratitude practices advise that you practice just after you wake up. First thing in the morning, your day is still full of possibilities. If the first thing you do in the morning is check the news or go on social media, you are shifting your mental focus on the things that are wrong in the world or all the things missing in your own life. For the rest of the day, you'll be more likely to see all the things that are wrong, and you'll be looking for all the things you don't have. If the first thing you do in the morning is to write down three things you are grateful for, however, you're shifting your mental focus on the things you do have. Now, for the rest of the day, you're more likely to see the love and support that you already have. This attitude extends to opportunities as well, which is one of the reasons that practicing gratitude seems to bring more love and positivity into your life. When you have a mindset of gratitude, you are looking for all the opportunities you do have, instead of pining over the opportunities you don't have. If you can see the opportunities in front of you, you are more able to seize them and take actionable steps to improve your life. This gives you even more to be grateful for!

Developing a daily gratitude practice is taking action over your own feelings. When you wake up in the morning, you have control over the tone of your entire day. You can choose to begin your day feeling stressed and anxious, or you can begin your day feeling grateful and content. If you begin your day by doing something that makes you feel anxious, then you are far more likely to have a stressful day. Why? Because your mental focus will be on anxiety, stress, and fear, so those are all the things that you will see. If you begin your day with gratitude, on the other hand, you are far more likely to have a fulfilling and productive day. Why? Because your mental focus will be on success, abundance, and love.

A mindset of gratitude can also make it far easier to solve or handle problems. It's not that being grateful makes your problems disappear; it's just that situations that once seemed overwhelming or impossible seem far less frightening when you view them with gratitude. For example, imagine you get into a terrible car accident. Most people would agree that this is a tragedy. But if you have a mindset of gratitude, while you may still feel hurt or traumatized, you will also feel grateful that you are still alive and that your injuries are all treatable. That feeling of gratitude will help you make it through the tragedy with strength and grace. Keeping that grateful mindset will prevent the trauma of the accident from settling deeply into your subconscious, and so give your mind and body the ability to heal from any damage caused by the accident.

A daily gratitude habit will make this kind of thinking automatic. Instead of receiving ANTs from your subconscious, you will get messages of gratitude. This mindset won't make your problems go away (necessarily), but it will make your problems seem a lot smaller. This is how gratitude can free you from negative mental traps. Rather than feeling crushed and overwhelmed by life, you will slowly see the challenges and obstacles before you shrink down to small issues that you can confidently solve. Cynical people can sometimes sneer at the idea that gratitude can solve big life problems, but practicing gratitude isn't about ignoring your problems at all. In fact, it will help you see them with more clarity! Situations that once took up so much of your time and energy will be exposed for what they probably are — petty annoyances that can be solved by moving on to more important things.

Cultivating a mindset of gratitude is a skill. Like learning a new language or a musical instrument, learning how to be grateful is something that takes daily practice and repetition. When you first start, it will feel strange or unnatural. You may feel silly or wonder how something so simple could really be so powerful. But over time, the benefits of gratitude will appear in your life.

The first and most basic benefit of a mindset of gratitude is contentment. It's very difficult to be grateful and unhappy at the same time. Being grateful means focusing on what you have, which allows you to give up mental or emotional attachments to the things you don't have. It allows you to pursue the things you want in life without feeling bitter that you have to pursue them. It also allows you to see your life through a different lens.

There are many people, situations, and even physical things that appear in our lives we don't want. But a mindset of gratitude can show us how those things might still be beneficial, and this, in turn, will show us how to transform any situation into an opportunity for growth. Like the example of the car accident, a mindset of gratitude helps to build resilience against tragedy, and allows us to benefit from situations that would have paralyzed us before.

The true lesson to be learned from cultivating a mindset of gratitude is that all experiences have both positive and negative aspects. Nothing is objectively "good" or "bad" — these are judgments that we assign to certain situations to give them meaning. This is why two people can experience the same event and have a different perspective on what happened. A mindset of gratitude trains your subconscious to look for positivity, opportunity, and benefits in every situation, even situations that are painful and unpleasant.

Many people mistake being grateful for being in denial. But practicing gratitude isn't about ignoring the negative. Rather, it's about embracing the negative, and learning how to turn it into a positive. It's about accepting that life comes with goods and bads, but there are very few experiences in life that have no positive side to them. Gratitude trains the subconscious to look for positives, and this is what opens the doors of opportunity, insight, and creative solutions to even the most impossible of problems. Gratitude is a powerful antidote to helplessness and despair, two mindsets that can suppress even the most powerful or talented among us.

On a more day-to-day level, gratitude also teaches us that many of the "problems" we encounter in life aren't really problems at all. They're just annoyances, minor social hiccups that only blossom into real challenges when we feed them with our attention. Gratitude keeps us focused on the things that are important. With a mindset of gratitude, the minor annoyances of daily life will pass you by. Small things that once caused you to spiral down into mental traps of frustration, self-pity, and resentment will cease to affect you. In fact, you will probably stop noticing them altogether!

If you're still skeptical, you're not alone. Numerous scientists and psychologists have done studies in recent years to see if daily gratitude practices really do make a difference in the way our minds work. Many of these studies focused on people facing a great deal of adversity, including elderly people confronting death and people battling cancer or other chronic illnesses. You may (or may not) be surprised to learn that almost all of these studies yielded similar results. We now have a great deal of research to support the idea that a daily gratitude practice improves your mental wellness and facilitates contentment. There is overwhelming research that indicates gratitude improves relationships and even makes people more generous.

If that's not enough, scientists are also beginning to discover that gratitude can promote physical wellness too. Many studies showed that people who practiced gratitude saw decreases in blood pressure and increases in immune system strength. People battling chronic illnesses or pain saw a reduction in symptoms with a daily gratitude practice, and people struggling with insomnia or other sleep issues saw a great deal of improvement, even after coming off medication!

Gratitude is also an essential part of most addiction recovery or rehabilitation programs. More important than medications or psychological treatments, many recovered addicts have said that they would never have been able to quit their addiction without cultivating a mindset of gratitude. Along this line, more and more links are being drawn between addiction and gratitude (or lack thereof). Those who don't have a mindset of gratitude are at a much higher risk for developing addictions of all kinds. Once addicted, those who don't have a mindset of gratitude find it far more difficult, or even impossible, to kick their addictions. Cravings are based in want and dissatisfaction. You can't crave something that you feel you already have enough of. While the cravings that come with drug addictions have a chemical component, often the original impulse to drink or smoke to excess is not driven by brain chemistry, but by psychology. Drugs, alcohol, or even addictive behaviors like sex, shopping, or video games are initially sought out to fill an emotional void. The physical component of addiction develops much later than many people suppose. No matter your brain chemistry or family history, cultivating a mindset of gratitude will prevent you from engaging in anything to excess. You won't have any emotional voids to fill, because your mind will be focused on the abundances of love, support, and happiness that you already have.

Those who believe in the Law of Attraction believe that gratitude is an essential part of this law. A mindset of gratitude, they say, will bring more positivity into your life. Again, there's no magic behind this idea. Gratitude doesn't make your problems disappear, it helps you to see that your "problems" weren't really problems at all! Gratitude doesn't suddenly improve your life, it helps you to see the positives you were blind to before. However, there is a practical way that gratitude does bring more happiness into your life, and that has to do with opportunity. If you only see the things that you can't do, then you will never be able to see the things that you can do. If you are only resentful about the opportunities you missed, then you will never be able to see the opportunities that you have. Gratitude, however, allows us to see those opportunities. Being grateful for what you have means being grateful for all of the abilities, connections, achievements, relationships, and privileges that surround you on a daily basis. When your vision is filled with positives, your vision becomes filled with opportunities and solutions. This, in turn, helps you to take action to build the life that you want to live. As you solve problems and achieve your goals, you'll have even more to be grateful for, which will open your eyes to even more opportunities. If you have to be trapped in your own mind, then the gratitude trap is definitely the one you want to fall into!

Inner Transformation Task - Gratitude Journal

There are many ways to go about creating a gratitude journal. No way is right or wrong, better or worse. The goal is to find a strategy that works for you. While you can find different exercises and resources online, this chapter will outline three specific ways to contribute to your gratitude journal and begin cultivating a mindset of gratitude.

The first is to write gratitude letters. A gratitude letter is a letter you write to someone in your life to express appreciation for all the ways they have helped you or been there for you. This letter can be something that you send to that person, or something that you keep to yourself. It can be about something that happened in the past or something happening in the present. Whether you give the person your written letter or not, it's good to share your gratitude with that person in one way or another. A simple "thank you" can go a long way toward strengthening or repairing a relationship.

The second strategy is a gratitude list. Every day (or every week, if that feels more manageable for you), write down a list of 3-5 things that you are grateful for. These things can be small, like "I'm grateful that I have good coffee waiting for me in the cabinet," or big like "I'm grateful that my grandmother's surgery went well." They can be specific and you can say something like "I'm grateful that the bookstore had a copy of the book I wanted yesterday," or general like "I'm grateful that it's warm today."

An alternative strategy is to make your gratitude journal one giant list. Write the heading "MY GRATITUDE LIST" at the top of the first page. Every day, add at least one new thing or person to be grateful for. Eventually, every line in your journal will have something that you are grateful for. Once you've filled up your journal, you can save it as a reminder of all you have to be grateful for, or you can start a new journal and fill that, too, with gratitude.

The third strategy is a gratitude reflection. This begins the same way as the list — write down 3-5 people or things in your life that you are grateful for. But then, beneath your list, explain why you are grateful for those things. These explanations can be as long or as short as you wish. You can write the list and the reason all at once, or you can write your list in the morning after you wake up, and then write your explanations at night before you go to bed.

Chapter 6

This is the Person You Should Love the Most

This person is someone you see every single day. You have had more experiences, interactions, and spent more time with this person than with anyone else in your life. This person was with you from the moment you were born, and this person will never leave you, all the way to your death.

This person is you.

That's right. You are the person you should love the most. Self-love (or self-care, as many people call it) is never selfish. Those in your life who truly care for you will never resent you when you care for yourself, and will never reject you for doing what is best for you (Jacob, 2018).

Self-love isn't about being narcissistic or self-absorbed. Rather, it's about showing ourselves the same nurturing love and affection that we would show to a lover, friend, or family member. We can be extraordinarily harsh with ourselves, saying and doing things to ourselves that we would never dream of saying or doing to our loved ones. No matter how giving, nurturing, and loving we may be to others, if we don't show ourselves the same amount of love, we will find it more and more difficult to feel happy and satisfied.

The reason for this is confidence. When we don't love ourselves, we lose confidence. We stop believing in our own worth and our own ability to achieve great things. Even when good things come to us, we feel like we don't deserve them, or we give those things up for the sake of someone else's happiness. We believe that we are not worthy of love, affection, or rewards, and so we give up those things even when they come to us.

Self-love is an essential part of a happy and fulfilled life. Without it, we cannot feel happy or truly whole. You may have heard the idea that to be loved, you have to love yourself. This doesn't mean that you don't deserve to be loved if you have self-doubt, or that no one will love you if you can't care for yourself. What it really means is that, even if you are surrounded by love and support, you won't be able to accept or receive that love if you can't first love yourself. If you don't love yourself, then any good things that come your way you will reject, give up, or miss, because your inner voice is telling you you don't deserve to have those good things.

A poor self-image can destroy our happiness and well-being. Low self-esteem is what causes us to say "yes" when we want to say "no." It's what causes us to break our promises or put ourselves in harm's way. Those who have strong self-love don't feel compelled to agree to things they don't want to do. Sacrificing for others is beautiful and noble, but it is only an act of love if it's a voluntary act. Sacrificing because we feel obligated or compelled to put others before ourselves isn't an act of love for others — it's an act of hatred for ourselves (Procter, 2017).

When we make decisions that are based on guilt or the need to please others, we are not behaving in a selfless or altruistic way. Many cultures around the world value sacrifice and placing the needs of others before yourself, but too often these cultural values are manipulated to make others feel fearful or devalued. If you are putting others' needs before your own because you genuinely want them to feel happy or cared for, this is an act of love. But if you are putting others' needs before your own because you fear conflict or because you feel you owe them for past mistakes, then this is not an act of love. It's an act of punishment. When you give in to others because you believe their needs are more important than your own, then you are consciously and intentionally giving up your power because you believe that you aren't worthy to wield it. Caring for others should never leave us feeling powerless. In fact, truly caring for others often makes us feel even more empowered. If caring for others leaves you feeling drained, angry, or resentful, then it's time to examine the quality of your own self-care.

The idea that caring for yourself is selfish or demanding is an extremely toxic idea. If you allow this to become part of your core belief system, then all of your subconscious programs will be designed to deny yourself power, pleasure, and love. Instead, repeat this affirmation to yourself every day: "It's okay to put my needs first."

And it is! Loving yourself nurtures the highest version of yourself. Just as showing love to your partner, friends, or family inspires them to be the best person they can be, showing love to yourself inspires you to be the best person you can be. Showing love to yourself develops the core belief that you deserve happiness. Without this core belief, you cannot accept the love and support of others, even if you are surrounded by it from all sides.

Self-love comes in every form: physical, mental, spiritual, and emotional. It's not enough to just take care of one part of ourselves and ignore the rest. It's equally important to care for our bodies, minds, feelings, and spirits. Showing disrespect to one can manifest as problems in the others.

Self-love makes us better able to give love to others. If we love ourselves, then we have more energy, strength, and resources to give out to those around us. When we have love for ourselves, then we are generating energy from within. Our stores are limitless, and so when we give some of that energy to others, we feel even more energized than we did before! But when we don't love ourselves, we are no longer generating energy or strength from within. So when we give to others, we end up depleting ourselves, becoming weaker and weaker. When this happens, we have a tendency to blame or resent others for taking advantage of our good will or not appreciating all that we do for them. But in reality, it's very difficult to take advantage of someone who is practicing self-love and self-care. Often, a simple "no" would have stopped another person from taking advantage of us. But when we don't value ourselves, we agree to things we don't want to do. This isn't an act of love, it's an act of dishonesty, one that creates far more problems than it solves (Procter, 2018).

While it's true that we sometimes get stuck in our own mental traps, it's also true that no one knows you better than you know yourself. While loved ones and trained professionals can offer us insight and a new perspective on our own needs, the ultimate knowledge still comes from within. You know, on the deepest level, what is good for you and what isn't. You know what makes you happy and what leaves you feeling dissatisfied. While it's important to be open to the wisdom and advice of others (even if that advice is sometimes difficult to hear), the ultimate decision always resides with you. You always have the power to make your own decisions. Allowing someone to pressure or force you into doing something you don't want to do is not self-love, and it's not an expression of love from that other person. If someone routinely bullies you into doing things against your will, then it's time to distance yourself from that person. That may not be possible immediately, and your safety should always come first. But remaining in contact with someone who routinely tries to suppress your ability to make your own decisions is giving up your power to that person, and there will never be a time when that is the best thing for you to do.

Self-love bolsters your confidence, which, in turn, improves your decision making power. People who love themselves are more likely to make decisions that are good for them. Self-love empowers us to make good choices, which brings more good things into our lives. When we don't have self-love, we are more likely to make poor life choices that bring more harm and misery into our lives. Self-love translates into success and benefits, not because you are selfishly taking those things for yourself, but because you are naturally making decisions that bring those things into your life.

Having a good relationship with yourself also improves the quality of your relationships with others. If you treat yourself with love and respect, then you allow others to do the same. If you routinely undervalue or disrespect yourself, then you are also giving others permission to undervalue or disrespect you. Setting good boundaries can be difficult, especially with people we love. Sometimes setting boundaries leads to conflict, but more often than not, this conflict is necessary for our overall well-being. Toxic people are attracted to those with low confidence and poor self-esteem. If you want to be surrounded by supportive and nurturing people, then one of the most important things you can do is support and nurture yourself (Procter, 2016).

It's nearly impossible to be successful without self-love. People who are achieving their dreams are highly unlikely to look in the mirror every morning and think "I hate myself" or "I wish I was someone else." These thoughts are destructive, eating away at your ability to accomplish your goals. If your core belief system is based on the idea that you are worthless or undeserving of love, then your behaviors will mirror that belief system. Your subconscious programming is designed to devalue and disrespect yourself. No matter how much your conscious mind wants to be loved, your very behaviors and attitudes will be constantly undermining that very possibility.

Self-love is directly related to self-acceptance. If you love your partner, then you love them as they are, even when they do things that annoy or frustrate you. Love is unconditional, and it does not disappear when someone is not being their best self. Love for yourself works the same way. Self-love means accepting your flaws and fully understanding who you are. Self-love is not about punishing yourself when you fail to be your best self, nor is it about blaming others for your shortcomings. Self-love requires complete self-acceptance. We can't work on our flaws if we can't forgive ourselves for having them in the first place.

There are some simple things we can do to cultivate a mindset of self-love. One way is to focus on the things we are good at. If you are constantly thinking about fixing your weaknesses, then your mental focus is trained on all the things you are bad at. No matter how much improvement you make, all you will see are your flaws, and you will find it more and more difficult to love or appreciate yourself.

Instead, focus on improving your strengths. If you're good at something, focus on becoming even better. This attitude shifts your mental focus on what you're good at. The more you improve, the better you will feel, and the more confidence you will have. You will see and appreciate your improvement because you will be working on something you already love and respect in yourself. No one can be good at everything. Rather than obsessing over all the ways in which you are imperfect, hone your natural gifts into talents and skills that you can be proud to exhibit in the service of others.

Another huge way to cultivate self-love is to eliminate toxic relationships. It's almost impossible to love yourself if you are surrounded by people who make you feel bad about yourself. It's impossible to like everyone, but take steps to distance yourself as much as possible from people who make you feel worthless, frustrated, or guilty. Never feel afraid to set strong boundaries with people. Those who truly love you will never resent you for advocating for yourself.

Battling ANTs is another route to self-love. Negative self-talk ("I hate myself," "I'm ugly," "I don't deserve this," "I can't do this," etc.) can quickly take root in our subconscious and become part of our core belief systems. Whenever you catch yourself thinking negatively about yourself, immediately counter those ANTs with affirmations. If you look in the mirror and think "I hate myself," immediately counter that thought with "I love myself." At first, it will feel forced, silly, or unnatural. But over time, your ANTs will be replaced with affirmations, your negative self-talk will be replaced with positive self-talk, and your core belief system will be built on a foundation of self-love, not self-hatred.

One of the most challenging, but most powerful ways of cultivating self-love is to value authenticity. If you feel like you have to hide parts of yourself to live peacefully with others, make the necessary changes that will allow you to live as authentically as possible. If this means moving out of your parents' house or finding a new job, then so be it. The psychological cost of wearing a mask every day is too high. No matter what benefits you get from your current situation, it's never worth the price of lying to yourself and others about who you are.

Finally, allow yourself to have good things! If and when you are offered love, support, or good fortune, accept it with gratitude. Tell yourself that you deserve to be happy. If someone wants to give you something, allow them to care for you. If life wants to give you something, allow the universe to care for you. If you want to give you something, allow yourself to care for you. Feel pride when you do a good job. Cook yourself a delicious meal. Do something fun on your day off. If the thought of doing something fun makes you feel guilty, anxious, or irresponsible, then it's definitely time for you to examine your sense of self-worth.

Inner Transformation Task - Celebrating Strengths

Buy or make yourself a wall calendar. Every night before you go to sleep, write one achievement on that day's square. These achievements can be small (I woke up five minutes before my alarm) or big (I negotiated a $300,000 deal at work). They can be specific (I had a good conversation with my mom about respecting my boundaries) or vague (I was friendly in the office). Doing this every day will help you see all the things you can already achieve. At the end of the month, you'll have 30 accomplishments to look back on with pride. Better yet, you'll anticipate the moment that you write down your achievement at the end of the night. Throughout the day, you'll be looking for great moments to write down on your calendar, instead of ruminating over your failures or mistakes.

Inner Transformation Task - Setting Boundaries

Setting boundaries can be extraordinarily difficult if you have a low sense of self-worth. The fear of conflict and rejection can make us feel powerless. But good boundaries are critical for self-love. Though this kind of communication may feel uncomfortable at first, over time you will feel more and more empowered as you stand up for yourself. Thought you may lose some connections, you'll find yourself surrounded by people who love and respect you. This task may sound simple, but for some of you it will be difficult.

The task is a weekly one. Once a week, challenge yourself to say "no." That's it! Sounds easy, right? But once you set up this challenge, you'll probably find yourself in a situation where you really want to say "no," but somehow feel obligated or pressured to say "yes." The reason this is a weekly challenge is because it will take this happening a few times before you finally muster up the courage to say "I'm sorry, but I just can't do that," or "I'd love to, but I have another commitment." Saying "no" will always be difficult if you have a low sense of self-worth. You may feel like you're being difficult, ungrateful, or selfish. Depending on the nature of your relationship, the other person may even tell you those very things. But if "no" is what you want to say, then you should never feel guilty for saying it. The more you honor and respect your own boundaries, the easier it will be for you to communicate those feelings in the long run. Eventually, saying "no" will just be a natural part of your communication style. As the toxic relationships in your life are replaced by people who love and respect you, you may say "no" less often. It's far easier to give to others when you love yourself than when you don't.

Chapter 7

Getting in Our Own Way

There is a big difference between confidence and arrogance. Confidence comes from a place of self-love. Confident people believe in their own power to be the best that they can be. They accept and forgive themselves for their shortcomings and are willing to work hard and change to achieve their dreams. Confident people are flexible and accept the fact that change is necessary for growth.

Arrogance, on the other hand, actually comes from a place of self-hate. Arrogant people act like they are confident, but this mask is actually a way to hide feelings of fear and shame from themselves and from others. As such, arrogant people are rigid, inflexible, and unwilling to accept themselves for who they truly are. They refuse to admit their shortcomings, and refuse to make the changes that will allow themselves to grow and achieve their dreams (Amodeo, 2014).

Too often, people believe that, if a change needs to be made, that means they have somehow failed or made a mistake. Taking steps to make changes means admitting to that failure, and so they become hard and rigid to convince themselves and others that they have done nothing wrong.

But growth itself is a change. Healthy, strong, and capable people are constantly changing as they move through life. Changes in feelings, opinions, needs, and wants are all perfectly natural. The need for change is an indication that you are moving on into a new phase of your life and bears no judgment on who you are now or who you were before. If you perceive the need for change as a sign of failure, your rigidity will stunt your own growth. Worse, your attitude toward the change as a sign of failure will be projected out to the people around you, who will treat your need for change as a problem to be solved, rather than a moment of growth that should be celebrated.

If you approach life changes as exciting opportunities, new experiences, new beginnings, improvements, or necessary steps toward an achievement, then people around you will be excited as well. Weddings, housewarming parties, graduation ceremonies, and even birthdays are all examples of cultural traditions that celebrate big life changes. Looking for a new job doesn't mean that you somehow failed at your current job, it just means you're ready to move on and find new opportunities. Coming out as gay can be treated as a confession or as a celebration — it all depends on how you yourself perceive this change. Do you feel your sexuality is something to be ashamed or embarrassed of? If you do, then the way you come out to your friends and family will probably indicate to them that this is something they should be worried or concerned about. If you treat your coming out as the next step toward embracing your true self, then those around you who love and support you will feel that energy and celebrate with you.

The need to make a change can be difficult to accept because changes often require us to take a risk. Looking for a new job or apartment means taking a step out into the unknown. Coming out as gay or proposing marriage to your partner both mean entering a world of love, romance, and sex that you've never experienced before. Whatever the change may be, it often requires us to do something we have never done before, and when we step out into unknown territory, we usually encounter challenges and obstacles along with adventures and rewards. Sometimes we make mistakes, and sometimes we lose things that we wanted to save. But this is a natural and healthy part of life, and pretending that we do not have to change can quickly turn into rigidity, denial, and arrogance (Winch, 2018).

Arrogance is a defense mechanism against change. By insisting that they are fine and that everyone else is the problem, arrogant people are able to avoid taking the risks associated with change and stay firmly in their comfort zone. But the comfort zone is yet another mental trap. No matter how much we wish it otherwise, everything changes eventually. If a seed never changed, it would never become a tree. Likewise, if we never allow ourselves to change, then we will never reach our true potential. No matter how comfortable we are where we are, embracing change means embracing growth. Change can be an exciting adventure or a terrible tragedy. The more you embrace change, the more you can relish the challenges it brings. The more you fear change, the more threatening and destructive it appears.

Pretending to be superior to others is pretending that we do not have to change. People who act superior look for flaws in others because they are terrified that someone else will find flaws within them. They relish the opportunity to criticize others so they don't have to spend any time working on themselves. They hold grudges and refuse to forgive others because they are unable to forgive themselves for their own failures or imperfections. Though behaving with arrogance and superiority may help you gain power or prestige in the short term, in the long term it will only make you feel less and less happy. More and more people will distance themselves from you, and it will become more and more difficult to maintain healthy relationships with others.

It's ok to swell with pride when you've accomplished something worthwhile or done something that affirms your sense of self-worth. However, if our self-worth depends on achievements, praise, or material wealth, then we become more and more dependent on external factors to feel good about ourselves. Arrogance, pride, and cruelty are often defensive behaviors that arise when our sense of self-worth becomes dependent on the opinions of others. Fear of rejection causes us to hide all of our failings and vulnerabilities. If we can convince those around us we are perfect, then we will never be hurt by their scorn or judgment. This, however, is far from the truth. In fact, the more we cling to our arrogance, the less others want to be around us.

There is a difference between feeling proud of our accomplishments and believing that we are defined by our accomplishments. The idea that your inherent worth is tied to your achievements can be a destructive core belief. This idea can cause us to feel that, if we aren't doing or achieving great things, then we are worthless. This idea prevents us from taking risks or learning from our failures. It's also very difficult to feel gratitude for what you have if you feel like achievements are what make you worthy of love and respect. You can never rest on your accomplishments because you feel that, if you aren't always working toward something, then you are worthless, unmotivated, or lazy. This mindset is what eventually leads to greed (self-worth is dependent on material wealth), vanity (self-worth is dependent on physical beauty), and cruelty (self-worth is dependent on having power and authority over others) (Morin, 2018).

Buddhism teaches us that suffering comes from attachment. Clinging too tightly to things that are impermanent, says the Buddha, is what ultimately causes suffering. The ability to accept change is the root of contentment. If our self-worth is based on achievements or accomplishments, then we will never feel good about ourselves, because achievements, accomplishments, and even material things are impermanent. Wealth, for example, will fluctuate throughout our lifetime, but we are always worthy of love and respect. If our sense of worth is connected to our wealth, then we will become greedy and avaricious in order to prevent the loss of that wealth.

To truly feel content and fulfilled, we must base our self-worth, not on who we could or should be, but on who we are. In order to love yourself, you must embrace yourself exactly as you are, without wishing that you were different or shaming yourself for any flaws. True self-worth means living with dignity, and dignity does not wax or wane with material success or failure. If achieving bigger and better things is the only thing that makes us feel good, then we will never be able to appreciate the things we have already accomplished, or even reap the rewards of our achievements.

Dignity is the belief that we are worthy of love and respect, regardless of our successes or failures. Dignity doesn't have to be proven or earned, even to ourselves. When you live we dignity, you are able to take more risks, because you understand that if your projects fail, that doesn't mean that you are a failure. If you attempt to communicate your feelings honestly to a loved one and fail, you understand that you are still worthy of their love and respect. You'll be able to try again to grow and repair your relationship, secure in knowing that your ability to communicate is not a reflection of your self-worth.

Good people make mistakes all the time. Cruel or evil people make very good decisions all the time. Making mistakes has nothing to do with being a good or bad person. No matter how nurturing, loving, or compassionate we are, we will make mistakes. Some will be bigger than others. When we live with dignity, we are able to own up to our mistakes, accept the consequences of our decision, and learn what we need to learn from the situation. Being wrong is a terrible feeling. It never feels good to be wrong, no matter how spiritually enlightened you may be. But if you have a strong inner sense of self-worth, then you will be able to admit (at least partially) that you were wrong, feel bad for a while, and then ultimately grow from the experience.

Arrogance is being unable (even partially) to admit any kind of responsibility for our actions. If an arrogant person is late for work, for example, they will insist that they weren't actually late, or lash out at their boss as being demanding or tyrannical for expecting them to arrive on-time. Many of us have encountered people who are so unable to admit their flaws that they will literally distort reality to avoid admitting they may have made a mistake. This is the person who spends thirty minutes looking for their keys every morning, but when you suggest that they might be disorganized, they respond with anger, saying, "I'm not disorganized!" "Someone must have moved my keys," or "If you were neater, I'd easily be able to find my own things," or "It only took me five minutes, why are you so impatient?"

In Christian theology, "pride" is considered one of the seven deadly sins. In contemporary language, we often use "pride" to mean positive feelings of confidence and achievement, and so this can be difficult to understand. But what medieval Christians meant by "pride" is what we would today call "arrogance," and from that perspective, it's easy to see why this mindset would be considered "deadly." We've all met people who seem to have an inflated opinion of themselves. They may talk only about themselves or attempt to sabotage situations that don't revolve around them or their needs. When we are around arrogant people, we feel judged and criticized, and often respond by becoming defensive, which is another form of emotional rigidity.

Arrogance is acting better than or superior to others. This goes way beyond feeling good about yourself or wanting recognition for your achievements. Arrogance is about making others feel ashamed or worthless so we don't have to confront those feelings within ourselves.

Arrogance is a kind of defense mechanism. It's a way of convincing ourselves and others that we are perfect, with no flaws of any kind. Arrogant people, whether they admit it to themselves, are actually insecure. Their arrogance is a way of protecting themselves from their insecurity and overcompensating for their low self-esteem or feelings of fear.

Ultimately, arrogance is protection against vulnerability. When we admit that we were wrong or that we made a mistake, we are exposing ourselves as imperfect people. Exposing our imperfections means opening ourselves up to the judgment, disappointment, or rejection of the people around us, and it's this that makes emotional vulnerability so scary. To protect themselves from judgment or rejection, arrogant people build a hard shell around themselves, refusing to admit when they are wrong.

The number one problem that arrogant people face is maintaining their relationships. While arrogance can give us a certain amount of power over others, it's power that's earned by making others feel bad about themselves. Over time, people will distance themselves from us, as people who have strong feelings of self-worth won't feel obligated to spend time with someone that makes them feel unworthy.

People who live with arrogance ultimately invite conflict. Their cruelty, selfishness, and need to control others initiates defensive and combative responses in others. Ironically, the fear of being humiliated or rejected that causes us to become arrogant in the first place will ultimately come true if we can't let go of that arrogance. People who live with dignity find themselves surrounded by people who are loving and supportive. There are cruel people in the world who will intentionally seek to hurt us and take advantage when we are vulnerable. However, most people are moved to feel compassion, empathy, and respect when we drop our emotional defenses. When you live with dignity, people see you as approachable and friendly, rather than hostile and intimidating. The better people feel when they are around you, the more willing they are to love, support, and emotionally invest themselves in your well-being.

Living with dignity doesn't mean that we shouldn't have ambitions or pursue our dreams. It doesn't mean that we shouldn't feel proud of our accomplishments or celebrate our moments of strength. What it means is that we shouldn't base our entire identity on these moments. Achieving great things doesn't make us great, just as failing to achieve our goals doesn't make us a failure. Living with dignity means accepting that all people have strengths and weaknesses, good and bad, and that the pursuit of achievements is about striving to be our best selves, not proving to ourselves or others that we are worthy of love.

Ultimately, arrogance causes us to feel disconnected from others. We are unable to accept and embrace them for who they are because we are unable to accept or embrace ourselves in the same way. Living with dignity opens you up to receive the love of others, and allows you to give that love freely, without losing your identity or feelings of self-worth.

Inner Transformation Task - Letting Go of Fear

If you suspect that you may interact with people in an arrogant way, congratulations! The fact that you are willing to admit it means you are already taking steps to improve your self-worth and embrace your flaws and failures. This task is a meditation task, so find somewhere you can sit in comfort and privacy.

Sit with your back straight. Cross your legs, or plant your feet firmly on the ground. First, take a deep breath in, and then let it out. With your next breath in, think of someone who makes you feel judged, worthless, or insecure. As you breathe out, think the words *my self-worth does not depend on what others think of me.*

Breathe in again. This time, think of a mistake you made, whether it's recently or in the distant past. As you breathe out, think the words *my self-worth does not diminish with my failures.*

Breathe in again. Think of an achievement that was hard earned, something that required a lot of time and effort for you to gain. As you breathe out, think the words *my self-worth is not dependent on external factors. I alone have the power to make myself happy.*

Breathe in again. Think of a situation in which you felt powerless, victimized, or taken advantage of. As you breathe out, think the words *I cannot stop bad things from happening to me, but I can change how I respond to them. I am not a victim.*

Breathe in one more time. Think of a time when you were wrong, whether it was because you made a bad decision or because you misunderstood a situation. As you breathe out, think the words *I am an imperfect being. My imperfections do not make me unworthy of love.*

Chapter 8

The Most Important Step to Take

The most important step to take on the journey of inner transformation is action. Remember, your conscious mind is only 5% of your brain power. It's not enough to just think positive; you have to act positive. It's not enough to think healthy; you have to act healthy. Whatever or however you are trying to change, thoughts alone won't be enough to change your emotions and your behaviors. Subconscious programming happens through experiences. You can manufacture experiences through things like habit formation, spiritual practices, and mindfulness exercises.

If you feel like you're stuck at this step, don't worry! Many people get caught at this step. They know what they're problems are, but they just can't seem to take that first actionable step that would lead them on the path to change. The reason for this is fear. Taking action often leads to mistakes. Starting a new habit can feel very uncomfortable at first. Maybe other people will laugh at you. Maybe the routine you thought up in your head doesn't work in real life, and you have to make some adjustments to get it just right. The fear of failure becomes more powerful than the excitement of success, and so we spend our lives telling ourselves "I have to eat healthier" or "I'd really like to try meditation," but we never take the first step to make those changes a reality (Canfield, 2019).

We fear failure for a number of different reasons. For some of us, our self-esteem is so low or fragile that failing is too much for us to take. If we fail, we think our self-worth will become even lower, and that's a scary prospect. Some of us are afraid of other people's judgments. We think our loved ones might make fun of us, become angry with us, or even reject us outright for trying to change our lives. Unfortunately, when we make changes in our lives, it sometimes means losing friends or even family who can't accept that change. Knowing that this is a possibility is enough to paralyze many people, trapping them in emotional or behavioral habits that they know are bad for them.

Making a change means putting ourselves in a position to be judged. Whether it's a change in fashion, picking up a new hobby, or even a change in opinion, we are opening ourselves up to feedback from others. Usually, when we imagine that feedback, we assume that it's going to be negative. Part of this is natural and even evolutionarily based. Humans are highly social creatures, and a big part of our survival is thanks to being members of small groups. Hunter gatherer societies were rarely larger than 150 people. Some hunter-gatherer bands could be as small as 30! Being rejected from the group almost certainly meant death, as it was highly unlikely that another band would adopt you into their tribe.

However, the biggest part of this fear is our own subconscious programming. Too many of us learn as children that standing out or being different in some way is offensive, disturbing, or upsetting. Children freely play and experiment, but inevitably, there were games or experiments that your parents, teachers, other adults, or even other children responded to with punishment, humiliation, or even violence. Now, as an adult, variations of those games are still ingrained in your subconscious as bad or dangerous. When you imagine how others are going to react when they see that facial piercing or your new yoga mat, your subconscious floods your conscious mind with images of rejection and humiliation.

But feedback to change isn't always negative. Some people may laugh or even become angry with you, but others will respond with curiosity and admiration. Those that truly care about you will recognize that this change is something healthy and good for you, and they will respond in kind. Maybe they will laugh at first, but over time, they will come to support and respect you. For example, maybe you've decided to go vegan. Your parents, co-workers, and friends may laugh, or be concerned for your health, or assume that you're just "going through a phase." But after a few months, the people that really love you will change their attitude. Your parents will start happily informing you that the place they picked out for lunch has vegan meals. Your friends, whether or not they eat meat, will excitedly start talking about this new vegetarian cooking app they've been using. Those who can't accept the idea of you making positive change will slowly fade away when they realize that their negativity won't control your decision making. Not only will your self-esteem be increased by the fact that you took empowering actions to change your life for the better, but the love and support of the people around you will be both increased and affirmed (Edberg, 2019).

Taking action is the only way to move forward. Thoughts are important, but they aren't enough to make the change a reality. We would not have a single Shakespeare play if he hadn't taken the action of writing them down. We would live in a much harsher society if Martin Luther King, Jr. had settled for just thinking about how to stand up to racism. And you will never become a vegetarian if you just think about it — you have to start cooking yourself some meat-free meals!

Whether the change you want to make is big or small, the key is to begin with small steps. If you want to change the way you dress, for example, don't go out and buy yourself a whole new wardrobe! Make the change in small steps — a new pair of shoes, a belt, or a few new sweaters that were on sale — and slowly but surely your fashion sense will shift in the direction that you want. Many people find themselves unable to progress because they try to change too much all at once. If you want to live a healthier lifestyle, for example, you can't just change your entire way of life overnight! Even if you could, the thought of doing so would make the task seem impossible. Instead, start with small tasks. Make one change at a time, changes that seem feasible for you. Slowly but surely, your lifestyle will transform as you change one unhealthy habit at a time. Better yet, with each successful change, you will feel more and more confident in yourself. The prospect of future changes will stop scaring you and start exciting you.

Remember, too, that it's not just the change you have to get used to - it's the reactions and opinions of others. If you want to do yoga every morning, you don't just have to change your own routine. You also have to make space in the living room, figure out how to block out the sounds of your roommate making coffee in the next room, and get used to the guys making comments about your mat when they come over on Sunday to watch the football game. So imagine if you tried to do yoga in the morning, meditating in the afternoon, go vegan, and quit smoking all at once! You would inevitably feel overwhelmed and frustrated, which would signal to the people around you that these changes aren't good for you, which would make them go from curious and admiring to concerned and unhelpful. One small change in routine can have effects in more areas of your life than you realize. Making these changes one at a time will not only help you, it will help your loved ones to support and encourage you.

Here is an example: John has a great smile, but over a lifetime of drinking coffee in the morning, John's beautiful smile is a bit more yellow than white. This makes John feel more and more self-conscious, to the point where he actively hides his smile when interacting with others. Finally, John decides to make a change. He wants nice, white teeth. However, he lives in a small town, where major cosmetic changes are looked down on as extravagant or impractical, especially if they're expensive.

So John wants to improve the health and beauty of his smile, but he is worried that others will laugh at or look down on him. He feels that his family and friends will disapprove of him spending a lot of money on his teeth when he doesn't have a car and has been wearing the same pair of sneakers for years. He and his community have been socially conditioned to believe that spending time or money on your health and beauty is impractical and shallow. This belief even has religious and political implications — people will see him as vain and obsessed with his looks. They may dismiss him as just another millennial who spends too much time looking at people on the internet with perfect white teeth.

In short, this is a big decision for John. It doesn't matter that there are other parts of the world where making this kind of change would not only be socially acceptable, but expected. The people he loves and cares for live in a society that looks down on these kinds of changes, especially for men. Making this change means opening himself up to the judgment of others, and he knows that there is a possibility that the judgment could be negative.

John takes the first step — saving up. When he has the money, he takes the next step: getting his teeth whitened. Good for John! He's taken steps to change his life for the better. He's achieved one of his dreams — he now has a gorgeous white smile. He no longer feels the need to hide or cover his smile. But when he goes home to show his new teeth to his parents, the first thing his father says is, "Look at you! You think you're a model or something to spend all that money on new teeth? You have the money for that, but you don't have the money to get your own apartment?"

As you might imagine, this kind of reaction is hurtful and humiliating for John. Why would his father say something so hurtful? Is John's father abusive, negative, or angry? Not necessarily. Often people respond with anger or ridicule to decisions that they can't understand. John's father would have felt more self-conscious to be living with his parents in his twenties than he would have with yellow teeth. John's father would have made a different decision. Because he can't understand John's position, he responds with anger and dismissal.

John's mother, on the other hand, responds with curiosity, and even admiration. She was not able to give her support before he made the change because of her own fears of social rejection (It's just not what people do around here...). But once she sees how good John's smile looks, and how much more confident he is with his new white teeth, she knows right away that this was a good choice for him. She's proud and happy that he made this decision.

Later that evening, John is sitting at the kitchen table doing some work on his laptop. His father comes into the kitchen to get himself a beer. There is a moment of tense silence — the rejection from the afternoon is still in the air. John is still hurt and angry, and John's father is still confused and angry. However, because John's father loves him, instead of allowing the situation to remain as it is, John's father sits at the kitchen table instead of continuing on into the living room. Gruffly, he asks to see John's teeth again. He asks a few questions. At first, they are a bit accusatory, but slowly his tone changes to one of curiosity, and even envy.

There are a few things that we can learn from John's story. The first is the importance of taking that first step. No matter what the reaction may have been from others, if John had not decided to improve his teeth, he would have spent the rest of his life hiding his smile. He would have become more and more self-conscious. The idea that he is ugly would sink deep into his subconscious and affect other areas of his health, hygiene, and self-esteem. Even if his father had outright rejected him, or if both of his parents had responded belligerently, this still would have been the right choice for him. John made this decision for himself, and though it may cause trouble with his parents in the short term, it will improve his life in the long-run.

The second lesson from John's story is that his parents' reactions were not what he expected them to be. His mother, far from responding with anger or fear, was actually supportive. Though she may not have responded positively when he was still talking about fixing his teeth, her love for John far outweighed her cultural conditioning. Often, the people around us say things that aren't in alignment with how they truly feel. They, too, have deep subconscious programming that stops them from accessing their true beliefs or feelings. This is one of the biggest reasons that taking action is so important. Once John took action, his mother could sense immediately how much more happy and confident he was for having taken this step, and responded to it instantly. The next day, his siblings, friends, and co-workers may very well have given him similar reactions. If he had allowed his imagination to get the best of him, he would never have given his mother this opportunity to show her love and support for him. He may well have gone the rest of his life thinking she would have rejected him!

His father responded exactly as John was afraid he would. However, after just a few hours, his father began trying to make amends. Others in his life may have responded the same way as his father.

Perhaps the first month or two after getting his new teeth, he may have been surrounded by people giving him grief for his choice. But after six months, the attitude of the people around him would be different. Those who loved and cared about him would swell with pride every time John flashed that beautiful smile. Those who didn't would slowly fade from John's life. Toxic people that he may have clung to for years are eliminated from John's social life, allowing him to spend more time with the people who truly care for his happiness and well-being.

The third lesson from this story is that, while this was a huge step for John, it's a step that many other people in the world would never have given a second thought. There is absolutely nothing wrong with getting your teeth whitened — people do it all the time. John's fears were not based in reality. They were based in subconscious programs that made something perfectly normal seem like something dangerous and radical. Almost always, the things that seem dangerous to us seem perfectly benign to others. Even if the other people around us are confirming our fears, it doesn't mean that this is a bad or dangerous change. Remember that the people around you also have subconscious programs that are altering their perspective.

The only way to beat subconscious programming is to take action. This doesn't just apply to your subconscious programs; it applies to the subconscious programs of the people around you, too. After seeing how happy and healthy John was after whitening his teeth, maybe his mother got her teeth whitened, too! Seeing and experiencing John's healthy transformation changed his mother's opinions on teeth whitening and cosmetic changes. These opinions couldn't be changed by talking about it — John had to take action, and his mother had to experience the positive effects of that change, before she could work on changing her own core beliefs.

When we make a change, we are inevitably going to attract attention. But people stare out of curiosity just as often as they stare out of hostility. Whether you want to start a new job, go back to school, or spend a month living in Indonesia, people who continue to react negatively to your decision are often people who wish they had the courage to make similar changes in their own lives. Allowing those people's reactions to stop you from taking action is giving up your power to people who are powerless themselves!

No matter what kind of feedback you get, taking action always improves your confidence, and opens up doorways to new opportunities, new relationships, and new growth. Even if your change ends in failure, you still gain experience, wisdom, and courage. For example, imagine that your month in Indonesia is disastrous financially. You end up having to move in with your parents, you have two maxed-out credit cards, and you have no savings to speak of. But also imagine that you meet someone in Indonesia who ends up becoming your best friend. For the rest of your life, no matter where in the world you're living, this friend routinely calls and texts you, and brings an unprecedented amount of joy, love, and support into your life. So was your month in Indonesia a failure or a success? Should you curse yourself for going? Was everyone right to tell you it was a bad idea? Every gain comes with a risk. Very few experiences in our lives are 100% good or bad. Your experience in Indonesia gave you the confidence to make your own choices, exposed you to new ways of life, and introduced you to someone you would never otherwise have met. It also taught you how to save and budget your money, the realities of the cost of travel, and that credit cards shouldn't be treated like they're free money. Sounds like a success to me!

Not taking action because we are afraid of failure is often culturally coded as being "sensible," but this is misleading. Failure is a necessary part of our growth, and if we never allow ourselves to fail, then we emotionally stagnate, no matter how stable or secure a life we have. Unfortunately, as children we are often punished for failure, and rewarded for success. As we grow up, the idea that failure is bad becomes a part of our core belief system. We are afraid to try anything that we aren't already good at, because we are so desperately afraid of the negative consequences of failure. If we don't think we'll succeed, we won't even try, and we lose both the possibility of success and the benefits of failure.

How we learn in school has absolutely no reflection on the way we learn in real life. Often, the best way to learn something is to try it and fail! Think about budgeting your money. You learn how to spend and save, invest and borrow, by trial and error. You learn how to make good investments by losing money, and you learn how to maintain good credit by digging yourself out of debt. If you try nothing new because you're afraid to fail, then you will never learn, and never grow.

Inner Transformation Task - Take Action!

Your task today is the most difficult task in this entire book, and that's taking the first step on your path toward change. To help you do this, you're going to make an Inner Transformation Action Plan.

First, find yourself a notebook or open up a new document on your computer. Ask yourself the question *"If I could snap my fingers and instantly change one thing about my life, what would I change?"* Answer with complete honesty. If you could change one thing, anything at all, what would it be? It could be anything — I'd have a million dollars in savings, my mother-in-law would be nicer, I'd be beautiful, etc.

Now, underneath your answer, write one step you could take to make that change happen in real life. No matter how ridiculous or impossible your answer may seem, there is probably a way you could make it a reality. For example, if your answer was "I'd be a millionaire," your action step could be"Put $5 a week into savings." If your answer was

"I'd have a sweet and loving mother-in-law," think about why she might be cruel, manipulative, or nasty. Your action step could be "Invite her to Thanksgiving," or "Call her tomorrow morning to ask how she's doing," or even "Have an honest conversation with my husband about how his mother makes me feel." Your action step can be big or small, but the key is to be as specific as possible. *Be more healthy* is not a great action step. It's too vague, and it could mean too many things! "I will not get lunch at McDonald's tomorrow," on the other hand, is a great action step!

Finally, remember that no action step is too small. One day of not eating at McDonald's might not seem like a big deal, but that's your subconscious talking! Imagine that you go to McDonald's every day for lunch with the guy who sits next to you. Tomorrow you take your tiny action step — "There's a new sushi place in the food court. You want to try it today for lunch?" Maybe your co-worker agrees. Maybe you guys like it so much that you decide to get sushi every day. You only committed to not eat McDonald's for one day, but that tiny step turned into a whole new habit!

Chapter 9

The Goal Is to Set Goals

Sometimes referred to as intention setting, setting goals is an important part of making a change that often gets overlooked. The reason why setting goals is so important is because that's where your mental focus will be. If your goal is to publish a book by the end of the year, then all of your thoughts will be centered on publishing that book. Your habits, your actions, and your communications will all be centered on that goal of publication. If you don't set this goal for yourself, you won't have the focus you need to take action and achieve what you want to achieve.

Setting goals makes the invisible visible. It allows us to see opportunities and solutions that we couldn't see before. Often we become too mired in the details. We are afraid to chase our dreams because we don't see how we could make them happen. We are looking at life from a perspective that tells us what we want is impossible. However, if you set a goal, you are saying to yourself *"I will get this,"* or *"This will happen."* Now, your perspective has shifted. If you set a goal, that means whatever you want is possible. It's only a matter of when and how. Once you set your goal, the "how" will appear. It isn't magic. Those solutions were there the whole time. You just couldn't see them because your belief that your goal was impossible blinded you to any opportunities you may have had in the past to achieve it (Muchoki, 2016).

However, sometimes we sabotage ourselves by setting goals that we think we want, rather than setting the goals that we truly want. We set goals we think are possible, and dismiss the goals we think are impossible as dreams, wishes, or fantasies. The problem with this is that, even if you achieve those goals, you still aren't satisfied because it's not what you wanted. Even worse, if you fail to achieve those goals, you may be left feeling bitter or resentful that you wasted so much time and effort trying to achieve something that you didn't want in the first place.

To truly set a goal, choose something that you would consider a dream or a wish. Anything that makes you think *if only...,* change that sentence to *when...* Now you have a goal! Don't worry about whether or not it's "realistic" or "achievable." Once you've set your goal, your new shift in focus will make the solutions appear. Even if you fail to achieve that goal, you will grow and change so much through your failures that your dreams and wishes may change too! Instead of failing to achieve that goal, you will have learned more about who you are and what you want. But that learning would never have happened if you hadn't set out to achieve that goal in the first place.

Sometimes our situation or upbringing causes us to look at certain goals as "impossible" and certain goals as "achievable." You might feel that the goal of putting 10,000 dollars into savings by the end of the year is impossible, but someone else might see that as easy. It all depends on your income, your lifestyle, your financial support system, and your core beliefs about money and finances. This is why it's important to break up your goals into small action steps. Your goal might be *I want a better job* but your first action step should look something like *Send out one resume a week*. You might not think one resume a week is enough, but just wait. Setting the goal of getting a better job will change your mental focus. Instead of always thinking "I hate my job," you will be thinking "I want to have a better job." Before, all you could see was how horrible your job is. Now, you see new employment opportunities everywhere! To reveal those opportunities, set the goal that you think is impossible for yourself. Taking that small action step might seem like nothing, but saving is a habit. It's a mindset that will take you time to cultivate.

After a week or two of being in that mindset, however, you might start to think "Well, maybe I could start sending two resumes a week instead of one," or "If I set aside five minutes every morning, I could send out one resume a day!" Two weeks ago, the thought of sending out a resume every single day would have given you a panic attack. You needed to take the small step of just one per week to change the subconscious programming that's been telling you you don't have the time to look for a new job.

No matter what area of life you wish to change, whether you want to improve the quality of a relationship, learn something new, or run a marathon, the process of intention setting is the same. First, allow yourself to turn your wish into a goal. Then, set up a tiny action step to get yourself moving in the right direction. Often, the journey toward achieving a goal is not a straight line. Your small action steps and your new mental focus will open up doors of possibility all around you. The steps you take to achieve your goal may be steps you would never have imagined yourself taking. You may even uncover so many new things about yourself that your goal itself changes. That's ok! It's the processes of growth, and it's the path toward happiness (Goeke, 2019).

Don't try to micromanage every step of the journey. Set your goal (the end of the road) and your action step (the road right in front of you). Don't worry about what's going to happen in the middle. You have no idea what's out there because you can only look at the world through your current perspective. To change that perspective, you have to first take that tiny action step. Each step you take will reveal more and more of the map until you reach that goal you once thought would be impossible to get to. For example, if your goal is to work half the hours for the same money, don't worry about how you're going to achieve that goal. Just take your first action step of researching jobs and let your mind open itself to the possibilities. You can't plan every step of the way because you don't know what's out there. If you set too many goals for yourself or too many action steps all at once, then you are narrowing your perspective, rather than allowing it to open up to all the possibilities before you.

This is why CEOs make the money that they do. Their job is to set goals for the company. Sounds like a small task, but the goals they set can change the entire mission, environment, and identity of the company. CEOs don't worry about how those goals are going to be achieved — once they set their goals, they have meetings with executives and consultants to discuss the action steps required to make that goal a reality. Your conscious mind is the CEO of your life. Allow it to do its job of setting goals, and let your subconscious mind do its job of finding solutions and adjusting your perspective to fit your new mental focus (Walsh, 2019).

Sometimes it can be difficult to determine what it is we truly want. Our subconscious is subconscious, after all, and it influences our conscious thoughts whether we want it to or not. To get around your subconscious programming, ask yourself three questions that might seem wild or fanciful:

1. If I could be anything, what career or profession would I choose?

2. If money wasn't an issue, what would I do with my life? Where would I go? And who would I spend time with?

3. If I could be or do anything I wanted without limits, what would I choose?

The answers to these questions might surprise you if you take the time to answer them. The further away your real life is from the answers to these questions, the more dissatisfied or unfulfilled you probably feel. Pretending that we don't want the things we want is a defense mechanism. It's a way of saving ourselves from disappointment. Don't be afraid to admit to yourself what you want! That goal may seem impossible now, but it will absolutely never happen if you never even try to get it.

The importance of an honest goal setting is that, if we set goals that aren't in line with what we truly want, then we probably won't achieve them. If you convince yourself that you want a stable job and house, but what you really want is to travel the world, that stable job and house will constantly elude you. Your inner self will always sabotage your ability to find a stable job, because that's not what it really wants. On that same note, even if you find that stable job or house, you'll never be satisfied with it. You'll always find some flaw or some reason your job or home isn't perfect, because it's not what you truly want.

Another goal setting trap that many people fall into is setting goals of avoidance, not goals of achievement. In other words, we sometimes focus on what we don't want, rather than focusing on what we do want. *I hate my job* is not the same as *I want a better job.* The first goal doesn't tell you where you want to go, and worse, it puts all of your mental focus on the thing you're trying to avoid! If you're constantly thinking *I hate my job,* then the only thing you'll be able to see around you is how awful your job is. If your goal is *I want a better job,* on the other hand, your mental focus will be on finding better employment opportunities, and those opportunities will appear.

This idea is the core philosophy behind the Law of Attraction. The idea is that like attracts like. If you are constantly thinking about disaster, then disaster will plague you. If you are constantly thinking about money, then money will surround you. Wherever you place your focus, that's what you will see around you. Examine your goals carefully. Are you thinking to yourself *"I want stability,"* or are you thinking *"I don't want instability?"* Is your goal *"I want to be a writer,"* or is your goal *"I don't want to work in an office?"* If you can't seem to escape from your 9-5, you may need to re-word your goals and make the necessary shift in perspective.

It's also important to be as specific as you need to be when you set goals. *I want a partner* is actually quite a vague goal. You may end up achieving this goal, only to realize that having a partner wasn't the only thing you wanted, and you will still end up feeling unhappy. Often we avoid setting specific goals because we are afraid that setting those specifics is being unrealistic. However, knowing those details is important. You don't want just any partner — you want a tall, male partner with a good job who loves to cook. Allow yourself to want that. Setting yourself that goal shifts your mental focus. Now you aren't just on the internet looking for anyone — your mind is specifically scanning all potential partners for the qualities that you want. Allow yourself to set this goal, and it might amaze you how many tall men out there have good jobs and love to cook! More importantly, you'll feel much more fulfilled and satisfied when you do finally achieve this goal. If you fail to achieve it, you'll learn a lot more about who you are and what you want from your relationships by pursuing it. If you fail to find a partner, you'll end up feeling unloved and unwanted. But if you fail to find a tall, male partner with a good job who loves to cook, then with every failure, you'll learn exactly why you want those specific things. This might cause your goal to change (that's ok!) or it might uncover romantic needs that you never knew you had (this is also ok!). If you hadn't set such a specific goal, you would never have discovered those needs.

Inner Transformation Task - Setting your Goal

If you did the task at the end of Chapter Eight, you probably already have some idea of what your true goal or intention is. But now it's time to sit down with yourself and set your goal for real. The time has now come to ask yourself what it is you truly want.

To set your goal, follow these five steps:

1. **State your goal in the positive.** Don't ask yourself what you don't want, ask yourself what you want, and word your goal accordingly.

2. State your goal as if you've already achieved it: *"I will be rich,"* or even *"I am rich"* is far better than *"I want to be rich,"* or *"I wish I was rich."*

3. **Specify the outcome.** Don't just say what you want, say why you want it: *"When I am rich I will live with my family by the sea"* is better than *"I will be rich"* because it's more specific. "Rich" can mean many things to different people. By some scales, you are rich right now! You don't consider yourself rich right now, not because you don't have a lot of money, but because you don't have enough money to support a family or own your own home. Setting specific goals gives you a much better understanding of who you are and what you truly want.

4. **Want 100% of your goal.** If you're not sure whether you want a family, don't include it in your goal. On the same note, include everything that you 100% want in

your goal. Nothing is too specific, and nothing is unrealistic.

5. **Make sure your goal is self-initiated and self-maintained.** *"My mom will be more supportive of my sexuality"* is not a great goal, because it's dependent on your mom, not on you. *"I will have a good relationship with both my mom and my partner,"* on the other hand, is an excellent goal, because it depends on you. You have the power to change the quality of your relationships. Though it may seem impossible now to reconcile your mom and your partner, set that goal, and the solutions will appear.

6. **Provide context.** *"I will have enough money to buy a house in 10 years"* is a much better goal than *"I will have enough money to buy a house."* Setting the time-frame gives you a better understanding of what you want and why. It makes your goal much clearer, and will give you more discernment when it comes time to create your action steps.

Take your time when writing your goal and don't allow yourself to edit because what you want is "impossible" or "unrealistic." If you are not completely overwhelmed with happiness and motivation when you read your goal, then it's not the right goal for you. A true goal will give you goosebumps or excited butterflies in your stomach. Be patient with yourself. If you take several days or even weeks to write your goal, then allow yourself that time. Uncovering what we truly want can sometimes mean peeling back layers and layers of subconscious defense mechanisms and toxic core beliefs.

Don't underestimate the power of specificity. If your goal is too vague, then your subconscious has the freedom to alter your goal to make it easier to achieve. For example, if your goal is to have a romantic partner, then your subconscious will make it happen — by finding you the first available person! But you probably don't want just anyone, and so don't allow yourself to settle for just anyone. Write down exactly what you want in a romantic partner and don't be afraid to commit to finding that perfect person.

Once you're happy with your goal, commit to it! Read it every morning to set your mental focus. Read it again every night for the same reason. Ask yourself "What did I do today to help me achieve this goal?" and "What will I do tomorrow to help me achieve this goal?" Put your goal at the top of your calendar or your To-Do List, so you will have it in mind every time you make plans or set yourself tasks. Every time you take an action step toward your goal, you are sinking it deeper and deeper into your subconscious. Soon, every emotion, behavior, and belief that you have will be centered on achieving your goal, and opportunities will manifest as if by magic!

Chapter 10

Believe in Yourself, Believe in the Process, Have Faith

Faith is complete trust or confidence in someone or something. When religious people talk about faith, they mean complete trust in the existence and power of God. If you put your faith in another person, it means that you believe in them, without a trace of doubt. In order to transform your life, you, too, must have faith. Not in God or in other people. Have faith in yourself.

Believe fully in the process of change that you're about to initiate. Doubt and fear are natural feelings, but don't allow them to stop you from being the person you want to be. Believe fully that you can achieve everything and anything that you set out to do. Believe fully that you are good enough to have whatever you want and be whoever you want to be. If you can get yourself to this mental stage, you will be unstoppable, because the truth is that you can achieve anything you want to achieve. You absolutely have the power to do whatever you want and be whoever you want. The number one obstacle holding you back from achieving your dreams is you (James, 2019).

Self-doubt is a normal and natural part of being human. Even the most confident people have moments of doubt, insecurity, and fear. Life is full of gifts, beauty, and opportunity. But life can be cruel and difficult, too. Anyone who has survived abuse, war, or other traumas knows how terrible life can be. When these moments of darkness and tragedy strike, our pillars of faith can easily crumble. On a less dramatic note, even small, everyday moments of failure can cause us to question who we are and what we're capable of. True courage is not about feeling fear. True courage is about being afraid to do something and doing it anyway. Sometimes, to restore faith in yourself, you have to do exactly the thing you think you can't do. Even if you fail, what you will learn about yourself may be exactly the lesson you need to restore your faith in your own abilities. If you have a terrible fear of public speaking, for example, you may decide to overcome your fear by giving a speech at graduation. Imagine that the speech is a disaster — you bungle it horribly, your voice was too quiet, and you were shaking so much that you could barely read your notes. Everyone else may see this as a failure, but what did you learn? You learned that you are brave enough to not only face your fears, but to face them in public. You learned that you are a terrible speaker, but you may also have learned that you're an excellent writer. Just because you couldn't read your notes doesn't mean that those notes didn't contain amazing ideas! If you never took on the task of writing that speech, you may not be the bestselling author or award-winning journalist that you are today.

Faith is one of the most powerful mindsets any human can have, which is why it's so central to many religious ideologies. Faith is the antidote to self-doubt, self-consciousness, and helplessness. If you believe in yourself, then self-limiting core values or worldviews must shift or disappear. If you believe in yourself, then the negative and harmful words or actions of others will not stop you from achieving your goals. If you believe in yourself, then you will never give into despair, because no challenges will seem too big for you to overcome. Even if you meet a challenge that defeats you, faith in yourself will allow you to learn from your failures, instead of being defined by them (Kee, 2018).

Every single human is different. We all experience the world in a slightly unique way. Always be open to the advice and feedback of others — they can sometimes see things that we can't see ourselves. But don't allow others to decide for you. You know what's best for you. If the things others are telling you don't feel right, you are under no obligation to do what they say or follow their advice. Even if you make a mistake, and have to admit that you were wrong, that's ok! Being wrong is part of the learning process, and admitting that someone else saw what you couldn't see doesn't make you stubborn or silly. It makes you human.

It's also important to remember that others respond to social signals that we give them. If you don't believe in yourself, then you send the message out to your friends and family that this is something you can't or shouldn't do. Those who love us take cues from our confidence and happiness. If you believe in yourself, then the people who truly care about you will believe in you too. Belief in yourself also frees you from dependence on the opinions of others. When you are constantly seeking approval or validation from others, then you make many choices that are not good for you. You aren't making choices that will make you happy you are making choices that you hope will make others happy. This differs greatly from finding joy in caring for others. This is looking for an external solution to an internal problem. If you believe in yourself, then you will decide based on what genuinely makes you happy. If sacrificing for others brings you joy, then you will do so in a way that's healthy and beneficial for all. If it doesn't, that's ok!

Making choices that are good for you are good for your loved ones too. Have faith that you deserve to be happy and have faith that the people who love you want you to be happy.

No matter how lofty, impossible, or unimaginable your goals may feel, you didn't pull them out of a void. Somehow, your goals are based on things you have experienced, witnessed, or heard about. No matter how wild your goals may seem, they are almost certainly based on things that other people have done before. Impossibility is a perspective, not a reality. Whatever you want, someone somewhere has probably done it before. And if they had the power to do it, why not you?

So many humans have done things that, by all odds, they should never have been able to do. Some of those humans become cultural heroes, and most of those humans will never get the fame, praise, or recognition that they deserve. You are surrounded by people who do amazing things all the time. If you aren't achieving amazing things, it's not because there's something wrong with you, and it's not because there's something wrong with the people or situations around you. It's because your mind, in some way, is telling you that you aren't capable of achieving the things you want to achieve. You're stuck because your mind is telling you "This is it! There's no way out! Accept your fate and deal with it (Nichols, 2017)!"

This little voice in your mind is called your Inner Critic. This little voice does a great job of keeping you safe, but it also does a great job of stopping you from taking the risks you need to take to achieve your dreams. The Inner Critic tells you that you can't or shouldn't do something. It's the voice that tells us we aren't good enough, smart enough, or successful enough. It's the voice that tells us we deserve it when bad things happen to us, but it's also the voice that tells us the world is out to get us. If we listen to our Inner Critic and allow it to control our lives, then we can find us stuck in horrible patterns of unhappiness, anxiety, self-hatred, and self-pity.

Sometimes it's not just your mind that's telling you these things. If you've ever been bullied, abused, or attacked, you've learned the hard way that you can't control what other people think, do, or say. What you can control is how you respond to other people's behavior. If someone attacks or abuses you, you absolutely did not deserve it. But you don't have to lie down and let them attack or abuse you again. It can take years to get out of an abusive situation or a toxic social environment, but you'll never get out if you never even try. Believe that you are worthy of love and respect, and you will find people who love and respect you. Believe that you deserve to be treated with care and dignity, and you will find people who care for and value you.

There will always be people out there trying to knock you down, and there will always be circumstances that are out of your control. But your own thoughts, feelings, and behaviors are always within your power to control. You have the power to affect others as deeply as they have the power to affect you. Believe, not in the goodwill of others or the luck of the universe, but in your own power to change your life. Believe that you have what it takes to get what you want, and believe that you, deep within, are already the person you want to be. It's not the pettiness of others or the grim reality of life that's holding you back, it's your own subconscious trapping you in a limited worldview. Like Rapunzel in her tower, the traps your mind sets for you are meant to keep you safe. But just as Rapunzel couldn't be happy living a lonely life in her tower, so you can't be happy living inside your comfort zone.

To achieve your dreams, you have to step out of your comfort zone. It's called that for a reason. The comfort zone is the physical, mental, emotional, and spiritual places where we feel safe, secure, and...well, comfortable. But comfortable can only sustain you for so long. Growth means change.

Eventually, to grow, you are going to have to make a change, and that means stepping out into the unknown. It means leaving the safety of the comfort zone, and it means the possibility of making mistakes and being judged by others.

Sometimes the comfort zone can be difficult to see. Our fears can make the world outside the comfort zone seem far more dark and dangerous than it really is. Worse, our fears can convince us that there is no world out there at all! There is only the comfort zone, and anyone who dares to suggest another way of being is delusional, misguided, or dangerous.

Imagine if Rapunzel lived her whole life looking at the wall of her tower. She might even believe that the entire world is just her one little room! That belief would make her feel bitter, angry, and cheated by life. She would waste away, believing that this was just how the world was, and that there was nothing she could do to change it.

Now imagine the day she turns her chair around and looks out the window for the first time! When you set your goal, you're turning your chair around. Rapunzel couldn't plan her escape if she thought there was nothing beyond the tower. You can't find a way out of situations that make you feel angry, trapped, or frustrated if you, too, believe that there's nowhere else for you to go. Setting your goal is about changing that worldview. It's about showing your subconscious mind that there's a whole big world out there, filled with possibilities you can't even imagine! However, to take advantage of those possibilities, you have to leave the safety of your tower, and dare to step outside the comfort zone.

Believe that there's a world bigger than your perspective. Believe that, if you can set your mind to the right perspective, you can achieve anything that you wish to achieve. Believe that you are not defined by your successes and failures. Believe that you are powerful, worthy, and good, even when you make mistakes, and even when you're wrong. Have faith that you can do it and watch as the opportunities appear before you.

Inner Transformation Task - Achieve Your Goals!

Think about all the work you've done up to this point. You have already taken a huge step toward changing your mindset by reading this book. You have taken steps to become more aware of your hopes and dreams, fears and desires. You have become more aware of your core beliefs and your subconscious programs. You have taken steps to bring gratitude and positivity into your life. You have thought honestly about your life and what you want from it. Most importantly of all, you have made a promise to yourself to never again give away your power to others. You, alone, have the power to control your life. So now it's time to go out and be the person you want to be.

If you did the task at the end of Chapter Nine, you've already set a goal that fills you completely with happiness and motivation. You have a goal that gives you the chills every time you read it. Your task for the end of this chapter is to take the first step toward achieving that goal, and to never give up until it has been achieved. Know that there will be those around you who are negative and those who will say it can't be done. Accept that you can't change their attitudes and forge ahead. Those who truly love and care about you will change their tune. Those who are toxic and unsupportive will slowly drift away when they realize that they can no longer control you with their hurtful words.

Only give yourself one action step at a time. Watch as those steps blossom into new opportunities and unexpected changes in direction. When you finally achieve your goal, look back on your journey with awe and respect for yourself and for the processes. You did it! You achieved the impossible. More importantly, you know now that there is no such thing as impossible.

As you set out to achieve your goals, here are some final tips to keep you moving in the right direction:

1. **Define your goal properly.** If your goal is to get a job, then you'll find one — but it may not be one that makes you happy. Your goal should be your dream job, something that sends you straight into the land of daydreams whenever you think about it.

2. **Your action steps, on the other hand, should be very small and very achievable.** In fact, they should be so simple that they seem too easy. A great action step is something that makes you think *Well, I can obviously do that!* The point of taking such simple, easy steps is about changing your mindset. If you set an action step that seems too difficult, your fears will stop you from even trying, or your disappointment if you fail will shatter your confidence. But if you set something that's easily achievable, your understanding of what's "doable" will shift. An action step should be something like *"Send out one resume every week."* You may not think such a simple task could find you a dream job, but that's where faith comes in. Believe that you will find your dream job. Believe in the process.

3. **Don't settle for anything less than your goal!** Compromises may have to be made along the way, but don't settle for "close enough" because you feel like your goal is too hard to achieve or too specific to find in real life. You deserve to aim as high as you want. Your goal is out there. Settling for anything less is allowing yourself to believe that you don't deserve to have everything you want. Yes, you will encounter a number of challenges and experience many failures on the journey toward your goal, but that's ok! Those challenges and failures are part of the process and are not an indicator that you have done something wrong or have set yourself an unrealistic achievement.

4. **Think about someone you admire or respect.** Talk to yourself the way you would talk to that person. Talk to yourself like you are someone worthy of admiration and respect, and soon you will believe that you are someone worthy of admiration and respect. If your self-talk is negative, abusive, or fearful, then it will be nearly impossible for you to maintain faith in yourself. If you talk to yourself like you are worthless or unimportant, then slowly you will believe

that you are worthless and unimportant, no matter what you achieve or how others truly see you.

5. **Embrace your insecurities.** In the words of T. Harv Eker, remember that if you're insecure, so is everyone else. Everyone fighting their own battles and healing their own wounds. Don't allow someone else's self-defeating story become your own.

Conclusion

You have the power to live the life you want to live. The only thing that you need to change is... you! When you first opened this book, that was a difficult sentence to read. You may have felt angry, judged, or insulted. But now, you're ready to take back control over your own life. You are now ready to transform your life from the inside out, and build a mindset of success, power, and positivity.

Realizing your own perspective is a powerful enough awakening for so many people. Too many of us go through life believing that the way we view the world is how the world is. Opening yourself up to the understanding that your perspective is just one of many is freeing. There is always another way to look at a situation, another angle were solutions to problems may be found.

When you realize the inherent biases of your own perspective, you will also realize that everyone's perspective is limited. It's impossible to know everything — we can only see things from our own point of view. We have no other way to see the world. Knowing this, again, is freeing. If someone else doesn't believe in or agree with you, is it because they hate you, or is it because what you are doing is too new or unexpected for them to understand? Anger is the fight side of the fight-or-flight response, so, ultimately, anger is a response to fear. Now that you know this, you can see aggressive people for what they truly are, and that's scared people.

You now have so many tools at your disposal with which to shift and change your perspective. If something isn't working for you, take a moment to step back from the situation. What about this situation can you control? What can you do to make this work? What are you trying to accomplish? Asking yourself these questions will keep you in a mindset of power, and stop you from descending into a mindset of blame, helplessness, or frustration.

You have learned how negativity can trap you in a mindset that is limiting, toxic, and self-defeating. Negative people aren't more realistic. In fact, they are often more blinded to the truth than positive people! A negative mindset causes you to focus on what you don't have and what you can't do, and so that's all you will be able to see. A positive mindset causes you to focus on what you have and what you can do, and so those things will appear all around you.

Focusing on what you have is so powerful on its own that we have a special word for this kind of mindset: gratitude. Practicing gratitude every day can create such a dramatic shift in the way you view the world that it can literally make your problems disappear! This powerful practice is also easy. Saying "thank you" to someone once a day can make us feel happier, healthier, and more connected to the people around us.

You learned in this book about the power of self-esteem. Not treating yourself with love and respect can trap you in situations you don't want to be in, burden you with commitments that you can't keep, and sink you into a deep pit of depression and despair. Empower yourself with positive self-talk. Treat yourself with respect, and others will be invited to do the same. Treat yourself with disrespect, and others will be invited to do the same. Treat yourself like you are someone worthy of love and admiration, because that's the truth! It's only your perspective that stops you from believing it.

However, we also learned about the destructive power of arrogance. Pride may seem like it's the opposite of low self-esteem, but in fact, they both come from the same place. People who behave like they are better than others are just trying to hide their own fears and imperfections. If you constantly judge or criticize others, it may be time to give yourself some self-love, and accept your own failings, flaws, or insecurities. If you are around someone who is arrogant, judgmental, or overly critical, take steps to distance yourself from them. You can't change their behavior. The lesson of self-love is one they unfortunately have to learn for themselves. But what you can do is change the way you respond to their behavior. No matter what, you aren't obligated to give your time and energy to someone who can't respect or value you.

You learned that goals can't be accomplished through the power of thought alone. To make your dreams a reality, you have to act! Taking that first step toward change can be scary, and can sometimes be met with resistance and negativity from those around you. However, if you set action steps that are easy (yes, even too easy!) your understanding of what you can and can't achieve will shift, and you will feel more and more empowered to reach your goals.

And last, but certainly not least, you learned how to set a goal that is in line with your dreams and your desires. No longer are you obligated to chase goals that have been set for you by your situation or your upbringing. Don't be afraid to set the goal that you want — believe that you can achieve whatever you want, and trust in the process.

As promised at the beginning of this book, you now have the tools that you need to transform your life for the better, and achieve all the dreams you want to achieve. No matter what problems you are facing or what you want to change about your life, you now have the tools to make it happen!

If nothing else, the most important thing that I want you to bring from this book into your life is the lesson of self-love. Above all else, believe that you are worthy of love and respect. Never allow yourself to believe that you don't deserve happiness or respect. No human is perfect. Everyone has done things to be ashamed of, has done things that hurt others, and has acted from places of selfishness, anger, and fear. If you have done these things, it makes you no less worthy of love, dignity, and respect. You can not undo the past but you can reflect and learn from it. Believe that you are worthy, and that you deserve to have all the things you want. I believe that you have the power to change your life, no matter what problems you are facing. It's time now to set that next action step and know that there's at least one other person out there who's rooting for you!

References

Alban, D. (2019). Automatic Negative Thoughts (ANTs): How to Break the Habit. Retrieved from https://bebrainfit.com/automatic-negative-thoughts/

Amodeo, J. (2015). Why Pride Is Nothing to Be Proud Of. Retrieved from https://www.psychologytoday.com/us/blog/intimacy-path-toward-spirituality/201506/why-pride-is-nothing-be-proud

Bozak, S. (2019). Perspectives Retrieved from https://www.legacyproject.org/activities/perspectives.html

Byrne, R. (2006). *The Secret*. Hillsboro, OR: Atria Books/Beyond Words.

Canfield, J. (2019). Take Action to Achieve All of Your Goals In Life Retrieved from https://www.jackcanfield.com/blog/how-to-take-action/

Canfield, J., & Switzer, J. (2015). *The Success Principles(TM) - 10th Anniversary Edition: How to Get from Where You Are to Where You*

Want to Be. New York, NY: HarperCollins.

Edberg, H. (2019). How to Take Action: 12 Habits that Turn Dreams into Reality. Retrieved from https:// www.positivityblog.com/how-to-take-action/

Elmer, J. (2019). 5 Ways to Stop Spiraling Negative Thoughts from Taking Control. Retrieved from https:// www.healthline.com/health/mental-health/stop-automatic-negative-thoughts#1

Goeke, N. (2019). The Secret Summary + PDF - Four Minute Books. Retrieved from https://fourminutebooks.com/the-secret-summary/

How to Stop Being Negative: 37 Habits to Stop Negativity Forever. (2019). Retrieved from https:// www.developgoodhabits.com/how-to-stop-being-negative/

Jacob, C. (2018). Why Is Self Love Important? Retrieved from https:// upjourney.com/why-is-self-love-important

James, S. (2019, January 29). Believe In Yourself, Nothing Is Impossible: 4 Strategies To Build Unwavering Self-Belief. Retrieved from https://projectlifemastery.com/believe-in-yourself/

Kee, J. (2018). 7 steps to develop unshakeable belief in yourself. Retrieved from https://medium.com/the-mission/7-steps-to-develop-unshakeable-belief-in-yourself-c5ff5b7d55a1

Law of Attraction Gratitude. (2019). Retrieved from https://www.smart-goals-guide.com/law-of-attraction-gratitude.html

Lipton, B. (2016). Sucuri WebSite Firewall. Retrieved from https://www.brucelipton.com/blog/four-fundamental-ways-changing-your-mind

Lipton, B. (2012). Sucuri WebSite Firewall. Retrieved from https://www.brucelipton.com/resource/article/happy-healthy-child-holistic-approach

Lipton, B. (2012). Sucuri WebSite Firewall. Retrieved from https:// www.brucelipton.com/resource/ article/nature-nurture-and-human-development

Lipton, B. (2015). Sucuri WebSite Firewall. Retrieved from https:// www.brucelipton.com/blog/there-way-change-subconscious-patterns

Mager, D. (2014). The Benefits of Cultivating an Attitude of Gratitude. Retrieved from https:// www.psychologytoday.com/us/blog/ some-assembly-required/201411/the-benefits-cultivating-attitude-gratitude

Morin, A. (2019). 10 Things Mentally Strong People Give Up to Gain Inner Peace. Retrieved from https://www.inc.com/ amy-morin/10-things-mentally-strong-people-give-up-to-gain-inner-peace.html

Muchoki, B. (2016). The Secret To Getting What You Want: Goal-Setting. Retrieved from http:// www.whateverittakesmotivation.com/ 2015/11/11/the-secret-to-getting-what-you

-want-goal-setting/

Nichols, L. (2017). YouTube. Retrieved from https://www.youtube.com/watch?v=dkHPtlKh3GA

Procter, B. (2016). YouTube. Retrieved from https://www.youtube.com/watch?v=H3QhS4WDqcA

Proctor, B. (2017). What Is Self-Love? Retrieved from https://www.proctorgallagherinstitute.com/23395/what-is-self-love

Procter, B. (2018). YouTube. from https://www.youtube.com/watch?v=FV1iwG4WyjA

Walsh, P. (2019). How to get what you want through goal setting - The Law of Attraction Retrieved from https://www.paulwalsh.co/resources/view/GoalSetting#.XdKtU1dKio1

Winch, G. (2018). Why Certain People Will Never Admit They Were Wrong. Retrieved from https://www.psychologytoday.com/us/blog/the-squeaky-wheel/201811/why-certain-people-will-never-admit-they-were-wrong

Printed in Great Britain
by Amazon

SOLOMON ISLANDS

eta

oiseul

Santa Isabel

Munda

Auki   Malaita

Honiara
Guadalcanal   Wanione

San Cristobal

SEA

Espiritu Santo   Luganville

VANUATU

Malakula

Port-Vila

Éfaté

Poum

Le Cap

Nouméa

NEW CALEDONIA

TROPIC OF CAPRICORN

Halstead, Bob: Coral Sea Reef Guide
ISBN: 0-9700574-0-7

First edition published in the U.S.A 2000
and to be ordered directly by

Sea Challengers
Natural History Books etc.
35 Versailles Court
Danville, CA 94506-4454
Fax: (Int: ++1) 925-736-8982; e-mail: info@seachallengers.com

Layout: Helmut Debelius
Type-setting & Editing: Ralf Michael Hennemann
Print & Production: Grupo M&G Difusión, S.L.

Bob Halstead

CORAL SEA
REEF GUIDE

Great Barrier Reef • Papua New Guinea
Solomon Islands • Vanuatu • New Caledonia

Over 1,000 photographs
of coral reef animals
taken in their natural habitat

TABLE OF CONTENTS

Introduction . . . . 6 - 8

Class Cartilaginous Fishes	**CHONDRICHTHYES**	**9**
Family Wobbegong Sharks	Orectolobidae	10
Family Epaulette Sharks	Hemiscylliidae	10
Family Tawny Sharks.	Ginglymostomatidae	11
Family Whale Sharks.	Rhincodontidae	11
Family Whaler Sharks	Carcharhinidae	11
Family Weasel Sharks.	Hemigaleidae	13
Family Hammerhead Sharks	Sphyrnidae	13
Family Shovelnose Rays.	Rhinobatidae	16
Family Stingrays.	Dasyatididae	16
Family Eagle Rays	Myliobatididae	19
Family Devil Rays	Mobulidae	19
Class Bony Fishes	**OSTEICHTHYES**	**22**
Family Moray Eels	Muraenidae	22
Family Snake Eels	Ophichthidae	26
Family Conger Eels.	Congridae	27
Family Garden Eels	Heterocongridae	27
Family Catfishes	Plotosidae	31
Family Convict Blennies.	Pholidichthyidae	31
Family Lizardfishes	Synodontidae	32
Family Brotulas	Ophidiidae	32
Family Pearl Fishes	Carapidae	33
Family Toadfishes	Batrachoididae	33
Family Angler- or Frogfishes	Antennariidae	33
Family Clingfishes	Gobiesocidae	35
Family Halfbeaks.	Hemiramphidae	35
Family Longtoms or Needlefishes	Belonidae	36
Family Flashlightfishes.	Anomalopidae	36
Family Soldierfishes & Squirrelfishes.	Holocentridae	37
Family Sea Moths	Pegasidae	39
Family Trumpetfishes.	Aulostomidae	40
Family Flutefishes	Fistulariidae	40
Family Shrimpfishes	Centriscidae	41
Family Ghost Pipefishes	Solenostomidae	42
Family Pipefishes & Sea Horses	Syngnathidae	44
Family Flying Gurnards.	Dactylopteridae	50
Family Waspfishes	Tetrarogidae	50
Family Scorpionfishes	Scorpaenidae	51
Family Velvetfishes	Aploactinidae	60
Family Flatheads	Platycephalidae	60
Family Barramundi	Centropomidae	61
Family Fairy Basslets.	Serranidae	62
Family Rock Cods or Groupers.	Serranidae	68
Family Soapfishes.	Serranidae	79
Family Dottybacks	Pseudochromidae	80
Family Longfins.	Plesiopidae	81
Family Grunters	Teraponidae	81
Family Flagtails.	Kuhliidae	83
Family Bigeyes.	Priacanthidae	83
Family Cardinalfishes.	Apogonidae	84
Family Sand Tilefishes	Malacanthidae	86
Family Remoras	Echeneidae	88
Family Trevallies	Carangidae	89
Family Snappers.	Lutjanidae	91
Family Fusiliers	Caesionidae	100
Family Sweetlips	Haemulidae	102
Family Monocle Breams and Spinecheeks.	Nemipteridae	105
Family Emperors	Lethrinidae	107

2

Family Goatfishes . . . . Mullidae 112
Family Sweepers . . . . Pempheridae 115
Family Silver batfishes. . . . . Monodactylidae 115
Family Batfishes. . . . . Ephippidae 116
Family Butterflyfishes . . . . Chaetodontidae 120
Family Angelfishes . . . . Pomacanthidae 130
Family Damsels and Anemonefishes . . . . Pomacentridae 140
Family Hawkfishes. . . . . Cirrhitidae 152
Family Bandfishes. . . . . Cepolidae 154
Family Mullets . . . . Mugilidae 154
Family Barracudas. . . . . Sphyraenidae 155
Family Wrasses. . . . . Labridae 157
Family Parrotfishes . . . . Scaridae 167
Family Sandperches . . . . Pinguipedidae 169
Family Stargazers . . . . Uranoscopidae 170
Family Sand Lances . . . . Ammodytidae 170
Family Sand Divers. . . . . Trichonotidae 170
Family Blennies . . . . Blenniidae 173
Family Triplefins. . . . . Tripterygiidae 175
Family Dragonets. . . . . Callionymidae 176
Family Gobies . . . . Gobiidae 177
Family Dart gobies . . . . Microdesmidae 184
Family Surgeonfishes. . . . . Acanthuridae 187
Family Moorish Idols . . . . Zanclidae 194
Family Rabbitfishes . . . . Siganidae 194
Family Billfishes . . . . Istiophoridae 199
Family Mackerels and Tunas . . . . Scombridae 199
Family Flounders . . . . Bothidae 200
Family Soles. . . . . Soleidae 200
Family Triggerfishes. . . . . Balistidae 201
Family Filefishes . . . . Monacanthidae 205
Family Boxfishes. . . . . Ostraciidae 208
Family Pufferfishes . . . . Tetraodontidae 210
Family Porcupinefishes . . . . Diodontidae 214

Plants   **Algae**   **215**
Sponges   **Porifera**   **216**
Comb Jellies   **Ctenozoa**   **216**
Cnidarians   **Cnidaria**   **216**
Family Upside-down Sea Jellies . . . . Cassiopeidae 216
Family Sea Jellies . . . . Cyaneidae 217
Family Box Jellies . . . . Carybdeidae 217
Class Hydrozoans   **HYDROZOA**   **217**
Family Hydroids . . . . Plumaridae 217
Family Fire Corals. . . . . Milleporidae 218
Family Lace Corals. . . . . Stylasteridae 218
Class Anthozoans   **ANTHOZOA**   **218**
Subclass OCTOCORALLIA   218
Family Soft Corals . . . . Nephtheidae 218
Family Leather corals. . . . . Alcyoniidae 218
Family Sea Pens . . . . Pteroeididae 220
Family Gorgonian Fan Corals. . . . . Subergorgiidae 220
Family Knotted Fan Corals . . . . Melithaeidae 220
Family Whip Corals . . . . Ellisellidae 221
Subclass HEXACORALLIA   222
Order ACTINIARIA. . . . . Anemones 222
Family Sea Anemones . . . . Stichodactylidae 222
Family Secret Anemones. . . . . Thalassianthidae 222
Family Stinging Anemones . . . . Actinodendridae 223
Family Fire Anemones . . . . Aliciidae 223
Family Tube Anemones . . . . Cerianthidae 223
Family Disc Anemones . . . . Discosomatidae 224

Order SCLERACTINIA . . . . Stony Corals 226
Family Stony Corals . . . . Acroporidae 226
Family Stony Corals . . . . Agariciidae 226
Family Stony Corals. . . . . Dendrophylliidae 227
Family Solitary Corals . . . . Fungiidae 228
Order ANTIPATHARIA . . . . Black Corals 228
Family Black Corals . . . . Antipathidae 228

Phylum FLAT WORMS   PLATYHELMINTHES   229
Family Flat Worms. . . . . Pseudocerotidae 229
Phylum SEGMENTED WORMS   ANNELIDA   229
Family Scale Worms . . . . Polynoidae 230
Family Fan Worms . . . . Sabellidae 230
Family Tube Worms. . . . . Serpulidae 230
Family Jaw Worms. . . . . Eunicidae 231
Family Quill Worms . . . . Onuphidae 232
Family String Worms . . . . Terebellidae 232
Family Fire Worms . . . . Amphinomidae 232

Phylum MOLLUSCS   MOLLUSCA   233
Class Mussels   BIVALVIA   238
Family Giant Clams . . . . Tridacnidae 233
Family File Clams. . . . . Limidae 235
Family Thorny Oysters . . . . Spondylidae 235
Family Pearl Oysters . . . . Pteriidae 235

Class Snails   GASTROPODA   238
Subclass PROSOBRANCHIA   238
Family Turban Shells . . . . Turbinidae 238
Family Conchs . . . . Strombidae 238
Family Cowries . . . . Cypraeidae 240
Family Allied Cowries. . . . . Ovulidae 242
Family Helmet Shells . . . . Cassidae 245
Family Fig Shells . . . . Ficidae 246
Family Murex Shells . . . . Muricidae 246
Family Spindle Shells. . . . . Fasciolariidae 248
Family Volutes . . . . Volutidae 248
Family Harps . . . . Harpidae 249
Family Cone Shells. . . . . Conidae 249
Family Sundial Shells . . . . Architectonicidae 250
Family Wentletraps. . . . . Epitoniidae 252
Family Eulimids. . . . . Eulimidae 252
Family Tritons. . . . . Ranellidae 252
Family Frog Shells. . . . . Bursidae 253
Family Lamellarids . . . . Lamellariidae 253

Subclass OPISTHOBRANCHIA   271
Family Bubble Shells . . . . Hydatinidae 253
Family Tailed Sea Slugs . . . . Aglajidae 254
Family Sea Hares . . . . Aplysiidae 255
Family Side-Gilled Slugs . . . . Pleurobranchidae 256
Family Polybranchids . . . . Polybranchidae 257
Family Elysiids . . . . Elysiidae 257
Family Polycerids . . . . Polyceridae 258
Family Notodorids. . . . . Notodorididae 258
Family Hexabranchids. . . . . Hexabranchidae 259
Family Chromodorids. . . . . Chromodorididae 260
Family Miamirids. . . . . Miamiridae 262
Family Kentrodorids . . . . Kentrodorididae 263
Family Platydorids . . . . Platydorididae 263
Family Halgerdids . . . . Halgerdidae 264
Family Wart Slugs . . . . Phyllidiidae 264
Family Dendrodorids. . . . . Dendrodorididae 265
Family Triton Slugs . . . . Tritoniidae 265
Family Tethys Slugs . . . . Tethyidae 266

4

Family Arminids. . . . . Arminidae 266
Family Zephyrinids. . . . . Zephyrinidae 266
Family Flabellinids. . . . . Flabellinidae 268
Family Facelinids. . . . . Facelinidae 268
Class Cephalopods   CEPHALOPODA   280
Family Cuttlefishes . . . . Sepiidae 269
Family Squids. . . . . Loliginidae 271
Family Octopuses. . . . . Octopodidae 272
Family Nautiluses . . . . Nautilidae 274
Phylum ARTHROPODS   ARTHROPODA   276
Class Crustaceans   CRUSTACEA   276
Family Prawns. . . . . Penaeidae 276
Family Rock Shrimps . . . . Sicyoniidae 276
Family Solenocerid Shrimps . . . . Solenoceridae 276
Family Boxer Shrimps. . . . . Stenopodidae 277
Family Cleaner Shrimps. . . . . Hippolytidae 278
Family Hinge-beak Shrimps . . . . Rhynchocinetidae 280
Family Commensal Shrimps . . . . Palaemonidae 281
Family Reef Lobsters . . . . Enoplometopidae 282
Family Spiny Lobsters. . . . . Palinuridae 282
Family Slipper Lobsters. . . . . Scyllaridae 282
Family Hermit Crabs . . . . Diogenidae 283
Family Porcelain Crabs . . . . Porcellanidae 283
Family Swimming Crabs. . . . . Portunidae 284
Family Pebble Crabs. . . . . Leucosiidae 284
Family Mantis Shrimps . . . . Odontodactylidae, Gonodactylidae 285
Phylum ECHINODERMS   ECHINODERMATA   288
Class Feather Stars   CRINOIDEA   288
Family Feather Stars . . . . Comasteridae, Himerometridae 288
Class Sea Stars   ASTEROIDEA   289
Family Sea Stars. . . . . Acanthasteridae 289
Family Sea Stars . . . . Oreasteridae 290
Family Sea Stars . . . . Ophidiasteridae 292
Family Sea Stars. . . . . Echinasteridae, Mithrodiidae 294
Family Sea Stars. . . . . Goniasteridae, Astropectinidae 296
Class Brittle Stars   OPHIUROIDEA   297
Family Basket Stars. . . . . Gorgonocephalidae 297
Family Brittle Stars. . . . . Ophiotrichidae, Amphiuridae 298
Class Sea Urchins   ECHINOIDEA   299
Family Diadema Sea Urchins. . . . . Diadematidae 299
Family Sea Urchins . . . . Echinothuriidae, Cidaridae 300
Family Toxic Sea Urchins. . . . . Toxopneustidae 301
Family Sand Dollars. . . . . Loveniidae, Scutellidae 302
Class Sea Cucumbers   HOLOTHURIOIDEA   303
Family Worm-like Sea Cucumbers. . . . . Synaptidae 303
Family Anemone-like Sea Cucumbers . . . . Phyllophoridae 304
Family Sea Cucumbers. . . . . Holothuriidae 305
Family Sea Cucumbers . . . . Stichopodidae 306
Phylum CHORDATES   CHORDATA   307
Class Ascidians   ASCIDIACEA   307
Family Ascidians. . . . . Styelidae, Didemnidae 307
Class Reptiles   REPTILIA   310
Family Turtles . . . . Cheloniidae, Dermochelyidae 310
Family Sea Snakes . . . . Laticaudidae, Hydrophiidae 311
Class Mammals   MAMMALIA   313
Family Dugongs . . . . Dugongidae 312
Family Sperm Whales . . . . Physeteridae 315
Family Rorqual Whales . . . . Balaenopteridae 315

Index . . . . 316 - 319
Bibliography 320

INTRODUCTION

I never met my grandfather, but he spent a lifetime in the Royal Navy. No one else in my family was remotely connected to the sea so I have to assume that my own enthusiasm must have been inherited from him. Having been brought up in London my own early experiences were limited to the few one week family holidays spent at Hastings on the south coast of England. Memories are still strong of the excitement of the first glimpse of the sea, and of the fascinating fishes that were displayed for sale, some still flapping and wriggling, as the fishing fleet unloaded.

Papua New Guinea's first dedicated live-aboard dive boat, the Telita.

In an attempt to get on the water I joined a canoe club where I diligently practiced the art of the Eskimo roll. Since this entailed spending a lot of time upside down in a capsized canoe, I became quite good at holding my breath and became familiar with wearing a mask to protect my eyes.

I eventually joined the club on an expedition to canoe down a wild Welsh river. It was November, and, since none of us had any money, we pooled cars and were camping. After proceeding a short distance down the cursed river I hit a rock, smashed my canoe, and sank. The water was icy cold, but shallow, so I managed to drag myself to shore. Because of the car pool I could not go home. We camped, my air bed leaked, it was freezing. I spent the night huddled around the remains of a bonfire, dreaming of life in a tropical paradise.

The next summer, in 1968, I sailed for the Bahamas. The liner "Oriana" anchored off the harbour and I was taken ashore in a launch over the clear blue water. That afternoon I walked along one of the sparkling white beaches and planted my

The Coral Sea has the most modern fleet of live-aboard dive boats, and illustrates the investment being made to provide excellent services to divers and snorkellers.

feet in the tropical sea. The water was hot and transparent, and dozens of colourful fishes darted about my toes. The warm humid air charged my body with energy. A week later a new friend introduced me to Scuba diving. He explained the various skills, and I performed them easily. Slipping beneath the surface, I had found my true home.

In 1973, after qualifying as a Scuba Instructor, I moved to Papua New Guinea. Here I set out to systematically explore its incredible underwater paradise, and to learn what I could about the amazing marine life that surrounded me on every dive. It was, and still is, a

Cairns is one of many Queensland ports which harbour fleets of modern fast boats making daily cruises to the Great Barrier Reef.

marvellous adventure which I have been blessed to share with my wife Dinah, a wonderfully talented natural diver. Many reefs we explored were not even charted let alone dived, and on all of them we were confronted by the challenge of understanding and identifying our marine life discoveries.

In the early 1980's we built a 20 metre live-aboard dive boat, the Telita, to enable diving adventurers from around the world to join us. We were able cruise to the most remote of Papua New Guinea's islands and reefs. Our guests always surfaced full of excitement and wonder at what they had seen, and inevitably we were asked many questions about the identity of creatures discovered, and behaviour observed.

This book answers those questions, and all the questions that Dinah and I have asked others about marine life in the Coral Sea over the years. We needed a lot of help to find the answers and have been privileged to work with dozens of the world's top marine scientists, naturalists and photographers. I particularly wish to acknowledge Dr. Eugenie Clark and Dr. Jack Randall who have inspired us to great depths with their love of coral seas and their insatiable curiosity, and thank them for their generosity in sharing their knowledge. Should the book contain any errors, however, they are mine alone.

The Coral Sea region is an area which boasts astonishing biodiversity. Milne Bay in Papua New Guinea in particular has yielded the highest numbers yet recorded in marine biodiversity surveys anywhere in the world. Indonesia may be a close rival as far as biodiversity goes but the Coral Sea has a big advantage in that it has superb infrastructure that enables people to see these wonders.

Australia's Great Barrier Reef supports a huge tourist industry which, every day, welcomes thousands of people to go snorkelling, diving, or viewing from special semi-submersible boats. The reef itself is 2,300 kilometres long and anything from 30 to 260 kilometres off shore. It is a marine park, and has been zoned for different activities by the Great Barrier Reef Marine Park Authority, GBRMPA, charged with protecting the 20,300 square kilometres of actual submerged reef.

Outside the GBR, in the open Coral Sea, are a number of isolated coral reefs systems, Osprey, Flinder's, Lihou, Marion and so on, which are accessible from Australian ports on a regular basis. Here the water is usually extraordinarily clear, and the reefs are characterised by dramatic vertical outer walls, abundant pelagics, and lagoon bommies

Leru Cut in the Solomon Islands is one of several unusual and dramatic reef formations.

7

Coral Sea reefs are vibrant and have stunning biodiversity.

(isolated coral heads or small reefs) festooned with soft corals and gorgonians. Biodiversity is not as varied as the inshore reefs since habitats are limited, however some of the creatures that live here are rare elsewhere.

Papua New Guinea not only has an exceptionally long coastline, it boasts a great variety of different habitats, shared to a lesser extent by the other island nations of the Coral Sea. It has barrier reefs, lagoons, mangroves and atolls and even its own Coral Sea reef, Eastern Fields, but also something that is unknown in Australian waters - areas where the shore line lacks any continental shelf.

Here the mountains fall directly into the sea and continue down to the abyss with just a few metres of fringing reef in the shallows. Some of these sites are protected from the prevailing South East trade winds of the Coral Sea and the combination of shelter, nutrients from the land, and deep clear water produce extraordinary habitats, full of beautiful corals and exotic marine life, and easy to dive.

Papua New Guinea dive tourism is now well established and the country, which gained independence in 1975, boasts both land based resorts and excellent, state of the art, live-aboard dive boats. Although technically containing the Bismark and Solomon Seas and being bordered by the Pacific Ocean as well as the Coral Sea, the whole of Papua New Guinea is included here.

The independent nations of the Solomon Islands and Vanuatu form a chain of relatively small islands that define the north-eastern rim of the Coral Sea. Tourist snorkelling and diving facilities are again well established and form a major part of the total tourist industries of these countries. The Solomon Islands is particularly treasured for its splendid reefs and unusual reef formations, and Vanuatu boasts probably the world's most famous, and certainly the largest, regularly dived shipwreck, the SS President Coolidge, along with excellent coral reefs.

The south-east corner of the Coral Sea is defined by the French territory of New Caledonia and its off-shore, and seldom visited, Chesterfield Reef system. At the southern tip of New Caledonia the Isle of Pines is one of the best known diving destinations appreciated not only for its coral reefs but for stunning flooded limestone caves. Noumea has a famous aquarium that has specialised in displaying living corals, and is also a base for diving, snorkelling and coral viewing tours.

Divers move through several stages when observing Coral Sea marine life. The first stage is to be overwhelmed by the abundance and, particularly, the biodiversity - which is far greater than that observed in the Caribbean or Red Sea. The next stage is to learn to recognise common species by their colour and shape, and perhaps behaviour, and to find their identity. Further underwater study reveals subtle differences between species and sometimes the surprising revelation that what was considered to be one species is in fact two - or even more. I have tried to pay special attention in this book as to how divers may distinguish between what are, at first sight, two members of the same species. The details can be very important.

The Coral Sea is one of the richest areas of marine life on our planet both in terms of abundance and biodiversity. Much still awaits discovery and it is an area, perhaps threatened, but still not significantly damaged by pollution or over-population and over-fishing. The creatures in this book are only a small part of the total marine life that exists, but I hope that it will serve as a useful, accurate and entertaining guide that will help increase the enjoyment of every spectator viewing beneath CS waves.

Cairns, spring of 2000   **Bob Halstead**

Tasselled Wobbegong

Length: Rarely over 2 m.
Distribution: Southern parts of
PNG and all other CS.
Depth: 5 to 30 m.
General: Usually found resting
on bottom or under open
ledges, common on wrecks
and inside lagoons. Docile if
not molested but have large
jaw with sharp gripping teeth
and reluctant to let go once
they have bitten.

Previous page:
Silvertip Shark,
see also page 11.

Eucrossorhinus dasypogon   **Port Moresby, PNG**

**Freycinet's Epaulette
Shark**

Le: To 70 cm.
Di: All CS.
De: Shallow reef tops to 10 m.
Three of five species are shown
here, they are often confused
but careful observation of the
patterns of markings surrounding
the large black ocellus can help
identification. Usually seen by
divers partly hidden under coral
during the day time or out feeding at night mainly on bottom
dwelling invertebrates.

Hemiscyllium freycineti   **Milne Bay, PNG**

**Ocellated Epaulette
Shark**
Epaulette Sharks are sometimes
grabbed by foolish divers who
find the shark difficult to hold
on to as it struggles with surprising power, on one occasion
the shark freed itself immediately biting the, up until that
moment, girlfriend of its captor.
Below: *Hemiscyllium hallstromi.*

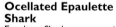
Hemiscyllium ocellatum   **GBR, Australia**

Tawny Shark

Le: Up to 3 m. Di: All CS. De: 5 to 50 m. Ge: Will usually find a cave, wreck or deep ledge to hide in during the day, and will take off with a wide thrashing motion which wrinkles their skin if disturbed. Can be attracted by baits. Below: *Stegostoma fasciatum*, family Stegostomatidae, rarely over 2 m, 0 - 50 m.

Nebrius ferrugineus   Milne Bay, PNG

Whale Shark

Le: Up to 12 m or more, usually less than 10 m. Di: All CS. De: Commonly seen from surface down to 10 m. Ge: Will often swim to an anchored boat but will take off if approached aggressively by swimmers or divers. Divers who approach carefully, swimming parallel rather than towards the shark, and who avoid touching it initially, are often rewarded by closer and repeated encounters. The world's largest fishes are plankton feeders and harmless. Up to 300 embryos found in pregnant ♀ which is record for all sharks.

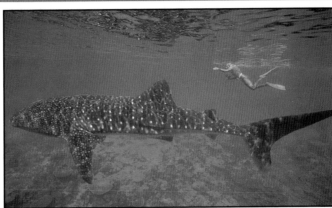

Rhincodon typus   Milne Bay, PNG

Silvertip Shark

Le: To 2.5 m.
Di: All CS.
De: Surface to 50 m plus.
Ge: This beautiful shark is easily distinguished from Oceanic and Reef Whitetip sharks in that it has silver edges to its fins rather than tips, yet is often confused with them. It may approach a diver head on when first investigating but turns away at the last moment, subsequent approaches are not so close unless baits are used. Groups of these sharks do not frenzy when feeding but are respectful to one another.

Carcharhinus albimarginatus   New Ireland, PNG

Grey Reef Shark
Le: Rarely over 1.8 m.
Di: All CS.
De: Surface to 50 m plus.
Ge: A curious, fast moving and competitive shark that often occurs in large numbers. The shark may frenzy in baited conditions. Displays threat display by arching its back, raising its head, lowering its pectorals and making exaggerated swimming motion. If ignored the shark will make a rapid biting attack. The sharks are easily attracted to baits and quickly learn to ignore divers, however, they are inaccurate close to baits and should not be hand-fed.
See also page 9.

Carcharhinus amblyrhynchos   **New Ireland, PNG**

Blacktip Shark

Le: Up to 140 cm.
Di: All CS.
De: Shallower than 10 m.
Ge: A common and distinctive species seen on reef tops or close to beaches or mangroves in very shallow water. Has been known to bite waders but usually considered harmless because of its small size. Territorial and a popular food fish.

Carcharhinus melanopterus   **New Ireland, PNG**

Silky Shark

Le: To 3 m, commonly much less.
Di: All CS.
De: Surface to 50 m plus.
Ge: This pelagic shark is rarely seen on coral reefs but common in deep water nearby. It is most often seen if divers or snorkellers attempt to swim with whales. The whales may rapidly disappear and the divers left with circling Silky Sharks in the blue water below, sometimes making aggressive close approaches. The shark is slim and has an elongated second dorsal twice as long, or more, as it is high.

Carcharhinus falciformis   **Milne Bay, PNG**

Bull Shark

Le: To 3.4 m.
Di: All CS.
De: Surface to 50 m plus.
Ge: An impressive, curious and dangerous shark which in my experience is far more bold and aggressive than the Tiger Shark. Known to enter fresh, shallow and turbid water systems. It has a large blunt head with large powerful jaws and the first dorsal fin is slightly caudate which is an important aid to identification.

Carcharhinus leucas Vanuatu

Whitetip Shark
Le: To 170 cm. Di: All CS. De: 8 to 40+ m. Ge: Often resting on or swimming close to bottom. Young (below) favour shelter of plate corals. Older specimens may loose white tip but skinny cigar-shaped body is distinct. May be ciguatoxic.

Triaenodon obesus Eastern Fields, Coral Sea

Scalloped Hammerhead Shark
Le: To 3.5 m. Di: All CS. De: Surface to 50 m plus. Ge: This hammerhead shark often forms large schools, one of the great sights of the underwater world. They favour reefs with steep dropoffs to very deep water, and avoid the warmest tropical waters. It has been speculated that the hammer-shaped head is an aid to blue water navigation. Generally shy and difficult to approach. Males will take baits but females are more wary. Experienced divers do not consider these sharks dangerous.

Sphyrna lewini Milne Bay, PNG

SHARK FEED IN THE CORAL SEA

My beginning dives in the Bahamas thirty years ago were preceded, usually as I tried to sleep the night before, by a nagging vision of being grabbed by a shark. Heroic stories abounded of miraculous escapes from shark attacks by super-human divers. Dive knives were purchased with their shark fighting qualities of first consideration, which is why they looked rather more like swords than knives, and divers were advised to leave the water if a shark was ever seen. In fact very few ever were, which of course just added to their terrible reputation, and if one was ever seen this became an excuse to huddle close to your buddy, and utter prayers for salvation while backing out of the water.

I moved on to PNG where, in the early days at least, making a dive without seeing a shark was about as easy as making one without getting wet. I quickly learned that sharks had been slandered and that the risk to a diver from a shark was minuscule. I also found that sharks preferred to stay away from sites regularly dived. This became a problem as better educated divers started to request dives where they would see sharks, and this led to dive operators selecting certain sites and deliberately attracting sharks to them by using baits.

Grey Reef Sharks *Carcharhinus amblyrhynchos* ignore the divers at this SCUBA ZOO gathering. All photographs on these two pages were taken at Flinder's Reef in the Coral Sea.

SCUBA ZOO was planned and developed by Mike Ball to give divers close-up experiences with sharks in controlled conditions. A carefully selected sheltered site at Flinder's Reef in the Coral Sea on a flat sandy bottom in 15 metres of water enables the vessel Spoil Sport to anchor nearby. Two huge shark cages have been constructed and anchored to the bottom making an L shape. Access is at the back through large doors. Baits are placed in a metal garbage can with holes in the side to allow the aroma to waft in the water.

Crew members of the Spoil Sport use lines to pull the baits closer to the divers.

All divers enter together and descend to the cages, where they may enter or just lie on top. Once everyone is in position the bait bin is connected to a series of lines which enable it to be pulled close to all the divers. Sharks follow the bin and approach the cages. The water is wonderfully clear and the white sand bottom makes everything bright even if the sun is not actually had a rain squall while on our dive, and never realised

The sharks gather around the bait bucket just before it is opened. Apparently the baits are much more attractive than divers well wrapped in neoprene.

until later. This is the best time for photographers as the sharks are slowly cruising and come as close as you want them to. They are obviously interested in the bait bin and not the divers.

Grey Reef Sharks were abundant, but there were also Whitetips and some magnificent Silvertips. It was impossible to count them all but I estimate between thirty and fifty sharks coming and going. If you were concerned that you could not watch your back - there were always sharks behind me - you can go into the cage, but the sharks were so well behaved that I never felt any threat at all.

After about twenty minutes of this everyone was instructed to enter the cages, the top of the bait bin was released and the string of baits floated out starting a frenzy of shark feeding. Now the pace was quite frantic but everyone could get a close up view with the absolute, but probably unnecessary, security of the cages. After only a couple of minutes the baits were consumed, sharks returned to their slow cruising and a frenzy of divers left the cages to look over the sand below where the baits had been to see if they could find any shark teeth.

Those low on air just followed the direct line from the cages to the stern of the Spoil Sport where later in the

day sharks were given another feed direct from the platform.

I rate this dive as truly excellent for both new and the most experienced divers. If you are a diver who has some nagging concern about a shark taking a nibble one day then you should definitely make the dive. The reality of shark diving is far more wondrous than any fantasies you may have, and far less fearsome.

On occasion a Silvertip Shark *Carcharhinus albimarginatus* joins the feed. Usually this species is more shy towards divers and patrols steep reef walls.

Sphyrna mokarran Milne Bay, PNG

Great Hammerhead Shark

Le: To 6 m.
Di: All CS but rare.
De: Surface to 50 m plus.
Ge: This awesome shark, which grows to enormous size is an unforgettable sight underwater. Grey Reef, Reef Whitetip and Silvertip sharks scatter at its approach, sharks and rays being its usual diet. The huge sickle shaped dorsal and other fins make it instantly recognisable. Only rarely seen but apparently fearless and considered dangerous though personal experience has not found the shark aggressive.

Giant Shovelnose Ray

Le: To 2.7 m.
Di: GBR, Southern PNG, Solomons.
De: Surface to 50 m plus.
Ge: Common on sandflats at Heron Island on GBR and similar habitats but also close inshore in estuaries. Rest during the daytime partly covered with sand and will allow close approach. Feed primarily on shellfish and have blunt crushing teeth. Possibly several different species in the CS area, some yet to be described.

Rhinobatos typus GBR, Australia

Dasyatis kuhlii Milne Bay, PNG

Blue-spotted Stingray

Wi: To 38 cm.
Di: GBR, PNG, Solomons, Vanuatu.
De: 1 to 50 m plus.
Ge: Shares a common name with *T. lymma*, following, but less brilliantly coloured, diamond shaped and prefers a sand habitat rather than reef. Very common. Can be a nuisance on night dives over sand when disturbed rays can blunder into divers. They have two sting barbs capable of inflicting serious injury.

Blue-spotted Fantail Ray

Wi: To 30 cm.
Di: GBR, PNG, Solomons.
De: 1 to 30 m.
Ge: Common and attractive stingray often found during the day partly hidden under coral ledges. Will take off rapidly if disturbed often startling un-aware divers. Twin sting barbs are located near the end of the tail. Most widely distributed from the Red Sea to the Central Pacific, probably the most common stingray to be found in coral reef habitats. Not to be confused with *Dasyatis kuhlii* (previous species).

Taeniura lymma   Eastern Fields, Coral Sea

Black-blotched Stingray

Wi: To 180 cm.
Di: GBR, PNG, Solomons.
De: 10 - 50 m plus.
Ge: A large easily recognised stingray found on reef dropoffs and wrecks. Has a single sting barb located half way along tail and is known to have caused at least one fatality. Often excavates large holes by blow-ing sand from the mouth, tak-en in by the large spiracles on top of the head, to dislodge molluscs and crabs, its primary diet.

Taeniura meyeni   Port Moresby, PNG

Thorny Stingray

Wi: To 100 cm.
Di: Throughout CS.
De: 5 to 20 m plus.
Ge: A very distinctive sting ray with thorny growths (fused dermal denticles) all over dor-sal surface. Only rarely encountered. Sometimes incorrectly identified as *U. africanus* which is a pseudo-nym. This species lacks a sting barb - which may account for its rarity.

Urogymnus asperrimus   Milne Bay, PNG

17

Jenkins Whipray

Wi: To 105 cm.
Di: Northern CS.
De: 20 to 50 m.
Ge: Large stingray with single sting barb. Distribution poorly defined but can be common in ideal habitats which appear to be soft sand/silty bottoms associated with coastal lagoons.

Himantura jenkinsii   **Madang, PNG**

Pink Whipray

Wi: To 150 cm.
Di: Northern CS.
De: 20 to 50 m.
Ge: This stingray occurs in large numbers and groups in the shallows surrounding Heron Island on the GBR and similar habitats. It has a very long tail, if unbroken its total length may exceed 5 m! Feeds on crustaceans and may have a taste for shrimps and prawns (as the author himself) as it is often caught in the nets of shrimp-trawlers. Dorsal surface is dark uniform brownish pink mottled with darker blotches.

Himantura fai   **GBR, Australia**

Cowtailed Ray

Wi: To at least 180 cm.
Di: All CS.
De: 5 to 50 m plus.
Ge: Easily identified by tail flap, single sting barb located at about half tail length. Often seen on and near coral reefs, and is curious, allowing close approach by divers.

Pastinachus sephen   **Port Moresby, PNG**

Eagle Ray

Wi: Reported to 300 cm but very rare above 180 cm.
Di: All CS.
De: Surface to 50 m plus.
Ge: Often swims in schools above reefs exposed to currents. Feeds in sand using projecting snout to dig for molluscs. Up to six stinging barbs near base of tail. Easily spooked, the rays will take off flapping and soaring if a diver approaches. Best technique for photographs is for the diver to hide until rays are very close.

Aetobatus narinari   New Ireland, PNG

Devil Ray

Wi: To 3 m, usually to 1.5 m. Di: All CS. De: 0-30 m. Ge: Distinct from manta rays by underslung mouth, narrow cephalic fins. In schools (below) just below surface. Sp. ID uncertain but listed as *M. japonica* or *M. tarapacana*. No sting barb, plankton feeders.

Mobula sp.   New Ireland, PNG

Manta Ray

Wi: Reported to 6 m or more, more commonly 4-5 m.
Di: All CS. De: 0-30 m.
Ge: These wonderful rays are plankton feeders, using their cephalic fins to funnel food into their gaping mouths. No sting barb, considered harmless. Will allow close careful approach but is spooked by touch. Best encounters are at cleaning stations (see following pages). Often seen feeding right at surface with dorsal fin and wing tips breaking the surface. Young rays will somersault completely out of the water, adults make leaping flops producing an enormous splash.

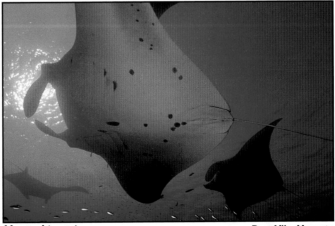

Manta birostris   Port Vila, Vanuatu

MANTA RAY DISCOVERY

The PNG dive tourism industry is more than twenty years old but there are still many coral reefs that have not even been charted, let alone dived. The PNG live-aboards Barbarian, Chertan, Febrina, Golden Dawn, Moonlighting, Paradise Sport, Star Dancer and Tiata have all made recent exploratory cruises in different regions of PNG. So when the opportunity came for my wife and me to join a special voyage of discovery aboard Golden Dawn we jumped at the chance.

The majestic Manta Ray *Manta birostris* at a bommie-based cleaning station.

The voyage was to start in Alotau in Milne Bay then immediately cruise to the islands south and east of the island of Samarai, continuing along the Papuan Coast and end, two weeks later, at Port Moresby. We planned to dive some known, but rarely dived, sites but the main aim was to explore and discover new ones.

A few days into the adventure we had made some very exciting dives which were added to the growing repertoire of great PNG dive sites. Inevitably we also had some disappointments where reefs that we were hoping would be first class turned out to be ordinary in both coral and fish life. But this is the way of exploration, and probably just a temporary condition for those reefs. Coral Reefs are very dynamic, they go through long periods of growth and lush life but also go through periods where the corals die back allowing rejuvenation of the reefs and an eventual increase in biodiversity.

The news was good, villagers told us that there were mantas around, and when the tide changed they would come close to the Island. We anchored up and started to send divers in different directions to explore the reef.

I surfaced to find that mantas had been seen feeding on the other side of the island and so I raced off in the inflatable with a couple of others to see if we could snorkel with them. Sure enough at least a dozen dark shapes moved just below the surface with an occasional dorsal fin or wingtip slicing into the air. I soon had some pictures of the magnificent beasts as they passed me, mouths agape and feeding, but trying to get close was difficult and exhausting.

On the way back to the boat we saw our skipper, Craig De Wit, waving to us. He was raving about giant mantas being cleaned at a rock he had

This close-up of the head region of a manta nicely shows its head flaps and large gill slits.

found in just 9 metres of water. I went back in the water and snorkelled over to the rock following the skipper's directions from his marker. I looked down to see two really big mantas just hovering near a rock as tiny Cleaner Wrasses worked them over. I held my breath, quietly dived down and glided towards them. The mantas allowed me to get some close photos before they slowly swam off.

Cleaner Wrasses eat tiny parasites and pieces of dead skin on fishes thus keeping them in top condition. Fishes recognise the wrasses and do not attempt to eat them. The wrasses live on certain areas of the reef called cleaning stations and although I have seen many reef cleaning stations over the years and watched countless numbers of small fishes being cleaned, this was the first time I had ever seen large mantas being cleaned.

Only a minute went by before the two mantas came again. I stopped breathing as one came right over my head only millimetres from me and filling the frame of my super-wide 16 mm fish-eye lens. I have learned in the past that it is not a good idea to touch mantas, tempting as that is, as they may get spooked, and when I finally had to breath out, I released my air in gentle controlled bubbles so as to not startle the manta. It must have worked because the mantas returned again and again each time pausing for more cleaning and more photos.

Manta Rays can reach wing spans of over 6 metres and weights of two tonnes but are completely harmless. Unlike Sting Rays they do not have spear-like barbs on their tails and they eat plankton and have no sharp teeth.

Mantas frequently somersault through the water. This behaviour is often associated with feeding on plankton.

They have the largest brain of any fish, and often perform elaborate three dimensional underwater ballets with each other which I have been privileged to see. It is a wondrous sight I will never forget.

Eventually others joined me in this close encounter of the miraculous kind but I had to

Note the gill openings (water outlets) inside the huge mouth cavity of this filter-feeding manta.

surface to reload my camera and refill my tank. It was one of the great dives of my life. I have dived with mantas before but never had I been able to get so close and have the mantas aware of, and welcoming, my presence. We had been eyeball to eyeball, a truly fabulous experience with a magnificent wild animal.

Another view of the cleaning station. Note the pair of cleaner wrasses right in front of the ray's mouth opening.

Echidna nebulosa **Port Moresby, PNG**

Starry Moray

Le: To 70 cm.
Di: All CS.
De: 1 to 10 m.
Ge: Attractive and distinctive moray is found in shallow water among coral heads. As with most moray eels this one is active at night, but can be seen peering from its lair during the day. Reported to feed mainly on crabs.

Gymnothorax fimbriatus **GBR, Australia**

Darkspotted Moray

Le: To 80 cm.
Di: All CS.
De: 1 to 10 m.
Ge: Usually solitary, distinctive shallow reef eel which is quite curious and easily approached. Often discovered in the company of cleaner shrimp which it allows to enter its mouth without risk of being eaten. Spot patterns on individuals are unique and can be used to identify them.

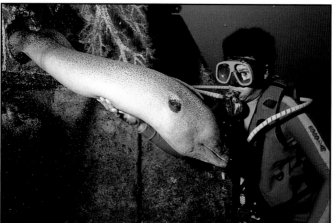

Gymnothorax javanicus **Port Moresby, PNG**

Giant Moray

Le: To 2.2 m.
Di: All CS.
De: 1 to 40 m plus.
Ge: The largest of the Coral Sea morays this is a very impressive creature. Easily attracted to baits but have poor eyesight and have been known to bite the hands of divers feeding them carelessly. However particular morays have been know to recognise certain divers who have been able to handle them with impunity. Wonderful silky smooth skin in natural habitat.

22

Masked Moray

Le: To 1 m.
Di: Uncommon but through-out CS.
De: 4 to 25 m.
Ge: This eel prefers oceanic and seaward reefs, sometimes sharing lair with a partner. Easily identified by black mark from eye to rear of mouth. Reported to be aggressive but author has found them docile.

Gymnothorax breedeni   Eastern Fields, Coral Sea

Yellowmargin Moray

Le: To 1.2 m but mostly less.
Di: All CS.
De: 1 to 50 m plus.
Ge: Common reef eel with distinctive orange eye. Similar to *G. javanicus* in that gill opening is in a black blotch but is much smaller and has a more speckled colouration. Easily attracted to baits. Often in the company of cleaner shrimps.

Gymnothorax flavimarginatus   Solomon Islands

Venomous Moray

Le: To 70 cm.
Di: Rarely encountered.
De: 1 to 10 m.
Ge: This unusual and distinctive moray is known to have a venomous bite and should not be handled. Seen mostly at night peeping from a coral lair. The range of this moray in the Coral Sea area is uncertain and reports would be welcome.

Gymnothorax chlamydatus   Milne Bay, PNG

Blackspotted Moray

Le: To at least 1.8 m.
Di: All CS.
De: 1 to 35 m.
Ge: The beautifully patterned
Blackspotted Moray is usually
encountered on outer reef
flats in areas with surge. The
animal is most often seen with
its head well up out of its hole.
The species is not usually
aggressive but has impressive
teeth and thus is potentially
dangerous like all large moray
species. Unprovoked animals
however will practically never
attack any divers since humans
are not part of their diet. The
Blackspotted Moray is less
common than the Giant
Moray.

Gymnothorax favagineus   Port Moresby, PNG

Barred Moray

Le: To 60 cm. Di: All CS. De: 1
to 15 m. Ge: Shallow reef
species found on clear coastal
flats and in lagoons. Has dark
bands across its body that fade
with age. *Gymnothorax zonipectis*
(below, to 47 cm, all CS, 20 m
and deeper) is similar. The tail
has dark bars which distinguish
it from other similar species.

Echidna polyzona   GBR, Australia

Tidepool Snake Moray

Le: To 28 cm. Di: All CS. Ge: In rubble of intertidal reef flats. Other small morays, such as the **White-eyed Moray** *Siderea thyrsoidea* (below, Milne Bay; to 66 cm, all CS, 1 to 20 m), share a similar habitat. Apparently variable in colour, reported grey. Several individuals often together in same coral crevice.

Uropterygius micropterus   Milne Bay, PNG

Ribbon Eel

Le: To 1.3 m. Di: All CS. De: 1 to 50 m plus. Ge: This beautiful eel is very popular with underwater photographers and has three colour phases. It is a protandrous hermaphrodite and can rapidly change sex and colouration. Males are black with a light stripe down back, females brilliant blue with yellow stripe (below) and old females are almost all yellow (vertical below; all photos Milne Bay, PNG). Favour small sand patches close to reefs and are usually seen with their heads well extended from their hole, they are rarely encountered completely outside their holes.

Rhinomuraena quaesita, **male**   Milne Bay, PNG

Rhinomuraena quaesita, **swimming female**   Milne Bay, PNG

Clown Snake Eel
Le: To 60 cm. Di: Northern
CS. De: I to 30 m.
Ge: This attractive snake eel
lives in sand and sea grass beds
and is mostly seen with just its
head peering from the sand.
Occasionally the whole eel is
found wandering along the
bottom. When disturbed it
uses its tail to dig into the
sand and can rapidly disappear.
It does not build a permanent
burrow. The banded body
mimics that of sea snakes and
probably provides some protection, however the tail is
pointed unlike the paddle tail
of sea snakes and therefore
easy for divers to distinguish.

Ophichthus bonaparti   Port Moresby, PNG

Stargazer Snake Eel
Le: To 1.25 m. Di: All CS.
De: I to 30 m. Ge: Usually
seen with head peering from
sand or loose rubble bottom,
rare to see whole eel. Very
similar species *B. crocodilinus*
has eyes further forward.
Ambushes small fishes and
crustaceans. Colour is variable
(below, Milne Bay, PNG).

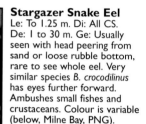

Brachysomophis cirrocheilos   Port Moresby, PNG

Banded Snake Eel

Le: To 88 cm.
Di: All CS.
De: 0 to 30 m.
Ge: This snake eel is mostly
seen completely exposed in
shallow water. At a glance it is
easily mistaken for the sea
snake *Laticauda colubrina* but
closer observation reveals a
pointed tail and long dorsal fin
compared to the snakes paddle
tail and no fins.

Myrichthys colubrinus   Port Moresby, PNG

Marbled Snake Eel

Le: To 57 cm.
Di: All CS but unusual.
De: 1 to 30 m.
Ge: Easily recognised widespread but uncommon snake eel found in sand patches near reefs. As with most snake eels it is more active at night. Spends time completely buried in sand. Much of our knowledge about snake eel identification comes from specimens collected incidentally when using poisons to collect fishes.

Callechelys marmorata　　　Milne Bay, PNG

Barred Sand Conger

Le: To 60 cm. Di: PNG, ? CS (rare). De: 2 to 25 m. Ge: Free swimming close to bottom or buried, only head emerging from sand (below). Prefers loose sand habitat. Only few specimens discovered but species widespread from Madagascar to Hawaii.

Poeciloconger fasciatus　　　Milne Bay, PNG

Many-toothed Garden Eel

Le: To 60 cm.
Di: Northern CS.
De: 2 to 50 m.
Ge: Wide range of habitats from shallow sea grass to deep sand slopes, easily distinguished by white blotch on side of head. As with all Garden eels favours sites with current and feeds on plankton drifting past its hole. Disappears into hole if it thinks it is threatened.

Heteroconger perissodon　　　New Britain, PNG

TAYLOR'S GARDEN EEL

Garden eels are the most frustrating of fishes for underwater photographers. Often occurring in vast colonies in sand and silty areas, in both shallow and deep water, they are common, and easy to find, but as a diver approaches they gradually slide back into their holes and when within shooting distance all that can be seen is the empty entrance to the hole. Waiting quietly and holding the breath a diver may see the head of the eel begin to appear - but by the time enough of the eel is out for a decent photograph another breath is needed, and the eel disappears again.

Close-up view of Taylor's Garden Eel *Heteroconger taylori* looking out from its hole.

Not only is it difficult for a diver to get close enough to photograph garden eels it is difficult to get close enough to identify them as well. Patience, good breath control and solo diving are usually required. Nevertheless it is because of scuba diving that the discovery of new species has been increasing. There is no doubt that silent rebreathers will be very useful for observing and photographing Garden Eels, and I predict that many new species will be discovered using this exciting equipment just becoming available for sport divers.

Garden eels are plankton feeders and rely on currents to bring food to them. They can be seen with their heads bobbing and weaving as they pick at plankton drifting past, their tails firmly rooted in their holes. On occasion pairs of eels are seen with their holes very close together - a manoeuvre necessary for mating.

One of the most common and widespread Garden Eels, *Heteroconger hassi*, was named after pioneer diver Hans Hass from specimens he observed diving in the Maldives. It is very distinctive. The basic coloration is white with numerous tiny black spots and it has two large black spots on its side and a third spot on its belly which can only be seen if the eel is well out of its hole. Other species include a beautiful but very shy eel which has orange bands around its body, and a shallow water species which has black bands like tiger stripes around it.

On a special cruise in December 1993 we were joined by film makers Ron and Valerie Taylor and Ichthyologist Jack Randall. Ron had been shooting video on his dive and when he came up asked Jack to look at some footage of a garden eel he had managed to shoot. On seeing the video Jack realised that Ron had been shooting an eel unknown to him so they went back in the water and collected a specimen by squirting a chemical irritant down the eel's hole. When the eel emerged they were able to trap it in a plastic bag.

The eel was pale yellow/green in colour with many small black blotches covering its body. It was relatively easy to approach and was a part of a colony of only six eels. The bottom was silty with sparse grass outcrops. Other sightings of the eel in Milne Bay indicate that it does not form the large colonies that other species do but occurs in small groups. An isolated specimen was photographed by Australian Rudie Kuiter at Tulamben, Bali. The known depth range is from 10 to 30 metres. The new eel was described in 1995 by Castle and Randall and named *Heteroconger taylori* in honour of Ron Taylor. As yet Taylor's Garden Eel has only been reported from Milne Bay, PNG and Tulamben, Bali.

Another Garden Eel species, *Heteroconger hassi,* which is distinct by two lateral black spots (Port Moresby, PNG).

A typical colony of Garden Eels on a coral sand slope in Vanuatu.

Spotted Garden Eel

Le: To 60 cm. Di: All CS. De: 2 to 50 m. Ge: Common garden eel named after famed underwater pioneer Hans Hass. Prefers coral sand near reefs. Often in very large colonies, which look like a garden of young plants. Below: **Taylor's Garden Eel** *Heteroconger taylori*, to 40 cm. See also the previous two pages.

Heteroconger hassi   **Solomon Islands**

Zebra Garden Eel

Le: To 40 cm.
Di: Probably throughout CS.
De: 1 to 10 m.
Ge: The author has only encountered this garden eel in very shallow water close to shore above sea grass beds. Other garden eels are known to favour sheltered shallow sand areas close to shore and can survive as long as there are slight tidal currents that run along the beach.

Heteroconger polyzona   **Milne Bay, PNG**

Splendid Garden Eel

Le: To 60 cm.
Di: Northern CS.
De: 5 to 40 m.
Ge: A splendidly coloured garden eel that is easily recognised even from a distance. Prefers coral sand patches near reefs. Difficult to approach and disappear into holes as diver breathes out. The advent of silent rebreathers for diving will make garden eel photography much easier.

Gorgasia preclara   **New Ireland, PNG**

CATFISHES PLOTOSIDAE

Striped Catfish

Le: To 32 cm, mostly smaller in range 3 to 12 cm.
Di: All CS.
De: 1 to 40 m.
Ge: Juveniles to 10 cm are commonly found in dense schools hiding in a coral cave or feeding over sand bottoms where the first row feeding are continually overtaken by catfish from the school. Both the dorsal and pectoral fin spines are venomous. Favour habitats close to shore or in lagoons. Adults are solitary and rarely seen in the daytime.

Plotosus lineatus   Port Moresby, PNG

CONVICT BLENNIES PHOLIDICHTHYIDAE

Convict Blenny

Le: To 34 cm.
Di: GBR, PNG and Solomon Islands otherwise uncertain.
De: 3 to 30 m.
Ge: Juveniles school in vast numbers over coral reefs. They are often mistaken for catfish *Plotosus lineatus* (previous species, the two species are not related and here placed together for direct comparison only) but lack whiskers and venomous spine. At night they retire into a sand burrow containing one or two adults. The adults maintain the burrows by collecting sand and spitting it out.

    Convict blennies are a single species family with a restricted distribution in the West Pacific. They are goby-like but apparently more closely related to blennies. Like blennies they lack scales but unlike them do not have the usually well-developed teeth and have small conical teeth instead. They also lack fin spines (see above) and a lateral line.
Below: Juveniles.

Pholidichthys leucotaenia, juvenile   GBR, Australia

Pholidichthys leucotaenia, adult   Solomon Islands

LIZARDFISHES

SYNODONTIDAE

Variegated Lizardfish

Le: To 28 cm.
Di: All CS.
De: 1 to 50 m.
Ge: A common reef dwelling lizardfish it is usually seen sitting up on a coral, often with one or two others. Easy to approach. There are several other similar species which are difficult to differentiate underwater.

Synodus variegatus   **Milne Bay, PNG**

Giant Lizardfish

Le: To 65 cm. Di: All CS. De: 1 to 50 m plus. Ge: Lives on soft bottom and often caught in trawls. *Trachinocephalus myops* (below, PNG) has similar habitat but eyes very far forward. Usually buried with only eyes protruding from bottom as it lies in wait for prey. If disturbed it will shoot off a distance and bury at once.

Saurida sp.   **Port Moresby, PNG**

BROTULAS

OPHIDIIDAE

Bearded Brotula

Le: To at least 60 cm, mostly much smaller.
Di: All CS.
De: 5 to 50 m.
Ge: Seldom seen in the daytime this fish is sometimes encountered on night dives on coastal reefs, but is shy of divers' lights. Has thread-like pelvic fins which are distinctive but still often confused with catfish because of mouth barbels. Feeds at night on crabs and fishes.

Brotula multibarbata   **Milne Bay, PNG**

PEARL FISHES   CARAPIDAE

Pearlfish

Le: To 10 cm. Di: All CS.
De: 1 to 50 m plus.
Ge: This extraordinary fish
lives inside sea cucumbers and
bivalves. The name Pearlfish
was derived from its common
appearance inside harvested
pearl shells. It is also regularly
encountered by Sea Cucumber
fishermen as the caught
cucumber expels the fish from
its anus. Usually only seen at
night when it emerges to feed.
Several closely related species.
Anus of the Pearlfish is situated close to the head so that
the fish can void without leaving its safe haven.

Onuxodon sp.   New Britain, PNG

TOADFISHES   BATRACHOIDIDAE

Toadfish

Le: To 26 cm.
Di: All CS.
De: 1 to 50 m plus.
Ge: Prefers silty or muddy
bottom but often seen by
divers close to wrecks or
inshore reefs. Spines are not
venomous but sting reported
to be painful. Has a wide variety of diet from fishes to
echinoderms and can be
caught on a baited hook.

Halophryne diemensis   GBR, Australia

ANGLER- OR FROGFISHES   ANTENNARIIDAE

Giant Frogfish

Le: To 30 cm. Di: All CS. De: 1
to 50 m. Ge: Largest frogfish,
extremely variable in colour
and pattern. Excellent camouflage, mostly mimics sponges. In
a wide range of habitats from
deep reef walls to silty lagoons,
though avoids areas of surge.

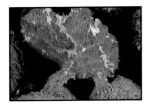

Antennarius commersonii   Port Moresby, PNG

Striped Frogfish

Le: To 22 cm. Di: All CS. De: 20 to 50 m. Ge: A very variable frogfish usually with distinct stripes (sometimes uniformly black or blotched). This contrasts with usual frogfish markings of circles imitating sponges. Some specimens have long hairlike growths. Deeper among debris or algae on sandy slopes.

Antennarius striatus   **Milne Bay, PNG**

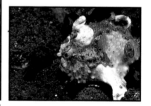

Warty Frogfish

Le: To 9 cm. Di: All CS. De: I to 20 m. Ge: In sheltered shallows in sea grass, among debris or on rocks close to shore. Markings clearly mimic sponges and also have disruptive patterns. Colour variable, mostly white, yellow or pink. Juv. may lack the sponge markings; found in the open possibly mimicking nudibranchs.

Antennarius maculatus   **New Britain, PNG**

Sargassumfish

Le: To 19 cm. Di: All CS. De: Surface. Ge: The sargassumfish is found floating with sargassum weed and is incredibly well camouflaged. The fish is abundant with nearly every clump of true sargassum hiding several fish, including juveniles. Sargassum occasionally drifts close to shore into sheltered water and if found in these circumstances should be investigated thoroughly as it harbours many fascinating creatures such as nudibranchs, shrimp and juvenile fishes as well as the bizarre sargassumfish.

Histrio histrio   **Port Moresby, PNG**

Urchin Clingfish

Le: To 5 cm.
Di: All CS.
De: 1 to 50 m.
Ge: Found on reefs free swimming near urchins or fine branching corals which it uses for shelter. Skin is reported to contain a toxin.

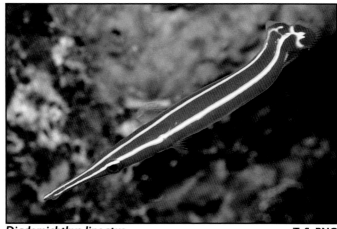

Diademichthys lineatus   Tufi, PNG

Featherstar Clingfish

Le: To 3 cm.
Di: All CS.
De: 5 to 40 m.
Ge: Always found associated with crinoids but usually well hidden. Colour depends on colour of host. Has a thoracic disc enabling it to cling to its host.
   This species is different to the well-known One-stripe Clingfish *Discotrema crinophila* (with one dorsal stripe) as it lacks a dorsal stripe.

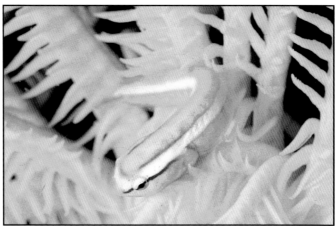

Discotrema sp.   GBR, Australia

Halfbeak

Le: To 35 cm. Di: CS. De: 0-1 m.
Ge: Common close to shore in sheltered areas (mangroves), feed at surface with elongated bottom jaw. Blotches on sides distinct, several similar spp. Tail forked in *Hyporhamphus*, truncated in *Zenarchopterus* (below) spp.

Hyporhamphus far   Milne Bay, PNG

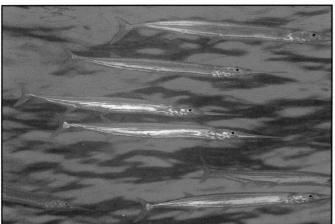

Platybelone platyura   Solomon Islands

Keeled Needlefish

Le: To 45 cm.
Di: All CS.
De: Surface to 1 m.
Ge: Occurs, sometimes in small schools, near the surface where it may be seen tail walking to escape predators or leaping from the water to dive into the schools of small bait-fish that it feeds on. The larger bottom tail lobe aids in the tail walking process.

Tylosurus crocodilus   Solomon Islands

Crocodile Longtom

Le: To 1.3 m.
Di: All CS.
De: Surface to 1 m.
Ge: The larger *Tylosurus croco-dilus* is a hazard for village fish-ermen in canoes particularly at night. Leaping fish have been known to spear fishermen causing fatal injuries. These fish are targeted by South Pacific fishermen using spiderweb lures skipping on the surface from lines trailing from kites. They have a greenish coloured flesh but are good eating.

Photoblepharon palpebratus   Milne Bay, PNG

Flashlightfish

Le: To 12 cm. Di: All CS. De: 1 to 40 m. Ge: A nocturnal fish which hides deep in caves or wrecks during daylight. At night the fish emerge, flashing a light organ beneath their eyes. The light is caused by symbiotic bacterium and can be flashed on and off by means of a shutter-like organ. They prefer moonless nights. Divers can approach the fish closely with their dive lights off, then freeze the fish motionless by turning their bright lights on making photography easy.

Shadowfin Soldierfish

Le: To 32 cm. Di: All CS. De: 5 to 50 m. Ge: A common large species seen in ledges and caves; easily distinguished by dark or black edges to fins. The smaller *M. vittata* (below, Solomon Isl., to 20 cm) has a splendid bright orange/red colour with fine white boarders to leading edges of fins.

Myripristis adusta   GBR, Australia

Splendid Soldierfish

Le: To 30 cm.
Di: All CS but not common.
De: 15 to 50 m.
Ge: This is a real beauty which inhabits coral reefs and is rarely seen shallower than 30 m. It is usually in pairs or small groups and unlike most soldier- and squirrelfishes is usually in the open although close to a hideaway. It may be approached closely by careful divers.

Myripristis melanosticta   Milne Bay, PNG

Blackfin Squirrelfish

Le: To 35 cm, usually 20 cm.
Di: All CS.
De: 1 to 40 m.
Ge: Widespread and easy to identify but usually partly hidden in daytime under small coral ledges. Can grow to 35 cm making it the largest in its genus but usually seen much smaller. Readily flashes its dorsal fin, a boon to photographers.

Neoniphon opercularis   Port Moresby, PNG

Crown Squirrelfish

Le: To 17 cm. Di: All CS. De: 2 to 30 m. Ge: Usually on lagoon reefs no deeper than 20 m. Similar to several other striped varieties such as S. *rubrum* (below, PNG) but has distinct dorsal fin markings, and finer white stripes. These are difficult to differentiate in the wild particularly if the fish does not display the dorsal fin.

Sargocentron diadema GBR, Australia

Blackspot Squirrelfish

Le: To 25 cm.
Di: All CS.
De: 5 to 50 m.
Ge: Usually found at depths of around 25 - 35 m this distinctive squirrelfish is easy to identify because of the obvious three black spots near the tail.

Sargocentron melanospilos Milne Bay, PNG

Violet Squirrelfish

Le: To 25 cm.
Di: Throughout CS, not yet recorded from New Caledonia.
De: 1 to 15 m.
Ge: Rarely encountered during the day but the author has seen individuals sheltering under "leaves" of Cabbage coral as shown in the photograph. The fish is uncommon and a prized find. The colouration is unique in squirrelfishes thus confirming identification.

Sargocentron violaceum Solomon Islands

Sabre Squirrelfish
Le: To 45 cm. Di: All CS. De: I
to 50 m plus. Ge: The largest
of the squirrelfishes, commonly
encountered under ledges or
large plate corals. Easy to
approach and a favourite with
photographers as it will sit still
looking at the camera. It has a
large spine on the preopercu-
lum. Below: New Ireland, PNG.

Sargocentron spiniferum   Eastern Fields, Coral Sea

White-tail Squirrelfish

Le: To 25 cm. Di: All CS. De: 6
to 50 m. Ge: Similar but smaller than the previous species. Is
also common in the CS area
but has white rather than yellow edging. Found from coastal
to outer protected reefs, in
lagoons, on walls in caves.
Singly or congregating into
large groups during the day
when the species is easily
recognised by the white tail
but turn entirely bright red at
night.

Sargocentron caudimaculatum   Eastern Fields, Coral Sea

SEA MOTHS   PEGASIDAE

Little Dragonfish

Le: To 10 cm. Di: All CS, close
to shore. De: 1 to 50 m plus.
Ge: May be found with careful
searching in sheltered bays
close to shore on sand or
gravel bottoms. More active in
the evening or at night and
usually in pairs. When captured will sometimes freeze in
displayed position and appear
dead. Surprisingly well camouflaged and reported to mimic
objects such as shells or rubble. Periodically sheds layer of
mucus to prevent build up of
growths on body.

Eurypegasus draconis   Port Moresby, PNG

39

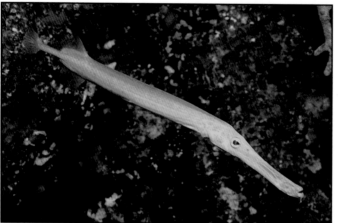

Trumpetfish

Le: To 60 cm.
Di: All CS.
De: I to 50 m.
Ge: A widespread and common species, found in a variety of habitats, which has colour variations. Juveniles (small photo below, Milne Bay, PNG) tend to be longitudinally striped, adults mainly brown but there is also a bright yellow variety. Adults will ride the backs of other fishes such as rockcod (second large photo) in order to approach fish prey. The yellow form often swims with huge schools of the yellow Bluestripe Snappers excellently camouflaged among them. Such a partnership is not beneficial for both sides. In this case the Trumpetfish simply takes advantage of the other fishes.

Aulostomus chinensis   GBR, Australia

Aulostomus chinensis   Tufi, PNG

Smooth Flutemouth

Le: To 1.5 m, usually less.
Di: All CS.
De: I to 20 m.
Ge: Usually appears in schools on top of shallow reefs. It has a long filament trailing from the middle of the tail. Pale green colouration, silver below but can become dark when close to the bottom. Easy to approach.

Fistularia commersonii   Solomon Islands

Coral Shrimpfish

Le: To 14 cm.
Di: All CS.
De: 1 to 30 m.
Ge: The species of this family
are sometimes called Razorfish
because of their laterally
extremely flattened body. They
may be found in a variety of
shallow water habitats from
fields of sea grass on sandy
bottom to all kinds of reef.
Shrimpfish most often are
encountered swimming in
schools in a head-down position but can take off horizontally when disturbed, although
they will often hide among
branches of staghorn coral.
Juveniles are sometimes seen
in huge schools.

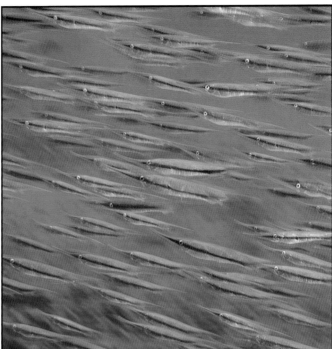

Aeoliscus strigatus   Milne Bay, PNG

Rigid Shrimpfish

Le: To 15 cm.
Di: All CS.
De: 3 to 30 m.
Ge: Coastal, often in muddy
habitats. Singly, in pairs or in
large dense schools. Individuals
are often found sheltering next
to sea pens or sea weeds out
in the open. Schools are found
in patches of rich coral growth
with fan corals or in sea whip
gardens.
   The species *Centriscus scutatus* has a rigid dorsal spine
whereas the dorsal spine is
hinged on *Aeoliscus strigatus* as
shown in the vertical photo
above.

Centriscus scutatus   Milne Bay, PNG

Solenostomus armatus   Milne Bay, PNG

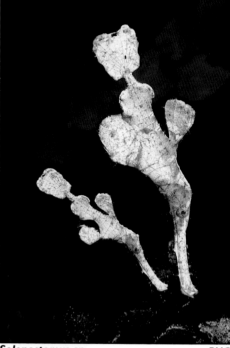

Solenostomus sp.   PNG

Solenostomus sp.   Solomon Islands

Solenostomus cyanopterus   Milne Bay, PNG

Top left: **Longtailed Ghost Pipefish**
Top right: **Halimeda Ghost Pipefish**
Left: **Hairy Ghost Pipefish**
There is debate as to whether some Ghost Pipefishes, e.g. the hairy one, are varieties only.
Bottom left:
Robust Ghost Pipefish
Le: To 15 cm. Di: All CS. De: 1 to 30 m. Ge: Caudal peduncle is wider than it is long. Also variable in colour and texture, but usually green or brown. Associated with sea grasses, dead leaves and fronds, and with some algae. Usually in pairs, female larger than male, and has brood pouch.
Right: *Solenostomus paradoxus*
Ornate Ghost Pipefish
Le: To 12 cm. Di: All CS. De: 1-30 m. Ge: Able to change body colour and texture to aid in camouflage with very variable habitat. In crinoids, gorgonians, soft and black corals and algae. Female larger, has brood pouch unlike sea horses. Usually in pairs but this unusual photo shows that they congregate to court and mate.

Reeftop Pipefish

Le: To 17 cm. Di: All CS. De: 1 to 20 m. Ge: A shallow water sp. which sometimes occurs in large numbers in favourable habitats such as sheltered bays with rubble or old concrete wharves. Below: *Corythoichthys ocellatus*, to 10 cm, northern CS, 1-25 m. Similar to older *C. schultzi* but has large ocellated golden spots.

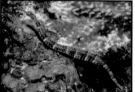

Corythoichthys haematopterus **Milne Bay, PNG**

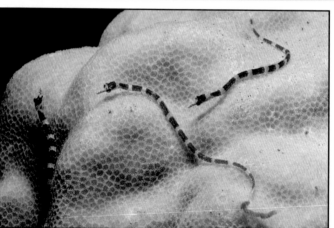

Brownbanded Pipefish

Le: To 10 cm. Di: All CS. De: 1 to 30 m. Ge: Common but hard to spot, with a wide depth range on coastal reefs and slopes rather than lagoons. Often in small active groups, but can be secretive. Male with brood pouch as in all genus members. Below: *Corythoichthys schultzi*, to 16 cm, all CS, 1 to 30 m.

Corythoichthys amplexus **Port Moresby, PNG**

Ringed Pipefish

Le: To 18 cm.
Di: All CS.
De: 1 to 50 m.
Ge: This distinctive pipefish species is often found in small groups near wharves or wrecks and favours sheltered water in nutrient rich lagoons. Females deposit their eggs on the ventral surface of the male as shown in the photograph. Both sexes of all genus members lack any pouch-like brooding structures.

Doryrhamphus dactyliophorus **Milne Bay, PNG**

Cleaning Pipefish
Le: To 13 cm. Di: All CS. De: I
to 35 m. Ge: Another inshore
sp. that favours wrecks and
wharves but more secretive and
less commonly seen than the
ringed pipefish. May share habitat with cleaner shrimps and,
along with the smaller *D. excisus*
(below, Tufi, PNG) is known to
clean parasites from fish skin.

Doryrhamphus janssi   Port Moresby, PNG

Ornate or Winged Pipefish
Le: To 16 cm. Di: All CS. De: I
to 25 m. Ge: A well camouflaged
pipefish with distinctive wings on
young to 10 cm length. Usually
shallow in weedy or rubble
areas. Its relative *H. dunkeri* (below, PNG) favours shallow sea
grass and algae beds, also floats
with sargassum on the surface.

Halicampus macrorhynchus   Eastern Fields, Coral Sea

Dwarf Pipehorse

Le: To 7 cm.
Di: Northern CS.
De: I to 10 m.
Ge: Almost impossible to spot,
this tiny pipefish has variable
colours and growths to suit its
habitat. May be found very
shallow on sea grasses or mangroves. Has a prehensile tail
like seahorses.

Acentronura breviperula   Madang, PNG

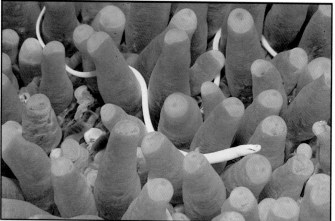

Siokunichthys nigrolineatus   Tufi, PNG

White Pipefish

Le: To 8 cm.
Di: Northern CS.
De: 5 to 20 m.
Ge: This is a commensal pipefish that lives among the tentacles of the solitary coral *Heliofungia actiniformis* which has tentacles similar to, and often mistaken for, those of a sea anemone. It has a tiny black line on its cheek from which it gets its scientific name, and probably feeds on organisms trapped in the coral's mucus. Usually several individuals in any one coral but likely absent from nearby corals.

Syngnathoides biaculeatus   Milne Bay, PNG

Double-ended Pipefish

Le: To 28 cm.
Di: All CS.
De: I to 10 m.
Ge: A large shallow water species usually found in sea grass beds but also hanging from floating weed. Extraordinary camouflage in sea grass and author has lost several specimens while turning away to attract other divers. Males carry eggs on ventral surface.

Short-tailed Pipefish

Le: To 40 cm. Di: All CS. De: I to 40 m. Ge: Often seen on bottom in the open where it will lie still and mimic a stick or twig. Dark brown to yellow to white, occasionally banded. On sand or rubble slopes with algae. Known to raise head off bottom, the close relative *T. longirostris* (below, Milne Bay) does not so.

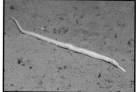

Trachyrhamphus bicoarctatus   Milne Bay, PNG

Common Seahorse

He: To 15 cm.
Di: All CS.
De: 1 to 40 m but most often seen in shallow water.
Ge: Usually found in sheltered habitats close to shore mainly in 1 to 5 m depth, but have been found deeper and also hanging on floating sargassum weed. Variable in colour but most commonly uniform grey (below) or yellow (right). Possibly includes several different species yet to be determined.

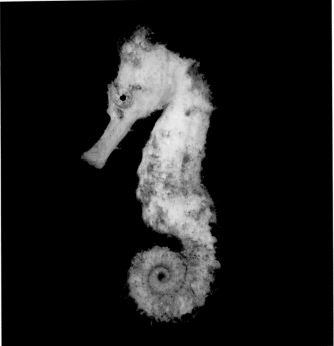

Hippocampus taeniopterus   **Solomon Islands**

Thorny Seahorse

He: 10 cm.
Di: Northern CS.
De: 1 to 35 m.
Ge: Covered in sharp spines with black tips, in sheltered bays often clinging to sponges, sea grass or soft corals. Colour variable.
   The Thorny Seahorse was described from Japanese waters and its distribution is not nearly as wide as has been suspected until now. For example similarly looking Red Sea species known under the name *H. histrix* are different species. The beautiful seahorse shown in the photo at the right is a typical *H. histrix* but the species is only rarely seen in our area. Seahorses often live in monogamous pairs, greeting each other every morning with a special, ritualised dance. Courtship and the transfer of eggs into the male's brooding pouch follow a species-specific pattern. The juveniles are born as miniature replicas of their parents without going through a true planktonic larval stage.

Hippocampus histrix   **Milne Bay, PNG**

47

Hippocampus spinosissimus   **Milne Bay, PNG**

Hedgehog Seahorse

He: 5.3 to 16 cm.
Di: All CS.
De: 25 to 50 m.
Ge: Males with very strongly developed spines bordering pouch. Colour pattern variable plain or pale, with darker saddles across dorso-lateral surface, and darker cross bands on tail. Has often been misidentified as *H. histrix.* Usually deeper than 25 m. Its exact range is uncertain.

Hippocampus bargibanti   **Milne Bay, PNG**

Pygmy Seahorse

He: 1 to 2 cm. Di: All CS.
De: 25 to 50 m.
Ge: Lives on, and mimics, sea fan *Murcella* sp. Very difficult to see, a magnifying glass is useful. Far more common than originally thought it is only recently that this tiny sea horse has been recorded from many countries in the Indo-Pacific. Original was described from specimens accidentally collected with a sea fan in New Caledonia. There appear to be varieties on different sea fans although they could be distinct species, particularly since many occur in shallower water.

Hippocampus sp.   **Port Moresby, PNG**

Gorgonian Seahorse

He: 1 to 2 cm. Di: All CS.
De: 25 to 50 m.
Ge: After the first photos of *H. bargibanti* from the natural habitat (up to 28 specimens were found on a single gorgonian!) were published in recent years dwarf seahorses attracted a lot of divers all over the world. Many underwater photographers started to look for these tiny beauties in gorgonians just as the author did. As a result further yet undescribed dwarf seahorses were discovered two of which are shown here to the left and right, respectively.

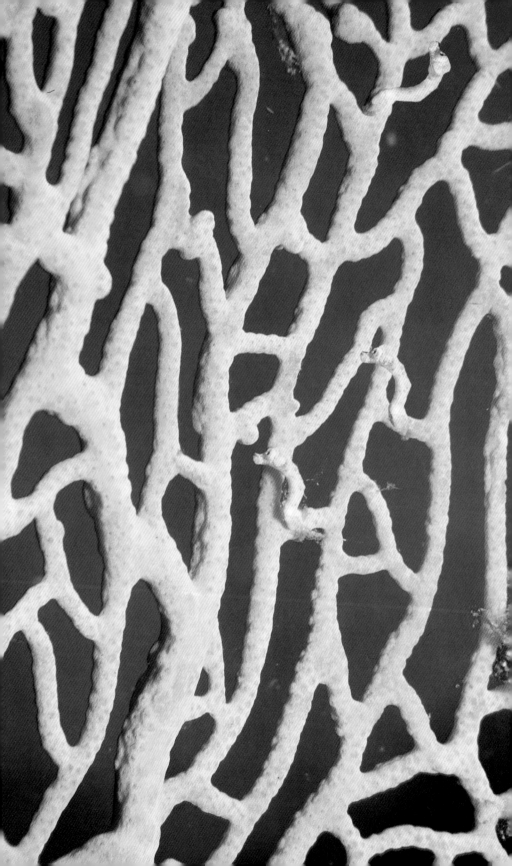

FLYING GURNARDS   DACTYLOPTERIDAE

Helmet Gurnard
Le: To 38 cm. Di: All CS. De: I
to 45+ m. Ge: Prefers soft bottom in which it can partly bury.
Active at dusk and night, feeds
on crustaceans, molluscs and
worms. If threatened it raises its
first two dorsal spines and extends its enormous pectoral fins
like wings, sometimes displaying
false eyespots (below, Milne Bay).

Dactyloptena orientalis   **Port Moresby, PNG**

WASPFISHES   TETRAROGIDAE

Spiny Waspfish
Le: To 15 cm. Di: All CS. De: I
to 20 m. Found close to shore in
shallow water, mimics dead leaf,
swaying from side to side, dorsal
spines venomous. Distinct from
scorpionfishes by dorsal spines
starting above or in front of eye.
Below: *A. macracanthus* (PNG).

Ablabys macracanthus   **GBR, Australia**

Whiteface Waspfish
Le: To 10 cm. Di: Northern
CS. De: 3 to 18 m plus.
Ge: Buries in soft bottom during day but emerges at night to
feed on crustaceans and
worms. Colour pattern quite
variable. The small photo
below (Milne Bay, PNG) shows
a flamboyant variety or a possibly undescribed relative.

Richardsonichthys leucogaster   **Port Moresby, PNG**

Zebra Lionfish

Le: To 18 cm.
Di: All CS.
De: 1 to 40 m.
Ge: Lacks long filaments from
pectoral fins, and lacks bands
of D. brachypterus. Lagoon
habitats, particularly associated
with sponges. As with all scorpionfishes it has venomous
dorsal spines. Stings are best
treated with very hot, but not
scalding, water. Scorpionfishes
are however not poisonous
and are eaten in some areas.

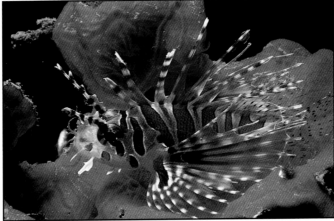

Dendrochirus zebra   Madang, PNG

Dwarf Lionfish

Le: To 17 cm, often much
smaller.
Di: All CS.
De: 2 to 30 m.
Ge: Pectoral fins lack long filaments and are distinctively
banded. Colour varies from
yellow to red. Usually not
associated with reefs but prefer sea grass, sand and rubble
habitats. Sometimes shelter
under the mantle of sand
anemones. Mainly feed on
crustaceans.

Dendrochirus brachypterus   Milne Bay, PNG

Twinspot Lionfish

Le: To 12 cm.
Di: Northern CS.
De: 1 to 40 m.
Ge: Very secretive during the
day when it hides in coral
caves and crevices. Active at
night but light sensitive and
will flee a diver's light. Easily
distinguished by ocelli on dorsal fin and barbels on upper
jaw.

Dendrochirus biocellatus   New Ireland, PNG

Spotfin Lionfish

Le: To 20 cm.
Di: All CS.
De: 1 to 50 m.
Ge: The long white pectoral filaments aid in this identification. A similar species (*P. radiata*) is rare in the Coral Sea region and has single white lines on its body compared to the doubled and wider lines on *P. antennata*. A reef dweller, usually hidden during the day.

Pterois antennata　　　　**Madang, PNG**

Deepwater Lionfish

Le: To 16 cm.
Di: Northern CS.
De: 15 to 40 m and deeper.
Ge: Similar to *P. antennata* but the pectoral filaments are shorter and often banded also the white striping near the tail is more confused. It has relatively large eyes. Prefers reef slopes.

Pterois mombasae　　　　**Milne Bay, PNG**

Common Lionfish
Le: To 38 cm. Di: All CS. De: 1 to 50+ m. Ge: Largest, most common and widespread lionfish, free pectoral rays distinct (gradually reduce in adulthood). Spreads fins and waves dorsal spines when hunting. Spines with small flag-like growths on their tips which resemble small fish moving when they are waved thus attracting prey. Quite fearless, will learn to follow divers with dive lights at night to get an easy feed on fishes caught in the light beam. Large adults often have the tentacles over their eyes missing (bitten off?). These sometimes have false eyespots so may be considered as lures.

Pterois volitans　　　　**Milne Bay, PNG**

Demon Stinger

Le: To 25 cm. Di: All CS. De: 1
to 40 m. Ge: A hazardous fish
for divers since it often buries
in sand during the day and can
deliver a vicious sting. Active at
night. Colour is variable, some
fish are bright red. Identified
from its pectoral fin pattern
which is displayed when the fish
is threatened (below, PNG).

Inimicus didactylus   Solomon Islands

Weedy Scorpionfish

Le: To 23 cm. Di: Northern
CS. De: 10 to 50 m plus. Ge:
Colours and body patterns
very variable (below, Milne Bay,
PNG), markings if present tend
to be nearly circular. Generally
deeper than 10 m and in
sheltered areas with slight
currents, not necessarily on
coral reefs.

Rhinopias frondosa   Milne Bay, PNG

Lacy Scorpionfish

Le: To 25 cm.
Di: All CS.
De: 3 to 25 m.
Ge: This spectacular scorpionfish was first discovered in
New Caledonia and described
in 1973. A second specimen
was discovered by the author's
wife in Port Moresby in 1980.
R. aphanes mimics crinoids and
has same wide range of
colours. Sits out on reefs in
the open preferring current
and surge areas. Often seen in
pairs and may remain in same
area for periods of at least
two years. A reluctant swimmer. See also following pages.

Rhinopias aphanes   Eastern Fields, Coral Sea

THE LACY SCORPIONFISH

Scorpionfishes are a very variable group of fishes which all have venomous dorsal spines and which have been known to injure divers. Since most scorpionfishes are masters of camouflage care should always be taken not to accidentally touch one. The spines are able to inject a potent venom producing immediate pain which can lead to shock and, rarely, even death. First aid is to immediately immerse the affected area in water as hot as can be tolerated. Although scorpionfishes are venomous, their flesh is typically not poisonous to eat. Some scorpionfishes regularly shed their skin which rids the fish of algae growths and external parasites.

In the reef habitat Lacy Scorpionfish *Rhinopias aphanes* mimick crinoids (all photos on these two pages from Milne Bay, PNG, unless otherwise noted).

Included in the Scorpionfish family are the Lionfishes, Stonefishes, Leaf Scorpionfish, Waspfishes, Demon Stingers and the most exotic of all, members of the genus *Rhinopias*. This group of four species is so rarely seen that they do not have a collective common name. The two fishes that may be found in the Coral Sea are the Weedy Scorpionfish, *Rhinopias frondosa,* and the Lacy (or Merlet's) Scorpionfish, *Rhinopias aphanes.* The other two species are known from Japan and Hawaii.

The Lacy Scorpionfish was first discovered in New Caledonia in 1964 but when found it was thought to be a Weedy Scorpionfish. Further study of the only known specimen showed it to be a new species and it was named by William Eschmeyer in 1973 as *Rhinopias aphanes.* The word "aphanes" comes from the Greek noun meaning "that which is inconspicuous", a very appropriate name since most divers fail to spot this brilliantly camouflaged fish even though it likes to sit out in the open.

In 1980, diving out of Port Moresby, my wife Dinah tried to describe a fish that she had just seen. I could not understand what she was saying so we went back in the water, Dinah found the fish again and I photographed it. We could not find the fish in any of our books so sent the photograph of to the Curator of

Note the dark spot on the dorsal fin of the Lacy Scorpionfish.

Fishes at the Smithsonian Institute. He wrote back with the splendid news that Dinah had found the second ever specimen of this fish. After that we found many more around the Port Moresby area and also in Milne Bay. We hosted expeditions from the New York Aquarium and caught a specimen which was hand carried, in a plastic bag inside a small insulated box with ice and oxygen, on flights all the way back to New York, and which survived in the Aquarium for several years.

A quite different colour variation of the Lacy Scorpionfish which was photographed near Port Moresby, PNG.

Lacy Scorpionfish prefer reefs exposed to swells and currents. They mimic crinoids (feather stars) so to find one a diver should carefully inspect all the crinoids on the reef - one may turn out to be a scorpionfish. Sitting out in the open they are usually shallower than 15 metres,

Portrait of the Weedy Scorpionfish *Rhinopias frondosa.*

often as shallow as 3-5 metres. They are more commonly seen in the late afternoon, but have been found at all times of the day and night.

Reluctant swimmers, they crawl over the reef to a likely spot and wait. They rely on their camouflage to ambush small fishes, sometimes rocking slightly backwards and forwards imitating the effect of surge on a crinoid, and feed by combining a forward lunge with a gaping mouth. This is a very clumsy movement, the fish sometimes falling off its perch after capturing its prey.

To match crinoids, Lacy Scorpionfishes occur in many different colours. Dark green seems to be the most common but reds, yellows and browns are also regularly found. The Lacy Scorpionfish is easily confused with the Weedy Scorpionfish, and unfortunately the common names have been swapped by some authors, however the markings on the latter are usually more circular - or even nearly invisible - and this fish tends to inhabit more sheltered habitats closer to shore where the water is less clear. Adult Lacy Scorpionfishes are larger than the Weedy variety and can grow to about 25 cm total length. Although the Weedy Scorpionfish has been reported from many locations in the Indian and Pacific Oceans, the range of the Lacy Scorpionfish appears limited to the Coral Sea region.

Another view of the excellently camouflaged Weedy Scorpionfish which seems to mimick algae rather than crinoids.

Ambon Scorpionfish

Le: To 8 cm. Di: Northern CS. De: 3 to 50+ m. Ge: Found in pairs crawling along dark sand bottom amongst debris. Horn-like growths above eyes and long mustaches distinct. Larger is probably ♀ (growths smooth), ♂ has antler-like branching growths. Active at night. Colour variable (below, Milne Bay).

Pteroidichthys amboinensis   **Milne Bay, PNG**

Leaf Scorpionfish

Le: To 10 cm. Di: All CS. De: 1 to 50+ m. Ge: The unusually thin body of this fish contributes to its leaf-like appearance. Often sits out on branches of staghorn or other corals. Colours include white, black, yellow and violet (below). Usually easy to photograph as it stays in place. If one is found there are others nearby.

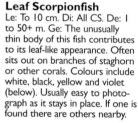

Taenianotus triacanthus   **Madang, PNG**

Blue-eyed Stingfish

Le: To 10 cm. Di: Northern CS, range uncertain. De: 5 to 50 m. Ge: Seen at night on soft sand or silt bottoms. Uses single modified pectoral ray to walk rather than swim. In some specimens white barbels grow from lower jaw. Large blue eye is distinctive. An unusual fish sometimes confused with lionfishes.

Minous trachycephalus   **Port Moresby, PNG**

Scorpaenopsis diabolus   **GBR, Australia**

False Stonefish

Le: To 30 cm.
Di: All CS.
De: 3 to 50 m plus.
Ge: Often confused with true stonefishes. Common in a variety of habitats and conditions, and variable as to colours and whether it has green algae growing on its back. It is however easily identified as the largest of the hump-backed scorpionfishes with a distinctive hump where the dorsal spines start. May be solitary or in pairs.

Scorpaenopsis macrochir   **Milne Bay, PNG**

Humpback Scorpionfish

Le: To 13 cm. Di: All CS. De: 1 to 15 m. Ge: Much smaller than *S. diabolus*, extraordinarily variable, even in same habitat. Prefers sheltered sand and rubble bottoms with debris. Often appears to have growths of algae and encrusting sponges on its body. Feeds on small fishes, active day and night.

Scorpaenopsis oxycephala   **Madang, PNG**

Tasselled Scorpionfish, Smallscale Scorpionfish

Le: To 36 cm.
Di: All CS.
De: 1 to 35 m.
Ge: This is the large scorpionfish often found in the open on clear water reefs relying on its effective camouflage. It will sit on hard or soft coral and is an attractive species - with a powerful sting. It is less variable in colour and decoration than other species of scorpionfish and readily identified. See also previous page.

Papuan Scorpionfish

Le: To 20 cm. Di: All CS. De: I to 40 m. Ge: One of a closely related spp. group that are difficult to distinguish in the field. Habitat is a clue as *S. papuensis* may be found on live coral reefs while *S. venosa* (below, Tufi, PNG) prefers more turbid habitats. All highly variable in colour, pattern and body growths.

Scorpaenopsis papuensis   **Port Moresby, PNG**

Horrid Stonefish, Estuarine Stonefish

Le: To 30 cm.
Di: Coastal bays throughout the Coral Sea region.
De: I to 40 m.
Ge: This truly horrible looking fish has a sting known to cause fatal injury. Very difficult to see and often partly hidden under debris or sand. Usually in habitats close to shore and reluctant to move if disturbed.

Synanceia horrida   **Milne Bay, PNG**

Reef Stonefish

Le: To 35 cm. Di: All CS. De: I to 30 m. Ge: In a variety of habitats including off-shore reefs. Will bury in sand or hide in coral caves to emerge at night, or remain in the open. Sometimes spectacularly coloured with red sponge-like growths. 13 dorsal spines which are highly venomous.

Synanceia verrucosa   **Madang, PNG**

Yellow-spotted Scorpionfish

Le: To 7 cm.
Di: All CS.
De: 1 to 15 m.
Ge: Very distinctive scorpionfish uniquely patterned with yellow blotches and white spots, found by searching among the branches of *Pocillopora* corals on reef tops of exposed coral reefs. Little known but actually quite common.

Sebastapistes cyanostigma   **New Britain, PNG**

VELVETFISHES   APLOACTINIDAE

Velvetfish
Le: To 8 cm. Di: Northern CS. De: 1 to 20 m. Ge: This sp. is becoming better known as divers explore more sand slopes. Dark varieties live on dark sand in association with logs and other debris, lighter ones in coral sand near dead coral (below).

Paraploactis sp.   **Solomon Islands**

FLATHEADS   PLATYCEPHALIDAE

Crocodilefish
Le: To 54 cm.
Di: All CS.
De: 1 to 30 m plus.
Ge: A favourite find for underwater photographers this species allows close approach, even gentle touching, before fleeing. Sometimes mistaken for a scorpionfish but the spines are not venomous. The eyes have intricate "lashes" - iris lappets. Most flatheads live on soft bottoms but this species can be found on coral reefs. Rarely they are coloured all black. See also p. 77 .

Cymbacephalus beauforti   **Milne Bay, PNG**

Spiny Flathead

Le: To 10 cm.
Di: Northern CS.
De: 4 to 15 m.
Ge: A small nocturnal species that buries in sand during the day. More colourful than other flatheads. Distinguished by its broad head which looks over-sized for its body.

Onigocia spinosa　　　Port Moresby, PNG

Welander's Flathead

Le: To 11 cm.
Di: Northern CS.
De: 6 to 12 m.
Ge: Welander's Flathead grows slightly larger than the Spiny Flathead, lacks the red colouration and has iris lappets that are not lacy but bilobed. It is found in sandy areas of lagoon and seaward reefs.

Sorsogona welanderi　　　Solomon Islands

BARRAMUNDI
CENTROPOMIDAE

Sand Bass

Le: To 47 cm.
Di: Northern CS.
De: 1 to 20 m.
Ge: True Barramundi, a table fish that delights gourmets, are rare outside river estuaries but the related, and equally tasty, Sand Bass can be found on inner, and coastal, reefs and sea grass beds. It is a nocturnal fish that hides deep in coral ledges during the day.

Psammoperca waigiensis　　　Port Moresby, PNG

Pseudanthias dispar   **Tufi, PNG**

Redfin Anthias

Le: To 9 cm. Di: All CS.
De: 1 to 15 m.
Ge: Anthias or Fairy Basslets are a group of small fishes that occur in large numbers on coral reefs. They are plankton feeders and swarm on top and down dropoffs, favouring areas with current activity. Males (left) are usually more extravagantly coloured than their harem of females. Dominant females can change sex if the male dies. The Redfin Anthias is found in shallow water and easily identified by its red dorsal. Yellow female similar to several other female anthias.

Pseudanthias huchtii   **Solomon Islands**

Threadfin Anthias

Le: To 12 cm.
Di: All CS.
De: 1 to 20 m.
Ge: Third dorsal spine elongated, red - orange stripe from eye to pectoral fin. Males have harems (see photo), though territories shared by groups of males. Found in large numbers on reef edges that experience currents.
   All Anthias or Fairy basslets belong into the subfamily Anthiinae of the family Serranidae.

Pseudanthias squamipinnis   **Eastern Fields, Coral Sea**

Scalefin Anthias

Le: To 15 cm.
Di: All CS.
De: 1 to 20 m.
Ge: Variable in colour throughout its range but typically purple. Third dorsal spine elongate in males (left). A common anthias on top or at the edges of coral reefs. See also facing page (harem of females with one male and a few specimens during sex/colour change).

Stocky Anthias

Le: To 19 cm. Di: All CS. De: 2 to 50 m. Ge: Prefers sheltered waters, though still relies on current to bring planktonic food. Males have spot on dorsal fin lacking in females (below), which have two spots joined with a fine margin on the tail. Often in small groups on isolated coral heads over sand or rubble bottom.

Pseudanthias hypselosoma, male   Milne Bay, PNG

Striped Anthias

Le: To 21 cm. Di: Northern CS. De: 25 to 60+ m. Ge: With this sp. the female (below, Port Moresby) is readily identified by its bright red stripe however males are far more scarce and tend to live deeper. Photos of the exquisite full grown males are rare because of their depth. The one shown here was found at 60 m.

Pseudanthias fasciatus, male   Milne Bay, PNG

Luzon Anthias

Le: To 14 cm. Di: Northern CS. De: 15 to 50 m.
Ge: Found in deeper water on outer reef dropoffs usually where vertical drop changes to reef slope. Usually in much smaller numbers than previous species of anthias. Below: Female (Eastern Fields, CS).

Pseudanthias luzonensis, male   Eastern Fields, Coral Sea

FAIRY BASSLETS AND SEX CHANGE

Fairy Basslets are one of the most common groups of fishes found in our area. They are often called *Anthias* although this is not strictly correct, as this term should be limited to Atlantic species, more correctly they belong to the genus *Pseudanthias*. They swarm on the tops, edges and slopes of coral reefs and, because they feed on drifting plankton, are particularly active if currents are running.

The orange female of the Squarespot Fairy Basslet *Pseudanthias pleurotaenia* (Milne Bay, PNG).

There are many different species but they are not evenly distributed and abundance of a particular species can change dramatically from one area to the next. A particular species often has defined depth ranges and different species are encountered as depth increases. Some of the most rare and beautiful species are found at extreme depths for divers. They are a small fish, usually in the order of 8 to 15 cm long.

Males are usually quite different in appearance from females. Although the males are usually easy to spot having more vibrant colours, they sometimes appear to be missing, only to be found in deeper water. There are far fewer males as each male maintains a harem of several females.

The fascinating sex life of these fishes revolves around the fact that if a harem loses its male a high ranking female will undergo a sex change and turn into a male to replace the one lost. No one knows exactly how long this process takes but it is thought to be weeks rather than days or months.

Observant divers are able to see this transformation taking place if they look carefully at groups of *Pseudanthias*. The illustrations show a series of photographs of Squarespot Fairy Basslets, *Pseudanthias pleurotaenia,* in the process of changing sex. This extraordinary fish is usually found on steep coral walls deeper than about 20 metres. It is large for a *Pseudanthias* and relatively easy to photograph. The female is yellow, then, as change takes place, becomes darker with markings appearing on her anal fin. Further into

In this fish the sex change is nearly complete. It has assumed the colouration of the male except for the large lateral squarish blotch.

the change, markings appear on all her fins including a darker red spot to the rear of the dorsal fin. Finally the male matures with a stunning and distinctive purple square spot on its sides.

Other groups of fishes also demonstrate sex change from female to male - Wrasses and Parrotfishes in particular. Since these groups have many different species it makes fish spotting very difficult as identification of both males and females have to be made. Do not feel too bad if you find this difficult - scientists have been known to describe a new species of fish only to find that it was the male or female (or juvenile) version of a known species. To complicate matters some wrasses are born male, while others of the same species are born female but eventually change into a male.

Anemonefishes are not only renown for their symbiotic relationship with anemones. They live in family groups with the largest and dominant fish being female. If the female is lost the largest adult male changes sex to female, a reversal of the more common change from female to male.

Sex change complete! A fully-coloured male of the Squarespot Fairy Basslet.

Pseudanthias pleurotaenia, male New Britain, PNG

Squarespot Anthias

Le: To 20 cm.
Di: All CS.
De: 15 to 50 m plus.
Ge: Common on outer reef walls usually deeper than 20 m. The male (left) is very distinctive with its purple square spot which stands out as blue in the natural environment. Easier to approach than many other anthias and a favourite with all Coral Sea photographers. See also previous page about the sex change of Fairy basslets demonstrated by the Squarespot Anthias.

Pseudanthias rubrizonatus Tufi, PNG

Redbar Anthias

Le: To 10 cm.
Di: All CS.
De: 3 to 50 m plus.
Ge: The author has seen this anthias in shallow water on isolated coral heads but it is more often encountered on current swept reefs or ship wrecks in deeper water where it may be the predominant anthias species. The bar on the side is much bigger and brighter than when found on P. cooperi following, and also on an undescribed deep water anthias.

Pseudanthias cooperi New Ireland, PNG

Cooper's Anthias

Le: To 14 cm. Di: Northern CS. De: 4 to 50 m plus.
Ge: Very variable in colour and boldness of stripe. The author has seen individuals in shallow water on top of current swept reefs, but usually deep. Below: Colour variation (Milne Bay, PNG).

Purple Anthias

Le: To 12 cm.
Di: Northern CS.
De: 2 to 30 m.
Ge: Also known as the Yellow-stripe Anthias because the females (small photo below, Milne Bay, PNG) have a yellow stripe along the back and tail. Males have a large dark blotch on the rear of the dorsal fin. In the Coral Sea area *P. tuka* is more common in the northern waters and the very similar *P. pascalus* in the southern, though they have been reported together. Female *P. pascalus* lack the yellow stripe and the males lack the dark blotch. Both species are abundant in their range.

Pseudanthias tuka   Eastern Fields, Coral Sea

Pseudanthias pascalus   Flinder's Reef, Coral Sea

Lori's Anthias

Le: To 12 cm. Di: All CS, but uncommon. De: 7 to 50+ m. Ge: Likes caves, arches and ledges where it occurs in small groups, often swimming upside down. *P. smithvanizi* (below) has a similar habitat for some of its range but in other areas (northern CS) is often the most common anthias, in huge numbers.

Pseudanthias lori   Milne Bay, PNG

Magenta Slender Anthias

Le: To 7 cm.
Di: Northern CS.
De: 1 to 30 m plus.
Ge: Often abundant where it occurs, this tiny anthias swarms around sea fans and soft corals. This genus does not show obvious differences between males and females, though we notice colour patterns, evident in the photo, with and without the red flash near the tail.

Luzonichthys waitei   **Eastern Fields, Coral Sea**

Longfinned Perchlet

Le: 3.5 cm. Di: All CS. De: 5 to 50+ m. Ge: Hard to spot due to small size and cryptic nature. Looks and behaves more like a Hawkfish. Usually sitting on the bottom. There are over 40 spp. in the genus, one (below), which features a high 3rd dorsal spine with a yellow flag-like flap, is undescribed or could be *P. inermis*.

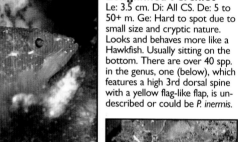

Plectranthias longimanus   **Milne Bay, PNG**

Hawk Anthias, Cave Anthias, Fathead Anthias

Le: To 13 cm.
Di: All CS.
De: 10 to 50 m plus.
Ge: This exquisite fish can be found on walls on outer reefs where it hovers, sometimes upside down, near or inside overhangs or crevices. Originally it was thought to be a Hawkfish, but turned out to be in the subfamily Anthiinae, and a relative of *Pseudanthias*. Uncommon north of latitude 10° S in the Coral Sea area.

Serranocirrhitus latus   **Port Moresby, PNG**

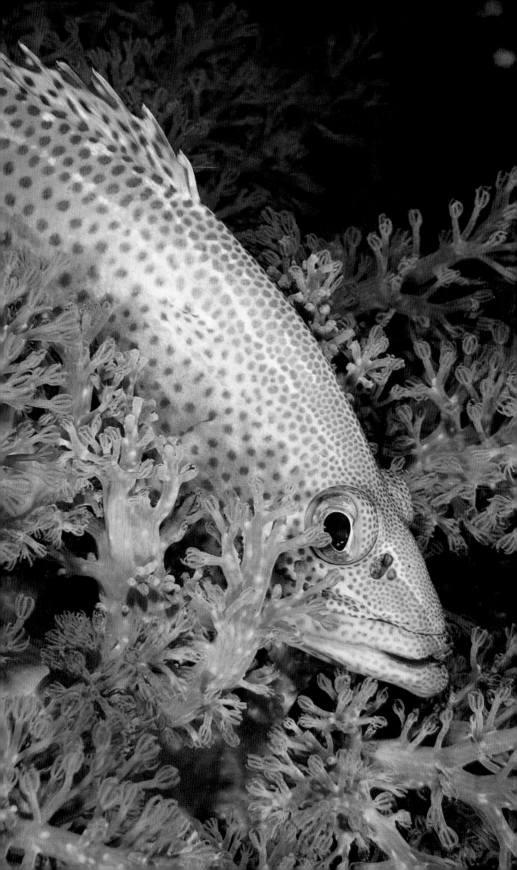

White-lined Rockcod
Le: To 52 cm. Di: All CS.
De: 3 to 50 m plus. Ge: A
very common and attractive
grouper that is easy to
approach. Often found nestled
in soft corals or gorgonians
where it patiently waits for fish
prey to swim close. Favours
protected rather than exposed
reefs. See also previous page.

Anyperodon leucogrammicus   **GBR, Australia**

Peacock Rockcod
Le: To 40 cm. Di: All CS.
De: 3 to 40 m. Ge: Prefers more
exposed reefs. As with most
groupers it mainly feeds on fishes but also may take crustaceans.
Can change its colour to a darker and less distinct pattern, as
with many groupers. Below
(GBR): *C. boenack* is smaller, all
brown and lives in silty areas.

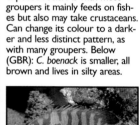

Cephalopholis argus   **Solomon Islands**

Blue-Spotted Rockcod

Le: To 35 cm. Di: All CS
except possibly Vanuatu and
New Caledonia. De: 1 to 50 m.
Ge: This species has a distinctive juvenile stage (below,
Solomon Islands) which is
often mistaken for a different
species. Prefers sheltered shallow reefs or sea grass.

Cephalopholis cyanostigma   **Solomon Islands**

Leopard Rockcod

Le: To 20 cm.
Di: Northern CS.
De: 3 to 40 m.
Ge: Easily identified by the
dark saddle on the base of the
tail. Not commonly noticed
because of its secretive habits
but very photogenic, particularly the head with its orange
spots on red base.

Cephalopholis leopardus   **Eastern Fields, Coral Sea**

Coral Cod

Le: To 40 cm. Di: All CS. De: 2
to 48 m. Ge: Abundant on
healthy reefs in current prone
areas. Easy to approach and photograph. Also banded, then very
similar to *C. sexmaculata* (below)
with blue lines rather than spots
on face, distinct dark bands with
blackish blotches at dorsal ends;
prefers to live in caves.

Cephalopholis miniata   **Milne Bay, PNG**

Tomato Rockcod

Le: To 50 cm. Di: All CS. De: 3
to 50+ m. Ge: Easily approached,
can change its colours readily
from dark red (below, Milne Bay,
PNG) to brown blotches. Usually reported from deep water but
resident in some areas at cleaning stations in only 3 m.

Cephalopholis sonnerati   **Milne Bay, PNG**

71

Barramundi Cod
Le: To 66 cm. Di: All CS. De: I to 30 m. Ge: Common name after distinct shape of head but not closely related to true Barramundi. Divers delight in finding juveniles (below) which are curious but will rarely stray far from their coral lairs. In a variety of habitats, occurs in both silty and clearwater habitats.

Cromileptes altivelis   **Port Moresby, PNG**

Flat-tail Grouper
Le: To 75 cm. Di: All CS. De: 4 to 50+ m. Ge: Larger and rarer than *E. areolatus* (below, to 45 cm, all CS, 5 to 50+ m) sometimes seen on wrecks in silty areas. Its spots are smaller and more numerous and it also has areas of dark blotching which have caused divers to have identified the fish as Potato Cod.

Epinephelus waandersii   **Milne Bay, PNG**

Malabar Grouper

Le: To 1.0 m.
Di: All CS.
De: 5 to 50 m.
Ge: A large grouper that is often misidentified. Easily tamed with fish baits but aggressive and competitive and will bite the hand that feeds them - and anything else that looks like food. Wide range of habitats including protected reefs, silty areas and wrecks.

Epinephelus malabaricus   **Port Moresby, PNG**

Giant Grouper

Le: To possibly 2.7 m.
Di: All CS.
De: I to 50 m plus.
Ge: The largest reef fish, the Giant Grouper is an impressive beast to meet underwater. They may be tamed by feeding however most are wary in the wild and difficult to approach. They inhabit caves and wrecks, but are also seen swimming in blue water off reef walls. They will compete with sharks for hooked tuna, though are said to prefer a diet of lobster.

Epinephelus lanceolatus   New Ireland, PNG

Potato Cod

Le: To 1.5 m.
Di: GBR, PNG.
De: 3 to 50 m plus.
Ge: An easily identified grouper made famous at the Cod Hole on the Great Barrier Reef where a protected family have been fed for many years. Otherwise rare on the GBR but small groups occur in the Coral Sea and PNG, and probably elsewhere in the region. Will approach divers and easily fed.

Epinephelus tukula   GBR, Australia

Flowery Cod

Le: To 90 cm. Di: All CS. De: 5 to 40 m. Ge: Large, mottled brown grouper with distinctive hollow above eye in head profile. It is shy and will rapidly disappear at the approach of a diver. Several specimens at the Cod Hole have become tame along with Potato Groupers. This grouper has also been implicated in Ciguatera poisoning. See also the following two species *E. polyphekadion* and *E. corallicola*, which are similar but smaller.

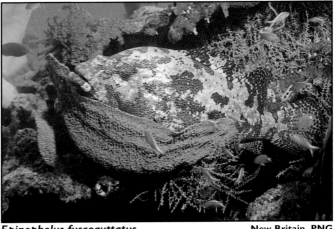

Epinephelus fuscoguttatus   New Britain, PNG

Snoutspot Grouper

Le: To 65 cm. Di: All CS. De: 2 to 46+ m. Ge: Similar to *E. fuscoguttatus* but smaller are the Snoutspot and the **Coral Grouper** *E. corallicola* (below, Solomon Islands). Both can be distinguished by dark blotches - a single one at the top base of the tail, and 3 or 4 along the base of the dorsal fin respectively.

Epinephelus polyphekadion   **Milne Bay, PNG**

White-spotted Grouper

Le: To 60 cm.
Di: All CS.
De: 2 to 20 m.
Ge: Generally found in shallow water under ledges or near coral caves. Has scattered large and small white spots. Ventures as far south as New South Wales in Australia. Will usually sit still and allow close approach by careful divers, following them with at least one eye.

Epinephelus caeruleopunctatus   **Eastern Fields, Coral Sea**

Speckled-Fin Rockcod

Le: To 40 cm. Di: All CS. De: 5 to 25 m. Ge: *E. ongus* also has white spots, generally more numerous and smaller than those of *E. caeruleopunctatus,* although some may combine to form white blotches. The juvenile (below, Milne Bay) is distinctive with many bright white spots over a dark brown base.

Epinephelus ongus   **Solomon Islands**

74

Blacktipped Grouper

Le: To 35 cm.
Di: All CS.
De: 3 to 50 m plus.
Ge: A very distinctive little grouper that will often be discovered staring at the diver from a coral perch. Tips of dorsal fin black. Common and widespread over a vast range From Red Sea to Pitcairn Island. Eats mainly crabs and fishes.

Epinephelus fasciatus   **Eastern Fields, Coral Sea**

Snubnose Grouper

Le: To 43 cm.
Di: Northern Coral Sea.
De: 5 to 30 m.
Ge: The Snubnose Grouper can be identified from its profile as shown in the photograph. Its colour patterns, particularly when juvenile, are similar to three other species. *E. maculatus* (bottom large photo) has two white and black blotches on its back and favours silty lagoons. *E. merra* (small photo below, Madang, PNG) has a more honeycombed pattern of dark spots, and with *E. quoyanus* (bottom small photo, Solomon Islands), the honeycombed spots are larger.

Epinephelus macrospilos   **New Caledonia**

Epinephelus maculatus   **Milne Bay, PNG**

Wavy-lined Grouper

Le: To 75 cm.
Di: Northern CS.
De: 5 to 50 m plus.
Ge: This grouper lives away
from coral reefs on sheltered
silt and sand bottoms close to
shore where it hides under
fallen logs and other debris. It
is wary and difficult to
approach but will study divers
from a distance. Known from
PNG and the Solomon Islands
it has not yet been reported
from elsewhere in the Coral
Sea.

Epinephelus undulosus   **Milne Bay, PNG**

Thinspine Rockcod
Le: To 40 cm. Di: All CS. De: 5
to 50 m plus. Ge: A common
rockcod prefering clearwater
coral reefs close to deep water.
The colour pattern is quite variable from moment to moment
(below, Eastern Fields). Juvenile,
with violet colouration and
orange trim, is surprisingly rare
considering abundance of adults.

Gracila albomarginata   **Solomon Islands**

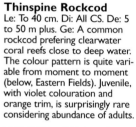

Coral Trout
Le: To 1.0 m. Di: All CS. De: 15
to 50+ m. Ge: Has two distinct
colour phases, the initial phase is
thought to mimic the poisonous
toby *Canthigaster valentini* however it rapidly grows to a much
larger size. Eventually becomes
more uniformly brown (below).
Esteemed as food fish but implicated in Ciguatera poisoning.

Plectropomus laevis   **Flinder's Reef, Coral Sea**

CROCODILE WITH GILLS

The Crocodile Fish is a member of the Flathead family all characterised by having, surprise, surprise, a flattened head shape. Their scientific family name is Platycephalidae, and, no surprise I am sure this time, platy is Greek for flat and cephal (kephale) is Greek for head. Scientific names are a mystery to many people but usually there is a strict logic to their application. You just need to know some Greek or Latin.

The Crocodile Fish *Cymbacephalus beauforti.*

Flatheads live in temperate as well as tropical seas, and indeed the temperate flatheads are regarded as excellent eating, tropical ones less so. There are several different species of tropical flatheads, most are small and found mainly on night dives over sand or silty bottom. The flathead stays on the bottom, often covered or partly covered with sand, and waits for unsuspecting prey to come close. They are reported to feed mainly on crabs and shrimp, and take the occasional small fish. But one giant inhabits coral reef areas, and what a magnificent beast it is, growing up to 75 cm long and with scientific name *Cymbacephalus beauforti.* Divers who knew no better thought the fish looked like a crocodile and simply called it a Crocodile Fish.

Unlike most flatheads the Crocodile Fish has elaborate frilly fins and a mottled colour pattern which helps to camouflage it on the reef. Probably the most impressive camouflage however is to the eye which has wonderful elaborate eyelashes. Eyes are a very important feature of a predator which is why so many other creatures use false eyes in their body patterns as a survival technique. They make the predator feel as though he is being preyed on!

These eyes are the reason that the Crocodile Fish is one of the most sought after creatures in the sea for underwater photographers. They are extraordinarily photogenic, and, as a bonus, the Crocodile Fish is so confident in its camouflage that it will sit still and allow close approach.

Close-up of the eye of the Crocodile Fish. Note the lace-like skin flap that covers most of the pupil.

77

Plectropomus oligocanthus   Eastern Fields, Coral Sea

Highfin Coral Trout

Le: To 65 cm.
Di: Northern CS.
De: 5 to 50 m.
Ge: An uncommon fish which is difficult to approach in daytime. It has spectacular luminous blue markings in the form of lines and dots.

Variola albimarginata   Milne Bay, PNG

Lyretail Trout

Le: To 60 cm.
Di: All CS.
De: 2 to 50 m plus.
Ge: This fish and *Variola louti* (following species) are often confused with each other. The Lyretail Trout can be recognised by having a fine white line margin. The brightly coloured fish has been seen following hunting octopus intent on stealing any prey the octopus flushes from beneath coral rocks.

Variola louti   Eastern Fields, Coral Sea

Coronation Trout

Le: To 65 cm.
Di: All CS.
De: 2 to 50 m plus.
Ge: The Coronation Trout can be distinguished from the similar previous species *Variola albimarginata* by a wider yellow margin. It is encountered on coastal shallow reef flats and outer reef crests and slopes. The juvenile lives secretively in rocky areas and has a distinct colour pattern with a light coloured band running on the midline from the chin to the dorsal fin.

Barred Soapfish

Le: To 25 cm, usually less.
Di: All CS.
De: 1 to 20 m.
Ge: A shallow water species often seen in silty harbours. This fish, along with other soapfishes, secretes a skin toxin called grammistin when stressed. This produces a soapy feel to the skin.
  All Soapfishes belong into the subfamily Grammistinae of the family Serranidae.

Diploprion bifasciatum   GBR, Australia

Arrowhead Soapfish

Le: To 15 cm.
Di: All CS.
De: 10 to 40 m.
Ge: A solitary fish which hangs motionless near the entrances to caves or crevices in outer reef walls. Dark colouration requires over exposure for good photographs, and a torch to see clearly.

Belonoperca chabanaudi   Tufi, PNG

Sixline Soapfish
Le: 27 cm, usually smaller. Di: All CS. De: Juv. 1 m, adults 20+ m.
Ge: Juveniles are quite common in sheltered habitats where they hide under boulders. Adults are harder to find and live deep down mud or silt slopes. Below: The rarer *Pogonoperca punctata*.

Grammistes sexlineatus   Milne Bay, PNG

79

Sailfin Dottyback

Le: To 12 cm.
Di: GBR.
De: 10 to 30 m.
Ge: A large and easily
approached Dottyback with a
distinctive long tail. Usually
deeper than 10 m on lagoon
reefs, and more often found in
the open although not far from
its hiding place.

Ogilbyina velifera   **GBR, Australia**

Oblique-lined Dottyback

Le: To 7.5 cm. Di: All CS. De:
10 to 40 m. Ge: Very variable,
some, probably males, with
dark ocellated spot on dorsal
fin (see left). All with fine diagonal striping. As with most
Dottybacks spends much time
hidden in small coral caves only
to make brief forays outside.
Below (Tufi): Colour variety.

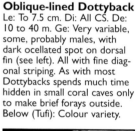

Cypho purpurescens   **Port Moresby, PNG**

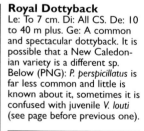

Royal Dottyback

Le: To 7 cm. Di: All CS. De: 10
to 40 m plus. Ge: A common
and spectacular dottyback. It is
possible that a New Caledon-
ian variety is a different sp.
Below (PNG): *P. perspicillatus* is
far less common and little is
known about it, sometimes it is
confused with juvenile *V. louti*
(see page before previous one).

Pseudochromis paccagnellae   **Milne Bay, PNG**

Yellow Devilfish

Le: To 6 cm. Di: Northern CS.
De: 5 to 40 m. Ge: Sometimes
called Scissortails because of
their highly forked tails the
Assessors swim, often upside-
down, along the roofs of caves,
rarely venturing outside. Below
(GBR, Australia): The **Blue
Devilfish,** A. *macneilli,* is found
in the southern part of the CS.

Assessor flavissimus New Britain, PNG

Comet

Le: To 16 cm.
Di: All CS.
De: 1 to 40 m.
Ge: The cave dweller emerges
from hiding at dusk. Will hover
near the entrance to its cave
at night, but slowly drifts back
if a light is shone on it. Moves
head first into small openings
inside cave, leaving tail to mimic head of spotted moray eel.
See also next page.

Calloplesiops altivelis New Caledonia

GRUNTERS

Crescent Grunter

Le: To 32 cm.
Di: All CS.
De: 0 to 5 m.
Ge: Usually seen by
snorkellers in very shallow
water along beaches or near
mangroves. Believed to have
evolved from freshwater
species and will enter brackish
water.

Terapon jarbua Milne Bay, PNG

THE COMET

One of the most fascinating things that divers can do on a dive is to take a torch and peer into the dark recesses of any crevices, small caves, overhangs and ledges that they find. A surprising number of different species of fishes live in these habitats. Many are nocturnal and emerge at night, but some spend their whole lives protected by these dark shelters. The best time to try this out is just before dusk as the nocturnal fishes start to migrate from the deeper recesses to the more open sections.

The wonderful Comet *Calloplesiops altivelis* near a reef crevice (Russell Group, Solomon Islands).

Cardinalfishes will be among the most common cave dwellers seen. There are very many different species of Cardinalfishes, some congregate in large numbers around isolated coral bommies, moving into the branches of the coral as a diver approaches. Those that prefer to live in caves usually hang motionless just inside the cave during the daytime and become more active as they feed on zooplankton at night. A particularly interesting behaviour of Cardinalfishes is "mouth-brooding". The female lays a gelatinous mass of eggs which the male immediately fertilises then takes in his mouth. After several days the eggs hatch out and by that time the male will be rather hungry as the egg mass in his mouth prevents him from feeding.

The Arrow-head Soapfish, *Belonoperca chabanaudi*, is another fish rarely seen far from the entrance of its cave during the day time. This is a solitary species which also likes to hang motionless and which is therefore easy to photograph once seen. The fish does absorb a lot of light however and needs a bit of extra exposure to capture its details. When stressed Soapfishes produce a soapy skin toxin called "grammistin" which protects it from predators.

Members of the family Plesiopidae, commonly called Longfins, are specialised cave dwellers. They generally have one continuous dorsal fin with a large extention towards the tail and large pelvic fins to match - hence "Longfins".

Devil fishes or "Assessors" are common Longfins. This small fish is usually found in groups upside down near the roofs of caves and ledges. In Papua New Guinea the beautiful *Assessor flavissimus* is the species most often found. This is bright yellow with a gold edge to its fins. On the Great Barrier Reef and other areas the blue *Assessor randalli* is more common. They have a diet of small fishes and crustaceans, with occasional gastropods and worms.

Probably the most exciting of the Longfin cave dwellers that a diver can find is a close relative of the Assessors, the Comet, *Calloplesiops altivelis*. This extraordinary fish grows to about 20 cm and during the day hides in the deep recesses of caves and is thus rarely seen. During the evening it moves nearer the opening of the cave and may be photographed. It is usually solitary though others may live in caves nearby. They are often shallow and I recently found three individuals in caves just a few metres apart in only 5 metres of water. When a diver disturbs a Comet it will sometimes move its head into a hole so that only its tail can be seen. The large ringed spot (ocellus) near its tail, and the shape of its enormous fins give the distinct appearance of the head of a moray eel, thus discouraging predators.

The juveniles have fewer but bigger white spots than the adults and for a time was considered to be a different species (juvenile fishes have fooled scientists on more than a few occasions!). The Comet is widespread and not considered rare. The reason it is not so well known is that divers just do not look in the right place at the right time.

The photograph shown here was taken in the Solomon Islands. I was aboard the dive boat Spirit of Solomons at a beautiful site called Karumolan Island in the Russell group. The reef came to a point and dropped off in ledges decorated with soft corals. The many crevices made this an ideal site for Comets though local operators claimed not to have seen the fish at all. I entered the water just before dark and dived into the night. As I scanned the wall with my dive light a familiar shape registered and I scanned the light back to see a Comet slowly glide out of view. I waited patiently with my light turned away, then scanned again getting a clear sight of the fish before it again slowly moved out of the light back into the depths of the crevice. Next time I set up to use my camera and as soon as I scanned and illuminated the Comet, I took the photograph.

FLAGTAILS KUHLIIDAE

Fiveband Flagtail

Le: To 20 cm.
Di: All CS.
De: 0 to 5 m.
Ge: This Flagtail, although
superficially similar to a Crescent Grunter without body
stripes, prefers a reef habitat
close to shore where it may
be found in the surf zone.
Often in large schools.

Kuhlia mugil Solomon Islands

BIGEYES PRIACANTHIDAE

Crescent-tail Bigeye

Le: To 40 cm.
Di: All CS.
De: 8 to 50 m plus.
Ge: Although the big eye suggests a nocturnal species this
fish can often be found in small
schools hovering over stands
of staghorn coral. Very easy to
approach. Can change colour
to silver with vertical red
bands. Crescent tail is distinctive.

Priacanthus hamrur New Britain, PNG

Glasseye

Le: To 32 cm.
Di: All CS.
De: 3 to 20 m.
Ge: A cave dweller usually only
seen at night. Silver blotching
variable, may be dominant
colour. Primarily plankton
feeders in spite of large mouth.

Heteropriacanthus cruentatus Port Moresby, PNG

83

Ring-tailed Cardinalfish
Le: To 12 cm. Di: All CS.
De: 1 to 20 m. Ge: The ringed
tail and blue lines readily identify this species which congregates in large schools among
the branches of staghorn coral.
They disperse at night to feed.
See also facing page (GBR).
A. crysopomus (below, Tufi) also
lives in coral branches.

Apogon aureus   **Milne Bay, PNG**

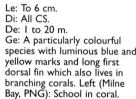
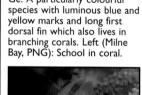

Longspine Cardinalfish

Le: To 6 cm.
Di: All CS.
De: 1 to 20 m.
Ge: A particularly colourful
species with luminous blue and
yellow marks and long first
dorsal fin which also lives in
branching corals. Left (Milne
Bay, PNG): School in coral.

Apogon leptacanthus   **Milne Bay, PNG**

Oblique-banded
Cardinalfish

Le: To 7 cm.
Di: Northern CS.
De: 1 to 20 m.
Ge: This cardinalfish is very
secretive and hard to find. It
lives in the crevices beneath
coral boulders and rarely ventures far. It is also usually solitary.

Apogon semiornatus   **Port Moresby, PNG**

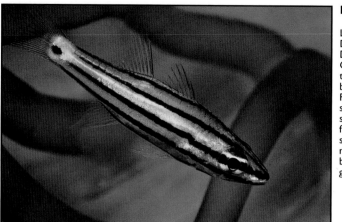

Five-lined Cardinalfish

Le: To 12 cm.
Di: All CS.
De: 5 to 40 m.
Ge: Usually found at entrances
to caves or ledges, or among
branches of staghorn corals.
Five black stripes bottom one
sometimes faint, and black
spot surrounded by yellow in
front of tail. Several similar
species distinguished by the
number of stripes and size of
black spot. Solitary or in small
groups.

Cheilodipterus quinquelineatus   **GBR, Australia**

Gelatinous Cardinalfish

Le: To 7 cm.
Di: All CS.
De: 1 to 40 m.
Ge: Body is translucent with
numerous dark spots. Lives
deep in caves during the day
and is only seen at night when
it emerges to feed. Prefers
sheltered coral reefs in clear
water. Several similar shaped
members of the genus in Coral
Sea area.

Pseudamia gelatinosa   **Milne Bay, PNG**

SAND TILEFISHES   MALACANTHIDAE

Blue Tilefish
Le: 15 cm. Di: All CS. De: 15 to
50 m. Ge: In pairs above home
which is a hole in a sand or rubble patch. Often seen by divers,
lives shallower than other genus
members. Juv.s in groups, may
be all blue. Below: *H. cuniculus* is
rarely seen shallower than 30 m.

Hoplolatilus starcki   **GBR, Australia**

Red-backed Tilefish

Le: To 12 cm. Di: Northern
CS. De: 25 to 50 m plus. Ge:
Easily recognised by the red
(black at depth) stripe along
the back, Lives in pairs in holes
on sand shelves. It may share
its habitat with the beautiful *H. purpureus* (below). Seeing
these two fishes usually
requires dives to at least 45 m.

Hoplolatilus marcosi   **Kavieng, PNG**

Chameleon Tilefish

Le: To 13 cm.
Di: Northern CS, other areas
uncertain.
De: 30 to 60 m.
Only recently discovered in its
natural habitat the fish lives in
holes on sand and rubble
ledges at depths of 45 to
60 m. It has the amazing ability,
unlike other tilefishes, to
instantly change its colour.

Hoplolatilus chlupatyi   **Milne Bay, PNG**

Stocky Tilefish

Le: To 20 cm. Di: Northern
CS, other areas uncertain. De:
Deeper than 50 m. Ge: Differs
from most other genus members by building huge mounds
from coral rubble which it lives
in. A second sp., now named
H. pohle (below), from 75 m
was discovered when a group
of mounds were investigated.

Hoplolatilus fronticinctus   **GBR, Australia**

Flagtail Blanquillo

Le: To 30 cm.
Di: All CS.
De: 15 to 50 m.
Ge: Lives in holes in sand and
rubble, particularly clear areas
between widely spaced reefs.
Hole is often under a dead
coral rock. Hovering motion is
very sinuous.

Malacanthus brevirostris   Solomon Islands

Blue Blanquillo

Le: To 35 cm. Di: All CS.
De: 3 to 15 m. Ge: In widely
spaced pairs hovering above
sand or rubble patches
between reefs, this fish is usually difficult to approach. The
juveniles (below) are far easier
to approach and photograph.

Malacanthus latovittatus   GBR, Australia

Suckerfish

Le: To 1 m. Di: All CS. De: 1 to
50 m. Ge: Uses sucking disc on
top of its head to attach itself to
large fishes or turtles. Scavenger,
usually feeds by picking at scraps
from host's meal although it also
cleans host of parasites. Sometimes attaches to divers (below).

Echeneis naucrates   Eastern Fields, Coral Sea

Diamond Trevally

Le: To 1.5 m.
Di: All CS.
De: 0 to 60 m plus.
Ge: The juveniles inhabit shallow water and have long trailing filaments from their dorsal and anal fins. Similar species *A. ciliaris* lacks concave head before eye in adults. Juveniles of both species swim in pairs and thought to mimic stinging sea jellies.

Alectis indicus   Bougainville, Coral Sea

Orangespotted Trevally

Le: To 53 cm. Di: Northern CS. De: 2 to 50 m. Ge: Orange spots may be on silver (below) or yellow body (right) colour. Will approach closely. Yellow variety sometimes seen swimming with yellow goatfish. Not to be confused with Golden Trevally - described next.

Carangoides bajad   Port Moresby, PNG

Golden Trevally

Le: To 1.1 m. Di: All CS. De: 1 to 50 m. Ge: Juveniles are golden with distinctive black vertical stripes (below), live in sea jellies initially, then often pilot large sharks or groupers. Adults feed in small groups (right) on invertebrates on sand and rubble. The vertical stripes fade in large adults.

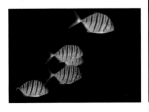

Gnathanodon speciosus   New Caledonia

89

Carangoides orthogrammus **Solomon Islands**

Yellowspotted Trevally

Le: To 70 cm.
Di: All CS.
De: 3 to 50 m plus.
Ge: This fish has far fewer spots than *C. bajad* and they are concentrated around the lateral line behind the pectoral fin. Feeds on invertebrates or small fishes buried in sand.

Caranx ignobilis **GBR, Australia**

Giant Trevally

Le: To 1.7 m.
Di: All CS.
De: 0 to 50 m plus.
Ge: A very impressive and unmistakable fish. Will feed around anchored boats at night on marine life attracted by the lights. Will sometimes approach divers closely and fast with unforgettable affect.

Caranx lugubris **Eastern Fields, Coral Sea**

Black Trevally

Le: To 80 cm.
Di: All CS.
De: 5 to 50 m plus.
Ge: Black body marks are distinctive. Not a common fish. Found on outer reef slopes and clearwater reefs, particularly in mid Coral Sea.

Bigeye Trevally
Le: To 94 cm. Di: All CS. De: I to 50+ m. Ge: Large eye and white tips to dorsal fin. Sometimes in huge schools that are attracted to divers who have the magnificent experience of them swooping past (see previous page). Feed at night so not fast swimmers during the day. One in a mating pair (left) is darker.

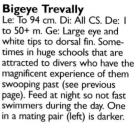

Caranx sexfasciatus   **Solomon Islands**

Bluefin Trevally
Le: To 1.00 m. Di: All CS. De: I to 50 m plus. Ge: A common fast moving trevally that will swoop in small groups on divers. Very attractive luminous blue, gold and black markings. Voracious hunter of small fishes. Below: *Caranx papuensis*, 88 cm, all CS, 2 to 30 m, with distinct point to rear top of operculum.

Caranx melampygus   **Solomon Islands**

Small-spotted Pompano

Le: 54 cm.
Di: All CS.
De: 0 to 20 m.
Ge: Usually seen swimming near the surface in small schools. Feeds on small fishes and enters the surge zone.

Trachinotus baillonii   **Solomon Islands**

Mangrove Jacks

Le: To 1,2 m. Di: All CS. De: 5 to 50+ m. Ge: Juveniles in estuaries but adults migrate to inshore reefs and wrecks where they are common. A good food fish which should be distinguished from the similar, but potentially ciguatoxic, Red Bass, L. bohar below, wich has deep pit in front of eye.

Lutjanus argentimaculatus   Port Moresby, PNG

Two-spot Snapper

Le: 20 cm. Di: North. CS. De: 3 to 40 m. Ge: Usually in schools hovering close over corals. Easily identified by stripes and two white spots. Its slender shape often causes misidentification as a fusilier by careless observers.

Lutjanus biguttatus   Kavieng, PNG

Golden-lined Snapper

Le: To 24 cm. Di: All CS. De: 15 to 50 m. Ge: Series of 10 or so horizontal yellow stripes along sides. Usually in schools often mixed with other snappers. A much rarer snapper, L. dodecacanthoides (below), has about 6 oblique stripes and is so far only recorded from PNG in the Coral Sea area.

Lutjanus rufolineatus   Madang, PNG

Spanish Flag, Stripey

Le: To 40 cm. Di: All CS. De: 2 to 35 m. Ge: An attractive but shy species with brown stripes that inhabits both lagoons and outer reefs. Lagoon specimens usually in small schools. Below: *L. argentimaculatus*, to 1.2 m, all CS, 5 to 50+ m. A good food fish but potentially Ciguatoxic Red Bass is very similar.

Lutjanus carponotatus

GBR, Australia

Blackspot Snapper

Le: To 35 cm. Di Northern CS. De: 1 to 20 m. Ge: Juveniles are commonly encountered in mangroves. This fish is sometimes confused with the **Longspot Snapper** *L. fulviflamma* (below), whose scales run diagonally above the lateral line.

Lutjanus ehrenbergii

Solomon Islands

Paddletail Snapper

Le: 50 cm. Di: All CS. De: 2 to 30 m. Ge: The paddle shaped tail makes it easy to identify. Often in large schools close over shallow reefs. Juv. (below) in very shallow water. Strangely this fish has been identified as potentially Ciguatoxic even though its diet consists of a high proportion of crustaceans as well as fishes.

Lutjanus gibbus

Flinder's Reef, Coral Sea

Bluelined Snapper

Le: To 35 cm. Di: All CS.
De: 2 to 50 m plus.
Ge: A beautiful schooling snapper with distinctive four blue
lines. Its close relative *L. quinquelineatus* (below) has 5 lines
and does not occur in such
large numbers. Both species
may be found together.

Lutjanus kasmira   **Milne Bay, PNG**

Bigeye Snapper

Le: To 30 cm. Di: Northern
CS. De: 2 to 50 m plus. Ge:
Sometimes mixed in schools
with other Snappers. Its big
eye separates it from the similar *L. vitta* (below). Possibly *L.
lutjanus* has been recorded as
L. lineolatus from New Caledonia in which case its distribution is all of the Coral Sea.

Lutjanus lutjanus   **GBR, Australia**

Maori Snapper

Le: To 65 cm. Di: Northern CS.
De: 3 to 50 m. Ge: A large shy
snapper often in groups of up
to 20 on top of reefs in 5 to 10
m depth, or solitary in deeper
water. Below: **Small Jobfish**
Aphareus furca, to 40 cm, all CS,
5 to 50+ m. Solitary, often
unnoticed, hangs around in mid
water near reef dropoffs.

Lutjanus rivulatus   **Eastern Fields, Coral Sea**

Onespot Snapper
Le: To 50 cm. Di: All CS. De: 5 to 30 m. Ge: On reefs usually close to caves, ledges or wrecks which provide shelter. Similar to *L. russelli* (below) and difficult to separate in the field, but *L. russelli* does not have yellow caudal fin and its spot is mainly above the lateral line rather than disected by it.

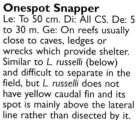

Lutjanus monostigma   **Vanuatu**

Black-banded Snapper

Le: To 35 cm.
Di: All CS.
De: 2 to 30 m.
Ge: Usually solitary and seen actively wandering on reef tops close to the bottom. Difficult to approach.

Lutjanus semicinctus   **Solomon Islands**

Red Emperor
Le: To 80 cm. Di: Western CS. De: I to 50 m plus. Ge: Not an Emperor at all, *L. sebae* is actually a Snapper. Juveniles with distinctive bands live in shallow water, often hiding in the spines of sea urchins (below and facing page). Adults move to deep water between or outside reefs and are prized food fish.

Lutjanus sebae   **New Britain, PNG**

BLACK AND WHITE SNAPPERS

When I am leading a dive cruise I encourage my fellow divers to tell me if they find anything that they cannot identify. Sometimes the descriptions defy logic and I have to wonder how deep the diver went, but often I can recognise the mysterious creature, even if I have to resort to my library. Over the years some descriptions crop up on a regular basis and I know immediately. "It's a small, black and white fish, spotted on top and striped below." Got it?

The exquisite black and white juvenile *Macolor macularis*.

Well, actually, it could be one of two closely related species of Snappers, or Sea Perch as they are known in Australia. OK! - the genus is *Macolor*, and the species could be either *M. macularis* or *M. niger*, and what the diver has seen is a juvenile whose colouration is much different from the adult.

Juveniles of both species tend to be solitary, and hang around close to black coral bushes or crinoids or other places where their body patterns make them difficult to spot. I think this is why they are so popular, often the divers are surprised and pleased when they notice the fish, which they may have been looking at for a while without realising it.

The most elegant of the two is the juvenile *M. macularis* since it has elongated fins, and it also grows to be the most elegant adult with a yellow

Adult Midnight Seaperch *M. macularis* (Solomon Islands).

eye and a mottled black, blue, brown and yellow body. The juvenile *M. niger*, as the name suggests, grows up to be an all black fish, sometimes with mottled grey patches which make it look dirty. Both these fishes, which grow to be about half a metre long, form schools - schools of *M. niger* may be very large indeed - which hang on the deep current side of coral reefs where they feed on drifting plankton.

The juveniles are surprisingly difficult to photograph. Not only do they tend to be continually on the move away from the photographer, their black colouration means that the fish disappears into any dark background.

Snappers are a large family of fishes and, although many of them are excellent eating, some are renown for harbouring Ciguatera toxin which causes anyone who eats them to become very sick - even if the fish is fresh and properly cooked. It is believed that Ciguatera accumulates in the body of a predatory fish which preys on certain reef fishes which in turn have digested a poisonous algae.

The likewise black and white juvenile *Macolor niger* (PNG).

There is also some evidence that this poisonous algae favours reefs which have been damaged, for example by storms or dynamiting. Strangely the poison does not affect the fishes, but has a devastating affect on humans. Minor symptoms include tingling in the palms of the hands which is accentuated by touching cold surfaces. Severe symptoms can lead to paralysis and death.

My favourite snapper is the exquisite Sailfin Snapper whose colour scheme has to be seen to be believed. Juveniles have trailing dorsal fin filaments and the adults feed on sand patches near coral reefs where they blow water down into the sand to disturb any small shrimp or crabs that may be hiding there. Usually the fish is solitary but the adults have been seen in huge congregations numbering in thousands of fish, presumably gathering for mating.

Adult Black Seaperch *Macolor niger* (Madang, PNG).

Pale Pinjalo

Le: To 50 cm.
Di: Northern CS, otherwise uncertain.
De: 5 to 50 m.
Ge: The Pinjalo snappers are represented by two similar species that congregate in schools on reef slopes. They are difficult to distinguish in life but *P. lewisi* (following species) is more red in colour and has a faint white mark on top of its caudal peduncle. Both species are widely distributed but seldom seen by divers as they are usually found deeper than other family members.

Pinjalo pinjalo   Madang, PNG

Red Pinjalo

Le: To 45 cm.
Di: Northern CS, otherwise uncertain.
De: 5 to 50 m.
Ge: The Red Pinjalo is more red in colour than the previous species and additionally has a faint white mark on top of the caudal peduncle.

Pinjalo lewisi   Tufi, PNG

Chinamanfish

Le: To 80 cm.
Di: Northern CS.
De: 5 to 50 m.
Ge: Juveniles (below) have trailing dorsal filaments. Smoothly rounded head is distinctive. This fish is known to carry Ciguatera toxin and should not be eaten.

Symphorus nematophorus   Milne Bay, PNG

99

Symphorichthys spilurus — Milne Bay, PNG

Sailfin Snapper

Le: To 60 cm.
Di: All CS.
De: 5 to 50 m.
Ge: One of the most beautiful of all reef fishes. They feed by blowing a jet of water on sand bottom to uncover marine invertebrate life which they devour. The centre photo shows a feeding adult specimen. Adults congregate in huge schools for mating. Juveniles have trailing filaments behind the dorsal and anal fin and a totally different colour pattern of mostly yellow fins and a broad black band running from the tip of the snout to the centre of the caudal fin. This bold lateral band runs across the eye and is lined with brilliant blue stripes already reminiscent of the adult pattern. It most certainly serves in disrupting the general shape of the fish in its natural coral reef environment. The distinctive black spot with white border on top of the caudal peduncle of adults is a remnant of this black band of juveniles. They also have some white areas in the caudal peduncle area nicely contrasting with the black band. Another distinctive feature of adults is their steep head profile. Juveniles have an elongated snout more typical for a snapper.

Symphorichthys spilurus — Milne Bay, PNG

FUSILIERS

CAESIONIDAE

Scissortail Fusilier

Le: To 25 cm.
Di: All CS.
De: 0 to 40 m.
Ge: Readily identified by black streaks on scissor tail and yellow band above lateral line. Often visits cleaning stations. Schools usually in midwater.

Caesio caerulaurea — Solomon Islands

Deep-bodied Fusilier

Le: To 25 cm. Di: All CS. De: 0 to 50 m. Ge: A large common fusilier in schools that are easy to approach. Fatter than others in genus, hence common name. *C. teres* (below) is slimmer and often has yellow continuing from tail along its back. Large schools of these fishes can be seen feeding on plankton at the surface.

Caesio cuning GBR, Australia

Two-lined Fusilier

Le: To 24 cm. Di: All CS. De: 0 to 50 m. Ge: A common schooling fusilier that can easily be confused with the similar *P. marri* (below). *P. digramma* has bottom stripe below lateral line, with *P. marri* stripe runs along lateral line.

Pterocaesio digramma Solomon Islands

Widestripe Fusilier

Le: To 13 cm. Di: Northern CS. De: 10 to 50 m. Ge: This fusilier lives in deeper water on reef dropoffs or even wrecks. The wide yellow stripe is distinctive. *P. pisang* (below), a shallow water fusilier, lacks any stripe but is otherwise similar.

Pterocaesio lativittata Solomon Islands

FUSILIERS

CAESIONIDAE

Tesselated Fusilier

Le: To 21 cm.
Di: All CS.
De: 0 to 50 m.
Ge: The scales have dark margins hence the common name Tesselated. Has single yellow line on top of lateral line. *P. trilineata* (below) has three brown lines.

Pterocaesio tessellata   Tufi, PNG

SWEETLIPS

HAEMULIDAE

Painted Sweetlips

Le: To 90 cm.
Di: All CS.
De: 1 to 40 m.
Ge: Photos show the progression from juvenile to full adult, and why there is some confusion with this species. Clockwise from top left to bottom large photo: Juvenile to full adult.

Diagramma pictum   Port Moresby, PNG

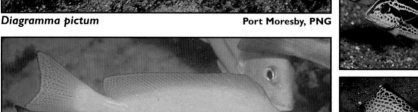

Diagramma pictum   Madang, PNG

Giant Sweetlips

Le: To 1.00 m.
Di: All CS.
De: 2 to 40 m.
Ge: Largest of the sweetlip family, usually solitary and shy. *P. obscura* is a synonym. Juveniles, as with most sweetlips, live in shallow coastal areas, and swim with an exaggerated sinuous motion.

Plectorhinchus albovittatus   Eastern Fields, Coral Sea

Goldstriped Sweetlips

Le: To 40 cm.
Di: All CS.
De: 2 to 40 m.
Ge: Adults form schools and sometimes this fish joins schools of other sweetlips. *P. celebicus* is a synonym.

Plectorhinchus chrysotaenia   New Britain, PNG

Harlequin Sweetlips

Le: To 72 cm.
Di: All CS.
De: 2 to 40 m.
Ge: Exquisite juvenile (below) usually found in silty water and much sought after by photographers. Adult easy to approach and forms small groups.

Plectorhinchus chaetodontoides   Solomon Islands

103

Brown Sweetlips

Le: To 60 cm.
Di: All CS.
De: 2 to 40 m.
Ge: Juvenile (below) mimics
dead leaf. Adult solitary and
difficult to approach.

Plectorhinchus gibbosus   **GBR, Australia**

Striped Sweetlips

Le: To 40 cm.
Di: All CS.
De: 2 to 40 m.
Ge: Photo shows typical adult
habitat under plate coral on
outer reef. Usually solitary.
Below: Juvenile.

Plectorhinchus lessoni   **Port Moresby, PNG**

Lined Sweetlips

Le: To 72 cm. Di: All CS.
De: 2 to 40 m. Ge: Since revision, no longer called Gold-
man's Sweetlips. Diagonal
stripes are distinctive, see *P.
vittatus* (small photo below).
Can form into large, closely
packed, schools particularly on
GBR. Easy to approach.

Plectorhinchus lineatus   **GBR, Australia**

Spotted Sweetlips

Le: To 84 cm.
Di: All CS.
De: 2 to 40 m.
Ge: Adults solitary and under ledges or plate corals. Sometimes confused with *P. chaetodonoides* but *P. picus* is black and white with no colour.

Plectorhinchus picus   Solomon Islands

MONOCLE BREAMS AND SPINECHEEKS   NEMIPTERIDAE

Two-line Spinecheek
Le: To 23 cm. Di: All CS.
De: 1 to 25 m. Ge: Often seen hovering close over sand patches close to corals. It will move a short distance then hover again. Feeds mainly on invertebrates in the sand. Easy to approach. Below: Juvenile.

Scolopsis bilineatus   Kavieng, PNG

Saw-jawed Spinecheek

Le: To 19 cm.
Di: All CS.
De: 1 to 25 m.
Ge: Easily identified by brilliant white stripe on back. Solitary or in small groups over sand near corals. *S. xenochrous* (below) lives in similar habitat and is easily distinguished.

Scolopsis ciliatus   Milne Bay, PNG

105

Scolopsis lineatus   **Solomon Islands**

Black and White Spinecheek

Le: To 23 cm. Di: All CS. De: I to 25 m. Ge: In small groups on reef edges, quite shy. Pattern on upper body is disruptive as is pattern on *Pentapodus trivittatus* (below). Both fishes tend to stay close to the bottom so pattern protects from above.

Scolopsis margaritifer   **Madang, PNG**

Pearly Spinecheek

Le: To 28 cm. Di: All CS. De: I to 25 m. Ge: Larger spinecheek also hovers close over sand near coral patches. *S. vosmeri* (below) has a deep body, prefers muddier bottoms, sometimes seen on wrecks but not seen on oceanic islands.

Pentapodus sp.   **New Britain, PNG**

Blue Whiptail

Le: To 20 cm.
Di: All CS.
De: 5 to 40 m.
Ge: Apparently undescribed, this luminous fish stands out from its surroundings - often volcanic sand. Adults are wary and difficult to approach. Below: Juvenile.

Gold-lined Sea Bream

Le: To 30 cm.
Di: All CS.
De: 1 - 20 m.
Ge: Found in schools hovering over hard corals on outer reefs. Bodies can be darker than shown here and gold lines almost obscured. Yellow spot near tail is distinctive. Feeds on bottom at night.

Gnathodentex aurolineatus   Solomon Islands

Spotted Sea Bream

Le: To 45 cm.
Di: All CS.
De: 2 to 40 m.
Ge: Apparently undescribed this fish is common in the Coral Sea area. The dark bar through the eye is more obvious in young. Scales on back have black spots. Hovers in mid water over corals and coral sand.

Gymnocranius sp.   GBR, Australia

Orangefin Emperor

Le: To 60 cm.
Di: All CS.
De: 18 to 50 m plus.
Ge: Solitary and difficult to approach this fish is commonly seen on outer reefs and drop-offs. Juveniles (below) seek shelter of caves and crevices. Feeds on shelled invertebrates.

Lethrinus erythracanthus   Tufi, PNG

Longfin Emperor

Le: To 50 cm.
Di: Northern CS.
De: 2 to 25 m.
Ge: Usually seen swimming slowly on top of coral reefs. Can be very colourful or change to drab, twin vertical white bars near tail identify. Solitary and difficult to approach.

Lethrinus erythropterus   **Flinder's Reef, Coral Sea**

Thumbprint Emperor

Le: To 60 cm.
Di: All CS.
De: 1 to 20 m.
Ge: Usually in shallow water over sheltered sand or sea grass bottoms. Oval blackish spot on side gives common name and identifies, but sometimes quite pale.

Lethrinus harak   **Milne Bay, PNG**

Smalltooth Emperor

Le: To 50 cm.
Di: Northern CS.
De: 5 to 50 m plus.
Ge: Usually seen on bottom on sand and rubble areas near reefs. Can change its appearance dramatically from pale to dark mottled brown (below).

Lethrinus microdon   **Port Moresby, PNG**

Spangled Emperor

Le: To 86 cm.
Di: All CS.
De: I to 50 m plus.
Ge: A large emperor reported
to be an excellent fish to eat.
Has blue spots and streaks
over pale yellow base. Sometimes in schools (right) usually
over sand or rubble.

Lethrinus nebulosus   GBR, Australia

Orange-striped Emperor

Le: To 40 cm. Di: All CS. De: 5
to 30 m. Ge: This emperor
can also darken its body sometimes obscuring the distinctive
yellow stripe. Over or near
coral reefs during daytime,
feeds on shelled invertebrates
at night. *L. lentjan* (below) is
identified by a red mark near
middle of operculum edge.

Lethrinus obsoletus   Solomon Islands

Long-nosed Emperor

Le: To 1.00 m. Di: All CS.
De: I to 50 m plus.
Ge: Emperor with the longest
snout. Adults seen actively
swimming over reefs. *L. xanthocheilus* (below) is similar but
has yellow lips and a red mark
at base of pectoral fin. Both
fishes can darken their colour.

Lethrinus olivaceus   GBR, Australia

109

Monotaxis grandoculis   GBR, Australia

Big-eye Bream

Le: To 60 cm.
Di: All CS.
De: 1 to 50 m plus.
Ge: A very interesting and common fish that hovers over coral reefs and is easy to approach. Its big eye is distinctive. Small juveniles are found singly on rubble or sand patches in shallow lagoons or on reef crests from clear coastal to outer reef habitats. The juvenile shows broad brown bars on a lighter background, which fade to an overall silvery colouration in adults. While juveniles are solitary adults sometimes congregate in small to large numbers to form loose aggregations during the day. At night they move out to feed on the substrate in deep water. The photographs show the stages of development of this species. Clockwise from top left to bottom large photo: Juvenile to full adult.

Monotaxis grandoculis   GBR, Australia

COURTING CODS

The cods (or groupers for the rest of the world, the members of the family Serranidae) are the largest of all the basses and most impressive inhabitants of coral reefs. The mightiest species may reach a length of up to 3 metres and a weight of over 400 kg. But even the largest specimens do not pose a threat to man. Helmut Debelius recalls his most exciting dive during his first visit to Australia's Great Barrier Reef where he was very lucky to witness the courtship of the Potato Cod.

This photo clearly shows the impressive size of the Potato Cod.

Almost all serranids are protogynous hermaphrodites, starting their life as females and changing sex if necessary. There is no sexual dimorphism (no externally visible difference between the sexes) except in size, males normally growing bigger than females. During the spawning season they migrate to spawning grounds which are located on the seaward face of a reef in the vicinity of deep water. As is the case in many pelagic spawners, according to literature courtship starts towards the end of the day, but this is not always observed in nature.

The courtship of the Potato Cod *Epinephelus tukula* was one of my most exciting experiences in over 20 years of diving and it happened around 6 o'clock in the morning. The day before I tried to take photographs of a 120-cm-long Potato Cod in a depth of 30 m right below our live-aboard. But it disappeared when I came too close with the camera. I wanted to take it by surprise, and so I went down again first thing in the morning while everyone else - including, hopefully, the cod - was still sound asleep. But the fish sensed the disturbance and retreated into the entrance of "its" cave in the reef. Suddenly it turned to face another even larger Potato Cod approaching from the open water. Both animals met near the reef and only then I noticed that the first one from the cave had a swollen belly: it was a female! The specimen that just had arrived started to slowly slide its head along her side until their lips touched. Immediately the large black spots typical for the species faded. Now I understood what was going on right in front of my eyes: the courtship of two Potato Cods. The pair no longer took any notice of me although in my excitement about being able to document this unusual spectacle on film my movements were rather more elaborate than usual. The courtship continued for

All their movements were gentle and loving...

about three minutes, the larger male repeatedly nudging the belly of the egg-laden female with its lips. Then, suddenly, both started to tremble violently. Fascinated, I watched the large cods gliding down into deeper water, pressed close together, and out of my sight. Unfortunately, due to low visibility I was unable to watch where and how they finally spawned.

...the newly arrived male caressing its partner.

111

Yellowstripe Goatfish

Le: To 43 cm.
Di: All CS.
De: 2 to 35 m.
Ge: Common in small groups
or large schools on sand
slopes where it feeds on invertebrates. Occasionally yellow
stripe fades and black spot is
prominent (below).

Mulloidichthys flavolineatus   **GBR, Australia**

Yellowfin Goatfish
Le: To 38 cm. Di: All CS.
De: 2 to 50 m plus.
Ge: Larger than *M. flavolineatus*
(previous species) and lacks
black spot although fish sometimes has a dirty appearance
with dark patches. On reefs
during daytime, feeds at night
by digging in sand for invertebrates. Left: School.

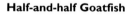

Mulloidichthys vanicolensis   **Milne Bay, PNG**

Half-and-half Goatfish

Le: To 25 cm. Di: All CS.
De: 2 to 25 m.
Ge: A small and distinctive
goatfish active on sand patches
near reefs in sheltered lagoons.
P. barberinus (below) grows to
50 cm, is the largest of the
goatfishes and usually found in
small groups.

Parupeneus barberinoides   **GBR, Australia**

Two-barred Goatfish

Le: To 35 cm. Di: All CS.
De: 1 to 50 m plus.
Ge: May be variable in colour
and bars less distinct. Solitary,
resting on coral during the day
though will feed if opportunity
arises. *P. ciliatus* (below) is less
common but also rests on
coral reefs during day.

Parupeneus bifasciatus   Santo, Vanuatu

Goldsaddle Goatfish

Le: To 45 cm. Di: All CS.
De: 1 to 50 m plus. Ge: Often
all golden yellow and swimming in small schools over
reefs, otherwise dark with gold
saddle near tail (below). Feeds
mainly on fishes. Very long
barbels used to chase small
fish out of holes in the reef.

Parupeneus cyclostomus   Kavieng, PNG

Indian Goatfish

Le: To 35 cm. Di: All CS.
De: 1 to 20 m.
Ge: Very variable but all phases have yellow blotch over lateral line. Can be similar to
P. barberinus (facing) but black
line much shorter. Shallow
sand or silty areas in lagoons
or near coasts.

Parupeneus indicus   GBR, Australia

Manybar Goatfish

Le: To 30 cm.
Di: All CS.
De: 1 to 50 m plus.
Ge: Colour and pattern variable but black bars, sometimes shortened to saddles, are distinctive. Adults usually deeper than young. *P. pleurostigma* (following) is similar but dark marks further forward.

Parupeneus multifasciatus **Eastern Fields, Coral Sea**

Roundspot Goatfish

Le: To 30 cm.
Di: All CS.
De: 5 to 40 m.
Ge: Found on clear water reefs in lagoons and on slopes. Usually singly or in small groups. Juveniles are coastal and often seen in small aggregations. They are similar in colouration to the adults but typically much more slender. The large black spot directly followed by the white area identifies the adults.

Parupeneus pleurostigma **GBR, Australia**

Freckled Goatfish

Le: To 30 cm.
Di: All CS.
De: 1 to 50 m plus.
Ge: A common goatfish often in pairs or small groups. Has other bar-tailed relatives. Sand or silty areas near coasts, will enter estuaries.

Upeneus tragula **Milne Bay, PNG**

SWEEPERS

Silver Sweeper

Le: To 15 cm.
Di: All CS.
De: 5 to 40 m.
Ge: There are several similar species in this genus, this one has a dark anal fin base. It is found usually in or near caves by day and feeds on plankton in open water at night.

The Sweeper family currently contains only two genera, *Pempheris* and *Parapriacanthus* (with a few species widespread in the Indo-Pacific region, not represented here). The family contains an estimated 20 species which are distributed globally in tropical to warm-temperate seas. They are closely related to the Silver Batfishes Monodactylidae (following) and share many features with them. Their bodies are oblong to moderately slender and compressed. In the genus *Pempheris* the lateral line scales extend to the posterior margin of the caudal fin. Small to large schools aggregate near reefs or in large caves during the day. At night they feed well away in open water on zoo-plankton, usually tiny crustaceans and cephalopods. Small juveniles are semi-transparent, often in very large cloud like formations along the front of small reefs in coastal estuaries Adults are usually secretive, staying in the shelter of the reef or live deep inside.

Pempheris schwenkii   Port Moresby, PNG

SILVER BATFISHES

Silver Batfish

Le: To 20 cm. Di: All CS.
De: 1 to 10 m.
Ge: Usually in schools (below) close to shore in silty water around wharves, wrecks or fringing reef. Will approach closely, swooping on divers.

Monodactylus argenteus   Milne Bay, PNG

115

FRIENDLIEST FISH IN THE SEA

If I was asked for the friendliest fishes in the sea I would have to vote for batfishes *(Platax* spp.). Even on sites dived for the first time resident batfish will approach closely - in fact several times I have been startled by a batfish approaching from behind then suddenly appearing in front of my mask. On regularly dived sites batfish follow divers around and can be a nuisance if you are trying to take wide angle photographs by continually swim into the frame. Batfish which have been fed will follow divers right to the surface and the boat. I have actually seen one lifted out of the water by a crew member on Telita and which allowed itself to be held without struggling.

Probably because they are so common, divers do not pay much attention to batfishes - in fact many divers do not realise that there are five different species in our area. Admittedly the adults do look very similar and distinguishing them requires some study, however the juveniles look nothing like the adults that they will grow to be. They live in different habitats to the adults and are well worth searching for. They are very beautiful fishes and make exquisite photographic subjects.

Batfishes are a small but interesting family comprising several genera, of which only *Platax* is commonly seen in our area. Members of other genera are found only deep or in the Atlantic Ocean. All known five species of *Platax* are shown here. Only recently the fifth species, *P. boersi*, was recognised as being distinct, previously it was confused with other species. Adult batfishes can be found from coastal lagoons to outer reefs where they may form large schools, and have been trawled from depths of up to 500 metres. They are thought to be pelagic spawners and their larvae transform into the tall juvenile when about 20 mm long. Juveniles are either pelagic or benthic, depending on the species, usually seeking quiet waters in coastal bays and estuaries. Diet consist of algae and a variety of invertebrates such as jellies or other plankton.

Possibly the most common is the juvenile Round

Batfish, *Platax orbicularis*. The adult has an almost perfectly round forehead from its snout to its dorsal fin. The juvenile can be found in very shallow water close to shore at a sheltered beach, typically near sea grass beds where it will lie on its side and drift around like a floating dead leaf. The colouration is a perfect mottled brown. Sometimes a small school of 3 - 10 will swim together. This fish is most often seen on night dives.

The **Round Batfish** *Platax orbicularis* grows to a length of 50 cm. It is found throughout the CS in depths from 1 to 30 m. Juveniles (above) mimic dead leaves and are found along sheltered beaches. Adults (right) live in small schools. Front of head is nearly perfectly round. Easily confused with very similar *P. boersi* (see fourth page on batfishes).

The most elegant of the juveniles is the Pinnate Batfish, *Platax pinnatus*. This gorgeous fish is completely black with a brilliant orange boarder all around it. The true juvenile is only a 5-6 cm tall and hard to find. Sub-adults, 20 cm or so tall, which have retained some of their juvenile markings but also have silvery patches on their bodies, are more often seen - particularly at night near staghorn corals or sheltered walls. I have found the true juvenile at sheltered sites close to shore. It is not easy to photograph as its eye is also jet black and hard to focus on, and because it is never still. Romantics might call it a dance, but more likely it is mimicking the very similar flatworm that is also found in the Coral Sea. The adult Pinnate Batfish is the easiest of the batfishes to identify, having a distinct snout. They are often in small schools on a wide variety of openwater reefs.

The **Pinnate Batfish** *Platax pinnatus* grows to a length of 30 cm. It is found in the northern Coral Sea region in depths from 1 to 30 m. The Juveniles (above, photo from Milne Bay, PNG, as both photos of *P. orbicularis* on the previous page) are exquisite and mimic a toxic flatworm in appearance and constant motion. Adults (left, photo from Solomon Islands) live in small groups on coral reefs and have have a pronounced snout which aids in identification.

The rarest is wonderful tiger-striped raggedly-finned beauty that prefers silty bottoms where it will hide close to a crinoid, fallen palm frond or other debris. This is juvenile Hump-headed Batfish, *Platax batavianus*. Once found it is easy to photograph and will stay in the same area until it reaches adult size. I was once able to revisit one that was only 6 cm high to start with then photographed it over a period of 6 months by which time it had grown to 25 cm. This juvenile seems to prefer water 10 to 20 m deep. The adult has a distinct double bump on its forehead and is unusual in that it is solitary and prefers to live at about 30 m or deeper.

The **Hump-headed Batfish** *Platax batavianus* grows to a length of 50 cm. It is found in the northern Coral Sea region in depths from 20 to 40 m. Juveniles (above, photo from Milne Bay, PNG) with black and white stripes may be encountered in sheltered coastal waters. They frequently associate with featherstars (crinoids) and have been observed nibbling on their arms. Adults (right, photo from Solomon Islands) are solitary or in small groups and live deep near coral reefs. The Hump-headed Batfish is the least observed batfish species in general.

The **Teira Batfish** *Platax teira* grows to a length of 60 cm. It is found in all of the Coral Sea region in depths from 0 to 60 m. Juveniles live in fields of sea grass (above, photo from Milne Bay, PNG), mangrove areas and floating sargassum weed. Adults (left, photo from Tufi, PNG) may be solitary or form huge schools. They are common on deep wrecks mainly in midwater above the wreck. They are very approachable and easily tamed by feeding (below, over wreck of St. Jacob, Tufi, PNG). **Boers Batfish** *Platax boersi* (top left) is easily confused with the very similar *Platax orbicularis*.

Threadfin Butterflyfish

Le: To 20 cm. Di: All CS.
De: 1 to 40 m. Ge: Most wide-spread of genus. Feeds on algae, worms, prawns and coral polyps. Distinguished from similar *C. vagabundus* (below) by having trailing filament and false eye-spot near tail. As with most butterflyfishes adults of both species are usually paired.

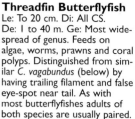

Chaetodon auriga   **Eastern Fields, Coral Sea**

Lined Butterflyfish

Le: To 30 cm. Di: All CS. De: 2 to 50 m plus. Ge: Largest of all the butterflyfishes and difficult to approach. Found in pairs but often solitary. *C. oxycephalus* (below) is similar but has distinct gap in black bar through eye. Both species may be found on the same reef.

Chaetodon lineolatus   **GBR, Australia**

Pacific Double-saddle Butterflyfish

Le: To 15 cm.
Di: All CS.
De: 1 to 30 m.
Ge: Prefers areas of rich coral on current fed reefs. Distinct black spot on tail base. Feeds on wide variety of invertebrates and algae. A very similar Indian Ocean species, *Chaetodon falcula,* is not found in the Coral Sea area.

Chaetodon ulietensis   **Tufi, PNG**

Spot-tail Butterflyfish

Le: To 14 cm. Di: Northern CS.
De: 3 to 50 m. Ge: The black
spot on the tail distinguishes
this sp. from the very close *C.
melannotus* (below). However in
the Southern Coral Sea only *C.
melannotus* is likely to be seen.
In the north both share many
reefs and careful observation is
needed to tell them apart.

Chaetodon ocellicaudus　　　　　Port Moresby, PNG

Bennett's Butterflyfish

Le: To 18 cm. Di: All CS.
De: 5 to 30 m.
Ge: An elegant butterfly fish
adorned with two sweeping
electric blue lines. Feeds mainly on coral polyps. The similar
species *C. speculum* (below)
lacks the blue lines and is usually solitary.

Chaetodon bennetti　　　　Guadalcanal, Solomon Islands

Teardrop Butterflyfish

Le: To 20 cm.
Di: All CS.
De: 5 to 50 m plus.
Ge: Young fishes display distinct tear line below black
spot, hence Teardrop common
name. Occur near leather
corals which appear to be part
of their diet. Also feed on hard
corals, worms, sponges and
algae. A very similar Indian
Ocean species, *Chaetodon interruptus*, is not found in the
Coral Sea area.

Chaetodon unimaculatus　　　　Vanuatu

Meyer's Butterflyfish

Le: To 18 cm.
Di: All CS.
De: 2 to 25 m.
Ge: Instantly recognisable this fish is not common and an exciting find. Usually in pairs, sometimes solitary, it feeds exclusively on coral polyps. Inhabits clear water outer reefs. Juveniles hide in branching corals.

Chaetodon meyeri   Solomon Islands

Ornate Butterflyfish

Le: To 18 cm. Di: All CS. De: 1 to 40 m. Ge: Prefers outer reefs often in the surge zone near dropoffs. Gold diagonal stripes make the fish easy to identify. With juveniles (below) the stripes are less distinct. Feeds on coral polyps and difficult to approach.

Chaetodon ornatissimus   Eastern Fields, Coral Sea

Racoon Butterflyfish

Le: To 20 cm.
Di: All CS.
De: 1 to 30 m.
Ge: Most other butterflyfishes sleep at night, often with their different night colouration but this butterflyfish is unusual in that it feeds at night. The only close relative is *Chaetodon fasciatus* from the Red Sea which is not found in the Coral Sea. Nudibranch lovers will be dismayed to find that this fish occasionally feeds on them - it must have ineffective taste buds.

Chaetodon lunula   Port Moresby, PNG

Black Butterflyfish

Le: To 20 cm.
Di: Southern CS.
De: 2 to 20 m.
Ge: Not known from mainland
PNG or Solomon Islands this
fish ranges as far west as Pitcairn Island. Typically on top of
reefs in 8 to 10 m of water
alone or in pairs not straying
far from coral shelter, but also
found near algae covered
rocks and in estuaries.

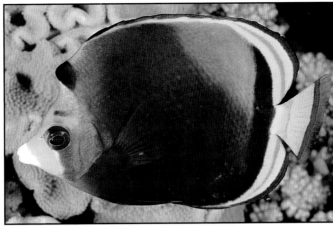

Chaetodon flavirostris   **Eastern Fields, Coral Sea**

Dotted Butterflyfish

Le: To 24 cm. Di: Northern CS,
not New Caledonia. De: 2 to
25 m. Ge: The fine black dots
and trailing filament distinguish
this fish from *C. rafflesi* (below)
which has a lattice-like body
pattern. Both fishes appear
absent from New Caledonia,
have a similar range and are
mostly found in shallow water.

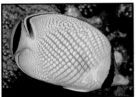

Chaetodon semeion   **Osprey Reef, Coral Sea**

Golden Striped Butterflyfish

Le: To 12 cm. Di: GBR. De: 5
to 15 m. Ge: Common on GBR
and reported from southern
PNG - but if so then rare.
Prefers coastal and inner reefs
and can tolerate brackish water.
Similar *C. rainfordi* (below)
shares habitat and range but
has vertical bands on the body.

Chaetodon aureofasciatus   **GBR, Australia**

123

Chaetodon lunulatus   New Ireland, PNG

Redfin Butterflyfish

Le: To 15 cm.
Di: All CS.
De: 1 to 20 m.
Ge: Should not be confused with the nearly identical C. trifasciatus from the Indian Ocean which does not occur in the Coral Sea area. Feeds on live corals. Usually in pairs or small groups.

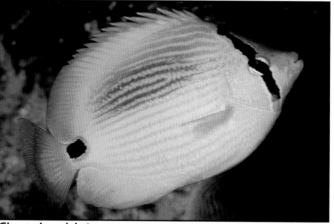

Chaetodon plebeius   New Britain, PNG

Bluespot Butterflyfish

Le: To 15 cm. Di: All CS. De: 1 to 10 m. Ge: Juveniles lack blue streak and have been seen cleaning other fishes. Adults feed mainly on coral polyps. Often in pairs but also solitary. Shares shallow habitat with C. kleinii (below) which is sometimes encountered in groups of 30 or so.

Spot-banded Butterflyfish

Le: To 12 cm. Di: All CS. De: 1 to 45 m. Ge: Easily confused with C. pelewensis (below) as both inhabit outer reef slopes and apparently produce hybrids with mixed patterns however C. punctatofasciatus has near vertical bands, C. pelewensis diagonal.

Chaetodon punctatofasciatus   GBR, Australia

Triangular Butterflyfish

Le: To 15 cm.
Di: All CS.
De: 1 to 10 m.
Ge: Feeds exclusively on *Acropora* coral polyps and is usually seen in pairs near plate and staghorn corals. Easily identified, as its only close relative *C. triangulum* is not found in the Coral Sea area.

Chaetodon baronessa　　Louisiade Archipelago

Chevroned Butterflyfish

Le: To 18 cm.
Di All CS.
De: 2 to 12 m.
Ge: The slimmest of all the butterflyfishes and actually classified as separate sub-genus, *Megaprotodon*, because of its unusual shape. Feeds on plate corals and will defend its territory. Mostly solitary but each male has a harem of two or three females.

Chaetodon trifascialis　　San Cristobal, Solomon Islands

Mertens' Butterflyfish

Le: To 12 cm.
Di: All CS.
De: 10 to 50 m plus.
Ge: Mostly encountered on outer dropoffs below 10 m, sometimes on wrecks, solitary or paired. May be distinguished from close relatives in that this is the only species in the Coral Sea area.

Chaetodon mertensii　　Port Moresby, PNG

Chaetodon citrinellus **New Caledonia**

Speckled Butterflyfish

Le: To 13 cm.
Di: All CS.
De: 1 to 25 m.
Ge: Favours rubble areas on edge of coral flats in areas of current or surge. Bottom of anal fin is black which helps distinguish it from other close species. Juveniles school in sea urchins for protection.

Chaetodon octofasciatus **Madang, PNG**

Eight-banded Butterflyfish

Le: To 12 cm.
Di: PNG and Solomons.
De: 3 to 20 m.
Ge: This fish can be found in sheltered areas close to shore where there is turbid water but also coral growth on which it exclusively feeds. It is common in these areas. Fish in Coral Sea are yellow, but silver in other areas. Adults alone or in pairs, sometimes small groups.

Chaetodon ephippium **GBR, Australia**

Saddled Butterflyfish
Le: To 23 cm. Di: All CS. De: 1 to 30 m. Ge: A stunning and easily identified species, note black saddle and trailing dorsal filament. Pairs can be found patrolling areas of rich coral growth. This fish obviously impressed the unknown artist who tried to paint it from memory - see below.

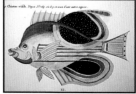

Burgess' Butterflyfish

Le: To 14 cm.
Di: Northern CS.
De: 15 to 50 m plus.
Ge: The specimen shown was photographed in the Solomon Islands where it swam up to only 15 m depth. Usually deep on walls in ledges. Solitary or in pairs. Other pairs may be close by. Possible range is wider but fish not often noticed.

Chaetodon burgessi   Guadalcanal, Solomon Islands

Pyramid Butterflyfish

Le: To 18 cm.
Di: All CS.
De: 3 to 50 m plus.
Ge: This distinctive and attractive fish forms large schools (right) which feed on plankton in midwater over the current face of outer reefs.

Hemitaurichthys polylepis   Bougainville, Solomon Islands

Beaked Coralfish

Le: To 20 cm.
Di: Northern CS and GBR.
De: 1 to 25 m.
Ge: Only found in inshore reefs usually in water that is slightly turbid. Commonly in pairs, this beautiful fish is surprisingly easy to approach. Is reported to enter estuaries.

Chelmon rostratus   Tufi, PNG

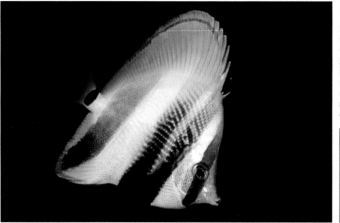

Highfin Coralfish

Le: To 15 cm. Di: Near major CS landmasses. De: 3 to 20 m. Ge: Very similar to *C. chryso-zonus* (below), which has not been reported from Vanuatu nor New Caledonia, however *C. altivelis* lacks dorsal spot in adult. Both fishes favour coastal reefs.

Coradion altivelis   **Milne Bay, PNG**

Ocellated Coralfish

Le: To 18 cm.
Di: Northern CS and GBR.
De: 1 to 25 m.
Ge: An easily recognised fish that inhabits silty and sheltered areas. High pointed dorsal fin is distinctive. Usually in pairs, reported to feed on sponges and bottom dwelling inverte-brates.

Parachaetodon ocellatus   **Osprey Reef, Coral Sea**

Longnose Butterflyfish

Le: To 22 cm. Di: All CS. De: 2 to 50 m plus. Ge: Easily con-fused with *F. longirostris* (below) but gill cover rounded rather than angled. In pairs but these can also consist of one of each species. Jaw opens like forceps but is more pipette-like in *F. longirostris* (almost no gape).

Forcipiger flavissimus   **Eastern Fields, Coral Sea**

Longfin Bannerfish

Le: To 25 cm. Di: All CS. De: 2 to 50 m plus. Ge: Usually in pairs while its close relative *H. diphreutes* (below) forms large, sometimes huge, schools. Another challenge to fish watchers, they may be identified by looking at the bottom corner of the anal fin which is more rounded in *H. acuminatus*.

Heniochus acuminatus   **Manus, PNG**

Pennant Bannerfish

Le: To 18 cm.
Di: All CS.
De: 2 to 40 m.
Ge: Often found with *H. varius* (below) partly hiding near coral caves or ledges. Both feed mainly on coral polyps and are difficult to photograph, melting into dark backgrounds.

Heniochus chrysostomus   **Madang, PNG**

Singular Bannerfish

Le: To 25 cm. Di: All CS. De: 2 to 50 m. Ge: Very similar to *H. monoceros* (below) sharing similar habitats, habits, size and colouration. Can be distinguished by sharp black - yellow boundary along base of dorsal fin of *H. singularius*. Both usually live in pairs.

Heniochus singularius   **Eastern Fields, Coral Sea**

ANGELS IN THE REEF

Angelfishes are considered to be among the most beautiful of all tropical reef fishes. They are similar in appearance to butterflyfishes but can be easily distinguished by the presence of a spine extending backwards from the gill covers. There are reported to be 85 different species worldwide however it would be exceptional to find more than 20 species in any one area. In the Coral Sea region they vary in size from the tiny White-tailed Angelfish, *Centropyge flavicauda*, at 6 cm to the Six-Banded Angelfish, *Pomacanthus sexstriatus*, which grows to nearly 50 cm.

Colin's Angelfish *Centropyge colini* (all photographs on these two pages are from Milne Bay, PNG).

The smallest angelfishes feed mainly on algae, but larger species supplement this with sponges, and other sedentary invertebrates. Members of the genus *Genicanthus* can often be seen swimming above the reef feeding on zooplankton.

Male angelfishes usually have a harem of 2 - 5 females but, except for a few angelfishes of the genus *Genicanthus*, males are indistinguishable from females by casual observation. They mate year round at sunset, the male spawning with each member of his harem in turn, rising off the bottom several metres before simultaneously releasing their gametes. Mating activity is less if there is no current to disperse the spawn.

The juveniles of some species are dramatically different from their adult form - the juvenile of the Emperor Angelfish, *Pomacanthus imperator*, is dark blue with white vertical stripes that become circular near the tail, while the adult

Juvenile Emperor Angelfish *Pomacanthus imperator*.

has a yellow, black and grey head with horizontal yellow and blue stripes. It is possible to find this exquisite fish in the intermediate colour phase as well. Many juveniles favour sheltered shallow reefs and a good place to find them is under wharves.

Emperor Angelfish, coloration intermediate between juvenile and adult patterns.

Those divers that love to wall dive should keep a look out for a beautiful little angelfish first discovered in the Cocos-Keeling Islands. It was named *Centropyge colini* after well known marine biologist Pat Colin. Colin's Pygmy Angelfish is easy to recognise being mainly yellow in colour with a distinctive blue patch covering the top of its back. Typically this species is about 8 - 10 cm long. It lives down deep on outer reef slopes and walls usually in ledges that cut back into the wall.

The specimen shown was photographed in Milne Bay, PNG. The site is known as Peer's Reef and descends as a steep slope to about 40 m where it plunges vertically for at least another 40 m en route to the abyss. At about 50 m a horizontal overhang slices back into the wall several metres ending in a narrow ledge. The top of the overhang is covered with yellow *Tubastrea* Corals, and Black Coral trees - many of which are infected with a parasitic white anemone which gives the site a weird appearance.

Lights are needed to see clearly and when I turned my light on I found myself surrounded by a blaze of colour and life which included several Colin's Pygmy Angelfishes swimming upside down on the overhang along with many small wrasses and other fishes. Initially startled by my light the angelfishes soon settled down and I was able to take a few photographs.

Colin's Pygmy Angelfish has also been reported from Guam, Palau and Fiji. My bet is that it is widespread through the Coral Sea but divers have not been looking for it. It is not always very deep and has been seen as shallow as 24m. Next time you wall dive, take a torch and have a good look in any ledges you come across.

Adult Emperor Angelfish.

Regal Angelfish

Le: To 25 cm. Di: All CS. De: I to 50 m. Ge: Juveniles (below), which have a distinct ocellated spot near the tail, live in caves and overhangs. Adults are common on current fed rich coral reefs either in lagoons or near dropoffs. Feed on sponges and tunicates and may be approached if patient.

Pygoplites diacanthus   **Holmes Reef, Coral Sea**

Three-spot Angelfish

Le: To 25 cm.
Di: All CS.
De: 10 to 50 m plus.
Ge: Three spots means a total of three, not three on each side - one on forehead and fainter ones on each side behind head. The lips are brilliant blue. Solitary or in pairs close to outer reef dropoffs, sometimes on lagoon reefs. Feed on sponges and tunicates. The only member of the genus in the Coral Sea area.

Apolemichthys trimaculatus   **GBR, Australia**

Coral Sea Angelfish

Le: To 8 cm.
Di: Northern CS.
De: 9 to 20 m.
Ge: Seen singly, in pairs or small groups among coral rubble as well as on open substrate. Very similar to and living sympatrically with the following species *C. heraldi* but with a blue-lined black blotch on the rear upper part of the dorsal fin. There are differences not only in the colouration but also in the morphology between both species. Juveniles lack the blotch and can not be distinguished from those of *C. heraldi*.

Centropyge woodheadi   **Eastern Fields, Coral Sea**

Herald's Angelfish

Le: To 10 cm.
Di: Offshore reefs, all CS.
De: 8 to 40 m.
Ge: Author has not seen this fish along PNG coast but has at Eastern Fields, PNG, and other Coral Sea reefs. Distinct from *C. flavissima* (below) by lack of any blue markings.

Centropyge heraldi　　　　　　　　Eastern Fields, Coral Sea

Two-spined Angelfish

Le: To 10 cm. Di: All CS.
De: 5 to 45 m. Ge: There are many colour variations of this fish to confuse fish-watchers, one shown below. The usual angelfish spine on gill cover has one or more smaller spines alongside. Rather shy and difficult to photograph hiding in coral when approached.

Centropyge bispinosa　　　　　　　　Solomon Islands

Bicolor Angelfish

Le: To 15 cm. Di: All CS. De: 3 to 25 m. Ge: Common, found in different habitats including shallow water fringing reefs, but mainly outer reef dropoffs. Singly, in pairs or small groups staying close to refuge under corals. *C. nox* (below) is another small angelfish seldom seen this time because of its colour, almost totally black.

Centropyge bicolor　　　　　　　　Bougainville Reef, Coral Sea

Flame Angelfish

Le: To 10 cm.
Di: Northeastern CS.
De: 5 to 50+ m.
Ge: Easy to identify but rare in some areas of the Coral Sea. Prefers clearwater oceanic reefs. The similar relative *C. shepardi* is not found in the Coral Sea area. Difficult to approach in the wild, and stays close to coral refuge. Sought after as an aquarium fish. Black bars on side are variable.

Centropyge loricula   **New Ireland, PNG**

Multi-barred Angelfish

Le: To 10 cm.
Di: All CS.
De: 10 to 50 m plus.
Ge: Secretive angelfish that lives in caves on reef walls. Usually solitary, but sometimes in pairs or small groups. A vertical zebra pattern of dark bars on light background combined with yellow snout, ventral and anal fins is distinctive. Juveniles with a large conspicuous spot on the rear of the dorsal fin. Has recently been placed into the new genus *Paracentropyge* due to morphological differences compared to *Centropyge* species.

Paracentropyge multifasciata   **Port Moresby, PNG**

Black Velvet Angelfish

Le: To 20 cm. Di: Only known from Samarai district, PNG, in CS area. De: 5 to 30 m.
Ge: Coral Sea variety from has uniformly black body colour behind head, possible different, new, species. Solitary or in small groups, one group under Samarai wharf in Milne Bay, PNG, now famous (left).

Chaetodontoplus melanosoma   **Milne Bay, PNG**

Vermiculated Angelfish

Le: To 18 cm.
Di: PNG, Solomons.
De: 1 to 20 m.
Ge: Common in PNG and
Solomon Islands on silty reefs
close to shore or in lagoons.
Tail may be grey or yellow,
which may represent two different species. Resembles butterflyfish with classic black
stripe through eye, but has gill
cover spine of angelfish. Feeds
mainly on sponges and tunicates.

Chaetodontoplus mesoleucus   **Tufi, PNG**

Masked Angelfish

Le: To 25 cm.
Di: GBR (northeastern coast of
Australia to Lord Howe Island).
De: 5 to 35 m.
Ge: Frequently encountered
among sponges which are its
main diet. Below: Subadult.

Chaetodontoplus meredithi   **GBR, Australia**

Black-spot Angelfish
Le: To 18 cm. Di: All CS.
De: 20 to 45 m. Ge: Males and
females easily distinguished.
Name comes from black spot
on breast of male, easier to
see in the wild. Plankton feeder. Below: Female. *Genicanthus*
spp. are the only angelfishes in
which sexes are distinctly
coloured.

Genicanthus melanospilos   **Solomon Islands**

135

Lamarck's Angelfish

Le: To 23 cm. Di: Northern CS and GBR, south to Vanuatu. De: 10 to 50 m. Ge: Thrives on coral reefs exposed to currents where it feeds on zooplankton. Males are larger and have yellow spot on forehead. Usually in groups, sometimes abundant. Below: Female.

Genicanthus lamarck   **Milne Bay, PNG**

Semicircle Angelfish

Le: To 35 cm.
Di: All CS.
De: 1 to 40 m.
Ge: Juveniles (below) are very shy, found in shallows, particularly under wharves. Adults (left) are relatively easy to approach, not common, reported solitary but usually seen pairs in the Coral Sea region. The species is found in reefs with rich coral growth, rarely more than one pair seen on any dive.

Already displayed on page 131 is the **Emperor Angelfish** *Pomacanthus imperator* which grows to a length of 38 cm. It is found in all of the Coral Sea region in depths from 3 to 50 metres. This spectacular yet common fish is easy to approach although it will emit knocking sounds if surprised. Juveniles are blue with white circular markings and found in sheltered areas, sometimes with adults.

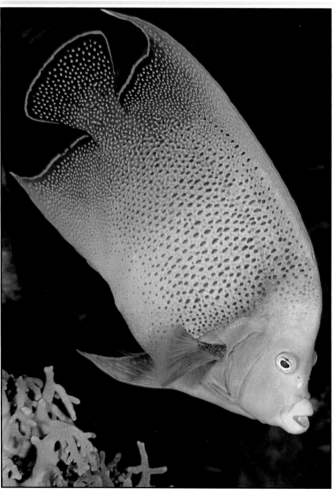

Pomacanthus semicirculatus   **Bougainville, Solomon Islands**

Blue girdled Angelfish

Le: To 25 cm.
Di: Northern CS.
De: 3 to 40 m.
Ge: Another spectacular fish, usually solitary but sometimes in pairs, that inhabits rich coral reefs, particularly near drop-offs. Not recorded from Vanuatu and New Caledonia, and only northern GBR. May be approached with care. Feeds on sponges and tunicates. A favourite with underwater photographers.

Pomacanthus navarchus   Milne Bay, PNG

Yellowmask Angelfish

Le: To 38 cm.
Di: Northern CS to Vanuatu.
De: 5 to 30 m.
Ge: A very shy species, difficult to approach and usually solitary, rarely in pairs. Makes a very loud thumping sound if suddenly disturbed. Large dark spot near tail unusual in angelfishes, more common in butterflyfishes. Feeds on sponges and tunicates. Reported to hybridize with *P. sexstriatus* and *P. narvarchus*.

Pomacanthus xanthometopon   Osprey Reef, Coral Sea

Six-banded Angelfish

Le: To 46 cm.
Di: All CS.
De: 3 to 50 m.
Ge: A very large angelfish found at a great variety of habitats from silty inshore reefs to outer dropoffs. Usually in pairs that swim close together. Five broad dark blue or black bars on sides produce six light coloured bands. Certain pairs may be approached closely, particularly if feeding, others are shy. Will grunt if suddenly disturbed.

Pomacanthus sexstriatus   Port Moresby, PNG

MUCK DIVING

One fine day I cruised our much loved live-aboard dive boat Telita into a sheltered bay with a black sand beach, dropped the anchor down the rubble slope and tied the stern to a tree ashore just a few metres behind the boat. The river mouth a hundred metres or so away was spewing a plume of brown mud after a recent downpour and the visibility appeared to be zilch. "What are we doing here?", one of our guests anxiously questioned "Trouble with the engine?, is there a storm coming? are we picking up some vegetables?" "No" I replied, to the assembled group, "this is a dive site."

Crinoids harbour small fishes...

My answer met with an explosive response. "We've paid thousands of dollars to come to dive PNG and we are not going to dive here, you lunatic, move the boat!"

They were seriously angry and I was in trouble. I had misjudged the sophistication of our dive group. Their expectations were for classic coral reefs and walls and crystal clear water - in fact just like the dives they had experienced during the first few days of our expedition.

I back-finned furiously, "I will move the boat straight away - but please just try the dive for a few minutes. The fresh muddy water you see is floating on top of the sea water, just go down 2 metres and the water will be clear,

...such as this juvenile batfish *Platax batavianus*.

and although this is not much of a reef you will see more creatures here than on all the reefs you have dived so far put together. Please try it for just five minutes, if you do not like it come up and I will move immediately." As a last resort I made the lawyer's plea - "Trust Me!"

I must have been persuasive because I managed to get them in the water but they were convinced that this was a big con and I was just trying to save fuel, or too lazy to take them to the great reefs.

The interesting thing was that no one surfaced for 40 minutes

A pipefish makes its home in a discarded typewriter covered by calcareous algae and other organisms.

Sand slopes in the Coral Sea region (and elsewhere in tropical reef areas) are far from being deserts. Many species live here but need a keen eye to be spotted.

or so and then it was because they were out of film and needed to reload - and get their tanks topped up at the same time. They boiled with excitement raving about the creatures they had seen and marvelling at each others discoveries. My reputation saved I announced:- "Welcome to the wonderful world of Muck Diving!"

Muck diving takes place at any site which does NOT have beautiful underwater scenery. Do not expect to see acres of beautiful corals. There may be patches with hard corals, gorgonians or sponges but these are usually isolated and not the main feature of the site. There may even be discarded human junk scattered around on the bottom. This does not sound very appetising so why would anyone want to dive a site like this? The answer is that Muck sites are habitats where many interesting and even bizarre marine creatures can be found, and extraordinary marine life behaviour can be observed. Be warned now - Muck diving is addictive!

Another venomous denizen of muck diving areas is the Cockatoo Waspfish *Ablabys taenianotus*.

One of the inhabitants of sand slopes is the stargazer (family Uranoscopidae).

139

Blackspot Sergeant

Le: To 20 cm. Di: All CS.
De: 0 to 3 m.
Ge: This and A. septemfasciatus
(below) inhabit shallow shore
line reefs exposed to waves.
A. sordidus has distinctive spot
on tail which separates otherwise very similar fish. Algae is
a part of both diets.

Abudefduf sordidus   **Solomon Islands**

Blacktail Sergeant

Le: To 18 cm.
Di: PNG, Solomon Islands.
De: 0 to 6 m.
Ge: This fish prefers more
sheltered habitats including
sandy beaches or near mangroves where it may be found
in very shallow water. Large
black mark on tail distinguishes
it from two species above. A
highly territorial species that
feeds mainly on algae.

Abudefduf lorenzi   **Vanuatu**

Scissortail Sergeant

Le: To 17 cm. Di: All CS. De: 5
to 20 m. Ge: Easily identified
by black streaks on tail. Similar
A. vaigiensis (below) has yellow
back and no tail streaks. Both
species can form large loose
schools and inhabit shallow
reefs which may be close to
shore or near dropoffs.

Abudefduf sexfasciatus   **GBR, Australia**

Spiny-tail Puller

Le: To 14 cm.
Di: Northern CS.
De: 1 to 50 m plus.
Ge: Difficult to identify in wild because of extreme geographic variations (see photos top and centre right). May be all black, brown with white rear, grey with white rear or all pale grey. Specimens may be identified by the 17 dorsal spines. Feeds on plankton and prefers clear water reefs with currents. Unique among damsels in taking care of young by guarding them closely after hatching. Juveniles (subadult below) school after leaving parents.

Acanthochromis polyacantha   Milne Bay, PNG

Acanthochromis polyacantha, colour variety   Milne Bay, PNG

Golden Damsel

Le: To 12 cm.
Di: All CS.
De: 3 to 45 m.
Ge: A common usually solitary species that is easy to approach and photograph. Often associated with gorgonians. Feeds on plankton so prefers current-fed reefs. Easily identified by its consistent bright yellow colour. Usually deeper than 12 m, lays eggs on sea whips and male will defend them against intruders.

Amblyglyphidodon aureus   Eastern Fields, Coral Sea

141

Blueline Damsel

Le: To 6.5 cm. Di: All CS. De: 20 to 50 m. Ge: A deep water sp. on rubble and rocky outcrops in sand channels on outer reef slopes. Similar to an adult colour variation, and juvenile form, of shallow water *C. brownriggii* (see centre). Several spp. have yellow juveniles with a blue stripe. Below: *Chromis viridis.*

Chrysiptera caeruleolineata   **Louisiade Archipelago**

Blue Devil

Le: 8.5 cm. Di: Coastal reefs in CS area, GBR to Vanuatu. De: 0 to 10 m. Ge: Brilliantly blue, lives in very shallow water on top of coral reefs close to shore or in lagoons. ♀ lacks orange tail and has black spot on rear base of dorsal fin. *C. brownriggii* (below) also lives in shallow water but prefers areas of strong surge.

Chrysiptera cyanea   **Milne Bay, PNG**

Yellowfin Damsel

Le: To 8.5 cm.Di: All CS. De: 3 to 38 m. Ge: Near or on reefs hiding in dead coral or rubble. Yellow colouration variable, sometimes just on dorsal fin and back. Damsels are believed to have a life span of at least 10 years. Most lay eggs on a clear patch on the bottom. Larvae pelagic. Below: *Chrysiptera talboti.*

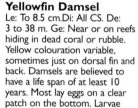

Chrysiptera flavipinnis   **Solomon Islands**

Threespot Damsel

Le: To 14 cm. Di: All CS. De: 1
to 50 m. Ge: Juveniles (below)
with total of three white spots,
often in large groups in sea
anemones with anemone fishes. Adults usually have just one
faint spot each side visible and
are in pairs. They defend their
nest fearlessly.

Dascyllus trimaculatus　　　　　　GBR, Australia

Humbug Damsel

Le: To 8.5 cm. Di: All CS. De: 1
to 12 m. Ge: Lives in crowded
group around small live coral
head on shallow sand or rubble
bottom. Takes shelter in coral
branches when threatened.
Feeds above coral head on
plankton. The similar *D. melanurus* (below) has a black tail.

Dascyllus aruanus　　　　Guadalcanal, Solomon Islands

Reticulated Damsel

Le: To 9 cm.
Di: All CS.
De: 1 to 50 m.
Ge: A distinctive and common
dascyllus that forms groups
associated with live corals.
Large adult shown has faded
black band that usually runs
full height of the body. Groups
typically consist of all age
groups and hence sizes. Similar
species *D. carneus* in Indian
Ocean but not found in the
Coral Sea.

Dascyllus reticulatus　　　　　　GBR, Australia

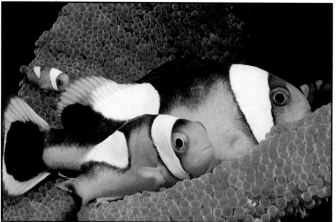

Panda Clownfish
Le: To 12 cm. Di: N-CS. De: 2-30 m. Ge: Distinctive white saddle on back. Not on reefs, on anemones in sand or sea grass, usually in sheltered areas close to shore. Lays eggs on debris or rock close under mantle of anemone, continually tended by adults. Below: Some large specimens all black and white.

Amphiprion polymnus   **Port Moresby, PNG**

Barrier Reef Anemonefish
Le: 12 cm. Di: GBR, oceanic CS, New Caledonia. De: 1 to 20 m. Ge: Two narrow white bars, tail base colour change not abrupt as in *A. clarkii* (below). Colour of latter quite variable, in all CS but not common on GBR, Vanuatu and New Caledonia specimens may be entirely yellow (not black), with white bars.

Amphiprion akindynos   **GBR, Australia**

Orangefin Anemonefish
Le: To 15 cm. Di: All CS, on GBR not common. De: 1 to 20 m. Ge: The two bars have a blue tint and 1st is wider than 2nd. May be brown rather than black. Specimens from Melanesia have black rather than orange pelvic fins. Largest fish in the genus *Amphiprion*. Below: Close-up of pelvic fins.

Amphiprion chrysopterus   **Eastern Fields, Coral Sea**

White-bonnet Anemonefish
Le: To 9 cm. Di: PNG, Solomon Isl. De: 1 to 10 m. Ge: Common in PNG where it usually is living solitarily in the same anemone as another sp., particularly *A. perideraion*, so this may actually be a hybrid rather than a valid sp. White bonnet sometimes joined to side bars (below).

Amphiprion leucokranos   Milne Bay, PNG

Black Anemonefish

Le: To 12 cm.
Di: All CS.
De: 1 to 10 m.
Ge: Usually in large numbers in colonies of the anemone *Entacmaea quadricolor*, the anemone with an inflatable bulbous tip to the tentacles, on top of rich shallow reefs. Colonies may measure up to about four metres square. Usually a single white bar on head but this is sometimes absent in Coral Sea, and in some areas the black patch is reduced.

Amphiprion melanopus   Flinder's Reef, Coral Sea

Clown Anemonefish
Le: 8 cm. Di: All CS except New Caledonia and oceanic reefs. De: 1 to 15 m. Ge: Orange with three white bars, in PNG white bars sometimes have black edging (below) which may fill first, usually orange, space. Without any black misidentified as the very similar *A. ocellaris* but this fish does not occur in CS area.

Amphiprion percula   Port Moresby, PNG

Pink Anemonefish

Le: 10 cm.
Di: All CS.
De: 3 to 20 m.
Ge: Easily identified by single narrow white bar through head and white line along back. Particularly adept at peering from its anemone at photographers. Commonly associated with anemone *Heteractis magnifica*, which can hide its tentacles in a colourful balled mantle. Lays eggs on rock close under the mantle of the anemone.

Amphiprion perideraion   **Milne Bay, PNG**

Orange Anemonefish

Le: To 13 cm. Di: PNG, Solomon Islands. De: 3 to 20 m. Ge: Single white stripe along back ending at upper lip. Not common in CS. Prefers shallow protected reef areas with significant current. As with all *Amphiprion* species largest fish are females and sex change can occur from male to female rather than the more common female to male. Pairs are usually bonded for several years, and males do not have harems.

Below and full page right:
Spinecheek Anemonefish
Premnas biaculeatus, to 16 cm, easily identified by conspicuous spine on cheek. 3 narrow white bands, and sometimes grey in females. Juveniles orange, colour deepens with age.

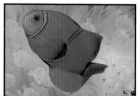

Amphiprion sandaracinos   **New Ireland, PNG**

Jewel Damsel

Le: To 11 cm. Di: All CS.
De: 2 to 12 m. Ge: Easily identified by jewel-like luminous
blue spots over body. These
fade somewhat with age. Base
colour variable from light grey
to dark brown. Lives on coral
reefs and feeds on algae.
Below: Adult.

Plectroglyphidodon lacrymatus, juvenile   New Britain, PNG

Ambon Damsel

Le: To 11 cm. Di: All CS. De: 3
to 40 m. Ge: Juveniles and
young adults have obvious ocellated spot on rear of dorsal fin
which fades or disappears in
adults. *P. bankanensis* (below)
retains spot through adulthood
and is distinguished from similar
P. vaiuli by stripe down centre
of head and white tail base.

Pomacentrus amboinensis   Milne Bay, PNG

Neon Damsel

Le: To 10 cm. Di: All CS. De: 1
to 12 m. Ge: Very noticeable
luminous blue colouration. Fish
often seen by snorkellers on
shallow reef tops. Below: Similar
Sapphire Damsel *Pomacentrus
pavo* to 10 cm, all CS, 1 to 12
m. Dark spot on upper gill cover, can vary blue intensity, prefers areas surrounded by sand.

Pomacentrus coelestis   Madang, PNG

THE HEART OF THE GREAT BARRIER REEF

G'day mate! Want to know the best place in the world if you want to take a Captain Cook at tropical fishes? Fair dinkum its Australia's Great Barrier Reef, and particularly the section between Townsville and Lizard Island, which includes Cairns, Australia's diving capital, Port Douglas and historic Cook Town. Its really ridgie didge.

Snorkelling for Minke Whales *Balaenoptera acutorostrata* around the Super Sport on the GBR.

We all know that the Great Barrier Reef is huge, in fact it is often touted as the World's Largest Living Organism. But it is not only huge in size, it also has prolific biodiversity. Compared to the Caribbean reefs you can expect to see at least four times as many different species of corals and invertebrates, and it is estimated that the incredible number of 1,500 species of fish swim in Great Barrier Reef waters.

I first dived the Great Barrier Reef in 1973 before moving up to Papua New Guinea. The few dive boats were small, slow and made a lot of exploratory dives searching for the best dive sites. Divers knew little about the marine life and fish were either edible, pretty or dangerous.

I recently returned to live in Cairns and found some big changes. The best sites are now well established and protected by moorings which also limit the number of boats on a site at any one time (usually just one). Fast comfortable dive boats visit these sites on an almost daily basis and the reef fishes have become fearless towards divers. Some areas have been declared Green by the Great Barrier Reef Marine Park Authority and all fishing and collecting is prohibited. On some sites, such as the famous Cod Hole where Potato Cod, Giant Maori Wrasse and other fishes are regularly fed, they have become not just tame but demanding of attention. At most sites there is no feeding and yet the fishes have learned that divers are harmless and approach very closely. Boats have an on-board marine life specialist and teach divers identification, and fascinating details of the life styles, of local marine creatures.

I took a live-aboard cruise from Cairns to Lizard Island, and, for the first time in my photographic life, ran out of film. Fishes that I had struggled for years to photograph in PNG swam up and posed in front of my camera lens. In just four days I had a fabulous collection of fish pictures, then had to book a return trip to get shots of the reef and the other critters.

Although it is possible to dive deep, by far the best part of the GBR is in the shallows. There are many exquisite coral gardens with a bounty of nudibranchs and other invertebrates, and the shallow depths enable divers to make multiple

Minke Whale watching has become popular on the Great Barrier Reef near Cairns.

dives and stack up considerable bottom time. Individual dives in my case were limited by the film in my camera rather than air or bottom time. Most dive sites are in sheltered water, protected by the outer barrier reef which actually dries in many areas at low tide. Snorkelling is enormously popular and in fact most visitors to the GBR see it snorkelling rather than scuba diving, and diving groups are usually small and do not overload the sites.

Note the characteristic white band across the base of the Minke Whale's flipper.

Night dives can be particularly rewarding for macro photographers, and are a good reason to take a live-aboard trip, even for just a couple of nights, rather than only day trips. The Great Barrier Reef is one of the few places in the world where the spawning of corals can be reliably predicted. The night time orgy of spawning after the full moon in November each year attracts a pilgrimage of divers to witness this wondrous event, and world record numbers of night dives are logged. If live-aboards do not appeal, then an option is to stay at one of the several island resorts right on the GBR, Lizard and Green Islands are probably the best known in the this section.

Beautiful reefs and a multitude of fishes would be more than enough for most divers, but when I surfaced after one early morning dive the crew pointed out that we had Minke Whales around the boat. I reloaded cameras and returned immediately to the water with my trusty snorkel to hang on a line conveniently trailing from the back of the boat. Minke Whales are common on the GBR from Cairns to Lizard Island from about May through September, with July being the month of choice. They are remarkably friendly and will approach a drifting or anchored dive boat. Divers are advised not to chase the whales and the best encounters are had by staying still and allowing the whales to swim right up to you. Humpback whales are also seen and recently a sensational and rare albino Humpback swam around the reefs for a month.

You will hear the word "Bommie" used a lot in Australia. Derived from an Aboriginal term it refers to an isolated coral head and can be quite small like an individual brain coral, or a complete coral tower such as Steve's Bommie. Steve's and other bommies such as Pixie Pinnacle, are spectacular dives, rising from deep water to just a few feet from the surface. The best dive plan is to go to a comfortable depth then spiral round the bommie making a gradual ascent. Reef passages such as the one at the Cod Hole provide big fish action since they are affected by tidal currents, however these are predictable and dive operators are skilled at avoiding the times of maximum flow.

At other sites coral labyrinths on top of the reef are particularly scenic with many channels, swim-throughs and

overhangs. This is beautiful relaxing diving with a multitude of interesting creatures to satisfy both beginning and experienced divers. Dive guides are available for those that want them, but experienced divers are not required to use a guide. Advanced Open Water diving skills are preferred for the Coral Sea reefs or on the renown wreck of the Yongala. The Coral Sea boasts vertiginous wall dives, sharks, large pelagics and deeper reefs sporting giant and gaudy soft corals and sea

Divers at the Great Barrier Reef's Cod Hole with Potato Cod (= Grouper) *Epinephelus tukula.*

Coral reef scene from Australia's Great Barrier Reef.

fans. Large fast boats have reduced the discomfort of the previously long bumpy Coral Sea voyage to an easy overnight passage, making these extraordinary reefs, with their legendary visibility, more accessible than ever before. The wreck of the Yongala is off-shore and exposed, and not always accessible because of the weather, however it is a truly awesome dive. Well distanced from any coral reef the wreck acts as an oasis attracting marine life from miles around. Giant grouper, sting rays, turtles, sea snakes and a multitude of other marine creatures are resident. The best months for the Yongala are usually October to December when the seas are calmest, but, as with the other sites on the Great Barrier Reef, all months have a possibility of excellent diving, and diving services are offered year round.

Visitors like to see our Aussie icons such as Uluru (Ayers Rock) or the Sydney Opera House but may not be familiar with the multitude of other activities available. In Tropical North Queensland tag and release big game fishing, and low level scenic flights, are thrilling reef activities but the rainforest is the other big attraction. You can trek or white-water raft through it, Skyrail or balloon over it, join an eco-tour and learn all about it, or just enjoy the ambience by staying in one of the many rainforest resorts. Visiting the "bush" inland or to the Cape can be an adventurous four wheel drive safari which may include

A coral bommie in the Wheeler Reef area of the GBR. Branching coral in foreground is *Acropora*.

barramundi fishing and crocodile spotting, or a more leisurely rail journey. And no trip to Australia would be complete without experiencing the fascinating Aboriginal culture, their art and dance unique and extraordinary. The really good news is that with the fall in the Aussie Dollar prices have never been better for a holiday in Australia. A true Blue experience with bommies, LBJ's and Noah's Arks on the reef, salties out at Woop Woop, and you wont have to put the bite on anyone. Now don't be a drongo, get on your dog and bone and call your travel agent, grab your cozzie and she'll be right!

Aussie slang

Amber fluid: beer
Awning over the toy shop: male beer belly
Put the billy on: boil some water
Put the bite on: ask for money
Blue heeler: police
You little bottler: expression of delight
Boofhead: a foolish friend
Chocker's full up
Captain Cook: look
Clobber: clothes
Cozzie: swimming costume
Crook: unwell, not working properly
Dinki-di: great Australian product

Dill or Drongo: someone not too smart
Dog and bone: telephone
Dead horse: tomato sauce, ketchup
Flat chat: fast as possible
Fair dinkum: genuine
Flaked out: laying down from exhaustion
Galah: loud, rude person
Idiot box: TV
Fix the Jack and Jill: pay the bill
LBJ's = little blue jobs: small fish
Lie doggo: hide
Mate: friend, either sex
Matilda: bed roll for camping
Noah's ark: shark

Ooroo: goodbye
Off like a bride's nightie: to leave quickly
Ridgie didge: genuine article
RS: lousy, useless (Nikonos please note)
Come the raw prawn: trying to deceive
Stickybeak: not minding your own business
Spat the dummie: lost his/her temper
Crack a tinnie: open a can of beer
True Blue: really Australian
Wowser: killjoy or prude
Woop woop: as far as possible from civilisation
Yakka: work

Cirrhitichthys aprinus   Manus, PNG

Threadfin Hawkfish

Le: To 12 cm.
Di: All CS.
De: 3 to 40 m.
Ge: Distinguished by filament at start of soft dorsal fin, dark blotch behind eye and four bars below eye. Has tufted tips to dorsal spines typical of hawkfishes. Hawkfishes have no swim bladder and are usually found resting on coral branches rather than free swimming. Feeds mainly on small fishes and crustaceans.
  Hawkfishes are a tropical family, 9 genera and 35 species are known which are mostly distributed in the Indo-Pacific, only 3 species occur in the Atlantic Ocean. These small fishes hug the substrate, perched on their thickened lower pectoral fin rays. But unlike most bottom dwellers they are very active, often restlessly changing position. Only one species regularly swims above the substrate to feed on zooplankton. Most species live in the shallows, on reef crests and in areas with strong surge, are habitat specific, found with certain sponges or corals and usually occur in loose aggregations. They are carnivores, feeding on small fishes and invertebrates, and spawn pelagic eggs. The filaments at the tips of the dorsal spines are often tufted and diagnostic for all family members.

Pixie Hawkfish

Le: To 9 cm. Di: All CS. De: 1 to 40 m. Ge: Body and tail covered with red brown blotches. Similar **Dwarf Hawkfish**, *C. falco* (below), is smaller and has distinct red bands laterally over body and dark brown blotches behind head. Both perch on coral.

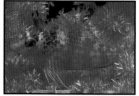

Cirrhitichthys oxycephalus   Vanuatu

Swallowtail Hawkfish

Le: To 15 cm.
Di: All CS.
De: 10 to 50 m plus.
Ge: Uniform orange brown colour with distinct swallow tail. Unique among hawkfishes in that it will leave perch to feed on plankton so sometimes seen free swimming. Usually found on edge of deep water on reef or rubble where currents bring food. Generally deeper than 20 m. Sometimes confused with Pseudanthias-species and may sometimes be seen swimming with them.

Cyprinocirrhites polyactis   Milne Bay, PNG

Longnosed Hawkfish

Le: To 13 cm.
Di: All CS.
De: 12 to 50 m plus.
Ge: A sought after and photogenic hawkfish typically found in large gorgonians or black corals deeper than 25 m. Once found, fish is easy to photograph allowing very close approach. Sometimes several on one gorgonian. Easily distinguished by long nose. Feeds mainly on crustaceans, including some pelagic larval stages that drift near the gorgonian or black coral.

Oxycirrhites typus   GBR, Australia

Arc-eye Hawkfish

Le: To 14 cm. Di: All CS. De: 1 to 40 m. Ge: Variable but always with multicoloured arc around rear of eye. Looks like small grouper. Sits patiently waiting for prey to pass near, mainly eats crustaceans. Common on clearwater reefs. Below: **Freckled Hawkfish** *Paracirrhites forsteri*, to 22 cm, all CS, 1 to 40 m.

Paracirrhites arcatus   New Ireland, PNG

Bandfish

Le: To 50 cm.
Di: All CS, coastal areas.
De: 3 to 40 m.
Ge: Live in holes in silt or mud bottoms generally close to shore. Mostly in small colonies. Individuals hover tail down over their hole. Larger adults tend to be deeper than young. Not commonly seen by divers because of their habitat.

Below:
Drummers, fam. Kyphosidae
Topsail Drummer
Kyphosus cinerascens, to 45 cm, all CS, 1 to 25 m. Often in small schools high over reefs, main diet is algae.
The similar species *Kyphosus vaigiensis* (below) has a yellow brown bar off mouth and more obvious striping.

Cepola sp.   **Milne Bay, PNG**

Fringelip Mullet

Le: To 40 cm. Di: All CS.
De: 0 to 5 m.
Ge: Inhabits sandy lagoons and reef flats, can come very close to shore in very shallow water. Usually in rapidly swimming schools which stop periodically to feed on the bottom. This species also occurs off shore. Has papillae on upper lip. Difficult to distinguish from *Valmugil seheli* in the wild, both have forked tail and dark spot over pectoral fin base. Feed on algae and detritus on surface of sand.

Crenimugil crenilabis   **Solomon Islands**

Pickhandle Barracuda
Le: To 1.5 m. Di: Probably all CS but not common. De: 10 to 40 m. Ge: Seen in schools of a few specimens to hundreds. Favours areas of current, often seen near wrecks. Large, yellow tail distinct. Bars on side may cause misidentification as the abundant S. qenie (below, previous page), without yellow tail.

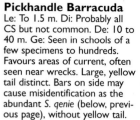

Sphyraena jello   **Holmes Reef, Coral Sea**

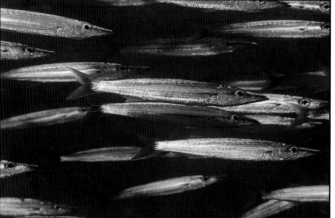

Yellowtail Barracuda

Le: To 37 cm.
Di: All CS.
De: 3 to 20 m.
Ge: Identified by yellow tail and twin light brown stripes along side, bottom line continues through the eye to the snout. A small barracuda always in schools. Usually found swimming above tops of lagoon and sheltered outer reefs or nearby sand patches. Curious and will approach closely. There are other similar species.

Sphyraena flavicauda   **New Britain, PNG**

Great Barracuda

Le: To 1.7 m.
Di: All CS.
De: 0 to 30 m.
Ge: Largest of the barracudas and usually solitary in Coral Sea area. Juveniles common in mangroves, adults sometimes in shallow water hanging motionless in a shadow or close to the bottom. Attacks usually caused by provocation, baits or a mistake in murky water. Considered safe in clearwater though capable of producing serious wounds. Identified by size and black blotches on side.

Sphyraena barracuda   **Flinder's Reef, Coral Sea**

Lyretail Hogfish

Le: To 21 cm.
Di: All CS.
De: 6 to 50 m plus.
Ge: A common and easily
identified hogfish with distinctive tail. Lives on outer reef
dropoffs in clear water. Usually
solitary. Juveniles similar
colour and pattern to adults.
Feeds on bottom dwelling
invertebrates.
    The wrasses are one of the
most speciose families of fishes
on tropical reefs, worldwide
they comprise more than 60
genera and an estimated 400
species many of which have
only recently been described.

Bodianus anthioides   Solomon Islands

Blackfin Hogfish
Le: To 40 cm. Di: All CS.
De: 3 to 40 m. Ge: Easily identified by black markings, body
colour can be darker in large
males. Found on clearwater
lagoon and outer reefs, usually
suspended a metre or so
above the bottom. Several
species in the genus, *B. diana*
(below) is a common one.

Bodianus loxozonus   GBR, Australia

Red-banded Wrasse

Le: To 38 cm. Di: All CS.
De: 4 to 40 m.
Ge: A common and colourful
wrasse that allows close
approach of divers. Often in
areas of mixed live corals and
coral rubble. Juveniles (below)
are more secretive and hide in
corals.

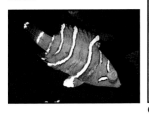

Cheilinus fasciatus   Madang, PNG

Cheilinus undulatus   **GBR, Australia**

Maori Wrasse

Le: To 2.29 m. Di: All CS.
De: I to 50 m plus.
Ge: This huge fish, the largest of the wrasses, is quite shy in the wild but easily tamed by feeding. Adults usually solitary but young may be in small groups. Highly sought after in the live fish trade, some populations are under threat, and require protection. Body patterns, various hues of green scolling, are extraordinary and beautiful. Usually found on outer reef slopes. Has a very broad diet, but should never be fed unnatural food such as eggs.

Oxycheilinus bimaculatus   **Milne Bay, PNG**

Two-spot Maori Wrasse

Le: To 15 cm. Di: All CS.
De: 2 to 50 m plus. Ge: The author has observed this fish among plant debris on sand slopes and although reported from coral reefs appears to favour rubble and sea grass areas. The tail shape is distinctive, pointed in the male and rounded in the female (below).

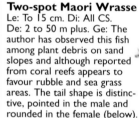

Oxycheilinus digrammus   **Louisiade Archipelago**

Cheeklined Maori Wrasse

Le: To 30 cm.
Di: All CS.
De: 3 to 50 m plus.
Ge: Has red to purple lines on green head. Similar to *O. unifasciatus* but does not have white band at tail base and clear patch free of lines behind eye. Reef dweller often feeding on rubble patches. One of a number of wrasses that will take advantage of a diver disturbing the bottom and follow divers around gaining the occasional easy meal.

Filamented Flasher

Le: To 8 cm.
Di: PNG, Solomon Islands.
De: 5 to 40 m.
Ge: One of a group of wrasses whose males have an elaborate fin display that they flash at females when mating. Since the flash is momentary, this is very difficult to photograph. Mating takes place each evening above the reef, each male servicing a harem of females. Females are similar but lack the display.

Paracheilinus filamentosus   **Port Moresby, PNG**

Whitebarred Wrasse

Le: To 5 cm.
Di: Oceanic CS, Vanuatu, Loyalty Islands.
De: 20 to 50 m.
Ge: This little known wrasse was scientifically described only in 1999. It has been seen by divers venturing to offshore reefs in the Coral Sea and other areas away from large land masses. Usually fairly deep on reef slopes and is cryptic, emerging from shelter only for brief periods. It is possible that this fish is more widespread than presently reported. Ocellated spot near tail is distinctive.

Pseudocheilinus ocellatus   **Eastern Fields, Coral Sea**

Blackspot Tuskfish

Le: To 90 cm.
Di: PNG, GBR.
De: 10 to 50 m plus.
Ge: Characteristic black spot on base of mid dorsal fin, sometimes faint. Inhabits flat areas of sand or rubble near coral reefs. Tuskfishes have prominent canine teeth in their upper and lower jaws. They move and rubble rocks in order to find food beneath, which they can pry loose with their teeth. Usually solitary.

Choerodon schoenleini   **GBR, Australia**

159

Harlequin Tuskfish
Le: To 25 cm. Di: Common GBR, very rare in PNG and Solomon Islands. De: I to 15 m. Ge: Usually swimming close to shallow coral walls or bommies in lagoons. Sought after by photographers and for aquariums because of stunning colours. Juveniles (below) in crevices.

Choerodon fasciatus

Flinder's Reef, Coral Sea

Dotted Wrasse

Le: To 13 cm.
Di: All CS.
De: 2 to 32 m.
Ge: Males have very long pelvic fins, both males and females have bodies covered with fine pink or blue dots. Males are territorial and have harems. Usually seen a short distance off the bottom. Cirrhilabrids have unusual eyes with a modified cornea effecting double lenses that may help them to focus close up on minute organisms such as plankton. Their small mouths suggest that this is what they feed on.

Cirrhilabrus punctatus

Milne Bay, PNG

Clown Coris
Le: To 100 cm. Di: All CS. De: I to 30 m. Ge: Large male adults are uncommon but the smaller females regularly seen. Juveniles are different again having two black ocellated eye spots surrounded by orange on their back. Large males have a strange ragged tail. Below: Adult.

Coris aygula

GBR, Australia

Yellowtail Coris

Le: To 40 cm. Di: All CS.
De: 2 to 50 m. Ge: Mostly
seen on exposed reef flats and
rubble areas close to live
coral. Brilliantly coloured and
easy to recognise. Juvenile
(below) is sought after by photographers. Has close relative
but not in Coral Sea area.

Coris gaimard   **San Cristobal, Solomon Islands**

Twospotted Wrasse

Le: To 12 cm. Di: All CS.
De: 7 to 35 m. Ge: Young
specimens and females have
two dark spots on dorsal fin
but these disappear with age
and the sex change to male.
The male **Canary Wrasse**,
H. chrysus (below), retains a
single black spot.

Halichoeres biocellatus   **Milne Bay, PNG**

Goldstripe Wrasse

Le: To 19 cm. Di: GBR, range in
CS uncertain. De: 10 to 30 m.
Ge: Inhabits the sheltered sand
or rubble slopes of outer barrier reefs. Male shown, females
have smoother edge to gold
stripe. *H. hortulanus* (below) is a
more common fish that inhabits
sand patches near reefs.

Halichoeres hartzfeldi   **GBR, Australia**

Tailspot Wrasse

Le: To 12 cm. Di: All CS. De: 1 to 20 m. Ge: Initial, female, stage has three spots including one near tail. These are lost in terminal male stage. Several wrasses similar to initial stage and also the juvenile of grouper *Anyperodon leucogrammicus* which mimics it. Below: Juvenile.

Halichoeres melanurus   Guadalcanal, Solomon Islands

Two-tone Wrasse

Le: To 13 cm.
Di: All CS.
De: 2 to 40 m.
Ge: Males and females similar, juveniles with four black longitudinal stripes. On live coral reefs. A common fish particularly on outer reef edges. Below: Female.

Halichoeres prosopeion   Tufi, PNG

Threespot Wrasse

Le: To 20 cm. Di: All CS. De: 1 to 20 m. Ge: Both males and females with black spot at upper base of tail. Lives in sheltered sandy areas near coral reefs. Sometimes very shallow. Has been seen with goatfish feeding where they are digging. Below: Female.

Halichoeres trimaculatus   Solomon Islands

Barred Thicklip
Le: To 50 cm, possibly longer.
Di: All CS. De: 1 to 20 m.
Ge: This genus has thicklips which help to identify. Feeds by filtering invertebrates from sand, also on larger invertebrates. Found on sheltered reefs with sandy areas. Juvenile (below) with white transverse lines on brown body.

Hemigymnus fasciatus   New Britain, PNG

Blackeye Thicklip

Le: To 60 cm, possibly longer.
Di: All CS. De: 1 to 30 m.
Ge: Juveniles have distinct white head, black body and yellow tail. The eye is black. As the fish ages the colour separations become less distinct and terminal phase is almost uniform green (below).

Hemigymnus melapterus   Eastern Fields, Coral Sea

Pastel Ringwrasse
Le: To 40 cm. Di: All CS. De: 1 to 30 m. Ge: On sand and rubble near reefs. 3 distinct phases. Juveniles (bottom) and females (below) very slender.

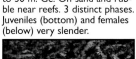

Hologymnosus doliatus, male   Solomon Islands

Labroides bicolor   Bougainville Reef, Coral Sea

Bicolor Cleanerfish

Le: To 14 cm. Di: All CS.
De: 1 to 40 m.
Ge: This genus clean parasites
from other fishes, even cleaning inside the gill covers, without being eaten themselves.
They use a distinct dancing
motion to attract customers.
Below: *Labroides alleni.*

Labroides dimidiatus   GBR, Australia

Striped Cleanerwrasse
Le: To 12 cm. Di: All CS. De: 1
to 40 m. Ge: Have been seen
cleaning large fishes such as
sharks and manta rays which
hover motionless while being
cleaned, usually in an unnatural
position. They set up cleaning
stations where several wrasses
work together. Below: Juvenile
cleaning anthias.

Leptojulis urostigma   Milne Bay, PNG

Tailspot Mudwrasse
Le: To 12 cm. Di: Only in Milne
Bay, PNG. De: 19 to 50+ m. Ge:
Named in 1996, on mud or silt,
hiding in holes of other animals
when threatened. Black spot
near tail distinct. Eats worms,
crustaceans. Body stripe may be
black. Below: *Novaculichthys* sp.,
to 11 cm, yet undescribed, discovered by author on deep
sand slopes in Milne Bay, PNG.

Rockmover Wrasse

Le: To 30 cm. Di: All CS. De: 2 to 25 m. Ge: Juveniles (below) are exquisite finds and flop about trying to mimic a piece of weed, found on sand or rubble patches on top of reefs. Adults are aggressive rock movers on rubble patches where they hunt for invertebrates.

Novaculichthys taeniourus   New Caledonia

Collared Knifefish

Le: To 12 cm.
Di: All CS.
De: 3 to 20 m.
Ge: This fish is able to dive straight into loose sand to avoid danger. Male, on right of photo, has a distinct black collar. The smaller female has more obvious bands across her body. Mating takes place high in the water and has been observed in the mid morning rather than evening as with most fishes.

Cymolutes torquatus   Milne Bay, PNG

Cryptic Wrasse

Le: To 9 cm. Di: All CS. De: 2 to 50 m plus. Ge: As the name suggests this wrasse spends most of the time hiding, usually in soft corals or algae. Distinctive ocellated spot on gill cover with white line running from snout over eye. Body colour is variable to suit hiding place. Below: Colour variation.

Pteragogus cryptus   Eastern Fields, Coral Sea

Whitepatch Razorfish

Le: To 20 cm. Di: All CS. De: 5 to 50 m plus. Ge: Razorfishes can dive into loose sand to avoid danger. In areas where sand compacts they maintain a soft spot and visit it regularly. Similar to *X. pavo* but black spot behind white patch on body and does not have a large first dorsal spine. Below: Juvenile.

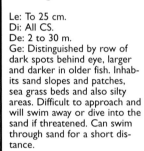

Xyrichtys aneitensis   **Madang, PNG**

Fivefinger Razorfish

Le: To 25 cm.
Di: All CS.
De: 2 to 30 m.
Ge: Distinguished by row of dark spots behind eye, larger and darker in older fish. Inhabits sand slopes and patches, sea grass beds and also silty areas. Difficult to approach and will swim away or dive into the sand if threatened. Can swim through sand for a short distance.

Xyrichtys pentadactylus   **Milne Bay, PNG**

Pavo Razorfish

Le: To 35 cm. Di: All CS. De: 2 to 50 m plus. Ge: Juveniles (below) in shallow water, variable in colour, mimic a dead leaf, long dorsal spine acting as stalk. Adults common and grow to large size. Note position of black spot relative to white patch.

Xyrichtys pavo   **Holmes Reef, Coral Sea**

Bumphead Parrotfish

Le: To 1.17 m. Di: All CS.
De: 1 to 30 m. Ge: Usually in groups of ten to fifty on reef tops. Feed on live corals by biting off chunks, absorbing the living tissue and producing coral sand. Difficult to approach unless used to divers. The largest of the parrotfishes. Below: Large adult.

Bolbometopon muricatum   New Caledonia

Bicolor Parrotfish

Le: To 80 cm. Di: All CS.
De: 1 to 30 m. Ge: Juvenile, female and male phases very different. Male has spectacular pink and green colouration. Reef tops and upper slopes of clear outer reefs. Juveniles (below) are solitary, males have harems.

Cetoscarus bicolor   Central Province, PNG

Bleeker's Parrotfish

Le: To 39 cm. Di: All CS.
De: 1 to 30 m.
Ge: Males with distinctive green edged yellow patch on cheek. Sleep in mucus enve-lope at night, reducing their scent, which may give some protection against parasites or predators.

Chlorurus bleekeri   Solomon Islands

167

Chlorurus microrhinos   Marion Reef, Coral Sea

Steephead Parrotfish

Le: To 70 cm. Di: All CS.
De: I to 30 m. Ge: Often seen
in groups feeding on algae
attached to coral rubble (large
photo). Bump head is distinctive in males in Coral Sea area
(below). Juveniles have dark
body with horizontal white
streaks.

Scarus altipinnis   Eastern Fields, Coral Sea

Minifin Parrotfish

Le: To 60 cm. Di: All CS.
De: I to 50 m plus. Ge: Has
unique mid-dorsal fin filament,
often seen by divers on night
dives tucked in a coral crevice.
Can also be distinguished from
similar *S. rubroviolaceus* (below)
by less rounded snout and blue
spotted cheeks.

Scarus chameleon   Solomon Islands

Chameleon Parrotfish
Le: To 31 cm. Di: All CS. De: I
to 30 m. Ge: Female phase usually drab brown but male has
splendid colours. Both can
change colours. Dark stripe
from snout passing below eye
and on to edge of gill cover with
2nd parallel stripe from behind
eye distinctive. Below: *Hipposcarus longiceps*, to 60 cm, all CS.

Latticed Sandperch

Le: To 17 cm. Di: All CS.
De: 3 to 50 m.
Ge: Distinguishing feature is a
pair of ocellated spots which
give the obvious appearance of
eyes when viewed from above.
A useful defence for a creature
that spends most of the time
sitting on the bottom.

Parapercis clathrata   Milne Bay, PNG

Lyretail Sandperch

Le: To 18 cm. Di: Northern CS,
rest uncertain. De: 8 to 30 m.
Ge: Reported deep but author
has seen fish in shallow water.
Has lunate tail. Juveniles with
spots rather than blotches.
Similar *P. snyderi* has yellow flag
with black tip on first dorsal
spines. Below: *Parapercis
hexophthalma*, to 26 cm, all CS.

Parapercis schauinslandii   Manus, PNG

Blackbarred Sandperch

Le: to 23 cm. Di: All CS. De: 1
to 25 m. Ge: Easily identified
with bold black and white patterns and yellow on lower lip.
Prefers sand and rubble patches
near clear water reefs. Feeds
mostly on benthic invertebrates
and small fishes. *P. snyderi*
(below) has yellow flag with
black tip on first dorsal spines.

Parapercis tetracantha   New Ireland, PNG

Whitemargin Stargazer
Le: To 35 cm. Di: All CS. De: 1 to 10 m. Ge: Lies buried in sand with only eyes and mouth visible. Cirri on mouth edges keep out sand during respiration. Large dangerous, venomous, spine on shoulders. If disturbed, the fish will quickly bury again. Has lure to attract prey to mouth. Eyes point upward.

Uranoscopus sulphureus   Louisiade Archipelago

SAND LANCES | AMMODYTIDAE

Milne Bay Sand Lance

Le: 10 cm.
Di: Unknown, only PNG as yet.
De: 5 to 20 m.
Ge: This small silver fish forms schools of a hundred or so individuals that move rapidly over soft sand and dive into the sand if threatened. Very difficult to approach. Seen in the same habitat as *Trichonotus*. This species awaits scientific description and naming.

Ammodytes sp.   Milne Bay, PNG

SAND DIVERS | TRICHONOTIDAE

Elegant Sand Diver
Le: To 15 cm. Di: Uncertain. De: 2 to 35 m. Ge: In swarms above soft sand bottom, feeds on passing zooplankton. Swarms of hundreds of fish, will dive into sand if threatened. Males have harems of ca. 8 females, mate at dawn. Sex change female to male.

Trichonotus elegans   Tufi, PNG

THE GOLDBAR SAND-DIVER

Sand-divers live in loose sand usually in areas which get slight currents, and clumsy divers never get to see them. This is because Sand-divers will detect an approaching diver before the diver sees them, and dive straight into the sand. They do not need a hole or burrow, their sharp pointed snouts can push sand out of the way and let the fish bury, wiggle a short distance through the sand, then carefully poke just its head out so that it can observe the approaching menace.

The most common Sand-diver is *Trichonotus setiger*. This fish completely buries in the sand at sunset, and emerges at dawn. Its first duty is to mate, and the male collects its harem of several females and proceeds to mate with them one by one. To do this he approaches the female, displays his dorsal fin and if she is interested they do a little dance together. The female lays her eggs and the male fertilises them. In less than one day the eggs have hatched and baby *Trichonotus* about 5 mm long hide among the particles of sand. Most fishes have a planktonic larval stage, apparently this is not so for Sand-divers.

Goldbar Sand-divers *Trichonotus halstead* emerge from the sand at dawn (Milne Bay, PNG).

Trichonotus setiger then spends the day sitting on the sand bottom, propped up on its clear pelvic fins, watching for food. It will rise a short distance off the bottom to catch tasty plankton drifting past.

Another species, *Trichonotus elegans,* spends most of its time a metre or so off the bottom continuously hovering in the current and pecking at passing plankton. These fishes are usually in large swarms and if disturbed dart into the sand *en masse,* a movement even the clumsiest of divers will notice - although probably not realising what it was.

The best way to observe Sand-divers is to slowly creep along the bottom looking carefully ahead. If they dive into the sand watch the place closely and sink your hand in under the sand. They will dash out, the males often making an elegant display, before diving into the sand again a short distance away.

Dinah and I found a magnificent site for Sand-divers in Milne Bay and reported it to Dr. Genie Clark who was studying the genus. Little did we realise how important our find was. It turned out that one of the species of Sand-divers, out of the four that lived there, was a species new to science. Although superficially similar to *T. setiger* the new species had a different number of body strips (9 rather than 11), and the male had black shaded pelvic fins and a wonderfully coloured dorsal fin featuring gold bars, black blotches and iridescent blue spots. The ventral and dorsal fins of the common *T. setiger* are clear.

My wife Dinah and I were honoured by the scientists who described the fish in 1996 and named it *Trichonotus halstead*. The males are about 13 cm long and females 9 cm. Females change into males as required. It is apparently a rare fish, known from a few locations in PNG and from Indonesia. Look out for it on sand slopes with fairly strong currents.

This Goldbar Sand-diver has spread its dorsal fin in a threat display.

A pair of the Goldbar Sand-diver *Trichonotus halstead* are mating on the sand in which they are buried during the night hours. The smaller and less colourful female is seen behind the larger male. The photo was taken in Milne Bay, PNG.

This male of the common Sand-diver *Trichonotus setiger* is preparing to mate. It tries to impress females by spreading fins and displaying colours. Note the clear dorsal fin of this species lacking the large black spots distinctive for *T. halstead*.

Reticulated Blenny

Le: To 12 cm.
Di: All CS.
De: 2 to 20 m.
Ge: Lives in surge areas of exposed coral reefs. Males generally much darker than female shown here. Distinguished form other blennies by having both spots and lines on side. Perch on algae covered corals but rapidly seek shelter on close approach. Many similar species which are difficult to differentiate in the wild.

Cirripectes stigmaticus   Eastern Fields, Coral Sea

Axelrod's Blenny

Le: To 4 cm. Di: North. Coral Sea. De: 2-25 m. Ge: Likes to perch on sponges, allows close approach. Very similar *E. tigris*, also in CS area lacks dark spot behind gill cover. Typical blenny features of blunt head and short tentacles on forehead make them different from gobies. Below: *Ecsenius bicolor*.

Ecsenius axelrodi   Milne Bay, PNG

Bath's Blenny

Le: To 4 cm. Di: Northern CS.
De: 5 to 40 m.
Ge: Although specimens shown are easily distinguished both *E. bathi* and *E. pictus*, below, are among a large group of similar small reef blennies and are individually variable.

Ecsenius bathi   Port Moresby, PNG

Leopard Blenny

Le: To 14 cm.
Di: All CS.
De: 2 to 20 m.
Ge: A very distinctive large
blenny often seen among
branches of live corals on reef
tops. Favours outer and clear
water reefs , sometimes with
surge. Feeds on coral polyps.
Males make a nest by feeding
on a coral patch until it dies,
then guard it while several
females lay eggs. Male colouration is brighter than that of
females.

Exallias brevis   **Eastern Fields, Coral Sea**

Yellowtail Fangblenny
Le: To 11 cm. Di: All CS. De: 1
to 30 m. Ge: This genus has a
pair of venomous fangs in lower
jaw used for defence only. This is
obviously effective as it appears
that several other blennies are
mimics, see *P. laudandus* at bottom. Below: *M. grammistes* is a
common shallow water fangblenny, usually solitary.

Meiacanthus atrodorsalis   **New Britain, PNG**

Mimikry Fangblenny
Le: To 8 cm. Di: All CS. De: 1 to
30 m. Ge: Mimics *M. atrodorsalis*,
holding fins erect to provide illu-
sion of deeper body. Colour
variable, often blue-grey shading
to yellow. Uses its fangs offen-
sively and its mimic status of the
inoffensive *M. atrodorsalis* enables
close approach to victims.
Below: *Meiacanthus rhinorhynchus.*

Plagiotremus laudandus   **Port Moresby, PNG**

Highfin Fangblenny

Le: To 8 cm. Di: All CS. De: I to 30 m. Ge: Uses high fin and patterns to mimic drifting algae for protection or to allow close approach to victims. Also hides in algae on sunken logs or other debris. Common in shallow sheltered habitats with sand and scattered corals. Nests in empty shells. Below: *Salarias fasciatus.*

Petroscirtes mitratus   Milne Bay, PNG

Snake Blenny

Le: To 53 cm. Di: CS. De: I-5 m. Ge: In shallow water in sand burrows often with only head appearing. Whole fish some-times emerges during daytime to swim over the sandy shallows, but more often at night. Backs into burrow tail first. Banded possibly to mimic sea snake. Below: *Salarias segmentatus.*

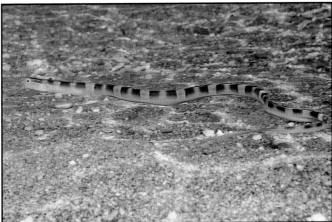

Xiphasia setifer   Milne Bay, PNG

Neon Triplefin

Le: 4 cm. Di: PNG and GBR. De: 3 to 25 m. Ge: Triplefins all have 3 dorsal fins. They sit on coral outcrops and feed on small invertebrates. Group little known, includes several unde-scribed but common species as shown below (*Ucla* sp.).

Helcogramma striata   Milne Bay, PNG

175

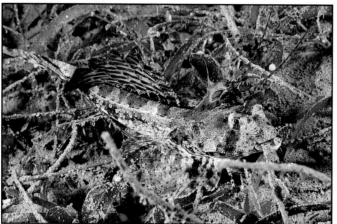

Fingered Dragonet
Le: To at least 18 cm. Di: All CS. De: 1 to 20 m. Ge: Found on weedy or sandy bottoms, often surprisingly difficult to recognise. Male has long filaments on first dorsal spines. Distinguished by detached first ray on pelvic fins, clearly shown in photographs. Below: Female.

Dactylopus dactylopus   **Milne Bay, PNG**

Ocellated Dragonet

Le: To 7 cm.
Di: All CS.
De: 1 to 30 m plus.
Ge: One of a number of small dragonets that are difficult to distinguish in the wild. Habitat is usually sheltered areas of sand or coral rubbLe: They stay on the bottom and are often only noticed when moving. Most males have elaborate and spectacular dorsal displays. This species has small ocellated spots on first dorsal fin.

Synchiropus ocellatus   **Bougainville Reef, Coral Sea**

Mandarinfish

Le: To 6 cm.
Di: All CS.
De: 1 to 18 m.
Ge: Spend most of the day hidden in coral rubble or dense branching corals, such as fire corals. Prefer shallow, sheltered and sometimes silty water free of significant currents. Seen at dusk or dawn as they emerge briefly. Mating takes place at dusk. Very distinctive pattern and colour, male has extended first dorsal spine. Difficult to photograph.

Synchiropus splendidus   **New Caledonia**

Giant Shrimp Goby

Le: To 25 cm. Di: Northern CS, rest uncertain.
De: 2 to 30 m.
Ge: The largest of the shrimp gobies. Lives on silt or mud bottoms on slopes usually leading to deep water. Habitat usually sheltered but experiences some current. Easily recognised by size, even dark bands, and yellow spots on head. Shrimp gobies live in symbiosis with blind shrimps. The shrimps dig and maintain burrows and the goby provides a warning system for the shrimp.

Amblyeleotris fontanesii   Milne Bay, PNG

Spotted Shrimp Goby

Le: To 8 cm.
Di: All CS.
De: 8 to 30 m.
Ge: A common shrimp goby easily recognised by orange spots and dark patch on belly. As shown here the blind shrimp maintains contact with the goby with one of its feelers. If danger approaches the goby signals the shrimp with a flick of its tail and the shrimp immediately retires to safety down the burrow.

Amblyeleotris guttata   San Cristobal, Solomon Islands

Randall's Shrimp Goby

Le: To 9 cm. Di: Northern CS.
De: 5 to 30 m plus. Ge: This spectacular shrimp goby is easily identified by the distinctive black spot on dorsal fin. Fin sometimes raised and lowered in possible threat display. Lives in sand patches beneath coral overhangs. Easy to approach.

Amblyeleotris randalli   New Ireland, PNG

177

Eye-brow Shrimp Goby
Le: To 10 cm. Di: Northern CS, rest uncertain. De: 5 to 25 m. Ge: There are a large number of similar shrimp gobies that are difficult to identify without a specimen in hand. Some are possibly still undescribed although quite common. A second species is shown below.

Amblyeleotris sp.   Milne Bay, PNG

Yellow Shrimp Goby

Le: To 8 cm.
Di: Probably all CS.
De: 3 to 25 m.
Ge: Has two colour forms, other is white or grey rather than yellow. Lives in open sand or silty areas in lagoons. A similar yellow species with barred pelvic fins has apparently not been scientifically named.

Cryptocentrus cinctus   Solomon Islands

Spotfin Shrimp Goby
Le: To 6 cm. Di: Northern CS. De: 2 to 20 m plus. Ge: Easily identified by white spot on pectoral fins together with gold marks on head. Often two gobies in same hole. *Vanderhorstia ambanoro* (below) is found in the same habitat but hovers above its hole rather than resting on bottom.

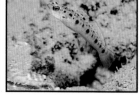

Ctenogobiops pomastictus   New Britain, PNG

Yellownose Shrimp Goby

Le: To 6 cm. Di: Northern CS. De: 3 to 45 m. Ge: Distinctive goby easily distinguished from Indonesian relative with high dorsal filament. Usually with *Alpheus randalli*, this shrimp can also be found with other shrimp gobies including undescribed *Tomiyamichthys* sp. below.

Stonogobiops xanthorhinica — Louisiade Archipelago

Crosshatch Goby

Le: To 8 cm. Di: All CS. De: 3 to 25 m. Ge: Orange cross hatch lines distinct though can be faint in some individuals. *Amblygobius* and *Valenciennea* gobies live in burrows but are not associated with shrimp. Exception *A. rainfordi* (below) is often mistaken for a wrasse and does not use a burrow.

Amblygobius decussatus — Milne Bay, PNG

Banded Goby

Le: To 15 cm. Di: All CS. De: 1 to 20 m. Ge: Lives in sand, rubble or areas of leaf debris. Almost always in pairs, there appears to be a subtle difference between male and female patterns. Build a burrow often under a rock or debris. Feed by filtering sand through the gills. Below: *Valenciennea helsdingeni*.

Amblygobius phalaena — GBR, Australia

Parva Goby

Le: To 7 cm.Di: All CS.
De: 2 to 20 m.
Ge: Smallest member of the genus. Has twin stripes but dorsal fin is clear. *V. randalli* (below) is larger, has gold stripes and brilliant electric blue longitudinal bar below eye.

Valenciennea parva   Port Moresby, PNG

Blueband Goby

Le: To 18 cm. Di: All CS. De: 1 to 20 m. Ge: Common and very large goby easily identified by brilliant blue band below eye and white body. Yellow on head typical for CS region specimens is not always present. Adults are in pairs and usually on rubble bottoms. Below: *V. wardi*, to 13 cm, rare.

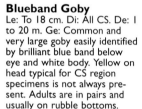

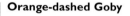

Valenciennea strigata   Tufi, PNG

Orange-dashed Goby

Le: To 14 cm. Di: Northern CS. De: 5 to 30 m. Ge: Occurs in pairs on sand or silty bottoms. Has electric blue spots on head below eye and orange spots and dashes along side. *V. sexguttata* (below) has six or more electric blue spots on head but no orange markings.

Valenciennea puellaris   Osprey Reef, Coral Sea

Blue-speckled Rubble Goby

Le: To 3.5 cm. Di: All CS. De: 6 to 40 m. Ge: Common on bare rubble slopes, usually in large numbers, look black at distance. Has a single spine on cheek. Below: **Beautiful Goby** Exyrias bellissimus, to 13 cm, all CS, 1 to 20 m, usually on silt near the base of corals.

Asterropteryx ensiferus　　　　Madang, PNG

Orange-spotted Sand Goby

Le: To 7.5 cm. Di: Uncertain, probably all CS. De: 2 to 30 m. Ge: A beautiful goby that is as yet undescribed. Sits on sand patches close to or under corals. Note white blotch between two dark blotches near tail. A number of different gobies in similar habitats. Below: *Priolepis cincta.*

Coryphopterus sp.　　　　Manus, PNG

Twinspot Goby

Le: To 6 cm.
Di: All CS.
De: 1 to 30 m.
Ge: Usually in pairs the Twinspot Goby lives in holes in sand. It prefers sheltered reefs and is often in silty areas. It can be completely in the open or at the base of small cliffs. It performs a unique hovering dance with its partner, with pelvic and anal fins extended horizontally. Possibly the motion is meant to imitate a large crab. A prized find for divers, but actually quite common.

Signigobius biocellatus　　　　New Ireland, PNG

181

Dinah's Goby
Le: To 3 cm. Di: PNG, rest uncertain. De: 5-35 m. Ge: Was first discovered by the author's wife Dinah. It lives on sponges and will enter their openings if threatened but also discarded bottles. Is currently being described. It prefers sheltered sand slopes with slight currents. Below: *Gobiodon okinawae*.

Lubricogobius sp.   Milne Bay, PNG

Hovering Goby
Le: To 2.5 cm. Di: All CS. De: 5 to 30 m. Ge: Is associated with black corals. Below: **Redeye Goby** *Bryaninops natans*, to 2.5 cm, all CS, usually in groups hovering above *Acropora* corals. Red eye distinctive. Several other similar species are associated with hard corals, sea whips and gorgonians.

Bryaninops youngei   Port Moresby, PNG

Doublebar Goby

Le: To 2.5 cm.
Di: Northern CS.
De: 1 to 10 m.
Ge: *Eviota* spp. are a large group of small gobies, some of which remain undescribed. Most identifications are based on colour patterns. Most live associated with algae covered rocks or rubble, or corals and are usually seen resting on, or hovering above, them. The *E. bifasciata* is one of the easiest to identify, distinguished by twin dark stripes along the body separated by a white stripe.

Eviota bifasciata   Central Province, PNG

Many Host Goby

Le: 2.6 cm. Di: CS. De: 2-30 m.
Ge: Transparent, variable in hue
depending on host (ascidians,
sponges, soft corals, sea cucumbers). Similar *P. boldinghi* (below)
is pink or white, lives below
20 m on soft corals, sea pens.

Pleurosicya mossambica   Guadalcanal, Solomon Islands

Ring-eye Pygmy Goby

Le: To 4 cm. Di: Probably all
CS. De: 2 to 30 m. Ge: Only
described in 1996 this is a
common goby on reef walls
and slopes usually seen resting
on sponges. White ring around
eye is distinctive. Relative *T.
tevegae* (below) prefers to hover, head up, in small reef caves.

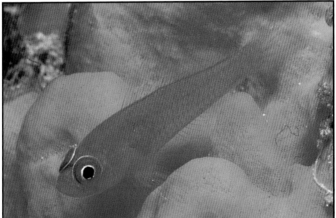

Trimma benjamini   New Britain, PNG

Banded Trimmatom

Le: To 4 cm.
Di: PNG and Micronesia, rest
uncertain, probably widespread.
De: 1 to 25 m.
Ge: One of a number of related
gobies that await description
and naming. Found resting on
live corals in sheltered habitats
often in very shallow water. This
one is readily identified by red-orange bands.

Trimmatom sp.   Milne Bay, PNG

183

Curious Worm Goby

Le: To 12 cm. Di: All CS. De: 4 to 25 m. Ge: Wormfishes live in open sand environments hovering just above the bottom and feeding mainly on zooplankton. They dive into burrows when threatened. *G. viridescens* (below) is smaller, lacks tail spot of *G. curiosus*.

Gunnelichthys curiosus   **New Ireland, PNG**

Fire Dart Goby

Le: To 8 cm.
Di: All CS.
De: 6 to 50 m plus.
Ge: Usually found in pairs hovering above burrow on small sand or rubble patch on outer edge of reef slopes. Clear water and current areas preferred. Relatively easy to approach and popular subject for photographers. Feeds on zooplankton, but rarely strays far from burrow. Common and widespread.

Nemateleotris magnifica   **GBR, Australia**

Decorated Dart Goby

Le: To 8 cm. Di: All CS. De: 25 to 50+ m. Ge: Habitat similar to that of the previous species but deeper than 25 m. Dorsal fin usually much shorter than in *N. magnifica* however a long finned variety, a possible hybrid with Fire Dart Goby have been found as shown below.

Nemateleotris decora   **New Ireland, PNG**

Blue-barred Ribbon Goby

Le: To 20 cm. Di: PNG, probably other CS. De: 20 to 40 m.
Ge: In burrow on mud or fine
silt bottom. Adults in pairs hovering tail down above burrow,
juveniles (below) in small
groups, always close to burrow.
Feed on passing zooplankton.
Burrows are slot shaped, match
flattened, ribbon like bodies.

Oxymetopon cyanoctenosum   Manus, PNG

Lined Dart Goby

Le: To 10 cm. Di: GBR & PNG.
De: 35 to 50+ m. Ge: Rarely
above 45 m, usually on deep
outer reef slopes where slope
flattens to a sand ledge with currents. Probably widespread but
not reported because of depth.
Feeds on zooplankton above
bottom but will retreat into
burrow. Below: *Ptereleotris evides.*

Ptereleotris grammica   New Ireland, PNG

Zebra Dart Goby

Le: To 11 cm.
Di: All CS.
De: 4 to 30 m.
Ge: The spectacular Zebra
Dart Goby is common on
exposed on seaward reefs usually seen by snorkellers in shallow water. It forms small
groups and is probably the
wariest of all Dart Gobies.
These fish are retreating into
their burrows so fast that it is
hard to follow them with the
eye left alone with a camera. It
is well known in aquaristic circles.

Ptereleotris zebra   San Cristobal, Solomon Islands

185

Threadfin Dart Goby
Le: To 12 cm. Di: Probably all CS. De: 2 to 45 m. Ge: Long trailing filaments from tail are distinct (TL to 16 cm). In pairs in burrows but commonly using burrows of various shrimp gobies. Do not appear to interact with gobies or shrimp, although the burrow must be crowded. Below: *Ptereleotris heteroptera.*

Ptereleotris hanae   **Milne Bay, PNG**

Pale Dart Goby

Le: To 13 cm.
Di: All CS.
De: 1 to 22 m.
Ge: Very similar to *Ptereleotris heteroptera* (small photo above) but does not have spot on tail also usually in more silty and sheltered habitats. Juveniles are apparently more common than the adults as this species is usually seen in groups.

Ptereleotris microlepis   **Tufi, PNG**

Bandtail Dart Goby

Le: To 8 cm. Di: Northern CS. De: 18 to 30 m.Ge: Lives in fine sand bottoms in burrow with raised lip. Sheltered lagoons are preferred and the fish is not common. Variety, or new species (below), with different tail markings has been observed in same habitat.

Ptereleotris uroditaenia   **Louisiade Archipelago**

Acanthurus guttatus　　　　　New Caledonia

Whitespotted Surgeonfish

Le: To 26 cm. Di: Most CS, not seen yet in PNG.
De: Surface to 5 m.
Ge: This fish lives in the surge zone on top of coral reefs, often in small schools. It is speculated that the white spots help to camouflage the fish in bubbling surf. The author has never seen this fish in PNG however has found it in the Solomon Islands, and it is reported on the GBR and from New Caledonia. It feeds mainly on filamentous algae. See also previous page.

Acanthurus fowleri　　　　　Solomon Islands

Fowler's Surgeonfish
Le: To 27 cm. Di: Northern CS, common in PNG.
De: 10 to 45 m.
Ge: One of several similar surgeonfishes which can be easily differentiated by distinct marks. This one has a dark horseshoe mark behind eye, *A. nigricauda* (below) has instead an elongated dark blotch.

Acanthurus dussumieri　　　　　Holmes Reef, Coral Sea

Eyestripe Surgeonfish

Le: To 50 cm.
Di: All CS.
De: 10 to 50 m plus.
Ge: A colourful and easily recognised surgeonfish which is usually encountered deeper than 10 m. Blue tail with dark spots is distinctive. Usually solitary but can be in small groups. Feeds on algae. Members of this genus have a single scalpel-like spine each side of the caudal peduncle, which folds into a groove. The spine is used for both defence and offence.

Striped Surgeonfish

Le: To 38 cm. Di: All CS. De: 1 to 10 m. Ge: Found shallow along the edge of outer reefs often in surge zone. Can be abundant in these areas, less common in lagoons. Its caudal spine is venomous and the fish reported territorial and aggressive. Males have harems. Juvenile, below, is popular aquarium fish.

Acanthurus lineatus   Solomon Islands

Mimic Surgeonfish

Le: To 25 cm.
Di: All CS.
De: 4 to 50 m plus.
Ge: Juveniles of this fish mimic angelfishes, either *Centropyge flavissimus* (yellow) or *C. vrolikii* (grey/black) depending on angelfish most common in area. The assumption is that the juvenile surgeonfish has a poorly developed caudal spine and gains protection because the angelfish spines are well developed. Even adults are variable having both light and dark colouration which they can change at will. Found on lagoon or outer coral reefs, usually solitary. Below: Two juvenile phases, yellow and grey/black, respectively.

Acanthurus pyroferus   Solomon Islands

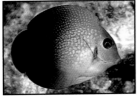

Acanthurus pyroferus, adult colour change   Milne Bay, PNG

Acanthurus olivaceus — **Marion Reef, Coral Sea**

Orangeband Surgeonfish

Le: To 35 cm. Di: All CS. De: 3 to 45 m.
Ge: Adults obvious and easy to identify even in dark body phase. Feed on algae on top of rubble areas of reefs. Usually shallow. Juveniles (below) yellow and similar to other juvenile surgeonfishes.

Acanthurus nigricans — **Solomon Islands**

Whitecheek Surgeonfish

Le: To 21 cm. Di: All CS. De: 1 to 50+ m. Ge: White patch below eye distinct. Usually on rubble patches on top of coral reefs feeding on algae, but can also be found in deep water. Widespread but not usually seen in large numbers, aggressive and territorial. Below: *Acanthurus mata,* to 50 cm, all CS, 1-40 m.

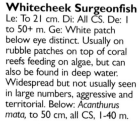

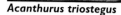

Acanthurus triostegus — **Port Vila, Vanuatu**

Convict Surgeonfish

Le: To 26 cm. Di: All CS. De: 1 to 50 m. Ge: Often forms huge schools to feed on algae on top of reefs. Has relatively small spine and thus may seek protection in numbers. Uncommon in PNG but reported to be abundant elsewhere in CS, Indian and Pacific Oceans. Unique colour pattern in CS area.

Yellowtip Bristletooth

Le: To 16 cm. Di: Common on outer reefs in PNG and Solomons but uncommon elsewhere. De: 1 to 30 m. Below: **Lined Bristletooth** *Ctenochaetus striatus*, to 26 cm, all CS, 1-30+ m. Yellow spots on head, blue lines on body, sometimes difficult to see in wild. Abundant, toxic because of algae it feeds on.

Ctenochaetus tominiensis   Solomon Islands

Whitemargin Unicornfish

Le: To 1 m. Di: All CS. De: 1 to 50 m. Ge: Schools in open water in front of reef dropoffs. Usually deeper than similar relative *N. brevirostris* (below) which has brown stripes and spots on its body. Both feed on zooplankton drifting towards the reef front.

Naso annulatus   GBR, Australia

Sleek Unicornfish

Le: To 75 cm. Di: All CS. De: 6 to 50 m plus. Ge: Schools on outer reef slopes where it feeds on large zooplankton, usually deeper than 18 m. Can change colour patterns from light to dark. Has two fixed knife-like caudal spines each side (see below).

Naso hexacanthus   New Ireland, PNG

Humpnose Unicornfish
Le: To 60 cm.
Di: All CS but not common.
De: 3 to 20 m.
Ge: Usually found in groups in shallow water on top of reefs, often in surge zones. Another strangely shaped unicornfish in similar habitat, *N. unicornis* (below), has a short horn, and blue spines.

Naso tuberosus   **Milne Bay, PNG**

Orangespine Unicornfish
Le: To 45 cm. Di: All CS.
De: 5 to 50 m plus.
Ge: A colourful unicornfish with paired, fixed, bright orange caudal spines (below). Solitary or in pairs usually close to reef where it feeds on algae. Difficult to approach during the day.

Naso lituratus   **Solomon Islands**

Bignose Unicornfish

Le: To 50 cm.
Di: All CS.
De: 4 to 50 m.
Ge: This can be a spectacular fish when it displays its brilliant colours, however it is often dark and can turn off the blue markings, usually just as a diver is about to take a photograph. It can also become very pale, particularly when visiting cleaning stations. Adults have long trailing filaments from tail. Usually in groups out from outer reef slopes and walls where it is thought to feed on zooplankton.

Naso vlamingii   **Solomon Islands**

Palette Surgeonfish

Le: To 31 cm. Di: All CS.
De: 2 to 40 m.
Ge: A spectacular surgeonfish instantly identified by its unique blue, black and yellow colouration. Juveniles have similar colour pattern to adults and stay near live branching *Acropora* or *Pocillopora* corals in which they seek shelter if approached. Adults are shy and hide in coral crevices. Prefer current areas where they feed mainly on zooplankton. Juveniles are popular aquarium fish, unfortunately easily captured by removal of the whole coral in which they are wedged.

Paracanthurus hepatus　　　　　　GBR, Australia

Brushtail Tang

Le: To 20 cm. Di: All CS.
De: 1 to 50 m plus.
Ge: Large adults have brush-like growths in front of single folding caudal spine. Solitary or in small groups on sheltered outer and lagoon reefs in rich coral. Below: Juvenile.

Zebrasoma scopas　　　　　　Eastern Fields, Coral Sea

Pacific Sailfin Tang

Le: To 40 cm. Di: All CS.
De: 3 to 40 m. Ge: Displaying its enormous fins will more than double the size of this spectacular fish. Usually found in small numbers browsing on reef tops. Juveniles (right, in crinoids) inhabit sheltered inshore areas and rapidly develop the characteristic fins.

Zebrasoma veliferum　　　　　　Milne Bay, PNG

193

Moorish Idol

Le: To 16 cm.
Di: All CS.
De: 2 to 50 m plus.
Ge: A common fish usually seen in pairs but occasionally in groups (see juveniles left). Sometimes confused with *Heniochus* (Bannerfish) by careless observers. Widespread and common, but juveniles surprisingly rare. Feeds mainly on sponges. The small photo below shows an adult.

This family is represented by a single species. It shares many characters with the closely related surgeonfishes. The snout is produced with a small mouth and teeth are long, slender and bristle like. They are mostly covered by the fleshy lips. Eggs of the Moorish Idols are pelagic floating over a great distance often into warm temperate zones and well beyond breeding areas. The Moorish Idol is one of the most widespread fish species seen in coral reefs from the East Africa in the West to the Americas in the East.

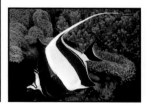

Zanclus cornutus   Osprey Reef, Coral Sea

Barred Rabbitfish

Le: To 25 cm. Di: All CS. De: 3 to 25 m. Ge: Some rabbitfishes have dark diagonal bars through the eye and head. The 2 species in CS area are *S. doliatus*, with two bars and *S. puellus* (below) with a single bar. Both are common and are usually in pairs.

Siganus doliatus   Tufi, PNG

Peppered Rabbitfish

Le: To 30 cm. Di: PNG & GBR, probably more CS. De: 3-30 m. Ge: Common in PNG and north. GBR but not yet recorded from much of the CS area. Peppered with light coloured spots. S. punctatus (below) has larger ocellated gold spots and occurs in all CS areas. Both in pairs, plain from a distance.

Siganus punctatissimus　　　　　　　　**GBR, Australia**

Coral Rabbitfish

Le: To 28 cm. Di: All CS. De: 3 to 25 m. Ge: Usually in pairs on shallow coral reefs feeding on algae. Because many rabbitfishes have similar fin counts identification is usually by colour patterns which has led to confusion. Spines venomous, however pain is reported to disappear after a few hours. Below: S. lineatus.

Siganus corallinus　　　　　　　　**GBR, Australia**

Forktail Rabbitfish

Le: To 37 cm. Di: All CS. De: 1 to 30 m plus. Ge: Most widespread rabbitfish. Schools over reef flats and will swim out into mid water. Young similar to S. canaliculatus (below) but distinguished by forked tail. S. canaliculatus apparently only from PNG in Coral Sea area.

Siganus argenteus　　　　　　　　**Louisiade Archipelago**

CUDDLE A CROCODILE

or **Everything You Always Wanted To Know About Diving With Crocodiles But Were Afraid To Even Think About**

First the bad news - salt water crocodiles, *Crocodylus porosus*, are common in parts of Australia, PNG, Solomon Islands and may occur in other Coral Sea countries. And the good news - divers virtually never encounter them.

Crocodiles typically live in areas that divers find unattractive. Muddy estuaries, rivers and mangrove swamps are their usual homes and most divers are happy that is so. Only twice in the past 20 years have I heard of divers having problems with crocodiles. In both cases the divers were at the surface (one was snorkelling) and in both cases the crocodile let go after an initial attack and the divers survived more shocked than seriously injured. To my knowledge there has never been a recorded attack by a crocodile on a scuba diver underwater.

A medium-sized salt water crocodile *Crocodylus porosus* rests among dry vegetation.

Occasionally villagers in PNG will tell us that they have seen a crocodile near the area we are diving, or that a crocodile has been stealing their pigs or dogs, favourite food for crocs. So some crocodiles do live close to reefs that divers visit. Crocodiles have also been known to swim many miles away from their usual homes. Once villagers at Garove Island in the Bali Vitu group complained to us about a large crocodile in the bay in the centre of the island, it must have swum over 60 km across open sea from the nearest swampy mainland.

A few years back we made an exploratory cruise around Goodenough Island In Milne Bay. This fantastic island is only 40 km long but has a mountain peak over 2,545 m high. We pulled into a large sheltered bay and anchored near the beach. The mountain towered above, with rain forest choking the slopes right down to the thin strip of white sand along the shore. Birds flapped and screeched, the insects buzzed and a

Practicing for live crocodile encounters with a plastic "dummy" in Milne Bay, PNG, waters.

wild primordial atmosphere settled as we realised that the place was completely uninhabited. It was Paradise, the sort of place that it is hard to imagine still exists on this overpopulated, people-polluted planet. A small creek ran into the bay and made an inviting landing place so our guests decided to take a walk ashore. They were just on the beach when I noticed that one of the logs floating in

This time it is the "real thing"! A live salt water crocodile, however, is a rare sight for divers.

the bay was making its way towards them. I yelled out and they were quickly in the boat, where they had the advantage over the crocodile and chased it for a while before returning to the ship. Strangely, that evening, no one brought up the subject of night diving and settled for a few stiff drinks instead.

The next day, further along the coast, Dinah and I were snorkelling off a white sand beach having carefully noted the absence of "floating logs". We headed for a school of bait fish in shallow water. As we swum through them and the school parted before us I was shocked to come face to face with a large crocodile that had been resting on the bottom under the bait school. It was facing me just a couple of metres away and my heart jumped a couple of beats. We had our pick-up boat with us so I jumped in and turned to Dinah, who was slightly behind me, and ordered her "Get in the boat!". Ordering my wife to do anything is generally a foolish idea and usually results in loss of visiting rights for a week or so - but Dinah thought I said "There's a croc!" and passed from surface to dinghy without touching the sides in one elegant movement, something she has never been able to do before or since.

Dinah prepares to dive with a salt water crocodile in the Milne Bay area, PNG.

The few moments I spent looking at the crocodile were very strange. I am very used to unexpected encounters with tropical sharks, including the occasional monster, but on seeing a shark I know immediately whether I should take any precautions or not. You can tell from the way the shark moves whether it is likely to be aggressive, in which case the best precaution is to stay

Then, suddenly and without warning, the crocodile turned towards the divers and opened its jaws....

still and stare it away. They hate that. I try to use the same technique with divers that I meet underwater, unfortunately they are far more unpredictable and potentially dangerous. But the crocodile did not move, it just lay there completely motionless. You cannot "feel" any danger, your senses are useless - you have to rely on your "knowledge" that crocodiles are supposedly dangerous. I am very sceptical about much of the so called knowledge we have about diving and so called "Dangerous Marine Animals", mainly because experience has shown me that most of the old "rules for diving" have turned out to be nonsense - and some of the really important ones - like "never diving deeper than your IQ" (Imperial units), generally ignored. Anyway in this instant, instead of making friends with the crocodile, indoctrination got the better of me and I made a swift exit from the water.

Recently we ran a charter aboard Telita with the "Living Legend of Diving", Stan Waterman, a gentleman, and scholar, famous for his exploits filming sharks and other giants of the sea. While approaching a favourite beach site "Observation Point" we saw a crocodile in the water right beside Telita. After anchoring Telita the crocodile was still there, 20m away. It was stalking a dog on the beach. The crocodile was of medium size - but still bigger than us.

Being aware that Stan was completely fearless, I suggested that we test the theory that crocodiles do not feed underwater, and scuba dive with it. This is one occasion I abandoned my "Always Dive Alone" golden rule, not because I had any naive misconceptions that Stan could rescue me, or I him, if the crocodile attacked, but simply that I figured (in a quiet assessment of the risks) that two of us together would probably be able to spook the crocodile for a while, where a single diver may well be thought fair game. I also had Telita's pick-up boat follow us with the driver using an oar to silently stay within range.

The crocodile obliged and although it was late in the day and overcast, Stan got some excellent video and I managed to take some presentable photographs. The crocodile moved away from the beach towards the open sea and we followed. It behaved itself until I began to sense that it had lost patience with us. Perhaps it was feeling threatened. Then its behaviour did change and instead of ignoring me or gradually swimming away, it kept on turning to face me and started to open and close its mouth. I was impressed. I turned round to Stan only to find that he had already run out of battery power on his video and had turned around to face the boat. Fortunately I finished my film at that time and so was honourably able to make my exit. I eventually made it back to the boat OK, and it has not taken me too long to get used to my new wooden leg.

Black Marlin

Le: To 5 m.
Di: Northern Coral Sea.
De: Surface to 50 m plus.
Ge: Black Marlin are famous in the Coral Sea, particularly off the northern GBR, for their abundance and great size, and are caught by game fishermen usually on a tag and release basis. Hooked fish make spectacular "tail walks" across the surface. This small individual has a large number of parasites infecting it. Black Marlin cannot fold their pectoral fins. They are occasionally seen by divers off steep dropoffs on outer barrier reefs.

Makaira indica   Milne Bay, PNG

MACKERELS AND TUNAS   SCOMBRIDAE

Shark Mackerel

Le: To 1.3 m. Di: All CS. De: 0-30 m. Ge: Distinctive twin lateral lines, bottom one forming a large downward loop behind pectoral fin. In schools or solitary, common near reefs. Has sharky smell but still a good food fish. Below: *Gymnosarda unicolor.*

Grammatorcynus bilineatus   Eastern Fields, Coral Sea

Long-jawed Mackerel

Le: To 35 cm. Di: All CS. De: 0-10 m. Ge: Common in dense schools in plankton rich waters of lagoons or passes. They usually swim at the surface with mouths wide agape scooping up plankton. With their mouths closed they are streamlined fast swimmers again. Below: *Scomberomorus commerson.*

Rastrelliger kanagurta   Solomon Islands

FLOUNDERS   BOTHIDAE

Flowery Flounder
Le: To 42 cm. Di: All CS.
De: 2 to 50 m plus.
Ge: Often found on hard bottom on reef top, not always sand. Flowery pattern distinctive. Three dark blotches usually noticeable on back. *Bothus pantherinus* (below) is smaller, always on sand, and has single dark blotch.

Bothus mancus   **GBR, Australia**

SOLES   SOLEIDAE

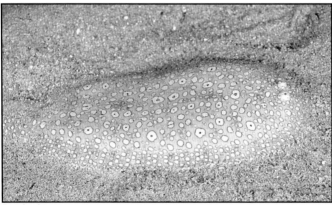

Peacock Sole
Le: To 25 cm. Di: All CS. De: 3-40 m. Ge: Small yellow spots over body distinctive. Has toxin glands that produce a bitter tasting fluid that provides protection against predators. Very small white sole (below) found on silty bottoms is, as yet, undescribed.

Pardachirus pavoninus   **Port Moresby, PNG**

Banded Sole
Le: To 15 cm. Di: All CS. De: 5 to 25 m. Ge: Rarely seen during the day. Prefers sheltered habitats, often silty areas. All soles have eyes on right side of the body. Only one right eyed flounder is found on coral reefs in CS, the tiny *Samariscus triocellatus* (below), to 7 cm, which lives under coral ledges.

Soleichthys heterorhinos   **Milne Bay, PNG**

Starry Triggerfish
Le: To 60 cm. Di: All CS.
De: 4 to 50 m plus.
Ge: Found on silty bottoms, not on coral reefs. Juveniles (below) will hide beneath sunken logs or other debris. Characteristic long caudal peduncle, unique for trigger-fishes. Three white blotches along back.

Abalistes stellatus   Tufi, PNG

Orangelined Triggerfish

Le: To 30 cm.
Di: All CS.
De: 2 to 50 m.
Ge: One of the most common of triggerfishes on a variety of live coral reef habitats. Solitary or in small groups, feeds on a wide assortment of inverte-brates including tips of *Acropora* corals. Spectacular colours with distinctive orange lines over body. Unusually in trig-gerfishes the males, as shown, may be distinguished from the females in that they lack stripes on most of the snout.

Balistapus undulatus   GBR, Australia

Clown Triggerfish

Le: To 50 cm.
Di: All CS.
De: 1 to 50 m plus.
Ge: Widespread and found on most clear water outer reefs in the Coral Sea area, this fish is never abundant and always a prized find. Its outrageous colour pattern makes it instantly recognised. Juveniles are usually in crevices on deep walls, or sometimes wrecks, and are hard to find. Mostly difficult to approach but occa-sionally a cooperative individ-ual is encountered.

Balistoides conspicillum   GBR, Australia

Balistoides viridescens   **New Britain, PNG**

Titan Triggerfish

Le: To 75 cm. Di: All CS. De: 1
to 40 m. Ge: The largest of
the triggerfishes is also the
most aggressive. Often in
pairs. When nesting large
craters are formed in sand or
rubble bottoms by the fish fan-
ning while on its side. These
have been mistaken for dyna-
mite craters by over-enthusias-
tic environmentalists. Eggs are
laid in the centre of the nest
and both adults, but usually
the female, will guard them.
Approaching divers will be
pursued and repeatedly and
furiously attacked. Wounds can
be significant, even through
clothing (see first small photo
below, bite through diving
hood). This triggerfish eats a
variety of invertebrates including the infamous Crown Of
Thorns Sea Star (second small
photo below).

Balistoides viridescens   **Solomon Islands**

Ocean Triggerfish

Le: To 50 cm.
Di: All CS.
De: 1 to 50 m.
Ge: This fish congregates
sometimes in large schools on
the edge of outer reefs, particularly in current areas. They
nest, also in groups, on outer
sand slopes sometimes as deep
as 40 to 50 m. Very difficult to
approach in the wild. Juveniles,
and some adults, are pelagic
and associated with drifting
weed or other floating objects.

Canthidermis maculatus   **Flinder's Reef, Coral Sea**

Yellowmargin Triggerfish

Le: To 60 cm.
Di: All CS.
De: 2 to 50 m.
Ge: Less aggressive than the Titan Trigger but, as with other triggerfishes, has been known to attack divers when protecting nests. Juveniles (first small photo below) found in sheltered sandy areas. Second small photo below shows the egg mass.

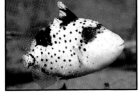

Pseudobalistes flavimarginatus   Manus, PNG

Pinktail Triggerfish

Le: To 35 cm. Di: All CS.
De: 4 to 50 m plus.
Ge: Large adults have yellow second dorsal and anal fins with black edges and pink tail, younger fish (below) mostly lack yellow and pink on these fins. Prefers tops of outer reefs in sparse coral areas and feeds mainly on algae.

Melichthys vidua   Solomon Islands

Odonus niger   Guadalcanal, Solomon Islands

Redtooth Triggerfish

Le: To 40 cm.
Di: All CS.
De: 2 to 35 m.
Ge: This fish can be found in small groups or huge loose schools swimming in front of reef slopes. Areas of strong currents are preferred as the fish feeds primarily on plankton. On approach the fish swims down to the coral where it finds a narrow crack to wedge itself often with its prolonged caudal lobes sticking out and crossed. Pulling a lobe will result in a loud grunt.

Sufflamen chrysopterus   Milne Bay, PNG

Halfmoon Triggerfish

Le: To 24 cm. Di: All CS. De: 1-30+ m. Can be light or dark, has similar stripe like S. *bursa* but different tail. Below: **Boomerang Triggerfish** *Sufflamen bursa*, to 24 cm, all CS, 3 to 50+ m. Boomerang shaped stripe through eye distinct. Prefers outer reefs with plenty of coral crevices to hide in. Solitary but common.

Rhinecanthus verrucosus   Bougainville, Solomon Islands

Blackbelly Triggerfish

Le: To 19 cm. Di: All CS. De: 1 to 20 m. Below: **Whiteband Triggerfish** *R. aculeatus*, to 25 cm, all CS, 1 to 4 m. Also known as Picassofish for its wonderful pattern. Inhabits shallow water particularly sand or rubble areas with rocks for shelter. Similar *R. verrucosus* is not so common, associated with sea grass.

Scribbled Filefish

Le: To 75 cm.
Di: All CS.
De: 2 to 50 m plus.
Ge: A strange fish which often hangs in odd positions trying to disguise its presence. Regularly encountered in Coral Sea area, and usually solitary. Feeds on a wide variety of invertebrates and algae. Generally easy to approach, though tends to turn away from divers. Beautifuly patterned with scribbled blue lines and dark spots. Has a worldwide tropical distribution.

Aluterus scriptus   Bougainville, Solomon Islands

Broom Filefish

Le: To 16 cm. Di: Northern CS. De: 3 to 18 m. Ge: Has large broom-like growth on body near tail, males growth longer than females. Quite common on clearwater reef tops with mixed sand and coral. *Cantherines fronticinctus* (below) has the same habitat but is much rarer.

Amanses scopas   Flinder's Reef, Coral Sea

Barred Filefish

Le: To 38 cm. Di: All CS. De: 1 to 35 m. Ge: Usually seen in pairs on outer reef edges. Two pairs of yellow spines in front of tail. Body colour can be much lighter. *C. pardalis* (below) has an intricate honeycomb pattern only visible close up.

Cantherines dumerilii   Solomon Islands

205

Oxymonacanthus longirostris   **New Britain, PNG**

Longnose Filefish

Le: To 9 cm.
Di: All CS.
De: 1 to 30 m.
Ge: Lives among the branches of *Acropora* corals, most often in pairs but can be solitary or small groups. Long nose helps it to feed on coral polyps. Easily recognised by rows of orange spots over blue-green base. Has black spot on tail. Rarely ventures in the open, and prefers reefs with minimum surge.

Mimic Filefish

Le: To 10 cm. Di: All CS. De: 1 to 25 m. Ge: Mimics the poisonous pufferfish *Canthigaster valentini*. Mimic pattern of older males (below) less convincing, but female pattern almost perfect, only close observation reveals the first dorsal spine and broad based second dorsal that confirms it is a filefish.

Paraluteres prionurus   **GBR, Australia**

Pervagor melanocephalus   **Port Moresby, PNG**

Blackheaded Filefish

Le: To 10 cm.
Di: All CS.
De: 10 to 40 m.
Ge: One of several similar filefishes that are difficult to distinguish in the wild. Museum specimens identified as this fish were found in fact to represent six different species as described in a revision of the genus in Indo-Pacific Fishes by J. Hutchins in 1986. The fishes are still mainly differentiated by relatively minor differences in colour patterns. A secretive fish, usually in pairs, that hides when approached.

Rhinoceros Filefish

Le: To 19 cm.
Di: All CS.
De: 1 to 50 m plus.
Ge: A common and distinctive filefish on sand or silty slopes in sheltered water, particularly in sea grass areas. Usually swimming free in the open water and makes no attempt to hide when approached. Note the unusual position of the dorsal spine in front of the eye.

Pseudaluterus nasicornis   Milne Bay, PNG

Strapweed Filefish

Le: To 18 cm.
Di: Northern CS, rest uncertain.
De: 1 to 20 m.
Ge: Very variable in colouration, will blend in with background. Usually found in sea grass beds in shallow water or on nearby sand slopes with algae patches. Small specimens are difficult to differentiate from other closely related filefishes. Often in pairs but can be solitary or in small groups.

Pseudomonacanthus macrurus   GBR, Australia

Whitebar Filefish

Le: To 13 cm. Di: Northern Coral Sea. De: 4 to 30 m. Ge: Photo juvenile. Colour variable from brown to black. Small size and deep diamond shape body help to identify. Commonly found around sea grass or crinoids on sandy slopes. Hard to detect. Below: *Rudarius minutus*.

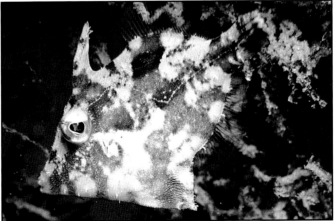

Paramonacanthus choirocephalus   Tufi, PNG

Radial Filefish

Le: To 7 cm. Di: All CS. De: 4 to 30 m. Ge: Also lives associated with soft corals particularly *Xenia* spp. and *Cespitularia* spp. Radial lines are distinctive. *Brachaluteres taylori* (below) is one of several very small file fishes that can inflate like a puffer, and can hold onto surfaces with its mouth.

Acreichthys radiatus

Milne Bay, PNG

BOXFISHES

OSTRACIIDAE

Longhorn Cowfish

Le: To 46 cm. Di: All CS. De: 1 to 50 m. Ge: Usually found by divers in shallow sea grass beds off sheltered beaches, and then specimens are usually less than 20 cm long. Expels a jet of water down into the sand to expose invertebrates on which it feeds. The fish is slow and a clumsy swimmer and often looses its prey to other faster fishes such as wrasses. Boxfishes are protected by bony plates which have small openings for mouth, gill vent, anus, and fins. They are also protected by spines and a toxic skin secretion.

Lactoria cornuta

GBR, Australia

Thornback Cowfish

Le: To 15 cm. Di: All CS. De: 20-50 m. Ge: The author has only observed this sp. in relatively deep water over sand or rubble, usually in areas with some current (fish is a poor swimmer!). Dorsal spine, blue lines and spots distinctive. Difficult to approach. Below: Juvenile *Ostracion cubicus*, see following sp.

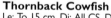

Lactoria fornasini

Milne Bay, PNG

Yellow Boxfish

Le: To 45 cm. Di: All CS.
De: 1 to 35 m. Ge: A common
fish regularly seen by divers in
all stages of growth from tiny 2
cm juveniles, which are yellow
with black spots, to full size
adults, which are quite variable
in colour. Usually solitary and
in a variety of habitats. Easy to
approach. Below: Female.

Ostracion cubicus   San Cristobal, Solomon Islands

Spotted Boxfish

Le: To 18 cm. Di: All CS.
De: 1 to 30 m. Ge: Most common and widespread of genus.
Males very colourful, brown
and blue with white and yellow
spots and lines, but female
(below) is dark brown with
white spots. On coral reefs,
usually close to coral shelter.

Ostracion meleagris   Flinder's Reef, Coral Sea

Striped Boxfish

Le: To 11 cm.
Di: Northern CS. De: 1-20 m.
Ge: A small boxfish probably
only found in northern Coral
Sea. Males blue, black and
white, females (below) just
brown and white. Prefers coral
rich areas, usually on outer
reefs.

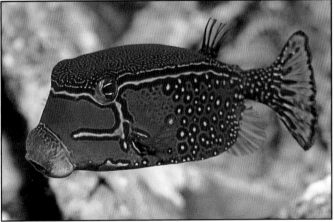

Ostracion solorensis   Eastern Fields, Coral Sea

209

Arothron manilensis   **Port Moresby, PNG**

Striped Puffer

Le: To 31 cm. Di: All CS. De: 5-30 m. Ge: Identified by its dark stripes, but never on clear water reefs. Prefers inshore areas in often turbid water on sand or silt bottoms. Very easy to photograph and usually sits still in a sand hollow looking at an approaching diver with large sorrowful dog-like eyes.

Pufferfishes are a large family of about 20 genera and at least 100 species with two distinct subfamilies: The sharp-nosed pufferfishes, Canthigasterinae, and the short-nosed pufferfishes, Tetraodontinae, the latter comprising the larger species as well as a great variety of small ones.

Arothron hispidus   **GBR, Australia**

Whitespotted Puffer

Le: To 48 cm. Di: All CS. De: 1 to 50 m. Ge: Reported to have highly varied diet which includes Crown of Thorns Sea Stars. Similar to *A. reticularis* but has spots, not lines, on snout. Found as far south as Sydney. Usually in shallow sheltered water. Below: Juvenile.

Arothron mappa   **Eastern Fields, Coral Sea**

Map Puffer

Le: To 65 cm. Di: All CS. De: 5 to 30 m. Ge: A large puffer with reticulated maze or map-like markings. Has dark lines radiating from eye. Usually solitary and not common. Juveniles (below) found in sheltered bays on sand bottom but adults inhabit reefs.

Arothron stellatus, **adult**   **Guadalcanal, Solomon Islands**

Arothron stellatus, **young juvenile**   **Central Province, PNG**

Starry Puffer
Le: To at least 90 cm, reported to 1.2 m. Di: All CS and south to New Zealand. De: 3-50 m. Ge: A very large puffer with small dark spots over body and fins. Variety of habitats including wrecks. Will sit in open and allow close approach. Its stomach often appears to be bulging with rocks which may be the case as its teeth are quite capable of biting off coral lumps, and coral is a part of its diet. When in this situation it is reluctant to swim. Below: Teeth. Previous page:

Blue-spotted Puffer *Arothron caeruleopunctatus*. To 80 cm, probably all CS, but only recorded from PNG, GBR and oceanic CS reefs, 5-40 m. The puffers on these two pages are closely related. This one is uncommon, large, easily confused with other spp. It has distinctive dark rings around eye with no radiating lines, and blue spots over body and fins. Found on gorgonian and current rich coral reefs. All puffers have the deadly poison tetrodotoxin in their organs and should not be eaten in case the flesh has been contaminated.

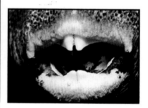

Blackspotted Puffer

Le: To 33 cm. Di: All CS. De: 1 to 30 m. Ge: A very common puffer in a variety of reef habitats. Often found sitting in sponge or on soft corals. Easy to capture, gentle stroking will produce inflation by fish gulping down water. Base colour can be grey (below) or yellow.

Arothron nigropunctatus   **Port Moresby, PNG**

Fingerprint Toby

Le: To 11 cm. Di: All CS.
De: 2 to 16 m. Ge: One of a
number of similar tobies with
dark spots below the dorsal
fin. This one is intricately patterned with fine lines compared to *C. papua* (below)
which has blue spots on sides
and lines over its head.

Canthigaster compressa   GBR, Australia

Lantern Toby

Le: To 12 cm. Di: All CS.
De: 9 to 36 m. Ge: Usually
seen deeper than 20 m on
outer reef walls and hides in
the reef crevices. Even harder
to find, *C. janthinoptera* (below)
rarely emerges from holes in
the reef and is usually only
detected by peering inside.

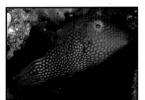

Canthigaster epilampra   New Ireland, PNG

Black-saddle Toby

Le: To 10 cm. Di: All CS. De: 1
to 50+ m. Ge: A very common
toby in a variety of habitats.
Mimicked by filefish *P. prionurus,* since toby is poisonous,
but also similar to *C. coronata*
(below) which has splendid
gold and blue spots and trim
round the black saddles.

Canthigaster valentini   Madang, PNG

213

Shortfin Pufferfish
Le: To 14 cm. De: 5 m. Ge: This sp. looks identical to *T. flavimaculatus* which is only known from around the Arabian Peninsula.

Below: **Silver Pufferfish**
Lagocephalus sceleratus, to 80 cm, all CS, 5 to 40 m. Juveniles in silty bays, rarely exceed 15 cm. Bury in silt but emerge at night.

Torquigener brevipinnis   Milne Bay, PNG

Rounded Porcupinefish
Le: To 20 cm. Di: All CS. De: 8-50 m. Ge: Active at night, hides in coral during day. Large eyes for night vision. Puffs up to near perfect and very hard sphere, choking would be predators. Crushes shelled prey (molluscs, crustaceans). Below: Mouth.

Cyclichthys orbicularis   Holmes Reef, Coral Sea

Black-spotted Porcupinefish
Le: To 70 cm. Di: All CS. De: 5 to 50 m plus. Ge: Will venture out during the day, but also may be seen under ledges or plate corals. Spines are quite short. *D. liturosus* (below) is similar but has large dark spots on body, hides during the day under ledges and is less common.

Diodon hystrix   Milne Bay, PNG

A SHORT LOOK ON ALGAE

Marine plants utilise sunlight and the nutrients in the water to produce what is in many cases the base of the ocean food chain. There are a myriad of forms from microscopic phytoplankton, to plants similar to terrestrial varieties such as sea grasses, to zooxanthellae which live in the flesh of marine animals and provide some of their nutrition, to plants whose calcareous skeletons contribute to bottom sediment or help cement reefs together. Here are three species of algae that may be of particular interest to divers.

Below: *Halimeda* sp. Its stalks consist of a string of tiny plate shaped "leaves". Found in a variety of habitats but often growing in small discrete clumps on shallow sandy sea beds to 30 m deep. Here as yet un-named ghost pipe fish, *Solenostomus* sp., whose body markings mimic the algae, is attempting to hide beside it (see also page 42).

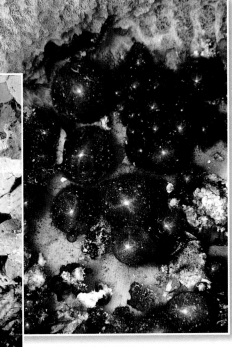

Above: **Sailor's Eyeball** *Valonia ventriosa*. These shiny globes, up to 5 cm across, have often mystified divers. They are actually a single celled green alga. As the alga ages it gets coated with an encrusting coralline alga and looses its sheen.

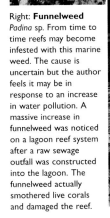

Right: **Funnelweed** *Padina* sp. From time to time reefs may become infested with this marine weed. The cause is uncertain but the author feels it may be in response to an increase in water pollution. A massive increase in funnelweed was noticed on a lagoon reef system after a raw sewage outfall was constructed into the lagoon. The funnelweed actually smothered live corals and damaged the reef.

Xestospongia testudinaria and *Ianthella basta*   Milne Bay, PNG

Sponges are sedentary filter feeders that have existed for more than half a billion years. There are more than 1,000 spp. in the CS area which are highly variable in size, colour and form. They are currently the subject of intense scientific research to examine their chemical make up with the hope of discovering new medical drugs. Two sponges of particular interest to divers are the **Giant Barrel Sponge,** *Xestospongia testudinaria* (brown barrel in foreground), and the **Elephant Ear Sponge** or **Sponge Fan,** *Ianthella basta* (yellow fan in background). Both grow to heights of about 1.5 m and are widely distributed.

COMB JELLIES   COELOPLANIDAE

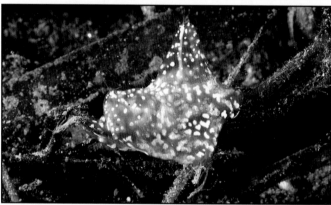

Coeloplana meteoris   Tufi, PNG

Crawling Comb Jelly

Le: To 5 cm.
Di: All CS.
Ge: These strange creatures mystified the author for many years. I filed my photographs of them with nudibranchs. They are actually Comb Jellies, or Ctenophores (phylum Ctenophora). Most are pelagic and look like sea jellies but some are bottom dwellers. The one shown is nocturnal. Two fine thread-like tentacles are used to catch planktonic prey.

UPSIDE-DOWN SEA JELLIES   CASSIOPEIDAE

Cassiopeia andromeda   GBR, Australia

Upside-down Sea Jelly
Le: To 15 cm diameter. Di: All CS. Ge: Usually encountered upside down on the sea bed (below) these are sea jellies and not attached to the bottom. They need sunlight for their symbiotic algae, hence the pose. Common, widespread.

SEA JELLIES

Crown Sea Jelly

Le: To 75 cm.
Di: Northern CS.
Ge: An elegantly coloured sea jelly that swims in depths from the surface to 15 m deep. Often seen by divers passing reefs near dropoffs. The sea jelly is often accompanied by juvenile fishes, particularly trevally, that can shelter within the open cavity at the base of the tentacles.

Netrostoma setouchina　　　　Milne Bay, PNG

BOX JELLIES

Sea Wasp

Le: To 1.5 m. Di: Northern CS, rest uncertain. Ge: This type of Box Jelly, or Sea Wasp, has a relatively benign sting. It occurs off shore as well as in shore. The extraordinarily venomous *Chironex fleckeri*, which has caused many fatalities, has a limited range and is encountered in turbid water close to the coast of northern Australia. It does not occur off shore on the Great Barrier Reef, and should not be a concern to divers. If diving or swimming inshore during the Sea Wasp season a full dive suit must be worn.

Carybdea marsupialis　　　　Solomon Islands

HYDROIDS

Stinging Hydroid

He: 30 cm.
Di: All CS.
Ge: Usually clumps of this hydroid are not noticed until the vicious sting is felt. The itch may last for several weeks after. Divers soon learn to look out for it and stay clear. Common on many reef environments the hydroid grows in small clumps or medium sized bushes up to a metre wide. There are several similar species but this is the biggest.

Aglaophenia cupressa　　　　Eastern Fields, Coral Sea

A large bush of fire coral   Solomon Islands

Fire Corals

Le: Fire Corals grow to a size of several metres.
Di: All CS.
Ge: The Fire Corals of the genus *Millepora* are found in all tropical seas and are extraordinarily variable in form and size but most are a yellow-olive colour with pale tips, and identity is confirmed by observation of the tiny hair like polyps as shown in the photographs. They can deliver a nasty sting to careless divers. Accurate determination of individual species is not possible in the wild. Fire corals grow in a variety of habitats which include sheltered silty reefs but also clearwater reefs with strong currents. They are a dominant species able to spread rapidly and smother other corals.
Below: A branching fire coral showing polyps extended.

Fire coral is smothering a large stony coral, *Pavona clavus*   Milne Bay

Stylaster sp.   Tufi, PNG

Lace Coral

Le: To about 25 cm.
Di: All CS.
Ge: Small, delicate coral that fastens to reef walls, usually under overhangs in small colonies. They do not have zooxanthellae and do not require sunlight. The genus contains about 70 different species world wide. Most are beautifully coloured but it is impossible to determine species identification in the wild and much scientific work remains to be done on their taxonomy.

Soft Coral

He: To 1.5 m.
Di: All CS.
Ge: Exact species determination is impossible in the wild but the genus is widespread and easily recognised. The coral inflates when there are currents, or at night, by absorbing water. The erect coral then feeds by capturing passing plankton. Most of these corals are extraordinarily beautiful with colours ranging from yellow to red to purple. They are often hosts to several other creatures including allied cowries, feather stars, brittle stars and crabs.

Dendronephthya sp.   Milne Bay, PNG

Mushroom Leather Coral

Le: Colonies may be several metres across.
Di: All CS.
Ge: A common shallow water soft coral. Exact species determination depends on internal structure and is difficult in the wild. This coral is preyed upon by nudibranchs such as *Phyllodesmium longicirra,* and by allied cowries including the Egg Cowrie, *Ovula ovum.* the photo shows a central section which has its polyps retracted. If touched the coral deposits a thick but harmless mucus.

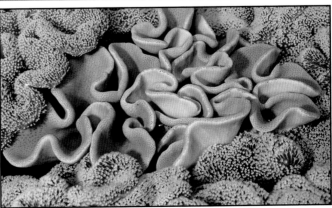

Sarcophyton sp.   Solomon Islands

Sea Pen

He: To 20 cm. Di: All CS.
Ge: Sea Pens are soft corals
that live on sand. They are
often hosts for a variety of
creatures including brittle stars
as shown here. There are
many different varieties, some
retract into the sand if
disturbed.

Pteroeides sp.   **Vanuatu**

GORGONIAN FAN CORALS   SUBERGORGIIDAE

Pink Sea Fan

He: To 2 m. Di: All CS.
Ge: These sea fans can grow
to a very large size. They need
sheltered water to survive in
the shallows and are more
often found deeper where
they are free from any large
surge action. They do however
require water movement,
usually in the form of gentle
currents in order to feed on
passing plankton. The sea fans
line up with their plane at right
angles to the prevailing
currents.

Anella mollis   **Flinder's Reef, Coral Sea**

KNOTTED FAN CORALS   MELITHAEIDAE

Orange Sea Fan

He: To 1.5 m. Di: All CS. Ge:
These corals are more common on top of reefs and are
able to withstand moderate
wave action. Close up inspection reveals knot-like bumps
on the branches as opposed to
the smooth parallel branches
of *A. mollis* above. Colours can
be very variable but orange is
the most common. Broken
branches of this fan can be
saved by sticking the end in a
convenient small hole in the
reef. A foot will generate and
the coral survive and grow.

Melithaea sp.   **Eastern Fields, Coral Sea**

220

Sea Whips are abundant on reefs in current areas at all diving depths in all of the Coral Sea. These whip-like gorgonians have a heavily calcified horny axis. They are found on reef slopes. Sexes are separate, but there also is an asexual reproduction by budding. The buds fall down and grow to become neighbours of the parent. **Red Sea Whips** *Ellisella* spp. (above right) reach a height of 1 metre and are sometimes host to a spindle shaped allied cowrie, *Aclyvolva* sp. (right), whose mantle mimics the white coral polyps of the whip which are retracted in the photograph. The **Olive Sea Whip** *Junceella fragilis* (above) can reach 2 metres in height.

Magnificent Sea Anemone

Le: 50 cm, reported to 1.0 m. Di: All CS. Ge: This anemone can lay flat, or ball up to the extent of almost enclosing all the tentacles. Its mantle is very variable in colour from white as shown to brown, red, blue and purple. Has blunt ended, parallel sided, tentacles. Found in the open on reef tops from 3 to 25 m deep. A common and widespread species that is host to a large number of different anemonefish species, shown here with *Amphiprion perideraion* and *Dascyllus trimaculatus*.

Heteractis magnifica　　　　　　**Milne Bay, PNG**

Beaded Sea Anemone

Le: To 25 cm.
Di: Northern CS.
Ge: The highly distinctive beaded tentacles make this anemone easily identified. There are also bold white and brown markings radiating from the mouth. This anemone lives in sand patches and may be attached to an object beneath the surface allowing it to retract into the sand. An uncommon but spectacular anemone shown here as host to a juvenile *Amphiprion clarkii*.

Heteractis aurora　　　　**Eastern Fields, Coral Sea**

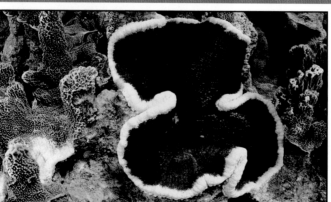

Adhesive Sea Anemone
Le: To 30 cm. Di: All CS. Ge: Usually without anemonefish. Highly variable colour, outer ring distinctive. If disturbed rapidly disappears. Its tentacles are very sticky and pack a powerful sting. Below: A young lady's backside after she sat in one.

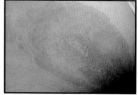

Cryptodendrum adhaesivum　　　　**GBR, Australia**

Snake Arm Anemone

Le: To 50 cm diameter. Di: Northern CS, rest uncertain. Ge: Large, lives on sand and rubble to depths of at least 30 m. Buries in the sand during the day but is fully extended at night. The long snake-like tentacles are covered with tubercules which may vary their length. Below: *Actinodendron glomeratum*.

Actinostephanus haeckeli   Milne Bay, PNG

Fire Anemone

Le: To 20 cm diameter.
Di: All CS.
Ge: This bizarre anemone inhabits coral reefs and is difficult to see. It is highly venomous and inflicts serious stings even from the slightest touch. Usually in shallow water from 1 to 10 m. on live coral, coral rocks or rubble. Reported nocturnal but author has seen several during daytime.

Phyllodiscus sp.   Milne Bay, PNG

Tube Anemone

He: To 25 cm.
Di: All CS.
Ge: This anemone lives in a tube that it builds in a sand or rubble bottom from 3 to 40 m deep. Usually the tentacles are extended but if disturbed will shoot back into the tube. Usually not considered to be harmful to humans however a report from New Caledonia indicates a problem species there. Often associated with a commensal shrimp. Identification to species is not possible without collection.

Cerianthus sp.   Solomon Islands

223

A PAINFUL EXPERIENCE

I was attempting to photograph a beautiful little Fairy Basslet called *Pseudanthias smithvanizi* which is common on reefs in northern parts of PNG. I tried to find a convenient place to settle on the reef but there was not a barren spot to be seen. The reef patches between the live coral had small, olive brown coloured, anemone like creatures all over it. I was wearing a Lycra suit that I assumed would protect me so I gently settled in the anemones, being careful not to harm them, and proceeded to make beautiful pictures.

A large colony of dangerously stinging corallimorpharians on a reef in New Britain, PNG.

I noticed a slight stinging sensation through the Lycra suit, but being a tough guy I continued my photography. Later in the week I did not feel so tough. Not satisfied with the first film through the camera I surfaced, reloaded and repeated the dive - and realised after a while that I was stung again. Marine stings have never affected me very much so, since at that stage it was not very painful, I ignored it.

When I had my evening shower I noticed a mass of stings on my left arm and shoulder. They looked and felt rather like sand fly bites. Later my shoulder felt strange and developed a deep ache and I considered that perhaps I had decompression illness, but that did not make much sense considering the modest depths and times of the dives I had made. The pain grew much worse over the next week, I tried to exercise the shoulder, but it hurt, especially if I moved my arm after it had been rested, and I had great difficulty sleeping. I went to a local doctor who thought I had pulled a muscle and I tried some pills and massage. Nothing helped and I noticed the arm was getting weaker. Feeling my back I found that the trapezius muscle on my left back was atrophying. Where I had a bulging muscle before, now there was a hollow.

I made some phone calls to a diving doctor who suggested that to eliminate the possibility of a bends bubble causing the problem I should do a six hour oxygen therapy. I was glad to receive this advice and so spent one morning in harbour sucking on a regulator connected to the ship's oxygen supply. It made no difference, and although I would gladly have felt better I was also sort of pleased that bends was eliminated as a cause. By that time I was investigating exactly what it was that had stung me and found out that there was a case history of a person badly stung by fire coral who had exercised after the sting and ended up with neuritis. Neuritis is painful and can cause muscular atrophy, and fire corals are in the same biological phylum as hydroids, jellies, and anemones, namely the Cnidaria.

Searching for more clues I also talked to some of my very experienced diving friends. Valerie Taylor told me of an expedition which had dived the very same reef and all the divers ended up in pain after coming into contact with the "little brown anemones".

These corallimorpharians are in their hunting mode and thus closed.

224

The brute turns out not to be an anemone at all, although it is a relative. The proper term is "Corallimorpharian" and there are several different species. They do not catch their food with their tentacles in the way that anemones do. During the day they spread themselves flat like a disc and I would be willing to guess that they need sunlight as many Cnidarians do, but, in the evenings, they curl up into a ball shape with a small opening at the top. Any fish or shrimp entering the hole causes it to immediately close thus trapping the prey. Fiendishly cunning eh!

These corallimorpharians of the genus *Discosoma* are fully open and have extended to flat discs, presumably to collect as much sunlight as possible (New Britain, PNG).

If a Corallimorpharian is molested it can produce a mass of special white filaments called "acontia" which have huge stinging nematocysts that pack a potent venom. These can easily penetrate a Lycra suit and these are what got me. Probably a few stings would not have bothered me very much but I had a large double dose, and then exercised, which almost certainly made the problem worse. The specimen that zapped me is of the genus *Discosoma* but the species is uncertain and is actually found throughout the Indo-Pacific but usually in small colonies. There may be several hundred animals in a colony since each is less than 10 cm. wide and they live touching their neighbours. On certain reefs, such as the one I dived, they form huge colonies covering the whole reef, hardly leaving any space for other organisms to grow there.

Disturbed corallimorpharians expell so-called "acontia", badly stinging white threads used in defense.

About six weeks after the injury the pain gradually disappeared but I was left with a very weak left arm which took a year of working out with weights to get back to normal. Now I am well, and wiser.

Another species *(Amplexidiscus fenestrafer)* has a large disc of 20 cm or more and is usually found in groups of less than ten. A small commensal shrimp lives on them. I have provoked this larger species and they do not produce as many acontia as the smaller, but whether they pack the same punch I do not know, and have no intention of testing.

Plate Coral, Table Coral

Le: To 3 m in diameter.
Di: All CS.
Ge: There are over 350 different species of *Acropora,* and
they have many different
forms. The main photo shows
a plate form, and the photo
below a branching form. These
are fast growing corals which
can eventually dominate a reef,
and whose loss is rapidly
repaired. Regeneration of
these corals can be good in as
little as five years.

Acropora sp.   **Osprey Reef, Coral Sea**

Some corals form massive
boulders several meters
across. *Pavona clavus*
(Agariciidae, Stony Corals) in
its short column form is
shown in the large photo at
the left.

  Below: *Lobophyllia hemprichii*
(Mussidae, Stony Corals). It is
estimated that large colonies
such as these may be several
hundred or even 1,000 years
old. Their loss is tragic.

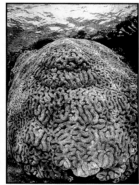

Pavona clavus   **Madang, PNG**

Cabbage Coral

Le: Colonies to several metres diameter. Di: All CS. Ge: A wonderfully sculptured coral, distinctively yellow-green with bright margins. Found on reef tops to 20 m depth. The author accidentally broke the coral shown below but was able to place the broken parts together and they fused within one year.

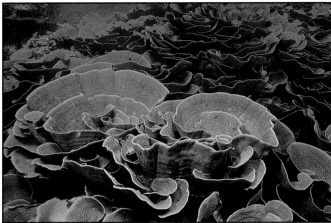

Turbinaria reniformis   **Solomon Islands**

Green Tree Coral

He: To 2.0 m.
Di: All CS.
Ge: This coral can be abundant on reefs with strong currents. Small fishes use its branches for shelter, and its surroundings are usually lush with coral reef life. This coral is very hardy and apparently ignored by Crown of Thorns Sea Stars and other coral predators.

Tubastraea micranthra   **Tufi, PNG**

Cave Coral

Le: Colonies from few centimetres to several metres across. Di: All CS.
Ge: *Tubastraea* are mostly impossible to distinguish from *Dendrophyllia* in the wild. Several species have bright yellow polyps and since they do not require sunlight can be found in shaded places under overhangs, on walls or even wharf pilings. The polyps are usually nocturnal though will respond to current on a dull day. Little surpasses the blaze of colour that greets a night diver when shining a light into a coral cave festooned with these corals.

Tubastraea sp.   **Eastern Fields, Coral Sea**

227

Fungia sp.   Milne Bay, PNG

Mushroom Coral

Le: To 20 cm. Di: All CS.
Ge: Mushroom corals are typically disc shaped solitary corals
that are not attached to the
reef or bottom. They sometimes appear to be dead but
come to life at night when the
single polyp's tentacles emerge.
They sometimes occur in large
numbers on shallow reefs.

Anemone Coral

Le: To 23 cm diameter.
Di: All CS.
Ge: This is not an anemone!
Probably the most misidentified animal on the reef it is a
solitary coral whose tentacles
are continuously exposed. A
small commensal pipe fish,
Siokunichthys nigrolineatus, may
be found (see page 46). On
the photo one can also see the
head of the commensal palae-
monid shrimp Periclimenes soror
between the tentacles.

Heliofungia actiniformis   GBR, Australia

Antipathes sp.   Milne Bay, PNG

Black Coral

He: To 2.0 m.
Di: All CS.
Ge: Only the skeleton of black
corals is actually black, most
have colours ranging from
white to yellow, green or
brown. They are a protected
species in most Coral Sea
countries but still often sought
by novice divers who do not
realise that their value is
grossly exaggerated. They may
be found in shallow water,
particularly in shaded areas
such as on wrecks. They are
slow growing corals.

Blue Flat Worm

Le: To 6 cm.
Di: Northern CS.
Ge: Flat worms are often confused with nudibranchs and this is not surprising as some are thought to mimic them. However flat worms are paper thin, and do not have gills nor rhinophores, although most do have a double fold in the body margin which at first glance may look like rhinophores. This species is easily identified by its blue colour and central purple edged white stripe.

Pseudoceros bifurcus   Madang, PNG

Yellow and Black Flat Worm

Le: To 5 cm. Di: All CS. Ge: A distinctive flat worm that is also quite variable with the outer black stripes sometimes breaking up into bars or becoming much wider. The margin is always orange.The beautifully coloured *P. ferrugineus* is shown below.

Pseudoceros dimidiatus   New Ireland, PNG

Giant Flat Worm

Le: To 30 cm. Di: Probably all CS. Ge: The author has seen 30 cm long specimens of this flat worm, and 20 cm is quite common. A nocturnal species that lives on sand. The elegant *P. bedfordi* (below) with its boomerang markings, can undulate its margins and swim.

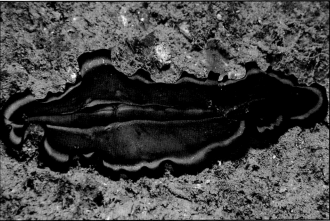

Pseudobiceros gratus   Bougainville Reef, Coral Sea

229

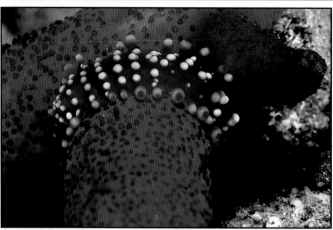

Asterophilia carlae   **Solomon Islands**

Carla's Scale Worm

Le: To 4 cm.
Di: All CS.
Ge: Similar in appearance to both flat worms and nudibranchs, but well camouflaged. They live commensally on sea stars and the white nodules on this species are thought to mimic the tube feet of the sea star. Sea Cucumbers also commonly have scale worms living on them which can be detected by turning the cucumber upside down.

FAN WORMS   SABELLIDAE

Common Fan Worm

He: To 12 cm. Di: All CS.
Ge: Sabellid worms are common on most reefs. They live in tubes into which they can rapidly retract it disturbed. Many have an operculum that acts as a trap door to close the tube, and protect the worm, as below.

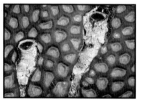

Sabellastarte sp.   **GBR, Australia**

TUBE WORMS   SERPULIDAE

Christmas Tree Worm

He: To 4 cm.
Di: All CS.
Ge: Each worm has twin spirals of tentacles which may be very variable in colour, and even multicoloured. The twin spirals retract into a single tube formed by boring into the living coral. Each tube has an operculum to close it off. Some coral rocks may have hundreds of worms bedded in them.

Spirobranchus giganteus   **GBR, Australia**

Delicate Tube Worm

Le: Colonies to 50 cm across.
Di: All CS.
Ge: These worms live in colonies and construct large masses of tubes so that they superficially resemble a coral growth. Inspection of the tentacles reveals that they are not polyps but worms. The colony is quite delicate and easily smashed by careless divers. The tentacles filter planktonic food from the water.

Filogranella elatensis   **Port Moresby, PNG**

Bobbit Worm

Le: To 1.0 m, perhaps much longer (some sources quote 3 metres!).
Di: Northern CS, probably all CS.
Ge: This worm lives in sandy or silty areas off sheltered beaches from 1 to 25 m deep. During the day it hides in its hole in the bottom but at night sticks its head 5 to 10 cm out of the hole and impales passing prey, including fish to 15 cm, in its fierce jaws. Unique in the animal kingdom, its massive jaw structure is twice the body width. Fortunately its body width is not more than a couple of centimetres, or it would be a real monster. Said to have attacked divers at night, but nobody really knows for sure...

Eunice sp.   **Milne Bay, PNG**

QUILL WORMS   ONUPHIDAE

Hyalinoecia tubicola   Milne Bay, PNG

Quill Worm

Le: To 7 cm.
Di: All CS.
Ge: This bizarre little worm
lives in a tube which it carries
with it. The worm moves by
reaching out about 2 cm, holding on to the bottom then
dragging the shell back over its
body. They live on sandy bottoms from 1 to 30 m and are
nocturnal.

STRING WORMS   TEREBELLIDAE

Reteterebella queenslandica   GBR, Australia

String Worm

Le: Tentacles to 1.0 m.
Di: All CS.
Ge: This worm, and a very
similar species, Loimia medusa,
which has banded tentacles,
are a common sight on coral
reefs. The tentacles spread out
and collect sediment which is
transferred along them to the
worm which lives safely in its
tube. Nutrition is removed
from the sediment which is
then spat out, or utilised for
tube building. If touched the
tentacles retract into the tube.

FIRE WORMS   AMPHINOMIDAE

Golden Bristle Worm
Le: 8 cm, reported much larger.
Di: All CS. Ge: Fire worms have
needle like bristles that can inflict
a painful sting if touched. C. flava
is distinguished by the dark
marks on top of each segment.
Similar C. fusca (below) has two
parallel lines along its back.

Chloea flava   New Ireland, PNG

232

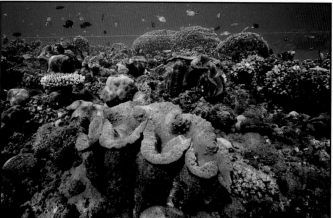

Tridacna gigas   **Milne Bay, PNG**

Tridacna gigas   **Milne Bay, PNG**

Giant Clam

Le: To 1.7 m.
Di: Northern CS.
Ge: Giant clams need sunlight for the symbiotic algae that lives in the mantle and provides some of the clam's nutrition. The colour in the mantle comes from the algae and is very variable. Clams grow very rapidly in their first two years and are suitable for farming however large clams are vital as breeding stock. In traditional societies in the Coral Sea area large clams are conserved and small clams taken or placed in front of villages to form clam gardens where they can grow and breed.

It takes about thirty years for adult size to be reached and clams will live for many years longer than that. Clam muscle is poached in the Coral Sea area. The magnificent clams shown with the diver (previous page), and with red soft coral growth (left) were recently illegally taken in Milne Bay PNG by a fishing company who paid villagers the equivalent of US$ 3.00 for clam meat from each clam worth up to 100 times that at retail.

Hippopus Clam

Le: To 40 cm.
Di: All CS.
Ge: Several other varieties of clam can be found on shallow reef flats. *H. hippopus* has a distinctive angular peaked shell, while *T. maxima* (below), has only slight convolutions to the shell mouth.

Hippopus hippopus   **Tufi, PNG**

FILE CLAMS LIMIDAE

File Shell

Le: To 3 cm.
Di: All CS.
File shells are ribbed, and each rib is covered with fine prickles so the surface resembles a file. This one has a delicate shell and is free swimming. The long banded tentacles help the animal to swim as well as feed. Usually seen on sandy bottoms no deeper than 20 m.

Limaria fragilis Solomon Islands

THORNY OYSTERS SPONDYLIDAE

Orange-mouth Thorny Oyster

Le: To 15 cm.
Di: Northern CS.
Ge: A common shell fixed on sheltered cliff faces, and under ledges, often covered with sponge and coral growth which obscures the short spines on the shell. The shell snaps closed if carelessly approached and is difficult to photograph open. Has rows of tiny eyes along each shell lip that can be seen in the photo.

Spondylus varius Solomon Islands

PEARL OYSTERS PTERIIDAE

Blacklip Pearl Shell
Le: To 20 cm. Di: All CS. Ge: Blacklip pearl shells are common and widespread on shallow coral reefs typically in sheltered areas 5 to 30 m deep. Below: **Goldlip Pearl Shell** *Pinctada maxima*, to 30 cm, all CS, 20 to 50 m, prefer areas of strong current flow.

Pinctada margaritifera Holmes Reef, Coral Sea

PEARLS FROM THE SEA

Pearl shells are farmed in the Coral Sea area. Young shells are collected from the wild by divers. The shells are cleaned and kept in baskets hanging from a cultivating raft. Older shells are often infested with burrowing worms which damage the shells, and are useless for cultivation but important for breeding and natural restocking.

Seeding a live Blacklip Pearl Shell with plastic forms, is a highly skilled process.

Harvested Blacklip Pearl Shells showing the blister pearls ready for manufacture into half-pearls.

The shells are then seeded with either hemispherical or spherical plastic forms around which the pearl shell will deposit nacre. They are placed back in the cultivating baskets and regularly cleaned for about one year. Eventually either a blister pearl or a sherical pearl is formed. Spherical pearls are more difficult to produce, and a large diameter, perfectly spherical high lustre pearl is rare and very valuable.

Natural pearls discovered in wild pearl shells are quite common but usually small in diameter and baroque (non spherical and uneven) in shape. Goldlip Pearl Shells produced the most highly prized pearls, however blacklip shells can produce sought after pearls particularly if the seed has been placed in the black part of the shell which produces black pearls. Blister pearls are cut from the shell, the plastic seed removed and a flat disc glued to the base, making a half-pearl.

Seeded pearl shells hanging in baskets from the cultivating raft, which is also providing shelter for a school of shrimpfish.

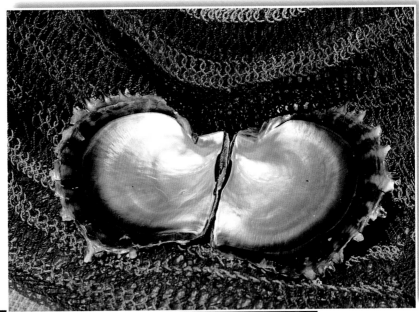

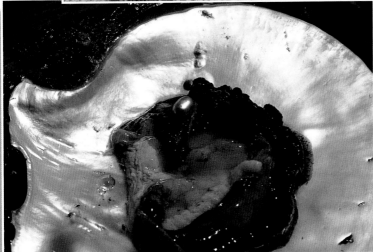

Above:
Blacklip Pearl Shells are not only used for pearl production but also prized for their natural beauty.

Left:
A natural baroque pearl in a **Goldlip Pearl Shell.**

Below:
A collection of manu-factured half-pearls, including black pearls, ready for setting in rings, earings or necklaces.

Cat's Eye Turban

Le: To 7.5 cm. Di: All CS. Ge: A beautiful shell with a highly polished operculum used in indigenous jewellery. Common on coral reef tops to 10 m. Below: *Turbo chrysostomus*, easily identified by its gold coloured mouth, is collected and eaten by slipper lobsters, mounds of shells accumulate near lair of lobster.

Turbo petholatus   **Port Moresby, PNG**

Bubble Stromb

Le: To 6 cm.
Di: All CS.
Ge: Strombs are fascinating molluscs, mainly because of their distinctive large stalked eyes. They have a large notch at the front end, and a shallower one beside it, through which the animal's eyes extend. Bubble strombs are common in sheltered sandy habitats where they feed on bottom algae. They are mostly buried during the day and emerge at night to feed.

Strombus bulla   **Port Moresby, PNG**

Purple Mouth Stromb

Le: To 10 cm. Di: All CS but uncommon. Ge: As with most strombs, shell back can be overgrown and well camouflaged. Turning the shell reveals the distinctive purple mouth of this species. Strombs are able to use their foot with operculum attached to turn themselves the right way up again (below).

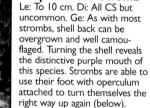

Strombus sinuatus   **Milne Bay, PNG**

Thersite Stromb

Le: To 14 cm. Di: All CS but rare. Ge: A heavy shell found offshore on sandy or algae covered rubble bottoms near coral reefs. Reported to depths of 30 m. The photos below the strombs following show how difficult it is to see them in their usual position (below).

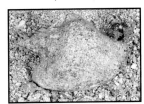

Strombus thersites   GBR, Australia

Orange Spider Stromb

Le: To 20 cm. Di: All CS but uncommon. Ge: Spider Strombs have a number of thorn-like "fingers" extending from the shell. This is one of the rarer spider strombs, similar to the common Scorpion Spider Stromb when first observed but revealing a magnificent orange mouth when turned upside down.

Lambis crocata   Milne Bay, PNG

Scorpion Spider Stromb

Le: To 15 cm.
Di: All CS.
Ge: A common find in shallow water to 12 m usually on sand or algae covered rubble areas close to coral reefs. Shells with clean backs are hard to find. Often in pairs.

Lambis scorpius   Solomon Islands

239

Giant Spider Stromb

Le: To 30 cm.
Di: All CS.
Ge: A common shell in small colonies on sand and rubble patches on top of shallow coral reefs. Most shells found are thick and overgrown and often damaged if they live in an area affected by surf.

Lambis truncata   **Tufi, PNG**

Milliped Spider Stromb

Le: To 12 cm.
Di: All CS.
Ge: Inhabits algae covered rubble near coral reefs to 10 m depth. Usually has nine fingers protruding from the shell.

Lambis millepeda   **Solomon Islands**

Golden Cowrie

Le: To 9 cm.
Di: PNG and Solomon Islands, very rare elsewhere in CS.
Ge: A beautiful and prized shell which is quite common in certain locations then very rare elsewhere. Live specimen shown has damaged shell worthless to collectors. Inhabit coral reefs, can be found during the day, this one was found under a plate coral.

Cypraea aurantium   **New Ireland, PNG**

Eyed Cowrie

Le: To 7.5 cm.
Di: All CS.
Ge: Cowries are nocturnal and
the Eyed Cowrie is usually
never seen alive during the day.
Its shell is however found surprisingly often by divers in
sand patches below coral reef
overhangs where the animal
has died, possibly killed by a
cone shell.

Cypraea argus   Port Moresby, PNG

Map Cowrie

Le: To 7.5 cm.
Di: All CS.
Ge: A shallow water cowrie
found on coral reefs. Active at
night but may be discovered by
turning (and replacing!) dead
coral slabs during the day. Has
a distinctive pattern resembling
a map. Map outline is formed
where the two sides of the
mantle meet when extended
over the shell. It is this mantle
which maintains the brilliant
shine of the cowrie shell.

Cypraea mappa   Eastern Fields, Coral Sea

Onyx Cowrie

Le: To 4 cm.
Di: All CS.
Ge: Many cowries prefer sand,
silt or even mud environments.
The author has found the
Onyx Cowrie at 20 m on a
sand slope at night but also a
colony on wooden wharf piles
in 2 m of water, during the day.
The camouflaged mantle covering the shell makes discovery
difficult. The shell is almost
black in colour with a lustrous
sheen. On revisiting the wharf
after 20 years the colony of
live Onyx Cowries was still
evident.

Cypraea onyx   Milne Bay, PNG

Humphrey's Cowrie

Le: To 2 cm. Di: All CS.
Ge: Humphrey's Cowrie is one of a number of small cowries that live on coral reefs that have red coloured mantles. These often blend in with red sponges growing on the coral making detection difficult. *C. cribraria* (below) is slightly larger but shares habitat.

Cypraea humphreysi   **Port Moresby, PNG**

Egg Cowrie

Le: To 7.5 cm. Di: All CS. Ge: Allied cowries are associated with soft corals and gorgonians. They can be readily distinguished from true cowries by inspecting the aperture of the shell. True cowries have "teeth" either side of the aperture (below), allied cowries have teeth on only one side or not at all (left). The Egg Cowrie is one of the most common cowries and heavily utilised as decoration in indigenous art in CS area. Fortunately they are abundant in very shallow water where they feed on *Sarcophyton* spp. The animal's mantle is jet black (bottom, adult).

Ovula ovum   **Madang, PNG**

Ovula ovum, juvenile   **Madang, PNG**

Elongated Egg Cowrie

Le: To 10 cm.
Di: Probably all CS.
Ge: This beautiful and delicate allied cowrie lives on soft corals, probably *Cavernulina* spp., growing on sandy sea beds. It is commonly taken by trawlers working deeper than 20 m but has also been seen by divers. Can be abundant in some areas but uncommon in others. The shell's shape and size is distinctive and the mantle pattern unmistakable.

Volva volva   Bougainville Reef, Coral Sea

Pink Sea Fan
Spindle Cowrie

Le: To 2.5 cm.
Di: PNG and Solomon Islands but probably all CS.
Ge: This shell lives on the common pink sea fan, *Anella mollis*. Some sea fans may have several specimens - but to the frustration of shell seekers - it appears that most have none, and finding the shell can be challenging. Although intricately patterned the mantle is not obvious except when viewed closely. The brown tips on the shell give it its scientific name.

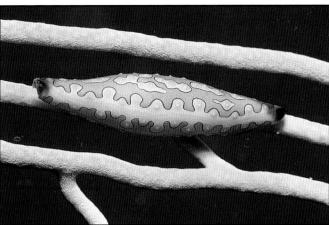

Haita brunneiterma   New Ireland, PNG

Tiger Ovulid

Le: To 1,5 cm. Di: Probably all CS. Ge: A spectacular shell which is easily discovered and identified. Usually 2 to 20 m deep. Strangely it shares its host gorgonian, probably *Euplexaura* sp., with one of the most brilliantly camouflaged of ovulids, *Prosimnia semperi* (below).

Crenavolva tigris   Madang, PNG

243

Dentiovula dorsuosa   Lizard Island, GBR

Soft Coral Ovulid

Le: To 1.5 cm.
Di: Northern CS.
Ge: One of a number of similar sized and shaped small ovulids that live in association with soft corals. Their mantles provide excellent camouflage for the particular coral they inhabit, and are usually extended day and night, only retracting when touched.

Globular Ovulid

Le: To 0.9 cm.
Di: Northern CS.
Ge: The first part of the genus name is derived from the Latin globus (= sphere) and stands for the globular shell. It is perfectly white in contrast to the brown spots on the mantle. The species is mainly found hidden among the branches of soft corals.

Globovula margarita   Milne Bay, PNG

Black Coral Ovulid

Le: To 2.5 cm.
Di: Northern CS.
Ge: This ovulid lives specifically on black corals and feeds on its polyps. It may be discovered by investigating black coral branches that have been denuded of polyps and therefore appear jet black in colour.

Phenacovolva weaveri   Tufi, PNG

HOW TO CATCH A SEA URCHIN

The Giant Helmet Shell *Cassis cornuta* grows to a length of 25 cm and occurs in all of the Coral Sea area. These robust animals are common on sandy slopes and plateaus from 5 to 40 m deep.

Giant Helmet Shell feed on echinoderms, including the occasional Crown of Thorns Sea Star, and the photo sequence shows a helmet detecting and trapping a sea urchin by lifting the lip of its shell over the top of the urchin and bringing it down firmly. The foot of the helmet is securely buried in the sand making escape impossible except for very large and powerful urchins.

These shells are a protected species on the GBR and collection is forbidden. Collection is discouraged by dive operators in other Coral Sea countries. Sometimes a diver will bring a live helmet back to the boat to show other divers and have the intention of putting the helmet back, however this must be done by physically placing the helmet back on the sand the correct way up. Shells thrown from a boat may land on their backs and be unable to get themselves the right way up, eventually starving to death. Australian marine naturalist Neville Coleman has reported witnessing a remarkable instance where two other helmet shells came to the rescue of an upside down shell enabling it to right itself.

Male helmets are smaller than the females, and have shorter spires. Some have mistaken these for juveniles or a different species. The only other large helmet shell in the Coral Sea area is the Bullmouth Helmet, *Cypraecassis rufa,* known from at least PNG and Solomon Islands.

Photo sequence of female helmet catching a sea urchin.

Above:
Male **Giant Helmet Shell** *Cassis cornuta* (Milne Bay, PNG).

Left:
Bullmouth Helmet *Cypraecassis rufa* (New Ireland, PNG).

Ficus subintermedia   **Port Moresby, PNG**

Underlined Fig Shell

Le: To 10 cm.
Di: All CS.
Ge: This animal has a very delicate shell suited to its environment of soft silt and mud.
It is reported to be common
in these areas - but divers are
less so! The animal lacks an
operculum and appears vulnerable to predation, however it
is active only at night, otherwise burying in the mud.

Venus Comb Murex

Le: To 12 cm. Di: Northern
CS, otherwise uncertain.
Ge: This animal has the most
exquisite shell covered with
many long comb-like spines. It
lives on silty sand bottoms
where it buries during the day.
At night it pushes up through
the surface and wanders in
search of small clams and other prey. The author has
observed the murex capture a
small clam by lifting itself over
the clam then forcing down so
that the clam is trapped in a
cage made by the spines.

Murex pecten   **Milne Bay, PNG**

Caltrop Murex

Le: To 10 cm.
Di: All CS.
Ge: This shell is a common
inhabitant of silty or sand bottoms and is sometimes abundant. Fishermen working at
night often find them tangled
in their nets where they touch
the bottom. It has fewer spines
than *M. pecten* but some
spines are very long and
straight, distinguishing it from
several similar species.

Murex tribulus   **Milne Bay, PNG**

Zambo's Murex

Le: To 5 cm. Di: Northern CS. Ge: Difficult to detect, may be on sand but more often on algae covered coral rocks. Two similar spp. are difficult to differentiate and require careful counting of spines. *H. zamboi* has three large funnel shaped spines on each whorl of the shell, *H. scorpio* has about six and *H. anatomica* four.

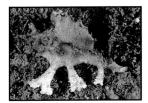

Homalocantha zamboi   **Port Moresby, PNG**

Giant Murex

Le: To 30 cm. Di: All CS. Ge: Largest murex, very common. Prefers sheltered sand or rubble near reefs but has an affinty for wrecks and wharves. Distinctive white tubular eggs packed in a honeycomb, laid on hard surface. Spires often worn. Right: 3 shells on a wreck, middle one is laying eggs. Below: With operculum.

Chicoreus ramosus   **Port Moresby, PNG**

Lacinate Murex

Le: To 5 cm. Di: All CS. Ge: One of a number of murex that become overgrown with a red sponge. Knowledgeable divers seeking shells will inspect all red objects illuminated in torch light at night. Easily identified by purple lip on mouth this uncommon murex lives on algae covered rubble at depths to 50 m.

Chicoreus lacinatus   **Milne Bay, PNG**

MUREX SHELLS | MURICIDAE

Dogwood Drupe

Le: To 5 cm. Di: All CS. Ge: This rather ordinary looking shell is hardly noticed in normal conditions especially if covered with marine growths. However it can reach plague proportions and, since it eats coral polyps, advertises itself by large areas of dead *Acropora* corals.

Drupella cornus   **New Ireland, PNG**

SPINDLE SHELLS | FASCIOLARIIDAE

Wavy-edge Spindle

Le: To 15 cm. Di: All CS. Ge: An uncommon shell. The author has found several, always on black sand slopes with coral rubble and isolated coral heads, to depths of 20 m. There are two similar species in the Coral Sea distinguished by pattern of knobs on spire whorls, and deeper habitat. Another, *F. colus* may be found in shallow water but has brown marks on the spire, *F. undatus* has a completely white shell, covered with a brown periostracum.

Fusinus undatus   **Milne Bay, PNG**

VOLUTES | VOLUTIDAE

Bailer Shell

Le: To 50 cm. Di: All CS. Ge: Baler Shells got their name because islanders used the shells to bail out water from their canoes. For some reason the "i" was dropped. There are several similar species but it also appears that different names are being used for the same species, and also that hybridisation takes place. Balers bury in the sand or mud bottom during the day, and emerge at night when they are fast voracious predators on other shelled molluscs, smothering them in their large foot.

Melo amphora   **Tufi, PNG**

Major Harp

Le: To 9 cm.
Di: All CS.
Ge: A common harp shell whose body is far too large to fit into the shell. If caught the animal will cast part of its foot in the same way that a lizard will cast its tail, hopefully distracting any predator and allowing escape. Several similar species usually distinguished by examining the ventral shell pattern. This one has two brown blotches separated by a white band. Becomes active in late afternoon and night.

Harpa major   Milne Bay, PNG

CONE SHELLS   CONIDAE

Striate Cone

Le: To 10 cm. Di: All CS. Ge: Has venomous radular teeth to spear prey. Most cones have narrow parallel apertures, feed on worms and are harmless (*C. generalis,* below left). Those with enlarged apertures (*C. striatus,* below right) may be harmful.

Conus striatus   GBR, Australia

Geography Cone

Le: To 12 cm.
Di: All CS.
Ge: A large and highly venomous cone that feeds mainly on fishes and has caused human deaths. Active at night, it seeks sleeping fishes and immobilises them with its venom which causes muscular paralysis. Its shell is surprisingly fragile and some fishes feed on the animal by biting through the shell apparently without harmful effect. Life support is essential for human victims until the effect of the venom fades.

Conus geographus   New Ireland, PNG

249

Textile Cone
Le: To 8 cm. Di: All CS. Ge: The textile cone feeds on other molluscs, but is still considered potentially harmful to humans. The photo shows a cone that has captured and envenomated another species of cone shell. A very common cone discovered in the day time under loose coral slabs. The proboscis holding the venomous spears of cone shells can stretch longer than the shell length and it is not safe to pick them up by either end. Shell collectors with warped minds have been known to keep Textile Cones in the aquarium and feed them small live cowries requiring cleaning.

Conus textile   **Port Moresby, PNG**

Spindle Cone

Le: To 3.5 cm.
Di: All CS.
Ge: This elegant little cone shell lives at depths greater than 25 m in silty sand environments. It is considered uncommon, but probably this reflects its environment. It has a narrow aperture, feeds on worms and is harmless to humans.

Conus aculeiformis   **Port Moresby, PNG**

Clear Sundial

Le: To 5 cm.
Di: Northern CS.
Ge: Sundial shells are common in shallow sandy and sea grass areas. They are active at night. When viewed from below the shell reveals that it tightly spirals around a central hollow umbilicus, an architectural marvel and hence the name. Males are smaller than females and lack a penis.

Architectonica perspectiva   **Port Moresby, PNG**

Port Moresby Wentletrap

Le: To 4 cm.
Di: PNG, rest uncertain.
Ge: This wentletrap is one of several different species found in association with sand anemones. They are apparently parasitic. Divers can find the wentletraps by disturbing the anemone with a gloved hand causing the anemone to disappear into the sand. Careful searching of the edges of the resulting hole often yields a shell. Gloves are essential as many of the sand anemones are highly venomous.

Epitonium sp.   **Port Moresby, PNG**

Fire Urchin Eulimid

Le: To 3 cm.
Di: Northern CS.
Ge: This small white shell lives parasitically on the upper surface of the venomous fire urchin, *Asthenosoma varium*. Often in small groups it not only feeds on the urchin but lays its eggs on it as well. In this case the eulimid is sharing the urchin with a pair of Coleman's shrimp, *Periclimenes colemani*.

Luetzenia asthenosomae   **Osprey Reef, Coral Sea**

Trumpet Triton
Le: To 33 cm. Di: All CS. Ge: A beautiful shell much sought after by collectors but now mostly protected. Many specimens covered with coralline algae and useless for display. It feeds on sea stars including the infamous Crown of Thorns Sea Star and infestations of this star were blamed on overcollecting of the triton, an unlikely explanation. Traditional use includes chipping a small hole near the end of the spire and blowing as an effective trumpet (previous page, note painted Egg Cowries on village house behind village boy).

Charonia tritonis   **Madang, PNG**

Giant Frog Shell

Le: To 18 cm.
Di: All CS.
Ge: Not easily discovered in
the wild as its shell is usually
covered with camouflaging
marine growths. Found by
divers on shallow coral reefs,
particularly areas of dead reef
or coral rubble.

Bursa bubo   **Solomon Islands**

Black Coriocella

Le: To 10 cm.
Di: Northern CS.
Ge: This is not a nudibranch
and has an internal shell completely covered by the flesh of
the animal. Uncommon and
may be found day or night on
shallow coral reef or rubble
areas. Colour ranges from
dark green to black.

Coriocella nigra   **Milne Bay, PNG**

Lined Bubble Shell
Le: To 4 cm. Di: All CS. Ge:
Bubble shells are very delicate
animals unable to entirely retract
into their shells. Nocturnal and
usually in shallow water. Similar
shell, *Micromelo undatus* (below)
distinguished by crossed lines on
shell and "out of focus" mantle.

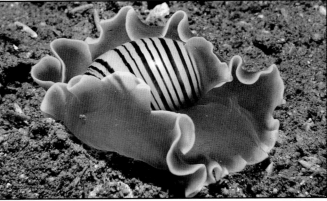

Hydatina physis   **Tufi, PNG**

253

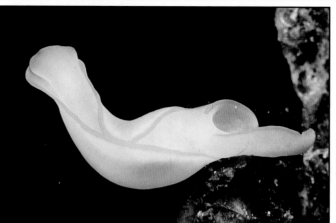

Electric Swallowtail

Le: To 7 cm.
Di: Northern CS.
Ge: *Chelidonura* spp. have an obvious pair of tails, one longer than the other. This slug has a white translucent body with yellow trim. The pair below have mated and are laying eggs.

Chelidonura electra   **New Britain, PNG**

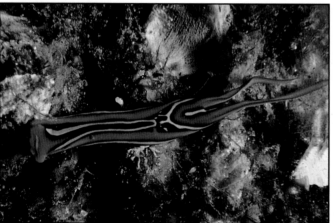

Striped Swallowtail

Le: To 3 cm.
Di: All CS.
Ge: This small slug can be variable in colour but is distinguished by its longitudinal stripes, typically black and yellow with blue or green. The head flap on all Swallowtails is reported to aid burrowing. The different tail lengths can be clearly seen in this photograph. The slug is sometimes erroneously reported as a flatworm, it is not, but does in fact feed on them.

Chelidonura hirundinina   **Milne Bay, PNG**

Black and Blue Swallowtail

Le: To 5 cm.
Di: All CS.
Ge: Distinguished from similar slugs by blue line along and across head. Very common on shallow sand where it can often be found mating and laying eggs (left).

Chelidonura varians   **New Ireland, PNG**

Black and Blue Slug

Le: To 4.5 cm. Di: All CS. Ge: Similar to the *Chelidonura* but with shorter tails and no hammer shaped head. Nocturnal, feeds on worms and sometimes confused with *C. varians* above. Relative *P. cyanea* (below) is variable in colour and feeds on other snails.

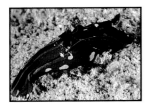

Philinopsis gardineri   GBR, Australia

Giant Sea Hare

Le: To 50 cm.
Di: All CS.
The Sea Hares have large rhinophores giving them a rabbit or hare like appearance. They are nocturnal feeders on algae and inhabit shallow reef tops. The Giant Sea Hare is common and easily identified by the chopped-in-half appearance of its sloping back. It will eject a purple dye from a pore in the middle of its back when disturbed.

Dolabella auricularia   Tufi, PNG

Swimming Sea Hare

Le: To 8 cm. Di: All CS. Ge: One of a number of sea hares that have large body flaps called parapodia on the body that assist in swimming. Variable in colour and found on shallow sand at night. Below: **Blue-spot Sea Hare** *Bursatella leachi*, to 13 cm, all CS. Body ornament and colour very variable depending on habitat.

Paraplysia geographica   Milne Bay, PNG

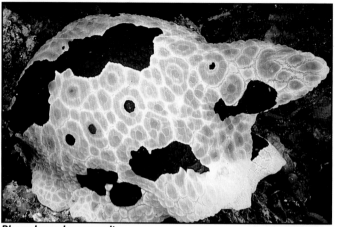

Pleurobranchus grandis   **New Ireland, PNG**

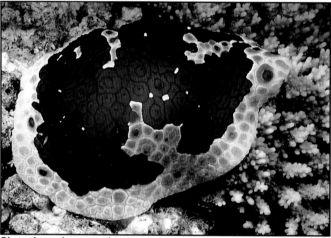

Pleurobranchus grandis   **Port Moresby, PNG**

Concentric Pleurobranch

Le: To 21 cm.
Di: All CS.
Ge: Pleurobranchs are nocturnal slugs that have rhinophores, and whose gills are located on the side under the mantle rather than on top of it as with most nudibranchs. *Pleurobranchus grandis* is distinguished from the similar *Pleurobranchus forskali* (below) by the pattern on its back which consists of concentric circles, but is haphazard on *P. forskali*. Colours with both species may be very variable.

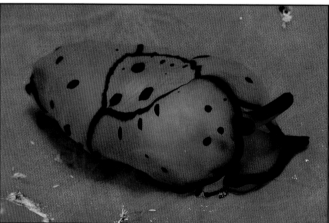

Berthella martensi   **Tufi, PNG**

Sponge-eating Berthella

Le: To 5 cm.
Di: All CS.
Ge: This side gilled slug has a multitude of different colours, patterns and bumps and is thus easily misidentified. It feeds upon tunicates and is reported to shed its mantle in three sections if threatened. These three sections are unique and the best way of identifying the species. Once a section of mantle is shed, the gills are exposed.

Leopard Slug

Le: To 7 cm.
Di: All CS.
Ge: This very strange looking slug can move over the bottom surprisingly fast and can even swim. It is found on sand or silt bottoms and buries during the day, only emerging at night.

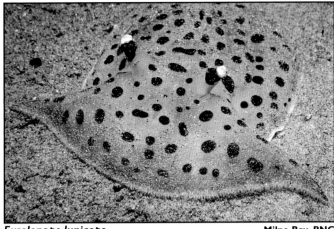

Euselenops luniceps   **Milne Bay, PNG**

POLYBRANCHIDS   POLYBRANCHIDAE

Leaf-gilled Slug

Le: To 2 cm.
Di: All CS.
Ge: An attractive and distinctive small slug which has flat leaf shaped gills called cerata. These contain a viscous mucus and may be discarded if the animal is disturbed. This slug feeds on algae.

Cyerce nigricans   **Milne Bay, PNG**

ELYSIIDS   ELYSIIDAE

Ornate Elysia

Le: To 4 cm.
Di: All CS.
Ge: Elysids are a large family with over 80 species in the Indo-Pacific region. This is one of the most common and well known. It feeds on algae and may be found in numbers in very shallow water during daytime. It has large parapodia and tiny rudimentary eyes situated just behind the rhinophores.

Elysia ornata   **GBR, Australia**

257

Lined Nembrotha

Le: To 4.5 cm. Di: All CS.
Ge: Long and slim, *Nembrotha*
and *Tambja* are some of the
most colourful and distinctive
nudibranchs. They feed on
tunicates and bryozoans
respectively. *Tambja affinis*
(below) is variable and may be
darker than shown.

Nembrotha lineolata   **Milne Bay, PNG**

NOTODORIDS

NOTODORIDIDAE

Minor Notodoris

Le: To 10 cm. Di: Northern
CS. Ge: This very distinctive
nudibranch is found on reef
tops from 5 to 25 m usually
adjascent to a dropoff. It has
an unusual shape and looks
even stranger because of the
disruptive effect of the black
lines. It is rigid to the touch
and will leave a yellow stain on
fingers. It feeds on sponges
and is seen in the open during
daylight. Presumably fishes
avoid it because of a foul taste.
This specimen is laying its yellow egg ribbon.

Notodoris minor   **Milne Bay, PNG**

Serene Notodoris

Le: To 10 cm.
Di: Northern CS.
Ge: An unusual notodorid that
is rigid to touch and of bizarre
shape, but lacks the yellow
colour of other notodorids.
The three large lobes protect
the animals gills. This species
has been found near, or on,
sheltered dropoffs, but is not
as common or conspicuous as
N. minor. It also feeds on
sponges.

Notodoris serenae   **Milne Bay, PNG**

Spanish Dancer

Le: To 50 cm.
Di: All CS.
Ge: Juveniles (centre) are found in sheltered habitats on sand or reef, but always close to sponges on which they feed. As the animal grows it moves to different habitats, the largest adults (top) are usually found 30 - 40 m deep on outer dropoffs. When released the Spanish Dancer lives up to its name with a flamboyant undulating swimming motion (bottom) that reveals the flapping skirts of a Spanish Dancer. The author has seen this nudibranch swimming just under the surface around an anchored boat at night evidently attracted to the lights.

The Spanish Dancer feeds on sponges that contain noxious substances making the slug distasteful. Its flamboyant colours may well serve as a warning for would be predators not to eat it.

The Spanish Dancer is, like many slugs and snails, a hermaphrodite, which means male and female at the same time. The eggs are laid as an orange-brown veil of myriads of tiny dots held together by a thin layer of mucus. When a slug has finished laying eggs this fragile veil is left behind in the coral reef without further care. After some time the larvae hatch and continue their life as part of the plankton.

A pair of commensal shrimp, *Periclimenes imperator*, live on the Spanish Dancer, typically around the gills (small photo below). The colour of the shrimp has been adapted to suit the environment, and is different on different hosts.

Hexabranchus sanguineus, adult   **Port Moresby, PNG**

Hexabranchus sanguineus, juvenile   **GBR, Australia**

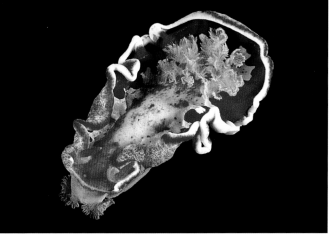

Hexabranchus sanguineus, swimming   **Milne Bay, PNG**

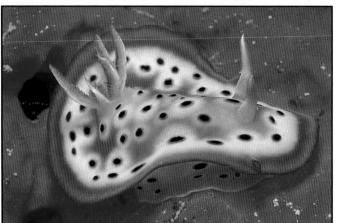

Chromodoris kuniei   **New Ireland, PNG**

Kuni Nudibranch

Le: To 5 cm.
Di: All CS.
Ge: A common and beautiful nudibranch whose colours appear luminescent under bright light. Should not be confused with *C. leopardus*, see following, which is marked with rings and blotches rather than ocellated spots. *C. kuniei* flaps its mantle as it moves along the bottom. Usually found in sheltered habitats where it feeds on sponges.

Chromodoris leopardus   **Milne Bay, PNG**

Leopard Nudibranch

Le: To 6 cm. Di: All CS. Ge: Also quite common and often seen in pairs. This pair are hosts to a pair of commensal shrimp often associated with nudibranchs, and some echinoderms, *Periclimenes imperator,* note colours compared to those on *H. sanguineus* above. *C. strigata* (below) is rarer, but shares habitat.

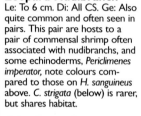

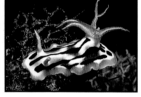

Heron Island Nudibranch

Le: To 10 cm.
Di: All CS.
Ge: A common but spectacular nudibranch because of its pure white colour with yellow trim, and relatively large size. Often seen wandering over shallow reef during daytime. It feeds on sponges and has been reported to 20 m depth. The type specimen came from Heron Island on the GBR, and the scientific name is derived from that of the common heron.

Ardeadoris egretta   **Solomon Islands**

Long-tail Ceratosoma

Le: To 8 cm.
Di: All CS.
Ge: This species has a couple of close relatives which are difficult to distinguish in the wild, particularly since all are very variable, but this appears to be the most common in the Coral Sea area. They are hard bodied and the mantle has fixed wing-like growths. The specimen shown is laying its red egg spiral on "leaves" of *Padina* algae.

Ceratosoma tenue   Solomon Islands

Black-margined Nudibranch

Le: To 10 cm. Di: All CS. Ge: A common, widespread and distinctive nudibranch that is easy to identify because of it black-lined undulating margin. Sometimes appears in groups which may be mating. It feeds on sponges and is usually shallower than 15 m.

Glossodoris atromarginata   Madang, PNG

Starry Nudibranch

Le: To 5 cm.
Di: PNG, possibly other northern CS.
Ge: First discovered in Milne Bay, PNG, by Austalian marine naturalist Neville Coleman this species was described in 1986 and named for the pattern of white dots over a dark background - stars. Usually found associated with sponges. Its distribution is still uncertain.

Glossodoris stellatus   Alotau, PNG

Hypselodoris obscura   Madang, PNG

Obscure Hypselodoris

Le: To 4 cm.
Di: All CS.
Ge: This uncommon nudibranch lives on silt and sand bottom and is sometimes found crawling on debris such as old logs. Its spectacular but variable colour pattern makes it readily identifiable however there appears to be a similar species *H. infucata*.

Mexichromis multituberculata   Tufi, PNG

Tuberculate Mexichromis

Le: To 5 cm.
Di: All CS.
Ge: *Mexichromis* spp. have small nodules, or tubercles, on their backs. This species has a large number, hence the scientific name. Their purple colour against a white background colour is distinctive and very attractive.

Miamira sinuata   Solomon Islands

Jolly Green Giant

Le: To 5 cm.
Di: All CS.
Ge: An unusual lumpy shaped nudibranch with a distinct reticulated pattern which is usually green but may be red in colour. Lives in association with sponges on which it feeds. Uncommon but widespread and found from 5 to 30 m deep.

KENTRODORIDS   KENTRODORIDIDAE

Red-lined Kentrodoris

Le: To 17 cm.
Di: All CS.
Ge: The author has only ever
seen one pair of this rare nudibranch. They were on black
silty sand at 24 m. The gills
and rhinophores can withdraw
into tube-like appendages. The
lines on the body are actually
brown rather than red.
Reported to feed on sponges.

Kentrodoris rubescens   **GBR, Australia**

PLATYDORIDS   PLATYDORIDIDAE

Formosa Platydoris

Le: To 10 cm.
Di: All CS.
Ge: Flat disc shaped nudibranch which is hard and rigid
to touch. Active at night and
early morning. Colour shown
is usual but there are colour
variations. Similar *P. cruenta* has
short lines rather than fine
spots over back. Inhabits shallow reef tops and is uncommon.

Platydoris formosa   **Milne Bay, PNG**

Nodulose Hoplodoris

Le: To 5 cm.
Di: All CS.
Ge: A well camouflaged small
species of Platydorid whose
back is covered with small
nodules. Reported to be widespread and common in some
areas. It inhabits shallow water
and is sometimes seen by
snorkellers.

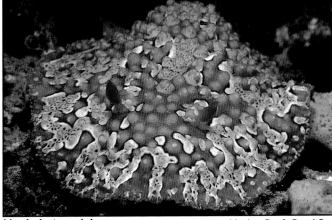

Hoplodoris nodulosa   **Marion Reef, Coral Sea**

Asteronotus caespitosus   Eastern Fields, Coral Sea

Knobbly Asteronotus

Le: To 22 cm.
Di: All CS.
Ge: A large easily identified nudibranch, however some authors have used the alternate spelling *A. cespitosus* leading to entertaining but incorrect interpretations. Quite common and widespread in a variety of habitats but not often recognised as its colour aids in camouflage. Feeds on sponges.

WART SLUGS   PHYLLIDIIDAE

Phyllidia ocellata   New Ireland, PNG

Eye-spot Slug

Le: To 6 cm. Di: All CS.
Ge: Phyllidiids have no gills on their back but have tiny leaf-like gills under the mantle. They are hard bodied and their backs are covered with nodules. *P. ocellata* is extremely variable and some specimens do not have ocellated nodules as photographed specimen does. It is found in shallow water in the open and is common and widespread. Most specimens do have large amounts of yellow or orange colouration.

Elegant Slug

Le: To 5 cm.
Di: All CS.
Ge: The species has black lines and spots over a grey or pink base. Nodules are tipped with white or yellow and rhinophores are yellow. Found on coral reefs from the shallows to depths of 40 m. Feeds on sponges.

Phyllidia elegans   New Britain, PNG

False Halgerda

Le: To 4 cm.
Di: All CS.
Ge: This gets its name because it is very similar in appearance to *Halgerda* nudibranchs, but it lacks dorsal gills and is in fact a Phyllidiid. *R. halgerda* is variable but the orange ridges, capped with white lines, on a black ground are almost distinctive. The only other similar species, *R. fungia,* has a pale skirt at the edge of the mantle, confirming identification.

Reticulidia halgerda   Eastern Fields, Coral Sea

Tubercular Nudibranch

Le: To 20 cm.
Di: All CS.
Ge: The author received a memorable introduction to this species when wiping his face after bringing one back to the boat to show other divers and handling it. The sting was very painful. It is a miserable looking creature, as realised by the scientist who described it. Generally inhabits shallow sand or silty areas near sheltered reefs.

Dendrodoris tuberculosa   Milne Bay, PNG

Soft Coral Slug

Le: To 5 cm.
Di: Northern CS, rest uncertain.
Ge: This nudibranch mimics soft corals and is very well disguised. It is considered to be rare, but this probably reflects the difficulty in seeing it rather than its actual abundance. It has been found in Milne Bay PNG but otherwise its range is uncertain. This species can be distinguished by the fine brown lines across its back. Members of this genus are predators on soft corals.

Marionia distincta   Milne Bay, PNG

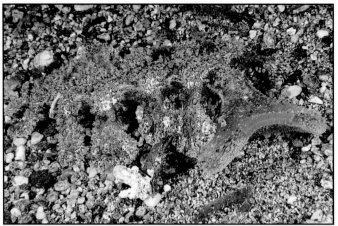

Melibe fimbriata   **GBR, Australia**

Giant Melibe

Le: To 20 cm or more. Di: All CS. Ge: This amazing creature, which looks like a piece of sea weed, crawls along shallow sandy bottoms to 20 m depth. As it moves it spreads its oral hood wide in front of it scooping the bottom and trapping small crustaceans. It also gains nutrition from symbiotic algae growing in its mantle which give it its green/brown colour. Widespread but not common, they sometimes occur in small groups.

Facing page: It is able to swim by flapping its body from side to side.

ARMINIDS   ARMINIDAE

Armina cygnaea   **Port Moresby, PNG**

Sea Pen Slug

Le: To 8 cm, possibly larger. Di: All CS.
Ge: This specimen was found by the author in a bed of sea pens on a sandy bottom at a depth of 40 m, but have also been reported from shallow water. The Arminids usually feed on sea pens but also soft corals. This species has a typical Arminid shape with a longitudinally ridged and lined back and no obvious gills. There are similar species. Usually nocturnal and bury in sand during the day.

ZEPHYRINIDS   ZEPHYRINIDAE

Janolus sp.   **Port Moresby, PNG**

Zephyr Slug

Le: To 4 cm.
Di: Northern CS, rest uncertain.
Ge: This species is found in strong current areas where it feeds on bryozoans. The bulbous cerata with purple tips are distinctive. There is a sensory organ clearly visible between the rhinophores.

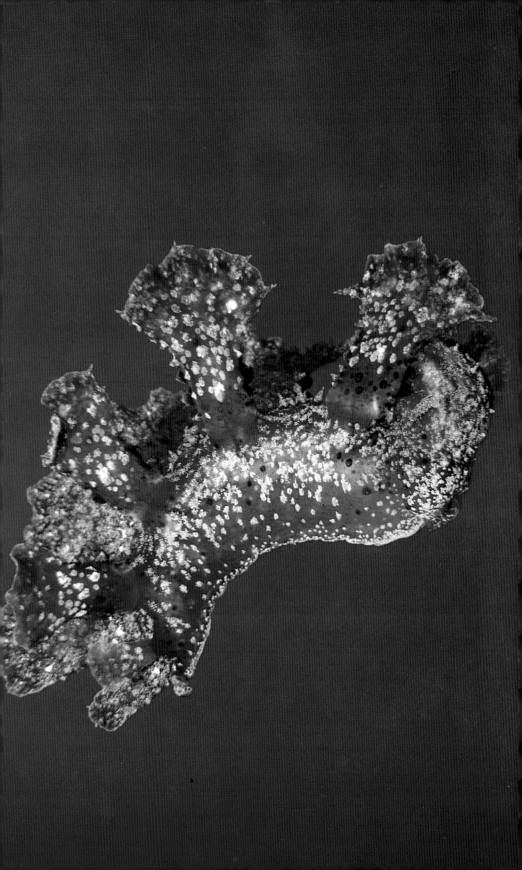

Purple Band Flabellina

Le: To 4 cm.
Di: All CS.
Ge: Members of this family lack distinct gills and use cerata for respiration. They feed on hydroids and, after digestion, are able to move undischarged nematocysts to the tips of their own cerata which provides a defence against predators. This species is common and distinguished by the cerata which have a white tip with a purple band below.

Flabellina exoptata   **Tufi, PNG**

FACELINIDS   FACELINIDAE

Solar Powered Slug

Le: To 14 cm. Di: All CS. Ge: Feeds on soft coral *Sarcophyton,* utilizes ingested zooxanthellae to produce nutrition. Plant cells clearly visible as brown patches in the flesh. If roughly handled the slug will discard cerata. On sand, 5 to 20 m deep (below).

Phyllodesmium longicirrum   **GBR, Australia**

Ianthina Slug

Le: To 15 cm.
Di: All CS.
Ge: This very long and distinctive slug is very variable in colour, typically green, brown and blue but also violet. It feeds on hydroids and is common particularly on shallow reefs and dropoffs. Has symbiotic zooxanthellae which provide significant nutrition and because of this is generally found in water not deeper than 10 m to take advantage of sunlight.

Pteraeolidia ianthina   **Eastern Fields, Coral Sea**

Sepia latimanus   **New Ireland, PNG**

Common Reef Cuttlefish

Le: To 50 cm.
Di: All CS.
Ge: This cuttlefish is common and widespread though not always noticed because of it remarkable ability to instantly match its colour to its surroundings. It usually is discovered hovering a few centimetres above the reef.
   Below: The cuttlebone of a dead cuttlefish floating with fallen leaves.

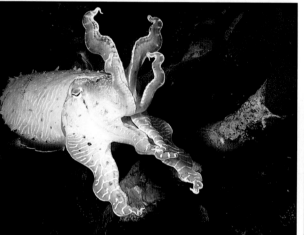

Sepia latimanus   **New Ireland, PNG**

Euprymna morsei   **Port Moresby, PNG**

Bobtail Squid

Le: To 8 cm.
Di: All CS.
Ge: This small colourful squid is recognised by its short rounded body. It lives in shallow sand and silty bottoms to 10 m deep, and hides by completely burying itself. It is reported to ambush passing prey, but the author has never witnessed this. It is active at night wandering just over the surface of the sand.

Flamboyant Cuttlefish

Le: To 12 cm.
Di: Northern CS.
Ge: This spectacular cuttlefish can switch from drab dark brown to a flamboyant flashing display. It lives in sheltered areas of sand where there is considerable bottom debris such as dead leaves, logs, human junk, and algae. It usually walks rather than swims along the bottom and catches its prey of small fishes and crustaceans with its pair of specialised extensible tentacles (first small photo below). Second small photo below: Its round eggs inside a discarded rusty can. An embryonic cuttlefish is clearly visible.

Metasepia pfefferi   Milne Bay, PNG

Metasepia pfefferi   Milne Bay, PNG

Bigfin Reef Squid

Le: To 30 cm. Di: All CS. Ge: The fins on this species extend right around the body, and this is distinctive. They are encountered in a variety of habitats - from boats they may be seen feeding at night on crustaceans or small fishes attracted by lights, or during the day, hover in formation near the surface around a boat's anchor chain. They may be deep or shallow near reefs. After mating they attach their eggs to the bottom, usually without any attempt to hide them.

Sepioteuthis lessoniana   Milne Bay, PNG

Octopus sp.   **Madang, PNG**

Wunderpus

Le: To 25 cm (armspan).
Di: Papua New Guinea to Vanuatu.
Ge: Scuba divers have discovered many new species of octopus over the pastten years, some of which remain scientifically undescribed. Wunderpus is one of these new discoveries.
This long-armed octopus lives on sand and rubble, generally emerging at dusk and dawn to prey on small fish and crustaceans. It feeds by spreading its thin arms over an area, like ribs of an umbrella, then closes the webs to trap everything caught inside the net.
This species is often confused with the Mimic Octopus which also occurs in the region. The Mimic Octopus has lines of dark and light running along the body and a distinct white "V" at the tip. It is able to mimic a wide range of animals from flounders to lionfish to jellies. Wunderpus is not such a good mimic, although it has been observed to mimic banded sea snakes.

Octopus sp.   **Vanuatu**

Blue Ringed Octopus

Le: To 15 cm.
Di: All CS.
Ge: This octopus has a highly toxic bite which may cause human fatality. The genus is distinguished by blue rings on the body which become more intense if the octopus is disturbed. Usually found in very shallow water among rocks or rubble. The author has been alarmed by seeing village children catch these octopus in their hands and poking them to see the bright colours. The children were not bitten but others have been.

Hapalochlaena lunulata   **Milne Bay, PNG**

MATING FROM A DISTANCE

The Common Reef Octopus *Octopus cyanea* is found on reef tops to 20 m depth. It grows to a length of 40 cm, is found in all of the Coral Sea region and may be identified by the dark oval spot below the eyes on the arm web as shown in the first photograph.

Octopus build lairs by collecting rocks and the rock pile, and obvious entrance hole, can be the first sign that a diver will have that an octopus is near. The octopus is usually seen poking its head out from the hole, and retreating on approach. Octopus can often be seen mating and, if approached with care, will usually ignore a diver. The male, at a distance, extends a specialised arm with a sperm packet on its end and inserts it into the female through the siphon opening, depositing the sperm packet near opening of the female's oviduct. Mating may continue for several hours.

Right: Adult Common Reef Octopus showing dark oval spot below eye which identifies species.

Two *Octopus cyanea* at entrances to their lairs and mating. Note extended arm of male.

Octopus are not necessarily nocturnal and are often encountered out foraging for food during the daytime. One method of feeding for the Common Reef Octopus is to spread its arms wide over a small coral head, completely enclosing it, then chase any small fishes or crustaceans out from under the coral with the tips of its arms. Feeding expeditions are often accompanied by predatory fishes, such as Lyretail Trout, who pick up any prey that escapes the clutches of the octopus.

Above: Male deposits sperm packet inside female mantle cavity. Right: Mating octopus ignoring diver photographing them.

273

ANCIENT CREATURES FROM THE DEPTHS

The Nautilus is a fantastic animal. It builds a chambered spiral shell whose curves have remained unchanged for 500 million years. We know this because ancient fossils show a perfect match. As the animal grows it builds a new chamber initially full of water, then, by the process of osmosis, removes the water from the chamber until it achieves perfect neutral buoyancy. The chamber does not contain gas but has a virtual vacuum inside. The shell, barely one millimetre thick, with a vacuum inside its chambers, withstands pressures of over 40 atmospheres.

Nautilus pompilius, note pearly umbilicus.

Nautilus are able to vary their buoyancy by controlling the amount of water inside the chambers and, by this means, move up or down in the water. They have no swim fins but they can pump water through a siphon giving them efficient jet propulsion. Up to ninety tentacles enable them to grasp food, though their lack of speed makes them scavengers rather than predators.

One of the tough problems with the Theory of Evolution is to give a rational explanation as to how eyes came to exist through the process of natural selection. The Nautilus provides one of the missing links with its primitive eyes which have no lens but act in the same way that a pinhole camera does.

I caught Nautilus on many occasions in PNG with a trap lowered to depths of 200 - 300 metres. The trap was baited with a fish carcass - or even chicken parts - and left overnight. In the morning the trap was hauled to the surface and inevitably there were nautilus inside. Nautilus must be abundant throughout PNG - on occasion I captured 45 at one time, though the usual haul was 5 - 15. Since they have no gas inside their shell the Nautilus were unharmed by their rapid ascent though they do not like the warmer surface waters. The standard procedure was to get them back in the water as soon as possible at a drop off near

Nautilus scrobiculatus, note hollow umbilicus and mossy periostracum.

274

where they were caught. Once down the drop off 20 metres or so they were released and soon orientated themselves, gave themselves slight negative buoyancy, and jet propelled themselves safely back down to their deep homes. I know they returned safely because marked specimens have been re-caught several times. Divers had enough time to watch and photograph the Nautilus and could control them easily in the water as they are quite slow movers.

The most common species is *Nautilus pompilius*. *Nautilus scrobiculatus* are rarer and require trapping at the deep end of the range. In New Caledonia, *Nautilus macromphalus* is the most common. On the GBR both *Nautilus pompilius* and *Nautilus stenomphalus* are found, along with hybrids of the two species.

When Nautilus die, and the body decays, the shell becomes positively buoyant, floats to the surface eventually drifts ashore. Those people that do not approve of shell collecting should have no qualms about buying Nautilus shells from villagers since they do not collect live Nautilus, they simply collect beached and drifting shells that have died naturally.

Right: A diver inspects the Nautilus caught in the trap.
Below: A close look at the Nautilus pinhole camera eye.

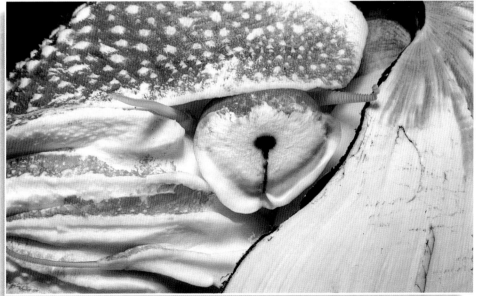

Great Barrier Reef King Prawn

Le: Up to 10 cm.
Di: Eastern Australia and Coral Sea.
Ge: At present more than 100 species of the prawn family Penaeidae are known in the Western Central Pacific alone. *Metapenaeus* contains economically most important species (second only to *Penaeus*), also extensively cultured in ponds.

Metapenaeus sp.   **GBR, Australia**

ROCK SHRIMPS   SICYONIIDAE

Stony Shrimp

Le: Up to 7 cm.
Di: Papua New Guinea.
Ge: The body of sicyoniid shrimps is generally robust, with a very hard shell, and of "stony" appearance. The abdomen often shows deep grooves and numerous tubercles. All family members are marine and found from shallow to over 400 m deep waters. Benthic on soft and hard bottoms. Sexes are easily distinguished by large copulatory organ (petasma) on 1st pair of pleopods of males. Eggs small, numerous, not carried.

Sicyonia sp.   **Milne Bay, PNG**

SOLENOCERID SHRIMPS   SOLENOCERIDAE

Faxon's Shrimp

Le: Up to about 12 cm.
Di: All CS.
Ge: Solenocerid shrimps are generally pink to red, sometimes with pale markings on antennae and tips of uropods. They are found offshore in a depth range of 2 - 5,700 m (usually deeper than 20 m). All are benthic, and prefer soft bottoms. Genus members burrow in mud during the day.

Solenocera faxoni   **Kavieng, PNG**

Banded Boxer Shrimp

Le: Up to 5 cm.
Di: One of the few larger crustacea found in all tropical seas.
Ge: A common cleaning boxer shrimp with spiny, bristly body and chelipeds. The species is always found in pairs and displays sexual dimorphism: Males are smaller. It is found in crevices from a depth of 3 m on downwards.

Probably all species of the genus *Stenopus* are cleaners that sit at the entrance of their cave and wave their antennae to attract fish customers.

Stenopus hispidus   GBR, Australia

Blue Boxer Shrimp

Le: Up to 2 cm.
Di: All CS.
Ge: One of the smallest genus members. Usually in pairs. During the spawning season the egg stalks that attach the blue eggs to the female are visible through the dorsal carapace.

Stenopus tenuirostris   Port Moresby, PNG

Crinoid Boxer Shrimp

Le: Up to 2 cm.
Di: Papua New Guinea.
Ge: This boxer shrimp has been found on the underside of a crinoid (feather star). Whether it is a cleaner, is unknown.

Odontozona sp.   Milne Bay, PNG

277

Lysmata debelius   Bougainville, Solomon Islands

Scarlet Cleaner Shrimp

Le: Up to 5 cm.
Di: All CS.
Ge: The Scarlet cleaner shrimp
is usually found in depths
greater than 10 m. It lives in
pairs or small groups and
defends territories against con-
specifics. There is no externally visible sexual dimorphism.
Although not the most important invertebrate cleaner in the
reef, the species readily cleans
fishes like the moray eel in the
photo.
    The colouration of the Scar-
let cleaner shrimp shows some
variation: In the Central Pacific
it has red legs.

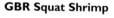

Lysmata amboinensis   Eastern Fields, Coral Sea

White-banded Cleaner Shrimp

Le: Up to 6 cm.
De: All CS.
Ge: One of the most
important invertebrate
cleaners of reef fishes.
Colouration distinctive: The
white line on the red back is
broken on the tail fan. Often in
pairs, groups of up to 100 have
been encountered in the reef.
    The cleaner shrimps of the
family Hippolytidae are known
to free especially large,
stationary reef fishes such as
morays and groupers (photo:
Cephalopholis miniatus) from
parasites and infected skin.

Thor spinosus   GBR, Australia

GBR Squat Shrimp

Le: Up to 1 cm.
Di: All CS.
Ge: A beautiful member of this
genus which is rarely seen by
divers.
    Below: The best known
member of this genus is
Thor amboinensis, often seen
close to anemones.

Pine Cone Marble Shrimp

Le: Up to 3 cm.
Di: All CS.
Ge: A laterally very compressed species, well demanded in the aquaristic trade. The large photo at the right shows a female, the small photo below shows a male.

Saron inermis   Milne Bay, PNG

Marble Shrimp

Le: Up to 9 cm.
Di: Northern CS.
Ge: This well-documented, distinct species is known since many years and should soon be described as a new species according to the Dutch carcinologist Charles Fransen.

Saron sp.   Port Moresby, PNG

Saw Blade Shrimp

Le: Up to 5 cm. Di: All CS.
Ge: The Saw blade shrimp is extremely elongated and its body is transparent with irregular transverse camouflaging bands. The rostrum makes up for nearly a third of the total length, but it is less than twice as long as the remainder of the carapace; rostrum without dorsal teeth but with 10 - 30 ventral teeth, giving it the appearance of a tiny saw blade. Abdominal somites 3 - 5 each carry a dorsal tooth, the one on the third somite is large and has a keel. On black coral, hard to spot.

Tozeuma armatum   Solomon Islands

279

Rhynchocinetes durbanensis   Marion Reef, GBR

Durban Hinge-beak Shrimp

Le: Up to 4 cm.
Di: All CS.
Ge: Often incorrectly reported as *R. uritai,* but differs in having a very long, toothed rostrum. Another difference concerns the colouration: The white inner lines are as bold as the red ones, and not of different width as in *R. uritai.* It lives deep in crevices and holes. The most common species of hinge-beak shrimp seen by divers is also active in the afternoon, especially when it is congregating into groups.

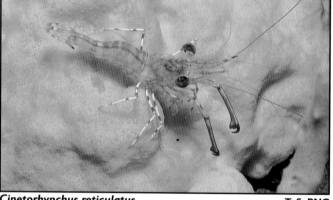

Cinetorhynchus reticulatus   Tufi, PNG

Reticulated Hinge-beak Shrimp

Le: Up to 6.5 cm.
Di: All CS.
Ge: With its blotchy red-brown body and banded legs, this shrimp resembles the smaller *C. hendersoni.* It is seen most often on vertical walls near caves and deep under-cuts, usually in small aggregations. Old males have long and enlarged chelipeds, see photo.

Cinetorhynchus striatus   Milne Bay, PNG

Striped Hinge-beak Shrimp

Le: Up to 6.5 cm.
Di: All CS.
General: Usually found on rocky reefs in a depth range of 1 - 20 m.

Ambon
Commensal Shrimp

Le: Up to 2.5 cm.
Di: All CS.
Ge: This shrimp is found on feather stars, e.g. *Oxycomanthus bennetti.* The colouration of the tiny commensal is variable, and always matches that of its crinoid host. The body is banded similar to the banding of the feather star. Colours include red or brown with white bands or red with yellow and orange banding. The eye stalks are thick and somewhat light in colour.

Periclimenes amboinensis Flinders Reef, GBR

Imperator
Commensal Shrimp

Le: Up to 2 cm.
Di: All CS.
Ge: The broad lamina of the antennal scales give this shrimp a duck-billed appearance. It is found on a variety of invertebrate hosts, mainly and often in pairs on the colourful nudibranch *Hexabranchus sanguineus*, also known as Spanish Dancer (below). The shrimp feeds near the gastropod's gills on fecal pellets and mucus of the snail. Other host species include the large nudibranchs *Dendrodoris tuberculosa, Asteronotus caespitosus* and *Risbecia tryoni* (bottom large photo) but also sea cucumbers of the genera *Stichopus, Bohadschia,* and *Opheodesoma* (top large photo). Like in many commensal shrimps, the individual colouration of *P. imperator* specimens varies to match the animal on which they live.

Periclimenes imperator Tufi, PNG

Periclimenes imperator Port Moresby, PNG

REEF LOBSTERS ENOPLOMETOPIDAE

Enoplometopus occidentalis   Alotua, PNG

Red Reef Lobster

Le: Up to 12 cm.
Di: All CS.
General: Reef lobsters are
spending the day hidden in the
deepest parts of caves and
crevices. Consequently, they
can be encountered only at
night. If a specimen or a pair
have been found, they will be
in the same area night after
night as long as they are not
molested.

SPINY LOBSTERS PALINURIDAE

Justitia japonica   Kavieng, PNG

Japanese Deep Lobster

. L: Up to 27 cm. D: All CS.
G: Depth range: 90 - 200 m. On
rocky substrates. Rarely seen by
divers but occasionally caught in
traps set for Nautilus. The photographer was lucky to find the
rare species in such a trap.

SLIPPER LOBSTERS SCYLLARIDAE

Thenus orientalis   Madang, PNG

Flathead Lobster

Le: Up to 25 cm, carapace
length up to 8 cm.
Di: Alll CS.
Ge: Carapace flattened, without sharp marginal teeth. Eyes
placed widely apart, near the
outer edges of the carapace.
Distinct central spine on rear
edge of 5th abdominal segment.
From the subtidal to a depth of
200 m, usually on sand or mud
bottoms. Mainly as bycatch
throughout its range.

Common Hermit Crab

Le: Up to 5 cm. Di: All CS.
Ge: Probably the most common species of hermit crab, it is identified by its spiny chelipeds, light coloured bristles, red and white striped eye stalks, and green eyes. The colouration often varies in intensity, some specimens being lighter or darker, leading some to believe that there may be more than one species. The shells used by this species are nearly always covered with small sea anemones. This relationship provides camouflage and protection for the crab, and gives the anemones the opportunity to feed in different locations.

Dardanus pedunculatus   GBR, Australia

Shell-breaking Hermit

Le: Up to 15 cm. Di: All CS.
Ge: One of the largest hermits, easily identified by red-orange colour with white spots and spines outlined with black. Numerous long thick brown bristles on the dark outlines. Feeds on molluscs, breaks open shells. Below: Eating a jelly.

Dardanus megistos   Port Moresby, PNG

PORCELAIN CRABS   PORCELLANIDAE

Small-dot Anemone Crab

Le: Up to 3 cm.
Di: All CS.
Ge: Carapace rounded, crab-like, surface smooth. Chelipeds broad, strong, with large claws. Creamy white with numerous small red spots. Among tentacles or under rim of sea anemones.
The Large-dot Anemone Crab *N. oshimai* lives in the same area and is distinguished by much larger dots more widely spaced apart.

Neopetrolisthes maculatus   San Cristobal, Solomon Islands

Pelagic Swimming Crab

Width: Up to 20 (male) cm
including lateral teeth.
Di: All CS.
Ge: Prefers sandy to sandy-
muddy substrates in shallow
waters down to a depth of
65 m, including areas near
reefs, mangroves, and in sea-
grass and algal beds. Juveniles
tend to occur in shallow intertidal areas. Matures at about 1
year of age. Caught commer-
cially in enormous numbers for
sale in local markets (fresh or
frozen) and for the crab flesh
canning industry. Shown
entangled in a set net.

Portunus pelagicus   **Kimbe Bay, PNG**

Tube Guardian

Wi: Up to 4 cm. Di: All CS.
Ge: Variable colour pattern of
brown and white, may be
reversed. Spines weak, interor-
bital smooth. Commensal on
tube anemones and sea
cucumbers. Below: The closely
related species *L. orbicularis* on
a sea cucumber.

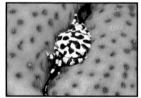

Lissocarcinus laevis   **GBR, Australia**

Pebble Crab

Wi: Up to 2.5 cm.
Di: Northern Australia to
Solomon Islands.
G: One of the most beautiful
crabs in the Coral Sea area.
The colouration of this small
species is very distinct. The
rounded markings on its back
vary from red to brown in
colour. The reader may interpret their significance. The
Pebble Crab is found on sand
near reefs in depths from 0 to
60 m.

Leucosia anatum   **Solomon Islands**

Peacock Smasher

Le: Up to 18 cm.
Di: All CS.
Ge: Depth range 1 to 50 m plus. This widespread species lives in u-shaped burrows constructed of small pieces of rubble. Adult males often have a bright green body colour. Females are more commonly olive while juveniles tend to be yellow.

The strike of this animal is quite potent and there have been several reports of human individuals suffering wounds to their hands when they attempted to grab them. In one case a finger required amputation.

Odontodactylus scyllarus   Madang, PNG

Rambo Smasher

Le: Up to 10 cm.
Di: All CS.
Ge: This species is common in the low intertidal, lives in cavities in coral rubble and rock bench. Gram for gram, *G. chiragra* is one of the most powerful of all smashing stomatopods, specialising on heavily armoured gastropods and hermit crabs. The cavities of these potent predators can often be identified by a midden of shell fragments near the entrance.

Gonodactylus chiragra   Lizard Island, GBR

Variable Smasher

Le: Up to 3 cm. Di: All CS.
Ge: 3 - 50 m. This is one of the most common gonodactyloids found below 3 m, usually living in cavities in coral and coral rubble. The species is highly variable in colour, although deep specimens tend to be pink or red.

The following two pages show the second large group of Mantis Shrimps, the **Spearers**. First a *Lysiosquillina* sp., followed by a description of the unusual behaviour of *Lysiosquillina maculata* and its significance for the evolution of animals.

Gonodactylus affinus   Port Moresby, PNG

285

WHAT REALLY HAPPENED TO THE DINOSAURS!

Many readers have heard the fantastic theory that a giant meteor crashed to earth, dramatically changed the world climate, and caused the extinction of the dinosaurs. It never ceases to amaze me how people can believe such nonsense. Giant meteors indeed - someone has been reading too much science fiction, and as for changing climate we all know that the climate changes all the time and although this is a cause of panic sales of suncream, umbrellas or overcoats, this does not cause mass extinctions. The time traveller Bob Halstead tells us the truth about the extinction of the dinosaurs.

Both contrahents oppose each other, ready to clash.

As usual the real explanation is much simpler and easily verified – when is the last time YOU saw a giant meteor, eh? The truth is that dinosaurs became extinct through the evolution of a voracious predator of the *Lysiosquillina* genus. Commonly called Mantis Shrimp today, they would not have been so called if Jurassic *Lysiosquillina* were still around, they were the big ancestors, and would undoubtedly be called Mantis Whoppers.

Students of Greek will recognise Lysio - to loose, and squilla - an onion or leek, thus *Lysiosquillina* means "to loose an onion" or, in other words, to cause a stink. And that is exactly what they did in the dinosaur world. *Lysiosquillina* formed lairs by digging holes in the Jurassic mud, interestingly they did this not by burrowing but by flapping their tails, expelling mud and forming a deep trench, which, when sufficiently deep, they allowed to fill in from behind, ending with a hole that they could comfortably, and securely, rest in while waiting for passing dinosaurs.

In a scientific experiment we performed, a live plastic dinosaur was allowed to roam close to the lair of *Lysiosquillina*. Illustrated here, in a world first, the dramatic photographs show the *Lysiosquillina* emerging from its lair to viciously attack the dinosaur. The incredibly sharp array of spears on the *Lysiosquillina's*

The dinosaur has no chance to escape the extremely fast attack of the mantis shrimp's claws, one of the fastest movements known in the marine world.

mandibles, thrown out with one of the fastest movements ever recorded underwater, can easily penetrate dinosaur armour and fatally impale the dinosaur. This instinctive behaviour, inherited from its Jurassic ancestors, proves without doubt what actually happened to the dinosaurs.

Finally, the dinosaurs have found their master: the predatory mantis shrimp prevails until today.

BUSHY FEATHER STARS   COMASTERIDAE

Comanthina schlegeli   GBR, Australia

Bushy Feather Star

Le: To 20 cm.
Di: All CS.
Ge: A very common feather
star (crinoid) on coral reefs
particularly where there are
consistent currents. Crinoids
sit on top of corals and feed
on drifting plankton. The
colouration is highly variable,
see opposite, and the best way
to distinguish this species from
the many other types of feather stars is by the densly
packed robust arms, about 130
of them, and size. Careless
handling by divers will result in
the sticky, but harmless, arms
being torn off.

SMALL FEATHER STARS   COLOBOMETRIDAE

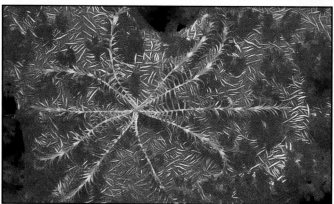

Oligometra serripinna   Madang, PNG

Small Feather Star

Le: To 10 cm.
Di: All CS.
Ge: This small and delicate
crinoid takes advantage of the
feeding habits of soft corals,
gorgonians and wire corals by
sitting on them thus elevating
itself into the currents. It only
has ten arms. A similar species
also with only ten arms,
Colobometra perspinosa, is one
of the crinoid species able to
actually swim through the
water by sequential flapping of
their arms, an amazing sight.

BEAUTIFUL FEATHER STARS   HIMEROMETRIDAE

Beautiful Feather Star

Le: To 15 cm.
Di: All CS.
Ge: Identified by its deep red
colouration this is a common
reef crinoid. Some crinoid
species are only active at night
and hide during the day but
this species stays holding onto
its coral perch day and night.

Himerometra robustipinna   Solomon Islands

Acanthaster planci   Flinder's Reef, Coral Sea

Crown of Thorns Sea Star

Le: To 50 cm. Di: All CS. Ge: Usually nocturnal this infamous coral-eating sea star typically feeds on fast growing *Acropora* corals and helps balance reef coral growth. Infestations reaching plague proportions sometimes occur in which case the sea star, competing for food, is also active in the day and may eat nearly all species of hard corals, and cause devastation. Regrowth, after infestation in an otherwise healthy environment has ceased, is usually rapid and results in increased biodiversity, however reefs already stressed, for example by pollution, may not fare as well. Giant Triton and Helmet Shells eat the COTs as do Maori Wrasse and Titan Trigger. Some blame overfishing as a cause of infestations. The author doubts this having witnessed an outbreak in PNG in the early 1980s in an area where fishing pressures were nil. At the end when live coral cover was very low, the author saw thousands of dying COTs apparently starving to death. Below: The poisonous spines of this species.

Acanthaster planci   Port Moresby, PNG

Granulated Sea Star

Le: To 30 cm.
Di: All CS.
Ge: An easily recognised large sea star common on reef tops throughout the Coral Sea area. Reported to be a scavenger on dead animal material which lives from 5 to 40 m.

Choriaster granulatus   Solomon Islands

Horned Sea Star

Le: To 30 cm. Di: All CS.
Ge: This common sea star inhabits shallow sand and sea grass beds, usually in sheltered habitats, and is reported to feed on sponges. It has horn shaped nodules which may be sharp or rounded. The sharp spines are not a hazard. Colours are very variable.

It is usual for echinoderms to have other creatures living commensally, or even parasitically, on them. Sea urchins have shrimp, crabs and shells. Crinoids often have shrimp, crabs and juvenile fishes.

On a dive in Milne Bay we discovered a single Horned Sea Star and photographed several types of creature living on it including a filefish (centre) and brittlestars (below).

Protoreaster nodosus   Milne Bay, PNG

Protoreaster nodosus   Milne Bay, PNG

Pin-cushion Sea Star

Le: To 25 cm. Di: All CS. Ge: Looks more like a soccer ball than a sea star, but turn it over (below) and its origin is obvious with 5 canals extending from the central mouth. Feeds on corals but is too inflexible to inflict the same kind of damage as Crown of Thorns. Colour very variable, often beautifully patterned.

Culcita novaguinea   Solomon Islands

291

Fromia monilis   GBR, Australia

Necklace Sea Star

Le: To 12 cm.
Di: All CS.
Ge: Colour and pattern distinct, the red disc has pores. Found in a variety of shallow reef habitats. This sea star is one of a number of sea stars of similar size and shape in the same genus each easily distinguished from each other by their different colours and patterns. They are usually in the open, some are quite deep to 30 m.

Leiaster speciosus   GBR, Australia

Spot Chain Sea Star

Le: To 50 cm.
Di: All CS.
Ge: A very large sea star with luminous orange-red colour and rows of low dark nodules. Lives on reefs, particularly outer walls, from 10 to 30 m deep.

Blue Sea Star

Le: To 40 cm.
Di: All CS.
Ge: A very common large sea star found in a variety of habitats, usually shallow but reported to 60 m. Can also be in several other colours, second most common is an olive brown (below).

Linckia laevigata   Eastern Fields, Coral Sea

Baby Watcher

Le: To 10 cm.
Di: All CS.
Ge: A small species of the genus with mottled red, white and yellow colours with blue tips to the arms. Sea stars can reproduce asexually by casting off an arm which then grows four more. The parent star can regenerate a new arm, as can all sea stars when damaged. This is an abundant sea star found in a variety of reef habitats to 30 m depth.

Linckia multifora   GBR, Australia

New Caledonian Sea Star

Le: To 20 cm. Di: All CS. Ge: Common on shallow reef flats and lagoon bottoms. The white nodules decrease in size towards the tip of the arms where there is an orange tint. *Gomophia egeria* (below) has sharp pointed cone shaped nodules with a dark ring around their base.

Nardoa novacaledoniae   GBR, Australia

Friant's Sea Star

Le: To 14 cm. Di: All CS. Ge: The star is covered with colourful rounded wart-like nodules. A shallow water species which is uncommon. Occasionally, with this and other sea stars, an oddity occurs which only has four symmetrical arms (right).

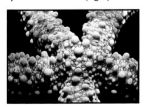

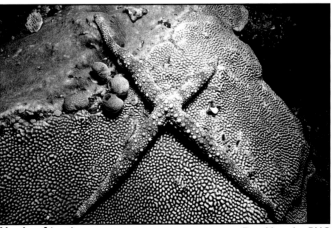

Nardoa frianti   Port Moresby, PNG

293

Lumpy Sea Star

Le: To 25 cm.
Di: All CS.
Ge: This unusual but spectacular sea star is instantly recognisable with its arms covered with lumpy nodules. The nodules join together along the arms forming bands. Appears particularly prone to losing arms. It lives on coral reefs but can also be found on sand patches. Uncommon in most areas.

Echinaster callosus   **Eastern Fields, Coral Sea**

Luzon Sea Star

Le: To 25 cm.
Di: All CS.
Ge: This sea star is very variable in colour and may be mottled or have a single colour. One of the distinguishing factors is that it nearly always has six, or even seven arms, as opposed to the usual five for similar species. Often one arm will only be a stub as the star has cast an arm which will form a complete new star in asexual reproduction.

Echinaster luzonicus   **Holmes Reef, Coral Sea**

Catala's Sea Star

Le: To 40 cm.
Di: All CS.
Ge: Usually found deeper than 10 m where the red tips of the arms appear green in natural light. The large thick arms and coloured tips are distinctive, although there is some variation. May be found to depths of 45 m in the open on coral reefs and walls.

Thromidia catalai   **GBR, Australia**

Icon Sea Star

Le: To 20 cm.
Di: All CS.
Ge: This beautifully propor-
tioned and elegantly coloured
sea star can be instantly identified. Unfortunately it is only
rarely encountered, usually
because it lives deep on rubble, coral reefs and walls usually between 30 and 50 m, and
deeper. The photo on the previous page shows a tiny relative, *Tosia queenslandensis,*
which only grows to a maximum of 3 cm but is usually
found between 5 and 20 m.

Iconaster longimanus   **Port Moresby, PNG**

Comb Sea Star

Le: To 26 cm.
Di: All CS.
Ge: A common and wide-
spread sea star that enters
temperate waters. It lives in
sand from near the surface
down to 40 m spending most
of its time buried. Easily identified by the long white spines
along the margin of the arms.
It feeds mainly on bivalves.

Astropecten polyacanthus   **Port Moresby, PNG**

Stinging Sea Star

Le: 15 cm.
Di: PNG, rest unknown.
The author discovered this sea
star in 60 m of water, carried
it to shallow water and in the
process was stung in the hand.
It is very unusual to find a
stinging sea star and, as yet, its
identity is uncertain. It is
possibly a new genus and
species.

Unknown genus and species   **Milne Bay, PNG**

BASKET STARS   GORGONOCEPHALIDAE

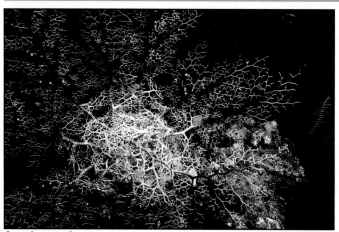

Giant Basket Star

Le: To 80 cm.
Di: All CS.
Ge: This creature hides in
coral crevices during the day,
emerging at night to perch on
top of the reef. Here it
extends its grasping tentacled
arms to feed on plankton. It is
very light sensitive and will
react to a diver's torch light.
A smaller unidentified relative,
shown on the previous page,
lives on soft corals, *Dendronephthya* spp., which always
grow in areas of current thus
ensuring a supply of plankton.

Astroboa nuda   **Madang, PNG**

BRITTLE STARS   OPHIOTRICHIDAE

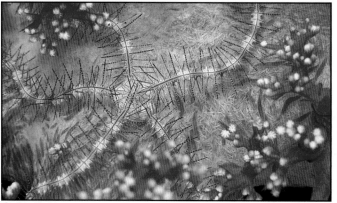

Brittle Star

Le: To 15 cm. Di: All CS. Ge:
The photos show two different
species of brittle stars, *Ophiothrix*
sp. There are several very similar
members of the genus, difficult
to differentiate in the wild. They
live in association with soft
corals, gorgonians and crinoids.

Ophiothrix sp.   **Port Moresby, PNG**

BURYING BRITTLE STARS   AMPHIURIDAE

Burying Brittle Star

Le: To 20 cm.
Di: All CS.
Ge: This interesting brittle star
lives in sand. It buries its disc
and uses one arm as an anchor
while the other four arms
catch passing plankton. It is
nocturnal and during the day
buries completely. Some fish,
particularly wrasses, will eat
brittle stars which explains
why the stars are usually nocturnal. Even so brittle stars will
sometimes have arms bitten
off. Fortunately they are able
to regenerate them.

Amphiura sp.   **Port Moresby, PNG**

Diadema setosum   **Milne Bay, PNG**

Long-spined Urchin

Le: To 50 cm. Di: All CS.
Ge: This urchin has impaled
countless careless swimmers,
snorkellers and divers. The
animal has no venom glands but
the long spines are coated with
toxin which increases the pain of
impalement. Injury is not usually
severe unless infected or the
spine lodges in a joint. The
spines break off and are very
difficult to remove. They live in
very shallow water down to
20 m and are not always black. A
white specimen is shown on the
previous page however identification can be made by the small
orange ring around the anus.

False Fire Urchin

Le: To 20 cm.
Di: All CS.
Ge: Easily identified by the
radiating lines of luminous blue
dots on a red base. Sometimes
called a Fire Urchin since some
can be very bright orange-red,
although most are coloured
much darker. However they
are not venomous. The ball
shaped organ on top of the
urchin is its anus. Requires a
sandy environment from 1 to
40 m deep.

Astropyga radiata   **Port Moresby, PNG**

SEA URCHINS   ECHINOTHURIIDAE

Fire Urchin

Le: To 20 cm. Di: All CS. Ge:
This creature gets its common
name of Fire Urchin both from
its colour and the burning sting
it can deliver through venomous
spines. The author can testify
that the pain is severe though,
strangely, the sting does not
leave a mark on the skin. These
fast moving urchins are usually
deeper during the day at 20 to
40 m moving to shallower water
at night. They are often hosts for
a pair of shrimp, *Periclimenes colemani*, a crab, *Zebrida adamsii*, and
shell, *Luetzenia asthenosomae*.

Asthenosoma varium   **Milne Bay, PNG**

DIADEMA SEA URCHINS DIADEMATIDAE

Calamari Sea Urchin

Le: To 12 cm. Di: All CS. Ge: Distinguished by long tubular spines, which may be all white or banded, short sharp brown spines, and an anal sac with white spots. *Echinometra mathaei* (below) has sharp but robust spines with a distinct white ring around their base.

Echinothrix calamaris Milne Bay, PNG

SEA URCHINS CIDARIDAE

Pencil Urchin

Le: To 17 cm.
Di: All CS.
Ge: One of a number of urchins with thick blunt spines. This one is common and wide-spread but rarely seen since it is purely nocturnal. It is able to use the spines to wedge inside coral crevices. Lives in shallow water in sheltered coral reefs. Spines from dead urchins are sometimes found laying on the reef mystifying divers.

Phyllacanthus imperialis Eastern Fields, Coral Sea

TOXIC SEA URCHINS TOXOPNEUSTIDAE

Flower Urchin

Le To 120 cm. Di: All CS. Ge: This urchin should never be handled with bare hands. It is extremely venomous and is reported to have caused fatali-ties. The flower-like discs are called pedicellariae which are grasping organs equipped with three jaws. If they are able to bite through the skin a venom is injected. The pedicellariae on the bottom of the urchin are reported to be most hazardous, and tender skin most vulnera-ble. In shallow water of shel-tered sand and rubble beaches.

Toxopneustes pileolus GBR, Australia

301

TOXIC SEA URCHINS   TOXOPNEUSTIDAE

Cake Urchin

Le: To 15 cm. Di: All CS.
Ge: A shallow water urchin
that also has venomous pedicellariae but far less hazardous
than *T. pileolus*. Colour variable, this urchin likes to disguise its presence by decorat-
ing itself with debris. Below:
Urchin with decoration.

Tripneustes gratilla   GBR, Australia

SEA URCHINS   LOVENIIDAE

Elongate Heart Urchin

Le: To 9 cm.
Di: All CS.
Ge: The author once
witnessed thousands moving
on top of sand in a bay in
PNG, however usually it lives
under the sand. Can be
variable in colour from
white to red-brown.

Lovenia elongata   New Ireland, PNG

SAND DOLLARS   SCUTELLIDAE

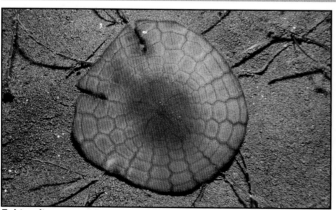

Purple Sand Dollar

Le: To 15 cm.
Di: All CS.
Ge: The Sand Dollar has a similar habitat as the previous
species. Its surface is covered
by many short, soft spines giving it a velvety appearance.
Mouth and anus are situated
on the bottom side. Buries in
sand just below the surface in
3 to 15 metres. Sand Dollars
feed on plant and animal detritus which they filter from the
upper layers of sand.

Echinodiscus auritus   Milne Bay, PNG

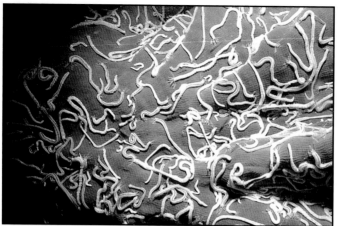

Lambert's Worm Sea Cucumber

Le: To 10 cm.
Di: All CS.
Ge: These small white sea cucumbers are often mistaken for worms. They live in large infestations on sponges, but appear to do the sponge no harm. In fact they may assist the sponge by cleaning off debris that the sponge has sucked onto itself, or by consuming waste products. The photo on the previous page shows a large vase sponge, *Kallypilidion* sp., covered with synaptids.

Synaptula lamberti   **New Britain, PNG**

Worm Sea Cucumber

Le: To 1.0 m, possibly longer.
Di: All CS.
Ge: This large synaptid can stretch out to a great length but is usually encountered at about one metre. Innocent divers sometimes mistake it for a snake. It has a very sticky surface and is unpleasant to touch. The adhesion is caused by minute calcium carbonate spicules observation of which can determine species. The commensal shrimp, *Periclimenes imperator,* can be seen on the sea cucumber.

Synapta sp.   **Milne Bay, PNG**

Large Burrowing Sea Cucumber

Le: To 30 cm above sand.
Di: All CS. Ge: The body of this sea cucumber remains buried in the sand and only the feeding tentacles and mouth can be seen. It can withdraw completely into the sand if disturbed. Sometimes mistaken for an anemone but distinguished by the fact that the tentacles continuously reach into the mouth in turn to have any captured food removed. Common on sandy bottoms to 30 m.

Neothyonidium magnum   **Solomon Islands**

Eyed Sea Cucumber

Le: To 45 cm.
Di: All CS.
Ge: The eye-spot markings of this sea cucumber are distinctive. If disturbed this, and some other, sea cucumbers discharge defensive white threads, called Cuvierian tubules, from the anus. They are very sticky, can cause intense skin irritation, and should be avoided. Shallow lagoons and rubble areas. This sea cucumber swallows sandy sediment at one end then discharges the cleaned - less any digestible matter - sand from the other.

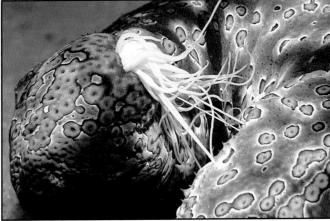

Bohadschia argus   GBR, Australia

Graeff's Sea Cucumber

Le: To 25 cm. Di: All CS.
Ge: This sea cucumber has feeding tentacles with pads on the end that it uses to pick up sediment and small animals. The juveniles (below) mimic nudibranchs, changing to adult form as soon and the nudibranch size is exceeded.

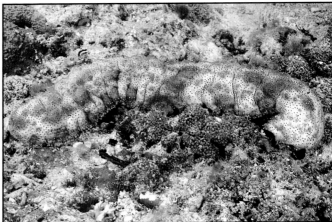

Bohadschia graeffei   Solomon Islands

Weight Watcher

Le: To 30 cm.
Di: New Caledonia and PNG, probably all CS.
Ge: A recently described shallow water species. The body is mainly white with black patches on its back. As sea cucumbers go this one is rather overweight for its length.

Holothuria fuscogilva   Marion Reef, Coral Sea

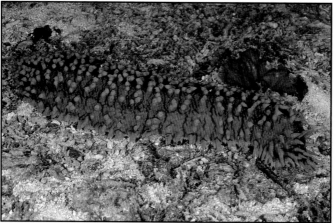

Pineapple Sea Cucumber
Le: To 50 cm. Di: All CS. Ge: An abundant and large sea cucumber with distinctive growths on its surface, hence the name. Photo below shows spawning which is timed simultaneously with several sea cucumbers standing erect so that gametes will mix in the current.

Thelenota ananas   **GBR, Australia**

Red-lined Sea Cucumber

Le: To 40 cm. Di: All CS. Ge: This magnificent sea cucumber was scientifically described only in 1991. It had probably avoided description by the fact that it is usually found deeper on sand patches down reef walls, and is nowhere abundant. Also at these depths the fantastic red colouration does not show in natural light. Original specimens were from PNG and Indonesia but it has since been reported to be far more widespread in the Coral Sea area. The photo also shows "cleaned" sand being excreted.

Thelenota rubralineata   **Milne Bay, PNG**

Anax Sea Cucumber
Le: 60 cm reported to 1 m. Di: All CS. Ge: The largest sea cucumber in the Coral Sea area and easily identified from its box shape with longitudinal lines along each side. *Stichopus chloronotus* (below) is also box shaped and identified by its dark colour and numerous horn like papillae along the edges.

Thelenota anax   **Solomon Islands**

Purple Sea Squirt

Le: To 10 cm. Di: All CS. Ge: A classic tunicate with two openings. If removed from the sea the tunicate will contract and squirt out water hence common name of sea squirt. Solitary or in groups, common, widespread. Below: An unusual colonial ascidian, *Citorclinum laboutei*, first discovered in New Caledonia.

Polycarpa aurata   Solomon Islands

Robust Sea Squirt

Le: To 3 cm.
Di: All CS.
Ge: Ascidians have larval stages whose structure relates them to other chordates. There are over 2,000 species which are found singly or in complex colonies attached to the bottom. Many resemble a sponge but can be differentiated since they responds to touch, something sponges never do. This one may be single or in groups of individuals.

Atriolum robustum   Eastern Fields, Coral Sea

Green Urn Sea Squirt

Le: To 3 cm.
Di: All CS.
Ge: The Robust Sea Squirt (previous species) should not be confused with this similar and very common species which is usually larger but with smaller oral siphons, the tiny holes on the sides of the ascidian. Green to brownish colour is caused by primitive symbiotic algae (*Prochloron* spp.).

Didemnum molle   GBR, Australia

307

THE GOLDBAR SAND-DIVER

I have been fortunate enough in my diving career to have experienced most of the great encounters that can be found in our amazing Indo - Pacific ocean. From awesome Great Hammerhead Sharks to exquisite nudibranchs, from common butterfly-fishes to undescribed gobies, from exquisite coral gardens to lonely, desolate, aircraft wrecks, our wonderful world underwater has never ceased to thrill me. However, until last year, I had never witnessed one of the tropical ocean's most magnificent displays - the annual orgy of coral spawning.

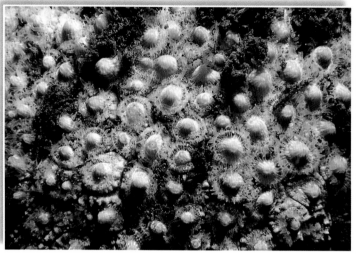

These coral polyps are bulging with spawn (all photographs from Eastern Fields, Coral Sea).

In certain parts of the world this is a highly predictable event. On the Great Barrier Reef diving the fifth night after the full moon in November will almost certainly guarantee synchronised coral spawning. In Western Australia at Ningaloo the coral spawns around March/April, and the plankton produced results in visits from Whale sharks which have made the place famous. April also appears to be the time for corals in the Solomon Islands to spawn.

In PNG we have seen the result of spawning at various times of the year, but have never been prepared for the event. There are probably different times for spawning in different parts of the country. So although I had seen and taken photos of sea cucumbers, clams, sponges and various other marine critters spawning, I had always missed synchronised coral spawning.

In November 1998 I joined a live-aboard for a cruise out into the Coral Sea to Eastern Fields. It is an exciting place to dive as the water is usually very clear, the hard and soft corals in excellent condition and there are plenty of big fishes. It was not until I was chatting with some of the other guests that I realised the cruise would include the November full moon and a week of diving after. Eastern Fields is not that far from the Great Barrier Reef, so it was very possible that coral spawning would take place during our cruise. We arranged with the captain to anchor the boat at a convenient night diving site on the fourth and fifth nights after the full moon.

On the fourth night we entered the water at about 8 pm and spent about an hour searching the coral heads for

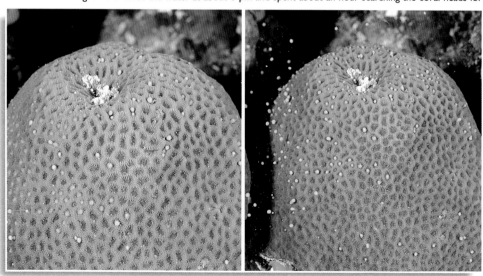

A coral shortly before and while releasing free-floating pink eggs by pulsing contractions from its polyps.

spawning. We saw a couple of large boulder corals producing a fog of spawn and a few small corals making brief and feeble attempts at spawning, but this was not the spectacular event that I had read about.

The next night we prepared to dive again and were excited to see that there was obviously something going on in the water - there was great activity in the plankton attracted to the boat's lights with lots of wiggly worms and bioluminescence. We went in early, before 7.30 pm, but when we looked at the corals there was still not much going on.

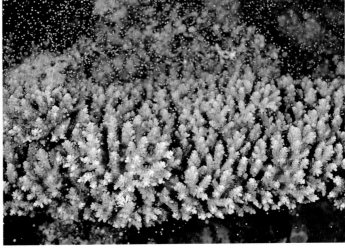

Huge amounts of spawn are released from the polyps of this branching coral.

As the dive progressed however I could see that more and more corals were showing signs of spawning. Coral polyps were obviously swollen, and tiny pink spheres of coral spawn started to show in the water. Schools of squirrelfishes were darting about and appeared to be feeding on the spawn. I had long slow dive but by 9.00 pm was just about out of both air and film. The other divers had returned to the boat and had hot showers, many were into the wine and rum and had obviously packed up for the night, but I had the feeling that the action was just about to start so had a refill of air, changed film in the camera and went straight back in.

I then experienced one of the most fantastic half hours I have ever spent underwater. Just a few moments after I returned the corals put on a magnificent display. All around me great pulses of coral spawn were being ejaculated from the reef - I was in the middle of a giant reef orgasm. The spawn squirted out from the coral heads, then drifted to the surface. It is such an unusual event that it is difficult to describe. Those that have seen it liken it to an underwater fireworks display, or upside-down snow storm. The big plate corals were particularly impressive producing huge amounts of spawn.

Most corals are hermaphrodites so the swelling I could see in individual coral polyps were bundles of eggs and sperm. The moon signals the corals so that they synchronise their spawning. This massed spawning produces so much spawn that it swamps predators with an over-abundance of food thus making survival more likely. The egg and sperm bundles quickly float to the surface of the water. Here the sperm leave the buddies to seek out an egg to fertilise. The fertilised egg will develop into a minute coral larvae which will eventually drift down to the bottom and seek a surface on which it may grow into a coral head.

Individual coral heads then grow by asexual reproduction where coral polyps bud from a parent polyp. Although most reefs grow by means of budding it is important to realise that without spawning it would be impossible for damaged reefs to regenerate or for artificial reefs to form on wrecks. If a reef is damaged, say by Crown of Thorns Starfish, the important factor in its regeneration are the feeder reefs from where coral spawn will originate to settle on the damaged reef.

I had soon finished all my film, but stayed underwater to witness this truly spectacular event. Gradually activity subsided and I made my way back through water thick with plankton some of which stung. On board I raved about the experience and was pleased that I had decided to continue my dive rather than settle for a tempting nightcap as my fellow divers had done - they missed the main event!

Another branching coral releasing eggs. Individuals of the same species spawn simultaneously.

Chelonia mydas   **Eastern Fields, Coral Sea**

Green Turtle

Le: To 1.5 m. Di: All CS.
Ge: Although Green Turtles are supposed to be protected from commercial exploitation they are still regularly traded by indigenous people in the Coral Sea area, and are still considered endangered. Adult Green Turtles are easy to identify however young are often confused with Hawksbill Turtles. The main distinguishing feature is that Green Turtles only have two plates between the eyes, Hawksbill Turtles have two pairs of plates, as shown in the photograph.

Eretmochelys imbricata   **New Ireland, PNG**

Hawksbill Turtle

Le: To 1.0 m.
Di: All CS.
Ge: Hawkbill Turtles are probably the most common turtle in the Coral Sea area. They are easy to befriend by careful divers who refrain from trying to grab the turtle and instead lift nearby loose coral slabs under which grows a sponge that the Hawksbill likes to feed on. The author has had Hawksbill Turtles follow him around on dives and allow gentle petting.

LEATHERBACK TURTLES   DERMOCHELYIDAE

Dermochelys coriacea   **Milne Bay, PNG**

Leatherback Turtle

Le: To at least 2.0 m.
Di: All CS but rare.
Ge: The huge Leatherback Turtle is pelagic and rarely seen underwater. It is encountered on the surface from time to time and unfortunately some are injured in collisions with boats, as was the one in the photograph. Fortunately it recovered and was released back into the sea. Its main diet is sea jellies and no doubt many are killed by trying to digest the plastic bags that pollute our oceans.

Black and White Sea Krait

Le: To 1.2 m.
Di: All CS.
Ge: Sea kraits are not entirely marine but sometimes come ashore. They lay eggs rather than bear live young as do the true sea snakes. They will also board moored boats and the author has witnessed several instances of people immediately jumping overboard after reaching their boats on discovering a sea krait ready for a marina cruise. They are venomous but usually not aggressive.

Laticauda colubrina   New Ireland, PNG

Laticauda colubrina   GBR, Australia

Olive Sea Snake

Le: To 1.5 m. Di: All CS. Ge: Widespread, populations are highly variable. Usually encountered as it searches in coral crevices for prey, may approach a diver but is almost never aggressive. Although highly venomous they rarely bite humans.

Aipysurus laevis   Port Moresby, PNG

DUGONG DUDLEY

Dudley the Dugong lived in a lagoon on Loh Island, a remote isle belonging to the independent state of Vanuatu, located on the very edge of the Coral Sea. That's how far one had to travel in the early 1990s in order to observe one of these rare marine animals in its natural environment! According to the natives, some of the children living in a nearby village found the small sirenian bull five years ago after a severe cyclone. It had apparently been separated from its parents during the storm. The children started to play with it in the shallow water and thereby saved the animal's life. Here is the story as the late Marjorie Bank told it.

Dugong Dudley in the shallow bay of Loh Island.

Normally the natives will kill sea cows for their savoury meat. In this case, however, they decided to spare Dudley for the sake of their children, who had adopted him as a playmate. The sea cows (scientific name Dugong dugon) of the Indo-Pacific area have almost become extinct. A few specimens have survived along the African and Indian coastlines, and herds of up to one hundred animals still exist in western and northern Australia. Once during the 1970s, about 600 dugongs were sighted from an aeroplane flying over a large bay located to the north of Cooktown, on the Great Barrier Reef. The closely related manatees, which prefer fresh water, live in the Atlantic region, particularly the Caribbean, the Amazon and in Senegal. The largest known species, the eight-metre-long Steller sea cow, was wiped out by humans during the 18th century. These marine animals, which grow to a maximum length of three metres and can weigh up to four hundred kilogrammes, are better known under the name of sirenians. Although they somewhat resemble porpoises in size and shape, they are actually more closely related to elephants. In contrast to other marine mammals, they do not communicate by echo lode, but by making bird-like guttural sounds - hence their popular designation. Dugongs, the only existing marine mammals that graze, can consume up to eighty pounds of sea grass and algae (preferably the genus Halophila and Thallasodendron) per day. They live for approximately seventy years, and the females are sexually mature when they reach the age of ten. The period of gestation is one year. Lengthy intervals

All strictly marine sea cows have a bi-lobed tail.

between reproduction, anywhere from three to seven years, and the rapid spread of their only adversary, mankind, are the main reasons why these marine animals have been included in the list of endangered species. At Vanuatu I was able to learn much about the habits of dugongs. They are keenly attuned to tidal fluctuations and changes in underwater visibility. They take advantage of the tides whenever they move from one place to another, as many fields of sea grass are so shallow that they dry up at low tide. Consequently, sea cows will only graze during high tide. At the same time, the fairly shallow waters they graze in (often no more than two metres in depth) need to be turbid enough so that they are not easily discovered by the ever present hunters. This does not always help them, however, for when the annual northwestern storms arrive they seek the turbid and sheltered bays of the islands, where the hunters are already waiting for them in their canoes.

Sirenians live in loose social groups, the size of which will vary depending on the food supply, environmental conditions and reproductive drive. Most of them "travel" in pairs, males with females or mothers with calves. I have never seen groups of more than ten. The harpooned animals are butchered on the beach. Females are in great demand because of their fatty meat. The choice parts fall to the harpooner and the crew, while the remainder goes to the harpooner's mother, followed by the

Dudley owes his life to the villagers of Loh Island.

rest of the relatives and other villagers. Approximately thirty per cent of the 400-kilogramme carcass is fit for human consumption. The same holds for green turtles, which are also grazers and live in the same area as the sea cows. They can weigh up to 150 kilogrammes in these parts and are regarded as a welcome additional catch by the natives.

The sea cow Dudley needs lots of cuddling.

Dudley is more fortunate. Not a single native of Loh Island has designs on his life. He has already become somewhat of an international celebrity, which is why I first heard of him in far-off America. I decided to pay him a visit together with few diving friends in order to take our first underwater photographs of a species that is otherwise known to be extremely shy. The water in the bay is no deeper than three metres and it doesn't take long for us divers to find Dudley grazing on the bottom. As soon as he spots us, he paddles over with elegant strokes and proceeds to embrace the first diver he comes upon. I nearly choke laughing, but do not forget to press the shutter on my

camera. Now he approaches my friend Wendy and rests his head affectionately upon her bosom. In a way I can empathize with him and his desire to cuddle. After all, this thoroughly social animal rarely ever gets the chance to live out his natural instincts for the simplereason that there is no adequate partner around.

I shouldn't have laughed so soon, because now the nearly two-metre-long young sirenian bull decides that I am next on his calling list. I

Dudley embraces a diver.

really don't mind being hugged by a male, but Dudley almost takes the wind out of me as he tenderly wraps his flippers around my body. A 600-pound admirer is a bit too much for me! Evidently I have underestimated the desires of a stripling dugong, for I suddenly feel some hectic motions. As I take a closer look, I quickly discover why Dudley is panting so much and just what it is that he has on his mind. While the other divers are nearly doubled over with laughter, I quickly release myself from his passion te embrace. But Dudley doesn't give up that easily. His next victim, Burt, shows a bit more consideration for a fellow male's emotional turmoil and romps

More cuddling wanted!

around with him for a while. Whereas sea cows are easily able to stay under water for fifteen minutes, our excited friend Dudley has to surface continually for a breath of fresh air. In shallower water, Burt finally manages to stand up and hold on to Dudley, stroking his neck. Suddenly the aroused sirenian bull becomes gentle as a lamb, almost purring like a cat. Now he floats motionless on the surface as we look on in amusement. Dudley has won our hearts.

Dugong Dudley calms down at the surface.

DUGONGS   DUGONGIDAE

Sea Cow, Dugong

Le: To 3 m.
Di: All CS.
Ge: Dugong are an endangered
species whose numbers are
still reported to be decreasing.
Most premature dugong deaths
are attributed to entanglement
in inshore fishing nets. They
usually occur on shallow sea
grass beds, but can be seen on
coral reefs and at depths to
20 m. Most are very shy but
occasionally they will approach
divers, and interact with them.

Dugong dugon   Milne Bay, PNG

SPERM WHALES   PHYSETERIDAE

Sperm Whale

Le: To 18 m.
Di: All CS.
Ge: Whale numbers in the
Coral Sea area appear to be
increasing for several species.
Whale watching is now an
important industry, and divers
are reporting regular encounters. Whales should not be
harassed and there are strict
laws against this in Australia. A
face to face meeting with a
great whale is an unforgettable
and awe inspiring experience.

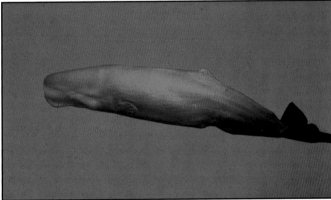

Physeter macrocephalus   New Britain, PNG

RORQUAL WHALES   BALAENOPTERIDAE

Minke Whale

Le: To 8.2 m.
Di: All CS.
Ge: Minke Whales occur quite
commonly in the Coral Sea
region however exceptional
encounters may be experi-
enced in the northern section
of the Great Barrier Reef
between May and August.
Whales actually approach
anchored dive boats.
Snorkellers and divers are
instructed to stay close to the
boat and not to swim towards
the whales, and are rewarded
with repeated close passes.

Balaenoptera acutorostrata   GBR, Australia

Abalistes stellatus 201
Ablabys macracanthus 50
Ablabys taenianotus 139
Abudefduf lorenzi 140
Abudefduf septemfasciatus 140
Abudefduf sexfasciatus 140
Abudefduf sordidus 140
Abudefduf vaigiensis 140
Acanthaster planci 289, 290
Acanthochromis polyacantha 141
Acanthurus dussumieri 188
Acanthurus fowleri 188
Acanthurus guttatus 188
Acanthurus lineatus 189
Acanthurus mata 190
Acanthurus nigricans 190
Acanthurus nigricauda 188
Acanthurus olivaceus 190
Acanthurus pyroferus 189
Acanthurus triostegus 190
Acreichthys radiatus 208
Acentronura breviperula 45
Acropora sp. 226
Actinodendron glomeratum 223
Actinostephanus haeckeli 223
Aeoliscus strigatus 41
Aetobatus narinari 19
Aglaophenia cupressa 217
Aipisurus laevis 311
Alectis indicus 89
Aluterus scriptus 205
Amanses scopas 205
Amblyeleotris fontanesii 177
Amblyeleotris guttata 177
Amblyeleotris randalli 177
Amblyeleotris sp. 178
Amblyglyphidodon aureus 141
Amblygobius decussatus 179
Amblygobius phalaena 179
Amblygobius rainfordi 179
Ammodytes sp. 170
Amphiprion akindynos 144
Amphiprion chrysopterus 144
Amphiprion clarkii 144
Amphiprion leucokranos 145
Amphiprion melanopus 145
Amphiprion percula 145
Amphiprion perideraion 146
Amphiprion polymnus 144
Amphiprion sandaracinos 146
Amphiura sp. 298
Amplexidiscus fenestrafer 225
Anella mollis 220
Antennarius commersonii 33
Antennarius maculatus 34
Antennarius striatus 34
Antipathes sp. 228
Anyperodon leucogrammicus 70, 162
Aphareus furca 95
Apogon aureus 84
Apogon crysopomus 84
Apogon leptacanthus 84
Apogon semiornatus 84
Apolemichthys trimaculatus 132
Architectonica perspectiva 250
Ardeadoris egretta 260
Armina cygnaea 266
Arothron caeruleopunctatus 212
Arothron hispidus 210
Arothron manilensis 210
Arothron mappa 210
Arothron nigropunctatus 212
Arothron reticularis 210
Arothron stellatus 212
Assessor flavissimus 81, 82
Assessor macneilli 81
Assessor randalli 82
Asteronotus caespitosus 264
Asterophilia carlae 230
Asterropteryx ensiferus 181
Asthenosoma varium 300
Astroboa nuda 298
Astropecten polyacanthus 296
Astropyga radiata 300
Atriolum robustum 307
Aulostomus chinensis 40
Balaenoptera acutorostrata 149, 315
Balistapus undulatus 201
Balistoides conspicillum 201
Balistoides viridescens 202
Belonoperca chabanaudi 79, 82
Berthella martensi 256
Bodianus anthioides 157
Bodianus diana 157
Bodianus loxozonus 157
Bohadschia argus 305
Bohadschia graeffei 305
Bolbometopon muricatum 167
Bothus mancus 200
Bothus pantherinus 200
Brachaluteres taylori 208
Brachysomophis cirrocheilos 26
Brachysomophis crocodilinus 26
Brotula multibarbata 32
Bryaninops natans 182
Bryaninops youngei 182
Bursa bubo 253
Bursatella leachi 255
Caesio caerulaurea 100
Caesio cuning 101
Caesio teres 101

Callechelys marmorata 27
Calloplesiops altivelis 81, 82
Cantherines dumerilii 205
Cantherines fronticinctus 205
Cantherines pardalis 205
Canthidermis maculatus 202
Canthigaster compressa 213
Canthigaster coronata 213
Canthigaster epilampra 213
Canthigaster janthinoptera 213
Canthigaster papua 213
Canthigaster valentini 206, 213
Carangoides bajad 89
Carangoides orthogrammus 90
Caranx ignobilis 90
Caranx lugubris 90
Caranx melampygus 92
Caranx papuensis 92
Caranx sexfasciatus 92
Carcharhinus albimarginatus 11, 15
Carcharhinus amblyrhynchos 12, 14
Carcharhinus falciformis 12
Carcharhinus leucas 13
Carcharhinus melanopterus 12
Carybdea marsupialis 217
Cassiopeia andromeda 216
Cassis cornuta 245
Centriscus scutatus 41
Centropyge bicolor 133
Centropyge bispinosa 133
Centropyge colini 130, 131
Centropyge flavicauda 130
Centropyge flavissima 133
Centropyge heraldi 133
Centropyge loricula 134
Centropyge nox 133
Centropyge shepardi 134
Centropyge woodheadi 132
Cephalopholis argus 70
Cephalopholis boenack 70
Cephalopholis cyanostigma 70
Cephalopholis leopardus 71
Cephalopholis miniata 71
Cephalopholis sexmaculata 71
Cephalopholis sonnerati 71
Cepola sp. 154
Ceratosoma tenue 261
Cerianthus sp. 223
Cetoscarus bicolor 167
Chaetodon aureofasciatus 123
Chaetodon auriga 120
Chaetodon baronessa 125
Chaetodon bennetti 121
Chaetodon burgessi 127
Chaetodon citrinellus 126
Chaetodon ephippium 126
Chaetodon falcula 120
Chaetodon fasciatus 122
Chaetodon flavirostris 123
Chaetodon interruptus 121
Chaetodon kleinii 124
Chaetodon lineolatus 120
Chaetodon lunula 122
Chaetodon lunulatus 124
Chaetodon melannotus 121
Chaetodon mertensii 125
Chaetodon meyeri 122
Chaetodon ocellicaudus 121
Chaetodon octofasciatus 126
Chaetodon ornatissimus 122
Chaetodon oxycephalus 120
Chaetodon pelewensis 124
Chaetodon plebeius 124
Chaetodon punctatofasciatus 124
Chaetodon rafflesi 123
Chaetodon rainfordi 123
Chaetodon semeion 123
Chaetodon speculum 121
Chaetodon triangulum 125
Chaetodon trifascialis 125
Chaetodon trifasciatus 124
Chaetodon ulietensis 120
Chaetodon unimaculatus 121
Chaetodon vagabundus 120
Chaetodontoplus melanosoma 134
Chaetodontoplus meredithi 135
Chaetodontoplus mesoleucus 135
Charonia tritonis 252
Cheilinus fasciatus 157
Cheilinus undulatus 158
Cheilodipterus quinquelineatus 86
Chelidonura electra 254
Chelidonura hirundinina 254
Chelidonura varians 254
Chelmon rostratus 127
Chelonia mydas 310
Chicoreus lacinatus 247
Chicoreus ramosus 247
Chloea flava 232
Chloea fusca 232
Chlorurus bleekeri 167
Chlorurus microrhinos 168
Choerodon fasciatus 160
Choerodon schoenleini 159
Choriaster granulatus 290
Chromis viridis 142
Chromodoris kuniei 260
Chromodoris leopardus 260
Chromodoris strigata 260
Chrysiptera brownriggii 142
Chrysiptera caeruleolineata 142

Chrysiptera cyanea 142
Chrysiptera flavipinnis 142
Chrysiptera talboti 142
Cinetorhynchus reticulatus 280
Cinetorhynchus striatus 280
Cirrhilabrus punctatus 160
Cirrhitichthys aprinus 152
Cirrhitichthys falco 152
Cirrhitichthys oxycephalus 152
Cirripectes stigmaticus 173
Citorclinum laboutei 307
Coeloplana meteoris 216
Colobometra perspinosa 288
Comanthina schlegeli 288
Conus aculeiformis 250
Conus generalis 249
Conus geographus 249
Conus striatus 249
Conus textile 250
Coradion altivelis 128
Coradion chrysozonus 128
Coriocella nigra 253
Coris aygula 160
Coris gaimard 161
Corythoichthys amplexus 44
Corythoichthys haematopterus 44
Corythoichthys ocellatus 44
Corythoichthys schultzi 44
Crenavolva tigris 243
Crenimugil crenilabis 154
Crocodylus porosus 196-198
Cromileptes altivelis 72
Cryptocentrus cinctus 178
Cryptodendrum adhaesivum 222
Ctenochaetus striatus 191
Ctenochaetus tominiensis 191
Ctenogobiops pomastictus 178
Culcita novaguinea 291
Cyclichthys orbicularis 214
Cyerce nigricans 257
Cymbacephalus beauforti 60, 77
Cymolutes torquatus 165
Cypho purpurescens 80
Cypraea argus 241
Cypraea aurantium 240
Cypraea cribraria 242
Cypraea humphreysi 242
Cypraea mappa 241
Cypraea onyx 241
Cypraecassis rufa 245
Cyprinocirrhites polyactis 153
Dactyloptena orientalis 50
Dactylopus dactylopus 176
Dardanus megistos 283
Dardanus pedunculatus 283
Dascyllus aruanus 143
Dascyllus carneus 143
Dascyllus melanurus 143
Dascyllus reticulatus 143
Dascyllus trimaculatus 143
Dasyatis kuhlii 16
Dendrochirus biocellatus 51
Dendrochirus brachypterus 51
Dendrochirus zebra 51
Dendrodoris tuberculosa 265
Dendronephthya sp. 219
Dentiovula dorsuosa 244
Dermochelys coriacea 310
Diadema setosum 300
Diademichthys lineatus 35
Diagramma pictum 102
Didemnum molle 307
Diodon hystrix 214
Diodon liturosus 214
Diploprion bifasciatum 79
Discotrema sp. 35, 225
Dolabella auricularia 255
Doryrhamphus dactyliophorus 44
Doryrhamphus excisus 45
Doryrhamphus janssi 45
Drupella cornus 248
Dugong dugon 312-315
Echeneis naucrates 88
Echidna nebulosa 22
Echidna polyzona 23
Echinaster callosus 294
Echinaster luzonicus 294
Echinodiscus auritus 302
Echinometra mathaei 301
Echinothrix calamaris 301
Ecsenius axelrodi 173
Ecsenius bathi 173
Ecsenius bicolor 173
Ecsenius pictus 173
Ecsenius tigris 173
Ellisella sp. 221
Elysia ornata 257
Enoplometopus occidentalis 282
Epinephelus areolatus 72
Epinephelus caeruleopunctatus 74
Epinephelus corallicola 74
Epinephelus fasciatus 75
Epinephelus fuscoguttatus 73
Epinephelus lanceolatus 73
Epinephelus macrospilos 75
Epinephelus maculatus 75
Epinephelus malabaricus 72
Epinephelus merra 75
Epinephelus ongus 74
Epinephelus polyphekadion 74

Epinephelus quoyanus 75
Epinephelus tukula 73, 111, 150
Epinephelus undulosus 76
Epinephelus waandersii 72
Epitonium sp. 252
Eretmochelys imbricata 310
Eucrossorhinus dasypogon 10
Eunice sp. 231
Euprymna morsei 270
Eurypegasus draconis 39
Euselenops luniceps 257
Eviota bifasciata 182
Exallias brevis 174
Exyrias bellissimus 181
Ficus subintermedia 246
Filogranella elatensis 231
Fistularia commersonii 40
Flabellina exoptata 268
Forcipiger flavissimus 128
Forcipiger longirostris 128
Fromia monilis 292
Fungia sp. 228
Fusinus colus 248
Fusinus undatus 248
Genicanthus lamarck 136
Genicanthus melanospilos 135
Globovula margarita 244
Glossodoris atromarginata 261
Glossodoris stellatus 261
Gnathanodon speciosus 89
Gnathodentex aurolineatus 107
Gobiodon okinawae 182
Gomophia egeria 293
Gonodactylus affinis 285
Gonodactylus chiragra 285
Gorgasia preclara 30
Gracila albomarginata 76
Grammatorcynus bicarinatus 199
Grammistes sexlineatus 79
Gunnellichthys curiosus 184
Gunnellichthys viridescens 184
Gymnocranius sp. 107
Gymnosarda unicolor 199
Gymnothorax breedeni 23
Gymnothorax chlamydatus 23
Gymnothorax favagineus 24
Gymnothorax fimbriatus 22
Gymnothorax flavimarginatus 23
Gymnothorax javanicus 22
Gymnothorax zonipectis 24
Haita brunneiterma 243
Halicampus dunkeri 45
Halicampus macrorhynchus 45
Halichoeres biocellatus 161
Halichoeres chrysus 161
Halichoeres hartzfeldi 161
Halichoeres hortulanus 161
Halichoeres melanurus 162
Halichoeres prosopeion 162
Halichoeres trimaculatus 162
Halimeda sp. 213
Halophryne diemensis 33
Hapalochlaena lunulata 272
Harpa major 249
Helcogramma striata 175
Heliofungia actiniformis 228
Hemigymnus fasciatus 163
Hemigymnus melapterus 163
Hemiscyllium freycineti 10
Hemiscyllium hallstromi 10
Hemiscyllium ocellatum 10
Hemitaurichthys polylepis 127
Heniochus acuminatus 129
Heniochus chrysostomus 129
Heniochus diphreutes 129
Heniochus monoceros 129
Heniochus singularius 129
Heniochus varius 129
Heteractis aurora 222
Heteractis magnifica 222
Heteroconger hassi 29, 30
Heteroconger perissodon 27
Heteroconger polyzona 30
Heteroconger taylori 28, 30
Heteropriacanthus cruentatus 83
Hexabranchus sanguineus 259
Himantura fai 18
Himantura jenkinsii 18
Himerometra robustipinna 288
Hippocampus bargibanti 48
Hippocampus histrix 47
Hippocampus sp. 48
Hippocampus spinosissimus 48
Hippocampus taeniopterus 47
Hippopus hippopus 234
Hipposcarus longiceps 168
Histrio histrio 34
Hologymnosus doliatus 163
Holothuria fuscogilva 305
Homalocantha anatomica 247
Homalocantha scorpio 247
Homalocantha zamboi 247
Hoplodoris nodulosa 263
Hoplolatilus chlupatyi 87
Hoplolatilus cuniculus 86
Hoplolatilus fronticinctus 87
Hoplolatilus marcosi 87
Hoplolatilus pohle 87
Hoplolatilus purpureus 87
Hoplolatilus starcki 86
Hyalinoecia tubicola 232

Hydatina physis 253
Hyporhamphus far 35
Hypselodoris infucata 262
Hypselodoris obscura 262
Ianthella basta 216
Iconaster longimanus 296
Inimicus didactylus 53
Janolus sp. 266
Junceella fragilis 221
Justitia japonica 282
Kallypilidion sp. 303, 304
Kentrodoris rubescens 263
Kuhlia mugil 83
Kyphosus cinerascens 154
Kyphosus vaigiensis 154
Labroides alleni 164
Labroides bicolor 164
Labroides dimidiatus 164
Lactoria cornuta 208
Lactoria fornasini 208
Lagocephalus sceleratus 214
Lambis crocata 239
Lambis millepeda 240
Lambis scorpius 239
Lambis truncata 240
Laticauda colubrina 311
Leiaster speciosus 292
Leptojulis urostigma 164
Lethrinus erythracanthus 107
Lethrinus erythropterus 108
Lethrinus harak 108
Lethrinus lentjan 109
Lethrinus microdon 108
Lethrinus nebulosus 109
Lethrinus obsoletus 109
Lethrinus olivaceus 109
Lethrinus xanthocheilus 109
Leucosia anatum 284
Limaria fragilis 235
Linckia laevigata 292
Linckia multiflora 293
Lissocarcinus laevis 284
Lissocarcinus orbicularis 284
Lobophyllia hemprichii 226
Loimia medusa 232
Lovenia elongata 302
Lubricogobius sp. 182
Luetzenia asthenosomae 252
Lutjanus argentimaculatus 93
Lutjanus biguttatus 93
Lutjanus bohar 93
Lutjanus carponotatus 94
Lutjanus dodecacanthoides 93
Lutjanus ehrenbergii 94
Lutjanus fulviflamma 94
Lutjanus gibbus 94
Lutjanus kasmira 95
Lutjanus lutjanus 95
Lutjanus monostigma 96
Lutjanus quinquelineatus 95
Lutjanus rivulatus 95
Lutjanus rufolineatus 93
Lutjanus russelli 96
Lutjanus sebae 96
Lutjanus semicinctus 96
Lutjanus vitta 95
Luzonichthys waitei 68
Lysiosquillina maculata 287
Lysiosquillina sp. 286
Lysmata amboinensis 278
Lysmata debelius 278
Macolor macularis 98
Macolor niger 98
Makaira indica 199
Malacanthus brevirostris 88
Malacanthus latovittatus 88
Manta birostris 19-21
Marionia distincta 265
Megaprotodon 125
Meiacanthus atrodorsalis 174
Meiacanthus grammistes 174
Meiacanthus rhinorhynchus 174
Melibe fimbriata 265, 266
Melichthys vidua 203
Melithaea sp. 220
Melo amphora 248
Metapenaeus sp. 276
Metasepia pfefferi 271
Mexichromis multituberculata 262
Miamira sinuata 262
Micromelo undatus 253
Millepora sp. 218
Minous trachycephalus 56
Mobula sp. 19
Monodactylus argenteus 115
Monotaxis grandoculis 110
Mulloidichthys flavolineatus 112
Mulloidichthys vanicolensis 112
Murex pecten 246
Murex tribulus 246
Myrichthys colubrinus 26
Myripristis adusta 37
Myripristis melanosticta 37
Myripristis vittata 37
Nardoa frianti 293
Nardoa novacaledoniae 293
Naso annulatus 191
Naso brevirostris 191
Naso hexacanthus 191
Naso lituratus 192
Naso tuberosus 192
Naso unicornis 192
Naso vlamingii 192
Nautilus macromphalus 275
Nautilus pompilius 274, 275
Nautilus scrobiculatus 274, 275
Nautilus stenomphalus 275
Nebrius ferrugineus 11
Nemateleotris decora 184
Nemateleotris magnifica 184
Nembrotha lineolata 258
Neoniphon opercularis 37
Neopetrolisthes maculatus 283
Neopetrolisthes oshimai 283
Neothyonidium magnum 304
Netrostoma setouchina 217
Notodoris minor 258
Notodoris serenae 258
Novaculichthys sp. 164
Novaculichthys taeniourus 165
Octopus cyanea 273
Octopus sp. 272
Odontodactylus scyllarus 285
Odontozona sp. 277
Odonus niger 204
Ogilbyina velifera 80
Oligometra serripinna 288
Onigocia spinosa 61
Onuxodon sp. 33
Ophichthus bonaparti 26
Ophiothrix sp. 298
Ostracion cubicus 208, 209
Ostracion meleagris 209
Ostracion solorensis 209
Ovula ovum 242
Oxycheilinus bimaculatus 158
Oxycheilinus digrammus 158
Oxycirrhites typus 153
Oxymetopon cyanoctenosum 185
Oxymonacanthus longirostris 206
Padina sp. 213
Paracanthurus hepatus 193
Paracentropyge multifasciata 134
Parachaetodon ocellatus 128
Paracheilinus filamentosus 159
Paracirrhites arcatus 153
Paracirrhites forsteri 153
Paraluteres prionurus 206, 213
Paramonacanthus choirocephalus 207
Parapercis clathrata 169
Parapercis hexophthalma 169
Parapercis schauinslandii 169
Parapercis snyderi 169
Parapercis tetracantha 169
Paraploactis sp. 60
Paraplysia geographica 255
Parapriacanthus 115
Pardachirus pavoninus 200
Parupeneus barberinoides 112
Parupeneus barberinus 112
Parupeneus bifasciatus 113
Parupeneus ciliatus 113
Parupeneus cyclostomus 113
Parupeneus indicus 113
Parupeneus multifasciatus 114
Parupeneus pleurostigma 114
Pastinachus sephen 18
Pavona clavus 218, 226
Pempheris schwenkii 115
Pentapodus sp. 106
Pentapodus trivittatus 106
Periclimenes amboinensis 281
Periclimenes imperator 281
Pervagor melanocephalus 206
Petroscirtes mitratus 175
Phenacovolva weaveri 244
Philinopsis cyanea 255
Philinopsis gardineri 255
Pholidichthys leucotaenia 31
Photoblepharon palpebratus 36
Phyllacanthus imperialis 301
Phyllidia elegans 264
Phyllidia ocellata 264
Phyllodesmium longicirrum 268
Phyllodiscus sp. 223
Physeter macrocephalus 315
Pinctada margaritifera 235-237
Pinctada maxima 235, 237
Pinjalo lewisi 99
Pinjalo pinjalo 99
Plagiotremus laudandus 174
Platax batavianus 118, 138
Platax boersi 119
Platax orbicularis 116
Platax pinnatus 117
Platax teira 119
Platybelone platyura 36
Platydoris cruenta 263
Platydoris formosa 263
Plectorhinchus albovittatus 103
Plectorhinchus celebicus 103
Plectorhinchus chaetodontoides 103
Plectorhinchus chrysotaenia 103
Plectorhinchus gibbosus 104
Plectorhinchus lessoni 104
Plectorhinchus lineatus 104
Plectorhinchus obscura 103
Plectorhinchus picus 105
Plectorhinchus vittatus 104
Plectranthias inermis 68
Plectranthias longimanus 68
Plectroglyphidodon lacrymatus 148
Plectropomus laevis 76
Plectropomus oligocanthus 78
Pleurobranchus forskali 256
Pleurobranchus grandis 256
Pleurosicya boldinghi 183
Pleurosicya mossambica 183
Plotosus lineatus 31
Poeciloconger fasciatus 27
Pogonoperca punctata 79
Polycarpa aurata 307
Pomacanthus imperator 131, 136
Pomacanthus navarchus 137
Pomacanthus semicirculatus 136
Pomacanthus sexstriatus 130, 137
Pomacanthus xanthometopon 137
Pomacentrus amboinensis 148
Pomacentrus bankanensis 148
Pomacentrus coelestis 148
Pomacentrus pavo 148
Pomacentrus vaiuli 148
Portunus pelagicus 284
Premnas biaculeatus 146, 147
Priacanthus hamrur 83
Priolepis cincta 181
Prosimnia semperi 243
Protoreaster nodosus 291
Psammoperca waigiensis 61
Pseudaluterus nasicornis 207
Pseudamia gelatinosa 86
Pseudanthias cooperi 66
Pseudanthias dispar 62
Pseudanthias fasciatus 64
Pseudanthias huchtii 62
Pseudanthias hypselosoma 64
Pseudanthias lori 67
Pseudanthias luzonensis 64
Pseudanthias pascalus 67
Pseudanthias pleurotaenia 65, 66
Pseudanthias rubrizonatus 66
Pseudanthias smithvanizi 67
Pseudanthias squamipinnis 62
Pseudanthias tuka 67
Pseudobalistes flavimarginatus 203
Pseudobiceros bedfordi 229
Pseudobiceros ferrugineus 229
Pseudobiceros gratus 229
Pseudoceros bifurcus 229
Pseudoceros dimidiatus 229
Pseudocheilinus ocellatus 159
Pseudochromis paccagnellae 80
Pseudochromis perspicillatus 80
Pseudomonacanthus macrurus 207
Pteraeolidia ianthina 268
Pteragogus cryptus 165
Ptereleotris evides 185
Ptereleotris grammica 185
Ptereleotris hanae 186
Ptereleotris heteroptera 186
Ptereleotris microlepis 186
Ptereleotris uroditaenia 186
Ptereleotris zebra 185
Pterocaesio digramma 101
Pterocaesio lativittata 101
Pterocaesio marri 101
Pterocaesio pisang 101
Pterocaesio tessellata 102
Pterocaesio trilineata 102
Pteroeides sp. 220
Pteroidichthys amboinensis 56
Pterois antennata 52
Pterois mombasae 52
Pterois volitans 52
Pygoplites diacanthus 132
Rastrelliger kanagurta 199
Reteterebella queenslandica 232
Reticulidia halgerda 265
Rhincodon typus 11
Rhinecanthus aculeatus 204
Rhinecanthus verrucosus 204
Rhinobatos typus 16
Rhinomuraena quaesita 25
Rhinopias aphanes 53, 54
Rhinopias frondosa 53, 55
Rhynchocinetes durbanensis 280
Richardsonichthys leucogaster 50
Rudarius minutus 207
Sabellastarte sp. 230
Salarias fasciatus 175
Salarias segmentatus 175
Samariscus triocellatus 200
Sarcophyton sp. 219
Sargocentron caudimaculatum 39
Sargocentron diadema 38
Sargocentron melanospilos 38
Sargocentron rubrum 38
Sargocentron spiniferum 39
Sargocentron violaceum 38
Saron inermis 279
Saron sp. 279
Saurida sp. 32
Scarus altipinnis 168
Scarus chameleon 168
Scarus rubroviolaceus 168
Scolopsis bilineatus 105
Scolopsis ciliatus 105
Scolopsis lineatus 106
Scolopsis margaritifer 106
Scolopsis vosmeri 106
Scolopsis xenochrous 105
Scomberomorus commerson 199
Scorpaenopsis diabolus 58
Scorpaenopsis macrochir 58
Scorpaenopsis oxycephala 58
Scorpaenopsis papuensis 59
Scorpaenopsis venosa 59
Sebastapistes cyanostigma 60
Sepia latimanus 270
Sepioteuthis lessoniana 271
Serranocirrhitus latus 68
Sicyonia sp. 276
Siderea thyrsoidea 25
Siganus argenteus 195
Siganus canaliculatus 195
Siganus corallinus 195
Siganus doliatus 194
Siganus lineatus 195
Siganus puellus 194
Siganus punctatissimus 195
Siganus punctatus 195
Signigobius biocellatus 181
Siokunichthys nigrolineatus 46
Soleichthys heterorhinos 200
Solenocera faxoni 276
Solenostomus armatus 42
Solenostomus cyanopterus 42
Solenostomus paradoxus 43
Solenostomus sp. 42, 213
Sorsogona welanderi 61
Sphyraena barracuda 156
Sphyraena flavicauda 156
Sphyraena jello 156
Sphyraena qenie 155, 156
Sphyrna lewini 13
Sphyrna mokarran 16
Spirobranchus giganteus 230
Spondylus varius 235
Stegostoma fasciatum 11
Stenopus hispidus 277
Stenopus tenuirostris 277
Stonogobiops xanthorhinica 179
Strombus bulla 238
Strombus sinuatus 238
Strombus thersites 239
Stylaster sp. 218
Sufflamen bursa 204
Sufflamen chrysopterus 204
Symphorichthys spilurus 100
Symphorus nematophorus 99
Synanceia horrida 59
Synanceia verrucosa 59
Synapta sp. 304
Synaptula lamberti 304
Synchiropus ocellatus 176
Synchiropus splendidus 176
Syngnathoides biaculeatus 46
Synodus variegatus 32
Taenianotus triacanthus 56
Taeniura lymma 17
Taeniura meyeni 17
Tambja affinis 258
Terapon jarbua 81
Thelenota ananas 306
Thelenota anax 306
Thelenota rubralineata 306
Thenus orientalis 282
Thor amboinensis 278
Thor spinosus 278
Thromidia catalai 294
Tomiyamichthys sp. 179
Torquigener brevipinnis 214
Tosia queenslandensis 295, 296
Toxopneustes pileolus 301
Tozeuma armatum 279
Trachinocephalus myops 32
Trachinotus baillonii 92
Trachyrhamphus bicoarctatus 46
Trachyrhamphus longirostris 46
Triaenodon obesus 13
Trichonotus elegans 170
Trichonotus halstead 271, 272
Trichonotus setiger 271, 272
Tridacna gigas 234
Tridacna maxima 234
Trimma benjamini 183
Trimma tevegae 183
Trimmatom sp. 183
Tripneustes gratilla 302
Tubastraea micanthra 227
Tubastraea sp. 227
Turbinaria reniformis 227
Turbo chrysostomus 238
Turbo petholatus 238
Tylosurus crocodilus 36
Ucla sp. 175
Upeneus tragula 114
Uranoscopus sulphureus 170
Urogymnus asperrimus 17
Uropterygius micropterus 25
Valenciennea helsdingeni 179
Valenciennea parva 180
Valenciennea puellaris 180
Valenciennea randalli 180
Valenciennea sexguttata 180
Valenciennea strigata 180
Valenciennea wardi 180
Valmugil seheli 154
Valonia ventriosa 213
Vanderhorstia ambanoro 178
Variola albimarginata 78
Variola louti 78
Volva volva 243
Xestospongia testudinaria 216
Xiphasia setifer 175
Xyrichtys aneitensis 166
Xyrichtys pavo 166
Xyrichtys pentadactylus 166
Zanclus cornutus 194
Zebrasoma scopas 193
Zebrasoma veliferum 193
Zenarchopterus sp. 35

INDEX: COMMON NAMES

Adhesive Sea Anemone 222
Ambon Commensal Shrimp 281
Ambon Damsel 148
Ambon Scorpionfish 56
Anax Sea Cucumber 306
Anemone Coral 228
Arc-eye Hawkfish 153
Arrowhead Soapfish 79
Axelrod's Blenny 173
Baby Watcher 293
Bailer Shell 248
Banded Boxer Shrimp 277
Banded Goby 179
Banded Snake Eel 26
Banded Sole 200
Banded Trimmatom 183
Bandfish 154
Bandtail Dart Goby 186
Barramundi Cod 72
Barred Filefish 205
Barred Moray 24
Barred Rabbitfish 194
Barred Sand Conger 27
Barred Soapfish 79
Barred Thicklip 163
Barrier Reef Anemonefish 144
Bath's Blenny 173
Beaded Sea Anemone 222
Beaked Coralfish 127
Bearded Brotula 32
Beautiful Feather Star 288
Beautiful Goby 181
Bennett's Butterflyfish 121
Bicolor Angelfish 133
Bicolor Cleanerfish 164
Bicolor Fangblenny 174
Bicolor Parrotfish 167
Big-eye Bream 110
Bigeye Snapper 95
Bigeye Trevally 92
Bigfin Reef Squid 271
Bignose Unicornfish 192
Black and Blue Slug 255
Black and Blue Swallowtail 254
Black and White Sea Krait 311
Black and White Spinecheek 106
Black Anemonefish 145
Black Butterflyfish 123
Black Coral 228
Black Coral Ovulid 244
Black Coriocella 253
Black Marlin 199
Black Seaperch 98
Black Trevally 90
Black Velvet Angelfish 134
Black-banded Snapper 96
Black-blotched Stingray 17
Black-margined Nudibranch 261
Black-saddle Toby 213
Black-spot Angelfish 135
Black-spotted Porcupinefish 214
Blackbarred Sandperch 169
Blackbelly Triggerfish 204
Blackeye Thicklip 163
Blackfin Hogfish 157
Blackfin Squirrelfish 37
Blackheaded Filefish 206
Blacklip Pearl Shell 235, 236
Blackspot Sergeant 140
Blackspot Snapper 94
Blackspot Squirrelfish 38
Blackspot Tuskfish 159
Blackspotted Moray 24
Blackspotted Puffer 212
Blacktail Sergeant 140
Blacktip Shark 12
Blacktipped Grouper 75
Bleeker's Parrotfish 167
Blue Blanquillo 88
Blue Boxer Shrimp 277
Blue Devil 142
Blue Flat Worm 229
Blue-girdled Angelfish 137
Blue-ringed Octopus 272
Blue Sea Star 292
Blue Tilefish 86
Blue Whiptail 106
Blue-barred Ribbon Goby 185
Blue-eyed Stingfish 56
Blue-speckled Rubble Goby 181
Blue-spot Sea Hare 255
Blue-Spotted Rockcod 70

Blue-spotted Fantail Ray 17
Blue-spotted Puffer 211, 212
Blue-spotted Stingray 16
Blueband Goby 180
Bluefin Trevally 92
Blueline Damsel 142
Bluelined Snapper 95
Bluespot Butterflyfish 124
Bobbit Worm 231
Bobtail Squid 270
Boer's Batfish 119
Boomerang Triggerfish 204
Brittle Star 298
Broom Filefish 205
Brown Sweetlips 104
Brownbanded Pipefish 44
Brushtail Tang 193
Bubble Stromb 238
Bull Shark 13
Bullmouth Helmet 245
Bumphead Parrotfish 167
Burgess' Butterflyfish 127
Burying Brittle Star 298
Bushy Feather Star 288
Cabbage Coral 227
Cake Urchin 302
Calamari Sea Urchin 301
Caltrop Murex 246
Canary Wrasse 161
Carla's Scale Worm 230
Cat's Eye Turban 238
Catala's Sea Star 294
Cave Anthias 68
Cave Coral 227
Chameleon Parrotfish 168
Chameleon Tilefish 87
Cheeklined Maori Wrasse 158
Chevroned Butterflyfish 125
Chinamanfish 99
Christmas Tree Worm 230
Cleaning Pipefish 45
Clear Sundial 250
Clown Anemonefish 145
Clown Coris 160
Clown Snake Eel 26
Clown Triggerfish 201
Cockatoo Waspfish 139
Colin's Pygmy Angelfish 130
Collared Knifefish 165
Colonial Anemonefish 145
Comb Sea Star 296
Comet 82
Common Fan Worm 230
Common Hermit Crab 283
Common Lionfish 52
Common Reef Cuttlefish 270
Common Reef Octopus 273
Common Sand-diver 172
Common Seahorse 47
Concentric Pleurobranch 256
Convict Blenny 31
Convict Surgeonfish 190
Cooper's Anthias 66
Coral Cod 71
Coral Grouper 74
Coral Rabbitfish 195
Coral Sea Angelfish 132
Coral Shrimpfish 41
Coral Trout 76
Corallimorpharian 224-225
Coronation Trout 78
Cowtailed Ray 18
Crawling Comb Jelly 216
Crescent-tail Bigeye 83
Crinoid Boxer Shrimp 277
Crocodile Fish 77
Crocodile Longtom 36
Crocodilefish 60
Crosshatch Goby 179
Crown of Thorns Sea Star 290
Crown Sea Jelly 217
Crown Squirrelfish 38
Cryptic Wrasse 165
Curious Worm Goby 184
Darkspotted Moray 22
Decorated Dart Goby 184
Deep-bodied Fusilier 101
Deepwater Lionfish 52
Delicate Tube Worm 231
Demon Stinger 53
Devil Ray 19
Diamond Trevally 89

Dinah's Goby 182
Disc Anemone 224-225
Dogwood Drupe 248
Dotted Butterflyfish 123
Dotted Wrasse 160
Double-ended Pipefish 46
Doublebar Goby 182
Dugong 312-315
Durban Hinge-beak Shrimp 280
Dwarf Hawkfish 152
Dwarf Lionfish 51
Dwarf Pipehorse 45
Eagle Ray 19
Egg Cowrie 242
Eight-banded Butterflyfish 126
Electric Swallowtail 254
Elegant Sand Diver 170
Elegant Slug 264
Elephant Ear Sponge 216
Elongate Heart Urchin 302
Elongated Egg Cowrie 243
Emperor Angelfish 131, 136
Estuarine Stonefish 59
Eye-brow Shrimp Goby 178
Eye-spot Slug 264
Eyed Cowrie 241
Eyed Sea Cucumber 305
Eyestripe Surgeonfish 188
False Fire Urchin 300
False Halgerda 265
False Stonefish 58
Fathead Anthias 68
Faxon's Shrimp 276
Featherstar Clingfish 35
Filamented Flasher 159
File Shell 235
Fingered Dragonet 176
Fingerprint Toby 213
Fire Anemone 223
Fire Coral 218
Fire Dart Goby 184
Fire Urchin 300
Fire Urchin Eulimid 252
Five-lined Cardinalfish 86
Fiveband Flagtail 83
Fivefinger Razorfish 166
Flagtail Blanquillo 88
Flamboyant Cuttlefish 271
Flame Angelfish 134
Flashlightfish 36
Flathead 77
Flathead Lobster 282
Flat-tail Grouper 72
Flower Urchin 301
Flowery Flounder 200
Flowery Cod 73
Forcepsfish 128
Forktail Rabbitfish 195
Formosa Platydoris 263
Fowler's Stingfish 188
Freckled Goatfish 114
Freckled Hawkfish 153
Freycinet's Epaulette Shark 10
Friant's Sea Star 293
Fringing Mullet 154
Funnelweed 215
GBR Squat Shrimp 278
Gelatinous Cardinalfish 86
Geography Cone 249
Giant Barrel Sponge 216
Giant Basket Star 298
Giant Clam 234
Giant Flat Worm 229
Giant Frog Shell 253
Giant Frogfish 33
Giant Grouper 73
Giant Helmet Shell 245
Giant Lizardfish 32
Giant Melibe 266, 267
Giant Moray 22
Giant Murex 247
Giant Sea Hare 255
Giant Shovelnose Ray 16
Giant Shrimp Goby 177
Giant Spider Stromb 240
Giant Sweetlips 103
Giant Trevally 90
Glasseye 83
Globular Ovulid 244
Gold-lined Sea Bream 107
Golden Bristle Worm 232

Golden Cowrie 240
Golden Dascyllus 141
Golden Striped Butterflyfish 123
Golden Trevally 89
Golden-lined Snapper 93
Goldlip Pearl Shell 235, 237
Goldsaddle Goatfish 113
Goldstripe Wrasse 161
Goldstriped Sweetlips 103
Gorgonian Seahorse 48
Graeff's Sea Cucumber 305
Granulated Sea Star 290
Great Barracuda 156
Great Barrier Reef King Prawn 276
Great Hammerhead Shark 16
Green Tree Coral 227
Green Turtle 310
Green Urn Sea Squirt 307
Grey Reef Shark 14
Half-and-half Goatfish 112
Halfbeak 35
Halfmoon Triggerfish 204
Halimeda Ghost Pipefish 42, 215
Harlequin Sweetlips 103
Harlequin Tuskfish 160
Hawk Anthias 68
Hawksbill Turtle 310
Hedgehog Seahorse 48
Helmet Gurnard 50
Herald's Angelfish 133
Heron Island Nudibranch 260
Highfin Coral Trout 78
Highfin Coralfish 128
Highfin Fangblenny 175
Hippopus Clam 234
Horned Sea Star 291
Horrid Stonefish 59
Hovering Goby 182
Humbug Damsel 143
Hump-headed Batfish 118
Humpback Scorpionfish 58
Humphrey's Cowrie 242
Humpnose Unicornfish 192
Ianthina Slug 268
Icon Sea Star 296
Imperator Commensal Shrimp 281
Indian Goatfish 113
Japanese Deep Lobster 282
Jenkins Whipray 18
Jewel Damsel 148
Jolly Green Giant 262
Keeled Needlefish 36
Knobbly Asteronotus 264
Kuni Nudibranch 260
Lace Coral 218
Lacinate Murex 247
Lacy Scorpionfish 53-54
Lamarck's Angelfish 136
Lambert's Worm Sea Cucumber 304
Lantern Toby 213
Large Burrowing Sea Cucumber 304
Latticed Sandperch 169
Leaf Scorpionfish 56
Leaf-gilled Slug 257
Leatherback Turtle 310
Leopard Blenny 174
Leopard Nudibranch 260
Leopard Rockcod 71
Leopard Slug 257
Lined Bristletooth 191
Lined Bubble Shell 253
Lined Butterflyfish 120
Lined Dart Goby 185
Lined Nembrotha 258
Lined Sweetlips 104
Little Dragonfish 39
Long-jawed Mackerel 199
Long-nosed Emperor 109
Long-spined Urchin 300
Long-tail Ceratosoma 261
Longfin Bannerfish 129
Longfin Emperor 108
Longfinned Perchlet 68
Longhorn Cowfish 208
Longnose Butterflyfish 128
Longnose Filefish 206
Longnosed Hawkfish 153
Longspine Cardinalfish 84
Longspot Snapper 94
Longtailed Ghost Pipefish 42
Lori's Anthias 67
Lumpy Sea Star 294

Luzon Anthias	64	Pin-cushion Sea Star	291
Luzon Sea Star	294	Pine Cone Marble Shrimp	279
Lyretail Hogfish	157	Pineapple Sea Cucumber	306
Lyretail Sandperch	169	Pink Anemonefish	146
Lyretail Trout	78	Pink Sea Fan	220
Magenta Slender Anthias	68	Pink Sea Fan Spindle Cowrie	243
Magnificent Sea Anemone	222	Pink Whipray	18
Major Harp	249	Pinktail Triggerfish	203
Malabar Grouper	72	Pinnate Batfish	117
Mandarinfish	176	Pixie Hawkfish	152
Mangrove Jack	93	Plate Coral	226
Manta Ray	19-21	Port Moresby Wentletrap	253
Many Host Goby	183	Potato Cod	73,150,111
Many-toothed Garden Eel	27	Potato Grouper	150
Manybar Goatfish	114	Purple Anthias	67
Maori Snapper	95	Purple Band Flabellina	268
Maori Wrasse	158	Purple Mouth Stromb	238
Map Cowrie	241	Purple Sand Dollar	302
Map Puffer	210	Purple Sea Squirt	307
Marble Shrimp	279	Pygmy Seahorse	48
Marbled Snake Eel	27	Pyramid Butterflyfish	127
Masked Angelfish	135	Quill Worm	232
Masked Moray	23	Raccoon Butterflyfish	122
Mertens' Butterflyfish	125	Radial Filefish	208
Meyer's Butterflyfish	122	Rambo Smasher	285
Midnight Seaperch	98	Randall's Shrimp Goby	177
Milliped Spider Stromb	240	Red Bass	93
Milne Bay Sand Lance	170	Red Emperor	96
Mimic Filefish	206	Red Pinjalo	99
Mimic Octopus	272	Red Reef Lobster	282
Mimic Surgeonfish	189	Red Sea Whip	221
Minifin Parrotfish	168	Red-backed Tilefish	87
Minke Whale	149, 150, 315	Red-banded Wrasse	157
Minor Notodoris	258	Red-lined Kentrodoris	263
Moorish Idol	194	Red-lined Sea Cucumber	306
Multi-barred Angelfish	134	Redbar Anthias	66
Mushroom Coral	228	Redeye Goby	182
Mushroom Leather Coral	219	Redfin Anthias	62
Nautilus	274-275	Redfin Butterflyfish	124
Necklace Sea Star	292	Redtooth Triggerfish	204
Neon Damsel	148	Reef Stonefish	59
Neon Triplefin	175	Reeftop Pipefish	44
New Caledonian Sea Star	293	Regal Angelfish	132
Nodulose Hoplodoris	263	Reticulated Blenny	173
Oblique-banded Cardinalfish	84	Reticulated Damsel	143
Oblique-lined Dottyback	80	Reticulated Hinge-beak Shrimp	280
Obscure Hypselodoris	262	Rhinoceros Filefish	207
Ocean Triggerfish	202	Ribbon Eel	25
Ocellated Coralfish	128	Rigid Shrimpfish	41
Ocellated Dragonet	176	Ring-eye Pygmy Goby	183
Ocellated Epaulette Shark	10	Ring-tailed Cardinalfish	84
Olive Sea Snake	311	Ringed Damsel	44
Olive Sea Whip	221	Robust Ghost Pipefish	42
Onespot Snapper	96	Robust Sea Squirt	307
Onyx Cowrie	241	Rockmover Wrasse	165
Orange Anemonefish	146	Round Batfish	116
Orange Sea Fan	220	Rounded Porcupinefish	214
Orange Spider Stromb	239	Roundspot Goatfish	114
Orange-dashed Goby	180	Royal Dottyback	80
Orange-mouth Thorny Oyster	235	Sabre Squirrelfish	39
Orange-spotted Sand Goby	181	Saddled Butterflyfish	126
Orange-striped Emperor	109	Sailfin Dottyback	80
Orangeband Surgeonfish	190	Sailfin Snapper	98, 100
Orangefin Anemonefish	144	Sailfin Tang	193
Orangefin Emperor	107	Sailor's Eyeball	215
Orangelined Triggerfish	201	Salt Water Crocodile	196-198
Orangespine Unicornfish	192	Sand Bass	61
Orangespotted Trevally	89	Sapphire Damsel	148
Ornate Butterflyfish	122	Sargassumfish	34
Ornate Elysia	257	Saw Blade Shrimp	279
Ornate Ghost Pipefish	42, 43	Saw-jawed Spinecheek	105
Ornate Pipefish	45	Scalefin Anthias	62
Pacific Double-saddle Butterflyfish	120	Scalloped Hammerhead Shark	13
Paddletail Snapper	94	Scarlet Cleaner Shrimp	278
Painted Sweetlips	102	Scissortail Fusilier	100
Pale Dart Goby	186	Scissortail Sergeant	140
Pale Pinjalo	99	Scorpion Spider Stromb	239
Palette Surgeonfish	193	Scribbled Filefish	205
Panda Clownfish	144	Sea Cow	315
Papuan Scorpionfish	59	Sea Pen	220
Parva Goby	180	Sea Pen Slug	266
Pastel Ringwrasse	163	Sea Wasp	217
Pavo Razorfish	166	Semicircle Angelfish	136
Peacock Rockcod	70	Serene Notodoris	258
Peacock Smasher	285	Shadowfin Soldierfish	37
Peacock Sole	200	Shark Mackerel	199
Pearlfish	33	Shell-breaking Hermit	283
Pearly Spinecheek	106	Shortfin Pufferfish	214
Pebble Crab	284	Short-tailed Pipefish	46
Pelagic Swimming Crab	284	Silky Shark	12
Pencil Urchin	301	Silver Batfish	115
Pennant Bannerfish	129	Silver Pufferfish	214
Peppered Rabbitfish	195	Silver Sweeper	115
Pickhandle Barracuda	156	Silvertip Shark	10, 11, 15

Singular Bannerfish	129	Threadfin Dart Goby	186
Six-Banded Angelfish	130, 137	Threadfin Hawkfish	152
Sixline Soapfish	79	Three-spot Angelfish	132
Sleek Unicornfish	191	Threespot Damsel	143
Small Feather Star	288	Threespot Wrasse	162
Small Jobfish	95	Thumbprint Emperor	108
Small-dot Anemone Crab	283	Tidepool Snake Moray	25
Small-spotted Pompano	92	Tiger Ovulid	243
Smallscale Scorpionfish	58	Titan Triggerfish	202
Smalltooth Emperor	108	Toadfish	33
Smooth Flutemouth	40	Tomato Rockcod	71
Snake Arm Anemone	223	Topsail Drummer	154
Snake Blenny	175	Triangular Butterflyfish	125
Snoutspot Grouper	74	Trumpet Triton	252
Snubnose Grouper	75	Trumpetfish	40
Soft Coral	219	Tube Anemone	223
Soft Coral Ovulid	244	Tube Guardian	284
Soft Coral Slug	265	Tubercular Nudibranch	265
Solar Powered Slug	268	Tuberculate Mexichromis	262
Spangled Emperor	109	Twinspot Goby	181
Spanish Dancer	259	Twinspot Lionfish	51
Spanish Flag	94	Two-barred Goatfish	113
Spearer	285-287	Two-line Spinecheek	105
Speckled Butterflyfish	126	Two-lined Fusilier	101
Speckled-Fin Rockcod	74	Two-spined Angelfish	133
Sperm Whale	315	Two-spot Maori Wrasse	158
Spindle Cone	250	Two-spot Snapper	93
Spinecheek Anemonefish	146, 147	Two-tone Wrasse	162
Spiny Flathead	61	Twospotted Wrasse	161
Spiny-tail Puller	141	Underlined Fig Shell	246
Spiny Waspfish	50	Upside-down Sea Jelly	216
Splendid Garden Eel	30	Urchin Clingfish	35
Splendid Soldierfish	37	Variable Smasher	285
Sponge Fan	216	Variegated Lizardfish	32
Sponge-eating Berthella	256	Velvetfish	60
Spot Chain Sea Star	292	Venomous Moray	23
Spot-banded Butterflyfish	124	Venus Comb Murex	246
Spot-tail Butterflyfish	121	Vermiculated Angelfish	135
Spotfin Lionfish	52	Violet Squirrelfish	38
Spotfin Shrimp Goby	178	Warty Frogfish	34
Spotted Boxfish	209	Wavy-edge Spindle	248
Spotted Garden Eel	30	Wavy-lined Grouper	76
Spotted Sea Bream	107	Weedy Scorpionfish	53, 55
Spotted Shrimp Goby	177	Weight Watcher	305
Spotted Sweetlips	105	Welander's Flathead	61
Squarespot Anthias	66	Whale Shark	11
Squarespot Fairy Basslet	65	White Pointer	46
Stargazer	139	White-banded Cleaner Shrimp	278
Stargazer Snake Eel	26	White-bonnet Anemonefish	145
Starry Moray	22	White-eyed Moray	25
Starry Nudibranch	261	White-lined Rockcod	70
Starry Puffer	212	White-spotted Grouper	74
Starry Triggerfish	201	White-tail Squirrelfish	39
Steephead Parrotfish	168	White-tailed Angelfish	130
Stinging Hydroid	217	Whiteband Triggerfish	204
Stinging Sea Star	296	Whitebar Filefish	207
Stocky Anthias	64	Whitebarred Wrasse	159
Stocky Tilefish	87	Whitecheek Surgeonfish	190
Stony Shrimp	276	Whiteface Waspfish	50
Strapweed Filefish	207	Whitemargin Stargazer	170
Striate Cone	249	Whitemargin Unicornfish	191
String Worm	232	Whitepatch Razorfish	166
Striped Anthias	64	Whitespotted Puffer	210
Striped Boxfish	209	Whitespotted Surgeonfish	188
Striped Catfish	31	Whitetip Shark	13
Striped Cleanerwrasse	164	Widestripe Fusilier	101
Striped Frogfish	34	Winged Pipefish	45
Striped Hinge-beak Shrimp	280	Worm Sea Cucumber	304
Striped Puffer	210	Yellow and Black Flat Worm	229
Striped Surgeonfish	189	Yellow Boxfish	209
Striped Swallowtail	254	Yellow Devilfish	81
Striped Sweetlips	104	Yellow Shrimp Goby	178
Stripey	94	Yellow-spotted Scorpionfish	60
Suckerfish	88	Yellowfin Damsel	142
Swallowtail Hawkfish	153	Yellowfin Goatfish	112
Swimming Sea Hare	255	Yellowmargin Moray	23
Table Cone	226	Yellowmargin Triggerfish	203
Tailspot Mudwrasse	164	Yellowmask Angelfish	137
Tailspot Wrasse	162	Yellownose Shrimp Goby	179
Tasselled Scorpionfish	58	Yellowspotted Trevally	90
Tasselled Wobbegong	10	Yellowstripe Goatfish	112
Tawny Shark	11	Yellowtail Barracuda	156
Taylor's Garden Eel	28, 30	Yellowtail Coris	161
Teardrop Butterflyfish	121	Yellowtail Fangblenny	174
Teira Batfish	119	Yellowtip Bristletooth	191
Tesselated Fusilier	102	Zambo's Murex	247
Textile Cone	250	Zebra Batfish	118
Thersite Stromb	239	Zebra Dart Goby	185
Thinspine Rockcod	76	Zebra Garden Eel	30
Thornback Cowfish	208	Zebra Lionfish	51
Thorny Seahorse	47	Zephyr Slug	266
Thorny Stingray	17		
Threadfin Anthias	62		
Threadfin Butterflyfish	120		

319

BIBLIOGRAPHY

Abbott, R.T. & Dance, S.P. (1982) Compendium of Seashells. American Malacologists, Melbourne, FL.

Allen, G.R. & Steene, R. (1994) Indo-Pacific Coral Reef Field Guide. Tropical Reef Res., Singapore.

Allen, G.R. Steene, R. & Allen, M. (1998) A Guide to Angelfishes & Butterflyfishes. Vanguard, Perth.

Allen, G.R. (1997) Marine Fishes of the Great Barrier Reef and South-East Asia. Western Australian Museum, Perth.

Clark, E. & Pohle, M. (1996) *Trichonotus halstead,* a new sand diving fish from Papua New Guinea. Environmental Biology of Fishes 45: 1-11, Kluwer Academic Publishers.

Clark, E. Pohle, J.F. & Halstead, R.A. (1998) Ecology and behavior of tilefishes, *Hoplolatilus starki, H. fronticinctus* and related species (Malacanthidae): non-mound and mound builders. Environmental Biology of Fishes 52: 395-417, Kluwer Academic Publishers.

Coleman, N. (1981) What Shell Is That? Ure Smith Press, Sydney.

Coleman, N. (1991) Encyclopedia of Marine Animals. Angus and Robertson, Pymble, NSW, Australia.

Coleman, N. (1989) Nudibranchs of the South Pacific. Sea Australia Resource Centre, Springwood, Qld, Australia.

Coleman, N. (1994) Sea Stars of Australasia. Neville Coleman's Underwater Geographic, Springwood, Qld, Australia.

Colin, P.L. & Arneson, C. (1995) Tropical Pacific Invertebrates. Coral Reef Press, Beverly Hills, CA.

Debelius, H. (1998) Nudibranchs and Sea Snails, Indo-Pacific Field Guide. 2nd ed. IKAN, Frankfurt, Germany.

Debelius, H. (1999) Crustacea Guide of the World. IKAN, Frankfurt, Germany.

Earle, J.L. & Pyle, R.L. (1997) *Hoplolatilus pohle,* a new species of sand tilefish from the deep reefs of the D'Entrecasteau Islands, Papua New Guinea. Copeia 1997: 382-387.

Fautin, G.F. & Allen, G.R. (1992) Field Guide to Anemonefishes and their Host Sea Anemones. Western Australian Museum, Perth.

George, J.D. & George, J.J. (1979) Marine Life. Lionel Leventhal Ltd, London.

Gosliner, T.M., Behrens, D.W. & Williams, G. C. (1996) Coral Reef Animals of the Indo-Pacific. Sea Challengers, Monterey, CA, USA.

Kuiter, R.H. (1996) Guide to Sea Fishes of Australia. New Holland, French's Forest, NSW. Australia.

Last, P.R. & Stevens, J.D. (1994) Sharks and Rays of Australia. CSIRO, Australia.

Lieske, E. & Myers, R. (1994) Collins Pocket Guide to Coral Reef Fishes. Harper Collins, London.

Michael, S.W. (1993) Reef Sharks and Rays of the World. Sea Challengers, Monterey, California.

Michael, S.W. (1998) Reef Fishes Vol 1. Shelburne, Vermont, USA.

Monniot, C. Monniot, F. & Laboute, P. (1991) Coral Reef Ascidians of New Caledonia. ORSTOM, Paris.

Myers, R.F. (1991) Micronesian Reef Fishes. Coral Graphics, Guam.

Surf Life Saving Qld., (1996) Venomous and Poisonous Marine Animals. UNSW press, Sydney.

Randall, J.E., Allen, G.R. & Steene, R. (1997) Fishes of the Great Barrier Reef and Coral Sea. University of Hawaii Press, Hawaii.

Randall, J.E. et al. (1982 - 1998) Indo-Pacific Fishes Vol. 1 - 27. Bernice Pauahi Bishop Museum, Honolulu, Hawaii.

Stafford-Deitsch, J. (1996) Mangrove, The Forgotten Habitat. Immel Publishing Ltd., London.

Talbot, F. & Steene, R. (1984) Reader's Digest Book of the Great Barrier Reef. Reader's Digest, Surry Hills, NSW, Australia.

Walls, J.G. (1980) Conchs, Tibias, and Harps. TFH Publications, Neptune City, NJ, USA.

Ward, P.D. (1988) In Search of Nautilus. Simon and Schuster, New York, USA.

Wells, F.E. & Bryce C.W. (1993) Sea Slugs And Their Relatives of Western Australia. Western Australian Museum, Perth.

PICTURE STORIES

SHARK FEED IN THE CORAL SEA . . . . 14 - 15
MANTA RAY DISCOVERY . . . . 20 - 21
TAYLOR'S GARDEN EEL. . . . . 28 - 29
THE LACY SCORPIONFISH . . . . 54 - 55
FAIRY BASSLETS AND SEX CHANGE 65
CROCODILE WITH GILLS. 77
THE COMET 82
BLACK AND WHITE SNAPPERS 98
COURTING CODS 111
FRIENDLIEST FISH IN THE SEA . . . . 116 - 119
ANGELS IN THE REEF. . . . . 130 - 131
MUCK DIVING . . . . 138 - 139
THE HEART OF THE GREAT BARRIER REEF . . . . 149 - 151
THE GOLDBAR SAND-DIVER. . . . . 171 - 172
CUDDLE A CROCODILE. . . . . 196 - 198
A SHORT LOOK ON ALGAE 215
A PAINFUL EXPERIENCE . . . . 224 - 225
PEARLS FROM THE SEA. . . . . 236 - 237
HOW TO CATCH A SEA URCHIN 245
MATING FROM A DISTANCE 273
ANCIENT CREATURES FROM THE DEPTHS . . . . 274 - 275
WHAT REALLY HAPPENED TO THE DINOSAURS! 287
CORAL SPAWNING. . . . . 308 - 309
DUGONG DUDLEY . . . . 312 - 314

PHOTO CREDITS

All photos by the author except
(**t** = top, **c** = centre, **b** = bottom, **w** = whole page)

FRED BAVENDAM: 277 b.
ROY CALDWELL: 285 c.
HELMUT DEBELIUS: 19 b 31 c
81 c 109 t 111 w 135 c 139 c 176 b
187 w 190 b 194 t 272 c 277 t.
GERD HAEGELE: 276 t 278 b.
DIETMAR SEIFERT: 167 t.
ROGER STEENE: 279 t 285 b.

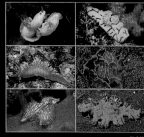